Surplus-Enjoyment

Also Available from Bloomsbury

Hegel in A Wired Brain, Slavoj Žižek
Sex and the Failed Absolute, Slavoj Žižek
Disparities, Slavoj Žižek
Antigone, Slavoj Žižek

Surplus-Enjoyment
A Guide for the Non-Perplexed

Slavoj Žižek

BLOOMSBURY ACADEMIC
LONDON • NEW YORK • OXFORD • NEW DELHI • SYDNEY

BLOOMSBURY ACADEMIC
Bloomsbury Publishing Plc
50 Bedford Square, London, WC1B 3DP, UK
1385 Broadway, New York, NY 10018, USA
29 Earlsfort Terrace, Dublin 2, Ireland

BLOOMSBURY, BLOOMSBURY ACADEMIC and the Diana logo are
trademarks of Bloomsbury Publishing Plc

First published in Great Britain 2022

ISBN: HB: 978-1-3502-2625-8
        ePDF: 978-1-3502-2626-5
        eBook: 978-1-3502-2627-2

Typeset by RefineCatch Limited, Bungay, Suffolk
Printed and bound in Great Britain

To find out more about our authors and books visit www.bloomsbury.com
and sign up for our newsletters.

Contents

Ouverture
Living in a Topsy-Turvy World

In his *Phenomenology of Spirit*, Hegel uses the term "*die verkehrte Welt*"—usually translated into English as "topsy-turvy world"—to designate the madness of the social reality of his time. "An example of topsy-turvy occurs when your carefully-made plans got messed up at the last minute and everyone is running every which way with no idea where to go."[1] Does this sentence from Yourdictionary. com entry for "topsy-turvy" not encapsulate perfectly the basic reversal in a Hegelian dialectical process in the course of which even the best-made projects turn into their opposite—a dream of freedom into terror, morality into hypocrisy, excessive wealth into poverty of the majority? Back in 1576, Thomas Rogers wrote in his *A Philosophical Discourse Entitled The Anatomy of the Mind*: "Devilish it is to destroy a city, but more than devilish to evert cities, to betray countries, to cause servants to kill their masters, parents their children, children their parents, wives their husbands, and to turn all things topsy turvy." Three basic relations of domination (masters over servants, parents over children, husbands over wives) are here turned around or, rather, inside out—is this not a succinct formula of Hegel's thought?

So is the present book yet another one on Hegel? In order to explain the logic of denial (*Verneinung*), Freud evokes a remark made by one of his patients: "You ask who that *woman* in my dream can be. Whoever she is, it's not my mother." Freud's reaction (which has since become proverbial) is: the question is settled then, we can be sure it is indeed his mother.[2] I can say exactly the same about this book of mine: whatever this book is about, it's not about Hegel, and this is not a Freudian denial but literally true. Yes, Hegel is ever-present in it. Even when he is not directly mentioned he lurks in the background, but the topic of the book is exactly what its title says:

it's about how the paradoxes of surplus-enjoyment sustain the topsy-turviness of our time.

From Catastrophe to Apocalypse . . . and Back

In an ideological space, different stances get connected into what Ernesto Laclau called a "chain of equivalences"—for example, extreme right-wing conspiracy theories about the COVID-19 pandemic get combined with New Age spirituality. Melissa Rein Lively's focus on wellness, natural health, organic food, yoga, ayurvedic healing, meditation, etc., led her into a violent rejection of vaccines as a source of dangerous contamination.[3] Today, this process is palpable all around us. We live in a weird moment where multiple catastrophes—pandemic, global warming, social tensions, the prospect of full digital control over our thinking . . .—compete for primacy, not just quantitatively but also in the sense of which of them will count as the "quilting point" (Lacan's *point-de-capiton*) which totalizes all others. Today, the main candidate in the public discourse is global warming, while lately the antagonism which, in our part of the world, at least, appears as the crucial one is that between partisans of vaccination and vaccine-sceptics. The problem here is that, for COVID-sceptics, the main catastrophe today is the fake vision of the (pandemic) catastrophe itself which is manipulated by those in power to strengthen social control and economic exploitation. If one takes a closer look at how the struggle against vaccination condenses other struggles (struggle against state control, struggle against science, struggle against corporate economic exploitation, struggle for the defense of our way of life . . .), it becomes clear that this key role of the struggle against vaccination is the outcome of an ideological mystification in some aspects even similar to anti-Semitism: in the same way that anti-Semitism is a displaced-mystified form of anti-capitalism, the struggle against vaccination is also a displaced-mystified form of class struggle against those in power.

To find a way in this mess, we should perhaps mobilize the distinction between apocalypse and catastrophe, reserving the term "catastrophe" for what Anders called "naked apocalypse." Apocalypse ("an uncovering" in Ancient Greek) is a disclosure or revelation of knowledge; in religious speech, what apocalypse discloses is something hidden, the ultimate truth we are blind to in our ordinary lives. Today we commonly refer to any larger-scale catastrophic event or chain of detrimental events to humanity or nature as "apocalyptic." Although it is easy to imagine the apocalypse-disclosure without the apocalypse-catastrophe (say, a religious revelation) and the apocalypse-catastrophe without the apocalypse-disclosure (say, an earthquake destroying an entire continent), there is an inner link between the two dimensions: when we (think that we) confront some higher and hitherto hidden truth, this truth is so different from our common opinions that it has to shatter our world, and vice versa, every catastrophic event, even if purely natural, reveals something ignored in our normal existence, places us face to face with an oppressed truth.

In his essay "Apocalypse without Kingdom," Anders introduced the concept of *naked apocalypse*: "the apocalypse that consists of mere downfall, which doesn't represent the opening of a new, positive state of affairs (of the 'kingdom')."[4] Anders's idea was that a nuclear catastrophe would be precisely such a naked apocalypse: no new kingdom will arise out of it, just the obliteration of ourselves and our world. And the question we should ask today is: what kind of apocalypse is announced in the plurality of catastrophes that today pose a threat to all of us? What if apocalypse in the full sense of the term which includes the disclosure of hitherto invisible truth never happens? What if truth is something that is constructed afterwards, as an attempt to make sense of the catastrophe? Some would argue that the disintegration of Communist regimes in Eastern Europe in 1990 was an authentic apocalypse: it brought out the truth that Socialism doesn't work, that liberal-democracy is the finally discovered best possible socio-economic system. But this Fukuyama dream of the end of history ended with a rude awakening a decade later, on September 11, so that we live today in an era that is best characterized as the end of the end— the circle is closed, we passed from catastrophe to apocalypse and then back to catastrophe. We hear again and again that we are at the end of history, but this end just drags on and even brings its own enjoyment.

Our usual notion of catastrophe is that it takes place when the intrusion of some brutal event—earthquake, war...—ruins the symbolic fiction which is our reality. But, perhaps, there is no less a catastrophe when reality remains as it is and just the symbolic fiction that sustains our approach to reality dissolves. Let's take the case of sexuality, since nowhere do fictions play a more crucial role than in sexuality. In an interesting comment on the role of consent in sexual relations, Eva Wiseman refers to "a moment in *The Butterfly Effect*, Jon Ronson's podcast series about internet porn. On the set of a porn film an actor lost his erection mid-scene—to coax it back, he turned away from the woman, naked below him, grabbed his phone and searched Pornhub. Which struck me as vaguely apocalyptic"—note the word "apocalypse" here. Wiseman concludes: "Something is rotten in the state of sex." I agree, but I would add the lesson of psychoanalysis: human sexuality is in itself perverted, exposed to sadomasochist reversals and, specifically, to the mixture of reality and fantasy. Even when I am alone with my partner, my (sexual) interaction with him/her is inextricably intertwined with my fantasies, i.e., every sexual interaction is potentially structured like "masturbation with a real partner," I use the flesh and body of my partner as a prop to realize/enact my fantasies. We cannot reduce this gap between the bodily reality of my partner and the universe of fantasies to a distortion opened up by patriarchy and social domination or exploitation—the gap is there from the very beginning. So I quite understand the actor who, in order to regain an erection, searched Pornbhub—he was looking for a fantasmatic support for his performance.

The rather sad conclusion we are forced to draw from all this is that a catastrophe is not something awaiting us in the future, something that can be avoided with a well-thought-out strategy. Catastrophe in (not only) its most basic ontological sense is something that always-already happened, and we, the surviving humans, are what remains—at all levels, even in the most empirical sense: do the immense reserves of oil and coal, until now our most important source of energy, not bear witness to immense catastrophes that took place on our earth before the rise of humankind? Our normality is by definition post-apocalyptic.

This brings us back to our main point: apart from a couple of "rational optimists," most of us agree that we—all of us, humanity—are caught in a multiple crisis: pandemic, global warming, social protests . . . We are entering a new era, and signs that we are doing so abound. The prospect of a war over access to the waters of the Nile is perhaps a model of wars to come: from the standpoint of nation-state sovereignty, Ethiopia is justified in reserving for itself as much as it wants or needs, but if it takes too much of it, this can threaten the very survival of Egypt which is reliant on the Nile. There is no abstract solution to this problem; there has to be a negotiated compromise from a global perspective. Now let's jump to a recent act of state terrorism: Belarus forcing a Ryanair plane, which was on its way from Athens to Vilnius, to land in order to get hold of Roman Protasevich, a Belarus dissident. (While unambiguously condemning this act of terror, one should remember that Austria did exactly the same thing—landing a flight crossing its air space—the plane of the Bolivian president Evo Morales; this was done on the order of the US which suspected Edward Snowden was on that plane trying to get from Russia to Latin America.) What do the two events have in common? They both exemplify a new type of conflict which will increasingly characterize our global era: the collision of state sovereignty and the interests of larger communities. Although capitalism nourishes itself from crises, using them to reappear stronger than ever, there is a growing suspicion that this time the well-tested formula will not work.

The focus of this book is not different crises as such, but how we fight them or reproduce them, sometimes doing both things in one and the same move. What I try to achieve is not just to analyze the mess we're in, but simultaneously to deploy how most of the critiques and protests against global capitalism effectively function as its ideological supplement and do not really question its basic premises. To see how this is possible, one needs to analyze ideology—not as an abstract system of principles but as a material force which structures our actual life. What this further necessitates is that we mobilize the complex apparatus of psychoanalytic theory which brings out the libidinal investments that regulate our daily lives.

An Unexpected *Lustgewinn*

We are thereby raising the old Freudian question: why do we enjoy oppression itself? That is to say, power asserts its hold over us not simply by oppression (and repression) which are sustained by a fear of punishment, but by bribing us for our obedience and enforced renunciations—what we get in exchange for our obedience and renunciations is a perverted pleasure in renunciation itself, a gain in loss itself. Lacan called this perverted pleasure surplus-enjoyment. Surplus-enjoyment implies the paradox of a thing which is always (and nothing but) an excess with regard to itself: in its "normal" state, it is nothing. This brings us to Lacan's notion of *objet a* as the surplus-enjoyment: there is no "basic enjoyment" to which one adds the surplus-enjoyment, enjoyment is always a surplus, in excess. *Objet a* has a long history in Lacan's teaching. It precedes by decades Lacan's systematic references to the analysis of commodities in Marx's *Capital*. But it is undoubtedly this reference to Marx, especially to Marx's notion of surplus-value (*Mehrwert*), that enabled Lacan to deploy his »mature« notion of *objet a* as surplus-enjoyment (*plus-de-jouir, Mehrlust*): the predominant motif which permeates all Lacan's references to Marx's analysis of commodities is the structural homology between Marx's surplus-value and what Lacan's named surplus-enjoyment, the phenomenon Freud calls *Lustgewinn*, a "gain of pleasure," which does not designate a simple stepping up of pleasure but the additional pleasure provided by the very formal detours in the subject's effort to attain pleasure. Another figure of *Lustgewinn* is the reversal that characterizes hysteria: renunciation of pleasure reverts to pleasure of/in renunciation, repression of desire reverts to desire of repression, etc. Such a reversal lies at the very heart of capitalist logic: as Lacan pointed out, modern capitalism began with *counting* the pleasure (of gaining profit), and this counting of pleasure immediately reverts to the *pleasure of counting* (profit). In all these cases, gain occurs at a "performative" level: it is generated by the very performance of working towards a goal, not by reaching the goal.[5]

A voluptuous woman from Portugal once told me a wonderful anecdote: when her most recent lover had first seen her fully naked, he told her that, if she lost just one or two kilos, her body would be perfect. The truth was, of course, that had she lost the weight, she would probably have looked more ordinary—the very element that seems to disturb perfection itself creates the illusion of the perfection it disturbs: if we take away the excessive element, we lose the perfection itself. So here is the paradox of *objet a* at its purest: there is an attractive but curvaceous woman lacking that something which generates a true charm—what should she do? *Not* make herself more perfect or beautiful but introduce onto her body some sign of imperfection, some detail disturbing perfection—this additional element *may* (nothing is guaranteed in this domain!) function as something that disturbs her perfection, so that it creates the mirage of perfection it disturbs. Let's take another (rather tasteless) example—hardcore pornographic movies. My spontaneous intuition tells me that it must be very uncomfortable to perform the ultimate intimate act before a camera very close to me, obeying the director's orders—utter sounds of pleasure or change the positions of bodily parts on demand ... Does this not present an obstacle which the performers can overcome only through long training which enables them emotionally to ignore their situation which seems to thwart surrender to ecstatic pleasures? Is sex not something that most of us are able to do only out of view of the public? However, what if we take into account the possibility that, with some people at least, the fact of finding oneself in such a de-stimulating situation can generate a pleasure of its own? Something along the lines of "it's even more pleasurable to perform the most intimate act as if it is a regulated activity requiring the following of external orders?" ...

If, then, every renunciation of pleasure gives birth to a pleasure in this renunciation itself, and if there is no "normal" direct pleasure, so that every pleasure caught in the symbolic cobweb is branded by this perverted twist, is there a way to get out of this vicious cycle of pleasure and pain? The answer Lacan hints at a couple of times is "subjective destitution," a mysterious move of acquiring a distance from all that forms the wealth of our "inner person," all the shit that is hidden deep in myself, while remaining a subject—a "pure" empty subject, a subject who resembles a living dead, a zombie-like subject. What—if anything—does this mean politically? The Finale of the book ventures some hypotheses in this direction.

However, before arriving at this final point, the book proceeds step by step. It begins with global capitalism as the social form and ultimate source of the madness of our world, focusing on the complex relationship between the Marxist critique of political economy and ecology. From here, it ventures upon what one might call the critique of libidinal economy: the deeply embedded forms of psychic life which sustain social relations of domination and exploitation. Then it deals directly with the basic de-rangement of our libidinal economy: surplus-enjoyment. Finally, the book proposes a way out of this predicament: the radical gesture of subjective destitution.

Every chapter is also in some sense a reader's report: each was instigated by an outstanding text. Kohei Saito enabled me to see in a new light the key role of ecology in Marxism; Gabriel Tupinamba shattered my Lacanian complacency with a sharp analysis of the ideological limitations not only of Lacanians but of Lacan himself; Yanis Varoufakis made me aware of how the deadlocks of desire affect the very core of our political projects; Frank Ruda's provocative call to abolish freedom brought out the theological roots of emancipatory projects; and, last but not least, Saroj Giri instantly converted me to his notion of subjective destitution as a key political category. So where is Hegel in all this? While these authors made visible the failings in our contemporary response to global emergencies, I had some liminal (but maybe important) disagreement with each of them, and, in each case, I found that how reading Hegel can supply that lack.

$2 + a$

So how does this book deal with the ambiguous signs of the new era? Its formula is $2 + a$. The first two chapters deal with Marx and Freud, the two founders of modern "hermeneutics of suspicion" which denounces the visible (socio-political and psychic) order as a "theatre of shadows" regulated by hidden mechanisms (of political economy, of the unconscious): Marx analyzed capitalist modernity in which the entire tradition is turned topsy-turvy; Freud deployed the antagonisms and reversals of our psychic lives. In both cases, the aim of my reading is to avoid the "reductionist" reading of Marx and Freud which claims that they both see social life as determined by "objective" mechanisms, and to assert the irreducible subjective dimension of social and psychic processes.

As with all philosophical works, this book is an ontology of its own (our, in this case) present, so the classics are read from our own historical experience: how do Marx and Freud enable us to grasp our present and its deadlocks? They are all rooted in a precise historical constellation: Marx witnessed the unheard-of capitalist expansion and analyzed its destructive effects; at the turn of the new century, Freud probed the dark recesses of the human mind against the background of what was called "decline of the West" and the traumatic shock of the Great War. The book reads Marx and Freud from our contemporary standpoint: Marx and ecological crisis; Freud and the socio-politics of psychoanalysis. Marx and Freud are past classics indispensable for an understanding of our present.

But what about our present itself? There is no classical author whose theory would allow us to directly grasp our epoch in its notional structure—we are fully caught in its mess, we are lacking a cognitive mapping, and the final chapter plunges directly into this mess. Lacan's notion of *objet a* or surplus-enjoyment (modeled upon Marx's surplus-enjoyment) was chosen here as a central point of reference because it functions exactly as the operator of topsy-turviness: you take a field of phenomena, you add to it surplus-enjoyment, and the balance of this field is irrevocably lost, everything turns around—pain becomes pleasure, lack becomes surplus, hatred becomes love … This chapter is the pivot of the book, and in order not to miss its point the reader must carefully follow the way it gradually approaches its central thesis. Starting with two opposed figures of the "big Other" (the virtual symbolic order, the Id-machine), it links the structural inconsistency of the symbolic order to the duality between the symbolic Law and the superego, and it then goes on to show how the superego injunction to enjoy regulates the libidinal economy of our "permissive" societies. The unavoidable result of such permissiveness is depression which can be defined as the suffocation of desire when its object is freely available—what is missing is surplus-enjoyment as the object-cause of desire. The book's Finale then tries to articulate the existential stance which would enable us to break out of the deadlock of permissiveness without regressing into old forms of fundamentalism. Relying on the work of Saroj Giri, I propose a political reading of the Lacanian notion of subjective destitution.

Does the book's rootedness in our present imply historicist relativism? The first move to make here is to radicalize historicism itself. Bruno Latour wrote that it is meaningless to talk about tuberculosis in Medieval times: tuberculosis is a modern scientific category which has no place in the Medieval horizon of thought— if we were to meet a man from that era and tell him "Your brother died of tuberculosis!", this would have meant nothing to him. The further step is that modernity (which, for Latour, doesn't exist) not only introduces a new horizon of understanding, it changes the entire field and also redefines what appears to us as "Medieval era"—our notion of the Medieval era is rooted in our epoch, it is always-already "mediated" by our contemporary experience, we cannot ever occupy a neutral place exempted from history from which we could compare different epochs.

So, again, does this mean that we cannot escape the trap of historicism? The way out of the historicist deadlock is indicated by the well-known passage from *Grundrisse*, where Marx deploys apropos the notion of labor how universal notions, although universal ("eternal," trans-historical, valid for all epochs), appear as such (become actual, part of our experience) only in a particular epoch. We don't reach universality by abstracting from concrete features of particular epochs but by focusing on a particular epoch in which the universality in question appears as such—this point is for Hegel the point of concrete universality. The hypothesis of this book is that the same holds for the topsy-turviness of human history: although universal, it becomes part of our daily experience only in our epoch, the epoch after "the end of history" in 1990 when new "post-historical" antagonisms exploded.

Today, the predominant idea of interpreting Hegel is that, in order to be of any use, Hegel should be read through some post-Hegelian theory. Liberal readers of Hegel (like Robert Brandom) who focus on mutual recognition submit him to pragmatic-linguistic reading. For eco-Marxists (like Saito), Hegel's notion of the self-movement of Idea should be reinterpreted as the collective productive process of humanity rooted in nature. Psychoanalysts who refer to Hegel (like Lacan) see in Hegel's dialectic a distorted expression of the processes of the Unconscious and its re-integration by the Self. The ongoing ideologico-political mess (populist violence that comes close to civil war) cannot be explained just by vested economic interests and ideological manipulations—one has to introduce (racist, sexist) enjoyment clearly discernible in alt-Right carnivalesque public events.

In each of these cases, the book will argue that there is more in Hegel than in his contemporary critical readings: Hegel's notion of nature is more open to contingencies than the Marxist focus on the productive process; instead of reading Hegel through Freud, one should read Freud (as well as Lacan) in a Hegelian way to detect his fateful limitations; finally, far from simply dismissing religion as a finite way to represent conceptual truth, Hegel clearly saw the role of surplus-enjoyment in religious collective rituals, the satisfaction they bring. So, again, the target of my critique is the already-mentioned predominant stance according to which we can retrieve what is alive in Hegel (as well as Marx and Freud) only if we read him through some later figure of orientation: Freud through Lacan, Marx through today's ecological problems, and Hegel himself through the liberal theory of mutual recognition. But what if the opposite move is also necessary: we have to read Hegel through later events and thoughts and then return back to Hegel to grasp what these new events and thoughts are really about? What if those who read Hegel's notion of freedom through the lenses of the gradual progress towards free mutual recognition miss radical negativity as the core of a dialectical process?[6] What if we can properly grasp the deadlocks of Marxism and ecology only if we read Marx through Hegel? What if we can grasp the radical break in Freud and Lacan only if we read them through Hegel?

So let's conclude with a Hegelian welcome to our viral time: all big battles today, at the beginning of the twenty-first century, are battles of viruses. Spirit is a virus parasitizing on the human animal, and this parasitizing got more dangerous with the prospect of a wired brain where our mental processes will be directly controlled by the big Other of a global digital network. Biochemical viruses threaten our survival: COVID-19 will for sure be followed by other and probably worse epidemics. And, last but not least, global Capital itself is a gigantic virus which ruthlessly uses us as means of its expanded self-reproduction . . . Yes, this century will be Hegelian.

"Good Luck, Mr Hegel!"

According to a legend (probably no more than that), the first words pronounced by Neil Armstrong after making the first step on the moon on July 20, 1969 were not the officially reported "That's one small step for man, one giant leap for mankind." but the enigmatic remark: "Good luck, Mr. Gorsky." Many people at NASA thought it was a casual remark concerning some rival Soviet Cosmonaut. We had to wait until July 5, 1995 when, while answering questions following a speech, enigma was explained: "In 1938, when he was a kid in a small mid-western town, he was playing baseball with a friend in the backyard. His friend hit the ball, which landed in his neighbor's yard by their bedroom window. His neighbors were Mr. and Mrs. Gorsky. As he leaned down to pick up the ball, young Armstrong heard Mrs. Gorsky shouting at Mr. Gorsky, 'sex! You want sex?! . . . You'll get sex when the kid next door walks on the moon!'"[7] This is what literally happened 31 years later . . . Upon hearing this anecdote, I imagined my own version. What if around 1800, when Hegel was still little-known, some old (and now forgotten) professor was heard to shout at him: "Fame! You want to be a famous philosophical classic? . . . You'll get fame when a guy from some little-known small Slavic country like Slovenia writes a big fat book about you which will be translated into many other languages?" This is what happened when my over-1,000 page *Less Than Nothing* appeared, although there is no doubt that some enemy of mine would immediately add: "This book may be a giant leap for Žižek, but it is a small step for philosophy."

Among those enemies was definitely Roger Scruton, who wrote some years ago: "Indeed, if there were no greater reason to regret the collapse of communism in Eastern Europe, the release of Žižek on the world of Western scholarship would perhaps already be a sufficient one."[8] One should stop for a moment to ponder the madness of this claim (even if one takes into account the moment of rhetorical exaggeration): that I am more dangerous and

destructive than all the horrors of Communist totalitarianism ...
(Incidentally, similar claims abounded in the 1990s: when Western
conservatives were reminded that Communism was undermined
by pop culture and sexual revolution much more than by traditional
values, some of them snapped back that this fact alone made one
regret the collapse of Communist regimes.) One can imagine how
this accusation feeds my megalomaniac fantasies: Hegel wrote that
the spiritual result of the Peloponnesian war is the book Thucydides
wrote on it—thousands had to die so that a book was written; in a
similar way, the spiritual result of Communism with its breath-
taking terror is my release on Western scholarship—the whole of
Eastern Europe had to go through dangerous turmoil so that I
could became known in Western academia ... If we step out of this
megalomaniac madness, there is a hint of what the role of an
intellectual is today. When a system that deserves to disappear (like
Soviet Communism) effectively disintegrates, and (almost)
everybody is enthusiastic about its fall, the task of thought—our
task today—is to envisage the dangerous potentials of the emerging
new order. Again, one should practice a critique of critique and
avoid at any cost the smug satisfaction of just kicking the head of a
system which already lies dead in front of us. That's why today, in
the mess of alt-Right obscenities and pseudo-Leftist PC moralist
rigidity, moderate conservatives are often the only reasonable
partners of (what remains of) the radical Left. In a recent phone
conversation with an editor of *Die Welt*, the moderately conservative
German daily, I expressed my amazement that they were prepared
to publish me, a self-declared moderately conservative Communist.
The wonderful answer I got was that I shouldn't be so surprised
since they are a moderately Communist conservative newspaper ...

There is, however, a feature of this book which will annoy many
readers, even some of those otherwise sympathetic to my ideas: the
style gets crazier and crazier, so that the book itself can appear as a
gradual drift into madness. While the first chapter could still pass as
an academic treatise, the text more and more reads as a confused
jumping from one example to another, from one quotation or image
to another ... (Incidentally, the same accusation befell Hegel in the
first reactions to his *Phenomenology of Spirit*.) My answer is that,
while I plead guilty to this reproach, I consider it a positive feature—a

strategy that is essential in unraveling the antagonisms of a text as well as of a historical epoch. Therein resides the fatal limitation of the effort to faithfully reconstruct the meaning intended by the author from whom we quote: what if the interpreted/quoted author is him/herself inconsistent, caught in historical antagonisms and tensions, so that the real violence is a reading which obfuscates these antagonisms? In this sense, I plead for (and practice) a violent reading, a reading which tears (what appears as) organic unities apart and the passages it quotes out of their context, establishing new unexpected links between fragments. These links do not operate at the level of continuous linear historical progress; they rather emerge at points of "dialectic at a standstill" (Benjamin) in which a present moment, in a kind of trans-historical short-circuit, directly echoes homologous moments in the past . . . in short, I try to practice what, in *Politically Red*, Eduardo Cadava and Sara Nadal-Melsio[9] have developed as a materialist practice of engaged reading, a reading which is in its very linguistic form political.

Such a reading breaks out of the space of the standard opposition between the immanent reading, which tries to remain faithful to the interpreted text, and the practice of quotation which just uses fragments of a text to justify present ideological and political measures. The exemplary case of such practice is found in Stalinism: the key to Leninism as (Stalinist) ideology is provided by Mikhail Suslov, the member of the Politburo responsible for ideology from Stalin's late years to Gorbachev. Neither Khrushchev nor Brezhnev would release any document until Suslov had looked over it. Why? Suslov had an enormous library of Lenin's quotes in his Kremlin office; they were written on library cards, organized by themes, and contained in wooden filing cabinets. Every time a new political campaign, economic measure, or international policy was introduced, Suslov found an appropriate quote from Lenin to support it. Lenin's quotes in Suslov's collection were isolated from their original contexts. Because Lenin was an extremely prolific writer who commented on all sorts of historical situations and political developments, Suslov could find appropriate quotes to legitimate as "Leninist" almost any argument or initiative, sometimes even if they opposed each other: "the very same quotes from the founders of Marxism-Leninism that Suslov successfully used under Stalin and for which Stalin so highly valued him, Suslov later employed to critique Stalin."[10] This was the truth of Soviet Leninism: Lenin served as the ultimate reference; a quote of his legitimized any political, economic or cultural measure, but in a totally pragmatic and arbitrary way—in exactly the same way, incidentally, that the Catholic Church referred to the Bible. The irony is thus that the two big orientations of Marxism, the Stalinist one and the authentic one, can be perfectly grasped through two different modes of quotation.

What Benjamin conceptualized and practiced (together with Hegel, Marx, Lenin, Brecht, Jameson, and numerous others) was a radically different practice of quotation, quotation as a form of struggle with the quoted text as well as with the writer's own predicament. Materialist quotation is internal to the quoted original through its very externality to it: its violent disfiguration of the original is in some sense more faithful to the original than the original itself since it echoes social struggles that traverse both.[11] That's why I jump from Hegel to Hollywood comedies, from Kant to vampires and the living dead in pop culture, from LGBT+ to Slovene vulgar expressions, from revolutionary subjectivity to *Joker*... with the hope that, in these crazy combinations, I—sometimes, at least—succeed in doing what Benjamin intended.

So this book is definitely a guide for the non-perplexed: it does not try to clarify things for the perplexed, it tries to perplex the non-perplexed who comfortably swim in the water of everyday ideology, not only trying to perplex them but demonstrating that their newly gained perplexity resides already in the thing itself. In the same vein, this book definitely does not provide a "safe space" for those exposed to racism and sexism. In a recent incident that occurred at the University of Alberta, Kathleen Lowrey, a professor at the school of anthropology, was under threat of losing her job for claiming sex is not just a cultural construct but primarily biological fact. Technically she was fired from her position as associate chair of undergraduate programs in the department of anthropology for creating an "unsafe" environment for students—how? In a nutshell, she doesn't believe that sex is a "social construct."[12] To clarify things, one should add here that the opposition between biological fact and symbolic construct is not an exhaustive one: there is a third option, sexual difference itself as real/impossible which is not a biological fact but a traumatic cut/antagonism that cannot be fully symbolized. But what should draw our attention is the word "unsafe": "unsafe" ultimately amounts to something that threatens the (self-declared) victim's views and self-perception. Let's take the case of a man who transforms into a woman: if gender identity is (also) biologically determined, this in no way limits his/her freedom to change gender identity. What it threatens is his/her idea that his/her identity is a purely cultural construct that ultimately depends on his/her free decision, the idea that I can freely reconstruct myself, play with multiple identities, and that all obstacles to this plasticity are to be located in cultural oppression.

One cannot but note how, in the case of sexual identities, the passage from one to another identity—like cross-dressing—is hailed as progressive, as undermining binary logic, while in the case of racial identities, transitions—especially whites dressing as blacks—are rejected as racial appropriation, as a form of racism. Here is a recent case: Bright Sheng is a world-class composer who has been teaching at the University of Michigan since 1995. On September 10 2021, David Gier, the dean of the University of Michigan School of Music, Theatre & Dance, announced that Sheng would stop teaching his undergraduate music composition course; the decision came a month after Sheng screened for the class the 1965 movie adaptation of Shakespeare's *Othello* featuring Laurence Olivier playing Othello with black make-up. Sheng was "turned in," according to the *Michigan Daily*, by one of his freshman students, Olivia Cook, who took note that Olivier was playing Othello in black make-up. She wrote. "In such a school that preaches diversity and making sure that they understand the history of POC (people of color) in America, I was shocked that (Sheng) would show something like this in something that's supposed to be a safe space." In a statement to the *Michigan Daily*, composition Professor Evan Chambers—who is replacing Sheng on the course—wrote: "To show the film now, especially without substantial framing, content advisory and a focus on its inherent racism, is in itself a racist act, regardless of the professor's intentions."[13]

The same was done in the Soviet Union around 1970 when the BBC production of *The Forsythe Saga* (1967) was shown on TV: to prevent ideological contamination, each episode was introduced by a five- to ten-minute commentary by a Soviet literary scientist who provided "substantial framing and content advisory," warning viewers of how, in spite of its universal humanism and occasional critical stance, the series celebrates the bourgeois way of life ... And, to go even further back, until a century or so ago, it was prohibited in Catholic countries for children (and in some cases even for adults) to read the Bible directly, without a proper comment providing "substantial framing and content advisory," since, without such a comment, many passages could incite impure or cruel thoughts (just think about the story of David and Bathsheba...). It is sad to see this tradition resuscitated today on behalf of Political Correctness ... In the case of *Othello*, to impose these conditions—"substantial framing, content advisory and a focus on its inherent racism"—on showing the film effectively is in itself a racist act, regardless of Chambers's intentions: he treats viewers in an extremely patronizing way, as naïve creatures who have to be protected from the direct impact of the text.

Upon a closer look, one can easily see that this is a double protection: by watching a movie like *Othello*, whites are reassured in their racism; blacks are not so much seduced into racism which humiliates them as insulted and furious at how racism goes on in culture (and their daily lives). But here problems begin. *Othello* offers a safe space for white racists, assuring them that even in an officially non-racist culture their privileges are safe; it violates campus as a safe space for blacks who are plagued even there by racism in high culture. But does the proposed strategy—"substantial framing, content advisory and a focus on its inherent racism"— work? No, because proper insults which affect the victim are impervious to negation: no matter how many qualifications are added, the insult remains an insult—this is why, among others, the N-word is prohibited and cannot be used, no matter how many qualifications we add. But direct prohibition of all works that may be perceived by someone as insults is also counter-productive: it cannot but generate an immense apparatus of censorship which would ultimately not only impoverish the presumed victims themselves but also open up the space for cynical irony that would even further insult the victims. The problem resides in the very concept of academia as a "safe space": we should fight to render the world *outside* academia safe for all, and if academia wants to contribute to this fight, it should be precisely the space where we openly confront all racist and sexist horrors. This book for sure does that.

1
Where is the Rift? Marx, Capitalism and Ecology

When, decades ago, ecology emerged as a crucial theoretical and practical issue, many Marxists (as well as critics of Marxism) noted that nature—more precisely, the exact ontological status of nature—is the one topic in which even the crudest dialectical materialism has an advantage over Western Marxism: dialectical materialism allows us to think of humanity as part of nature while Western Marxism considers socio-historical dialectics as the ultimate horizon of reference and ultimately reduces nature to a background of the historical process—nature is a historical category, as Georg Lukacs put it. Kohei Saito's *Karl Marx's Ecosocialism*[1] is the latest most consistent attempt to redress the balance and think of humanity's embeddedness in nature without regressing to dialectical-materialist general ontology.

Since the main philosophical reference of Western Marxism is Hegel, no wonder that Saito aggressively rejects the Hegelian inheritance. In contrast to Saito and other eco-Socialists, our premise is that the problems we are confronting now (pandemic, global warming) compel us not to abandon Hegel but to return from Marx to Hegel—with one proviso: we should return to Hegel *after passing through Marx*, through his critique of political economy. When Robert Brandom points out that Hegel is ultimately telling the same story again and again, the story of the rise of modernity, of the passage from traditional "organic" society to a modern "alienated" one, he focuses on two aspects of this passage, arguably the most radical passage in the entire history of humanity after the rise of the Neolithic: the break in religion and philosophy (Protestantism, Cartesian subjectivity), and the French Revolution—what is missing here? Although Hegel read Smith and other early political economists, he ignores the key role of capitalism and industrial revolution. Duane Rouelle perspicuously noted the basic ambiguity of the desperate search for the alternatives to capitalism:

> If the radical philosophers, including Marx and Bakunin, were quick to ask "what about the alternatives?", then it was because they sometimes failed to see that capitalism has assumed the position of "alternative." Capitalism is the alternative (to authoritarianism, dogmatism, socialism and so on).[2]

It is not only that capitalism can only thrive through permanent self-revolutionizing, as Marx pointed out; it is that capitalism again and again emerges as the only alternative, the only way to move forward, the dynamic force which intervenes when social life gets stuck into some fixed form. Today, capitalism is much more revolutionary than the traditional Left, which is obsessed with protecting the old achievements of the welfare state—just recall how much capitalism has changed the entire texture of our societies in recent decades. Many Leftists in the West are so obsessed with the critique of neoliberal capitalism that they neglect the big change, the passage from neoliberal capitalism to a strange post-capitalism which some analysts call "corporate neo-feudalism." How did it come to this?

Neoconservative Communism

When, due to the crucial role of the "general intellect" (social knowledge and cooperation) in the creation of wealth, forms of wealth are more and more out of all proportion to the direct labor time spent on their production, the result is not, as Marx expected, the self-dissolution of capitalism, but the gradual transformation of the profit generated by the exploitation of labor into rent appropriated by the privatization of the "general intellect" and other commons. Let us take the case of Bill Gates: how did he become one of the richest men in the world? Because Microsoft imposed itself as an almost universal standard, (almost) monopolizing the field, a kind of direct embodiment of the "general intellect." Things are similar with Jeff Bezos and Amazon, with Apple, Facebook, etc. etc.—in all these cases, commons themselves— the platforms (spaces of our social exchange and interaction)—are privatized, which puts us, their users, into the position of serfs paying a rent to the owner of a common as our feudal master. We recently learn that "2% of Elon Musk's wealth could solve world hunger, says director of UN food scarcity organization"[3]—a clear indication of corporate neofeudalism. With regard to Facebook, "Mark Zuckerberg 'has unilateral control over 3 billion people' due to his unassailable position at the top of Facebook, the whistleblower Frances Haugen told the British MPs as she called for urgent external regulation to rein in the tech company's management and reduce the harm being done to society."[4] The big achievement of modernity, the public space, is thus disappearing.

This new phase of global economy also implies a different functioning of the financial sphere. Yanis Varoufakis[5] noted a weird fact that became evident in the spring of 2020: on the same day that state statistics in the US and the UK registered a breath-taking fall in GDP, comparable to the fall at the time of the Great Recession, stock markets registered a gigantic rise. In short, although the "real" economy is stagnating or even shrinking, stock markets go up—an indication that fictitious financial capital is caught in its own circle, decoupled from the "real" economy. This is where the financial measures justified by the pandemic entered the game: they in a way turn around the traditional Keynesian procedure, i.e., their aim was not to help the "real" economy but to invest enormous amounts of money in the financial sphere (to prevent a financial collapse like the one of 2008) while making sure that most of this money will *not* flow into the "real" economy (as this could cause hyperinflation).

But what makes the situation really dangerous, pushing us into a new barbarism, is that privatized commons co-exist with a new wave of strong nation-state competition which runs directly against the urgent need to establish a new mode of relating to our environs—a radical politico-economic change which Peter Sloterdijk calls "the domestication of the wild animal Culture." Until now, each culture disciplined/educated its own members and guaranteed civic peace among them, but the relationship between different cultures and states was permanently under the shadow of potential war, with each period of peace nothing more than a temporary armistice. The entire ethic of a state culminates in the highest act of heroism, the readiness to sacrifice one's life for one's nation-state, which means that the wild barbarian relations between states serve as the foundation of the ethical life within a state.[6]

Today, things are getting even worse. Instead of civilizing (the relations between) cultures, the ongoing privatization of commons undermines the ethical substance within each culture, pushing us back into barbarism. However, the moment we fully accept the fact that we live on a Spaceship Earth, the task that urgently imposes itself is that of forging universal solidarity and cooperation among all human communities. There is no higher historical necessity that pushes us in this direction—history is not on our side, it tends towards our collective suicide. As Walter Benjamin wrote, our task today is not to push forward the train of historical progress but to pull the emergency break before we all end in post-capitalist barbarism. In recent months, the often alarming ways in which the crisis of the COVID-19 pandemic has been intertwined with ongoing social, political, climatic, and economic crises are increasingly apparent. The pandemic must be treated together with global warming, erupting class antagonisms, patriarchy and misogyny, and the many other ongoing crises which resonate with it and with each other in a complex interplay. This interplay is uncontrollable and full of dangers, and we cannot count on any guarantee in Heaven to make the solution clearly imaginable. Such a risky situation makes our moment an eminently political one.

It is only against this background that we can understand what is going on now in China. The recent Chinese campaign against big corporations and the opening of a new stock exchange in Beijing dedicated to the promotion of small firms can also be seen as moves against neo-feudal corporatism, i.e., as attempts to bring back "normal" capitalism. The irony of the situation is obvious: a strong Communist regime is needed to keep capitalism alive against the threat of neo-feudal corporatist post-capitalism . . . This is why one should follow with great interest the writings of Wang Huning, a current member of the party's Politburo Standing Committee and the director of the Central Guidance Commission on Building Spiritual Civilization. Wang is correct in emphasizing the key role of culture, of the domain of symbolic fictions. The true materialist way to oppose the topic of the "fiction of reality" (subjectivist doubts in the style of "is what we perceive as reality not just another fiction?") is not to strictly distinguish between fiction and reality but to focus on the *reality of fictions*. Fictions are not outside reality, they are materialized in our social interactions, in our institutions and customs—as we can see in today's mess, if we destroy fictions on which our social interactions are based, our social reality itself begins to fall apart.

Wang designated himself as a neo-conservative—what does this mean? If one is to trust our big media, Wang is the leading light against the recent new orientation of Chinese politics. When I read that one of the measures lately imposed by the Chinese government is the prohibition of "996," I must admit my first association was a sexual one: in our parlance "69" means the position in which the man performs cunnilingus on the woman and the woman fellatio on the man, and I thought "996" must refer to some more perverted sexual practice becoming widespread in China and involving two men and a woman (as there is a relative lack of women there). Then I learned that "996" means a brutal work rhythm imposed by many corporations in China (a working day from 9am to 9pm, six days a week). But in some sense I was not completely wrong: the ongoing campaign in China has a double target: more economic equality, inclusive of better conditions of work, and the elimination of Westernized popular culture focused on sex, consumerism and fandom.

So what does being a neo-conservative mean in today's conditions? In mid-October 2019, the Chinese media launched an offensive promoting the claim that "demonstrations in Europe and South America are the direct result of Western tolerance of Hong Kong unrest." In a commentary published in *Beijing News*, former Chinese diplomat Wang Zhen wrote that "the disastrous impact of a 'chaotic Hong Kong' has begun to influence the Western world," i.e., that demonstrators in Chile and Spain were taking their cues from Hong Kong. Along the same lines, an editorial in the *Global Times* accused Hong Kong demonstrators of "exporting revolution to the world":

> The West is paying the price for supporting riots in Hong Kong, which has quickly kindled violence in other parts of the world and foreboded the political risks that the West can't manage ... There are many problems in the West and all kinds of undercurrents of dissatisfaction. Many of them will eventually manifest in the way the Hong Kong protests did.

The ominous conclusion was that "Catalonia is probably just the beginning."[7]

Although the idea that demonstrations in Barcelona and Chile are taking their cues from Hong Kong is far-fetched. These outbursts exploded into a general discontent which was obviously already there, lurking, waiting for a contingent trigger to explode, so that even when the particular law or measure was repealed, protests persisted. Communist China discreetly plays on the solidarity of those in power all around the world against the rebellious populace, warning the West not to underestimate dissatisfaction in their own countries—as if, beneath ideological and geo-political tensions, they all share the same basic interest in holding onto power ... But will this defense work?

Wang sees his task as imposing a new common ethical substance, and we should not dismiss this as an excuse to impose the full control of the Communist Party over social life. Wang is addressing a real problem. Thirty years ago, he wrote a book, *America against America*, where he perspicuously noted the antagonisms of the American way of life, including its darker sides: social disintegration, lack of solidarity and shared values, nihilist consumerism and individualism ...[8] Trump's populism was a false way out: it was the climax of social disintegration because it introduced obscenity into public speech and thus deprived it of its dignity—something not only prohibited but totally unimaginable in China. We will definitely never see a senior Chinese politician doing what Trump did publicly: talk about the size of his penis, imitating a woman's orgasmic sounds ... Wang's fear was that the same disease might spread to China—which is now happening at the popular level of mass culture, and the ongoing reforms are a desperate attempt to put a stop to this trend. Again, will it work? It is easy to perceive in the ongoing campaign a tension between content and form: the content—the establishment of stable values that hold a society together—is enforced in the form of mobilization which is experienced as a kind of emergency state imposed by the state apparatus. Although the goal is the opposite of the Cultural Revolution, there are similarities with it in the way the campaign is carried out. The danger is that such tensions can produce cynical disbelief in the population. More generally, the ongoing campaign in China seems all too close to standard conservative attempts to enjoy the benefits of capitalist dynamism, but to control its destructive aspects through a strong nation state pushing forward patriotic values.

Therein resides the trap. Carlo Ginzburg proposed the notion that shame for one's country, not love of it, may be the true mark of belonging to it.[9] A supreme example of such shame occurred back in 2014 when hundreds of Holocaust survivors and descendants of survivors bought an ad in Saturday's *New York Times* condemning what they referred to as "the massacre of Palestinians in Gaza and the ongoing occupation and colonization of historic Palestine": "We are alarmed by the extreme, racist dehumanization of Palestinians in Israeli society, which has reached a fever-pitch," said the statement. Maybe, today, some Israelis will gather the courage to feel shame apropos of what the Israelis are doing on the West Bank and in Israel itself—not, of course, in the sense of feeling ashamed to be Jewish but, on the contrary, of feeling shame for what Israeli politics in the West Bank is doing to the most precious legacy of Judaism itself. "My country right or wrong" is one of the most disgusting of mottos, and it illustrates perfectly what is wrong with unconditional patriotism. The same holds for China today. The space in which we can develop such critical thinking is the space of the public use of reason. In the famous passage of his "What is Enlightenment?," Immanuel Kant opposes the "public" and the "private" use of reason: "private" is not one's individual space as opposed to communal ties, but the very communal-institutional order of one's particular identification; while "public" is the trans-national universality of the exercise of one's Reason:

> The public use of one's reason must always be free, and it alone can bring about enlightenment among men. The private use of one's reason, on the other hand, may often be very narrowly

restricted without particularly hindering the progress of enlightenment. By public use of one's reason I understand the use which a person makes of it as a scholar before the reading public. Private use I call that which one may make of it in a particular civil post or office which is entrusted to him.[10]

This is why Kant's formula of Enlightenment is not "Don't obey, think freely!" and is not "Don't obey, think and rebel!" but: "Think freely, state your thoughts publicly, *and obey*!" The same holds for vaccine doubters: debate, publish your doubts, but obey regulations once the public authority imposes them. Without such practical consensus we will slowly drift into a society composed of tribal factions, as is happening in many Western countries. But without the space for the public use of reason, the state itself courts the danger of becoming just another instance of the private use of reason. The space for the public use of reason is not the same as democracy in the Western liberal sense—in his last active year, Lenin himself saw the necessity of such an organ embodying the public use of reason. While admitting the dictatorial nature of the Soviet regime, he proposed the establishment of a Central Control Commission—an independent, educational and controlling body with an "apolitical" edge, consisting of the best teachers and technocratic specialists monitoring the "politicized" CC and its organs. In "dreaming" (his expression) about the kind of work to be done by the CCC, he describes how this body should resort

> to some semi-humorous trick, cunning device, piece of trickery or something of that sort. I know that in the staid and earnest states of Western Europe such an idea would horrify people and that not a single decent official would even entertain it. I hope, however, that we have not yet become as bureaucratic as all that and that in our midst the discussion of this idea will give rise to nothing more than amusement. Indeed, why not combine pleasure with utility? Why not resort to some humorous or semi-humorous trick to expose something ridiculous, something harmful, something semi-ridiculous, semi-harmful, etc.?[11]

Maybe, China needs a similar Central Control Commission. With the neoconservative turn in China, a whole cycle of emancipatory politics has closed. In his *Notes Towards a Definition of Culture*, the great conservative T.S. Eliot remarked that there are moments when the only choice is the one between heresy and non-belief, when the only way to keep a religion alive is to perform a sectarian split from its main corpse. Lenin did this with regard to traditional Marxism, Mao did this in his own way, and this is what has to be done today.

When, in 1922, after achieving victory in the Civil War against all the odds, the Bolsheviks had to retreat into the NEP (the "New Economic Policy" of allowing a much wider scope for the market economy and private property), Lenin wrote a short text "On Ascending a High Mountain." He uses the simile of a climber who has to retreat back to the valley from his first attempt to reach a new mountain peak in order to describe what a retreat means in a revolutionary process, i.e., how does one retreat without opportunistically betraying one's fidelity to the Cause. After enumerating the achievements and the failures of the Soviet state, Lenin concludes: "Communists who have no illusions, who do not give way to despondency, and who preserve their strength and flexibility 'to begin from the beginning' over and over again in approaching an extremely difficult task, are not doomed (and in all probability will not perish)."[12] This is Lenin at his Beckettian best, echoing the line from *Worstward Ho*: "Try again. Fail again. Fail better." His conclusion—"to begin from the beginning over and over again"—makes it clear that he is not talking merely of slowing down progress and consolidating what has already been achieved, but precisely of *descending back to the starting point*: one should "begin from the beginning," not from where one succeeded in ascending in the previous effort. In Kierkegaard's terms, a revolutionary process is not a gradual progress, but a repetitive movement, a movement of *repeating the beginning* again and again . . . and this, exactly, is where we are today, after the "obscure disaster" of 1989, the definitive end of the epoch which began with the October Revolution. One should therefore reject the continuity with what Left meant in the last two centuries. Although sublime moments like the Jacobin climax of the French Revolution and the October Revolution will forever remain a key part of our memory, that story is over, everything should be re-thought, one should begin from the zero-point.

As noted above, capitalism is more revolutionary today than the traditional Left, which is obsessed with protecting the achievements of the welfare state. Again, we should remember how capitalism has changed our societies over recent decades. This is why the strategy of the radical Left today should combine pragmatism with a principled stance in a way which cannot but recall Lenin's New Economic Policy (NEP) from the early 1920s when Soviet power allowed a certain degree of private property and market economy. The NEP was obviously the original model for Deng Hsiao-Ping's reforms which opened the way to a capitalist free market (under the control of the ruling Communist Party)—instead of a half decade of market liberalization, we already have in China half a century of what they euphemistically call "socialism with Chinese characteristics." So has China, for over half a century, been following a gigantic New Economic Policy? Instead of making fun of these measures or simply denouncing them as a defeat of Socialism, as a step towards (authoritarian) capitalism, we should take the risk of extending this logic to its extreme. After the disintegration of East European Socialism in 1990, a joke circulated, according to which Socialism is a transition from capitalism back to capitalism.

But what if we make the opposite move and define *capitalism itself* as a socialist New Economic Policy, as *a passage from feudalism (or premodern societies of domination in general) to socialism*? With the abolishment of premodern direct personal relations of servitude and domination, with the assertion of principles of personal freedom and human rights, capitalist modernity is in itself already socialist—no wonder that modernity again and again gave birth to revolts against domination which already pointed towards economic equality (large peasants' revolts in Germany in the early 1500s, the Jacobins, etc.). Capitalism is a passage from premodernity to socialism in the sense of a compromise formation: it accepts the end of direct relations of domination, i.e., the principle of personal freedom and equality, but (as Marx put it in his classic formulation) it transposes domination from relations between people to relations between things (commodities): as individuals, we are all free, but domination persists in the relationship between commodities that we exchange on the market. This is why, for Marxism, the only way to reach an actual life of freedom is to abolish capitalism. For partisans of capitalism, of course, this solution is utopian: is the lesson of Stalinism not precisely that, if you abolish capitalism, freedom is also abolished and personal domination returns in a direct and brutal way. And when capitalism is in crisis, it can also resuscitate feudal elements to survive—is this not going on today with the role of mega-corporations, which prompted some economists and social analysts to speak about neo-feudal corporate capitalism? This, then, is the true alternative today: neither "capitalism or socialism" nor "liberal democracy or Rightist populism" but *what kind of post-capitalism*, corporate neo-feudalism or socialism. Will capitalism ultimately be just a passage from a lower to a higher stage of feudalism, or will it be a passage from feudalism to socialism?

So we are back to Lenin's question: what is to be done? *"Ne demande que faire, que celui dont le désir s'éteint."* ("Only the one whose desire is waning asks what is to be done.") Is Lacan's wonderful formula to be read as an implicit critique of Lenin? No. Although Lenin's title is a question, the book is a clear answer, it provides precise guidelines as to what is to be done. The title works like similar titles of introductory textbooks: What is Quantum Physics?, What is Biogenetics?, etc. When today's post-Marxists write treatises where they ponder endlessly on what to do, on who might be the agent of radical change, their desperate doubt and search effectively bears witness to the waning of their desire to really embark on a radical change: they don't really desire change, they rather enjoy the endless self-critical pondering which, as they know well, will not lead to any clear result.

Referring to Lenin's shift towards NEP in the last years of his life, Alvaro Garcia Linera[13] provided a precise analysis of how, when an authentic radical Leftist party takes state power through elections, it shouldn't attempt to impose radical measures (like the abolition of capitalism) directly through state decisions and laws: he warns that nationalization (the change from private to state property) does not eliminate the gap between producers and means of production, and that one should proceed very cautiously in the overcoming of capitalism. Every authentic socialization of the means of production should not be imposed by the state but should grow out of self-organization of civil society, and, in the meantime, the Leftist state power should find a way to co-exist with private business, even with big corporations, to prevent economic crisis, in the same way that the equality of women cannot just be imposed by the state but should grow out of women's self-organized struggle. While I fully support these premises, I think that Linera still puts too much weight on grassroots democracy in local communities or, in general, on society versus state: in today's complex societies, something *like* the state is needed to provide a well-functioning background of self-organized local communities (the global network of health and education services, of water and electricity, etc.), and this network cannot grow "from below," out of cooperation among local communities, since it must always-already be here for communities to survive. This network is also needed in order to prevent local communities or interest groups getting caught in competition for privileges—in short, however "alienated," the global interest has to exist in a "reified" institutional form to control the excesses of local communities, as well as to coordinate their interaction. Parliamentary democracy is definitely not the only way to establish and control the institutional form which gives body to the global interest: if we understand by "democracy" what this term predominantly means today (parliamentary representative democracy), then I am definitely not a democratic socialist but rather a non-democratic Communist. However, what we should be aware of is the fateful limit of anarchism. An anarchist replies to the reproach that he is not able to provide a positive model of how the future society should look: "I don't want to tell people what to think, I want them to think." Although this is a nice rhetorically effective answer, it rests on a false presupposition: that "people" want to think for themselves if given the opportunity. As Deleuze insisted, "people" spontaneously don't want to think, thinking is an effort that goes against the grain of our spontaneous inclinations, so that strong pressure is needed to make them think.

If we want to perceive clearly the Communist potential of what goes on today, we should bear in mind the fundamental break in the relationship between the two sexes that is already taking place in movements like LGBT+ and MeToo: these movements threaten to undermine the most elementary patriarchal order that emerged before the rise of class society itself, with the Neolithic which led to the establishment of permanent settlements. Marx neglected the significance of this break, the importance of which is equal to the capitalist industrial revolution. In the entire history of humanity, there have only been two truly radical breaks, the Neolithic and capitalist industrial revolution.[14] Critics of patriarchy who attack it as if it is still a hegemonic position, ignore what Marx and Engels wrote more than 150 years ago, in the first chapter of *The Communist Manifesto*: "The bourgeoisie, wherever it has got the upper hand, has put an end to all feudal, *patriarchal*, idyllic relations." What becomes of patriarchal family values when a child can sue his parents for neglect and abuse, i.e., when family and parenthood itself are *de iure* reduced to a temporary and dissolvable contract between independent individuals? Although late capitalism is still a class society, it thus undermines the patriarchal order which arose back in pre-class societies, and this aspect of capitalism should be unconditionally supported by all partisans of radical emancipation. (This, of course, in no way means that we should not ferociously resist temporary setbacks like the ongoing "disaster patriarchy," a process parallel to disaster capitalism where "men exploit a crisis to reassert control and dominance, and rapidly erase hard-earned women's rights. All over the world, patriarchy has taken full advantage of the virus to reclaim power—on the one hand, escalating danger and violence to women, and on the other, stepping in as their supposed controller and protector."[15] The disaster is here, of course, that of the COVID-19 pandemic.)

Marx was here more Hegelian than Hegel: what he saw was precisely the "Hegelian" structure of the reproduction of Capital. But here an ambiguity arises: there are two opposite ways in which Hegel's dialectics and the logic of capital are linked.

Hegel in the Critique of Political Economy

Broadly speaking, there are four basic forms of reference to Hegel in Marxism, but we can safely discard two of them as irrelevant to a serious study of Hegel's thought: Hegel as a predecessor of a new materialist general ontology ("dialectical materialism"); the early Althusser's idea that Marx was just "flirting" with Hegelian dialectics in order to formulate ideas (overdetermination, etc.) which are totally foreign to Hegel.[16] The two remaining Marxist readings of Hegel are the one deployed in Lukacs's *History and Class Consciousness* (Hegel's notion of substance-becoming-subject as a mystified idealist version of the historical-materialist notion of the proletariat as the subject of history which, in the act of revolution, re-appropriates its alienated substance), and the one deployed in Frankfurt School and later in the so-called "logic of capital" orientation (Hegel's dialectics as a mystified idealist version of the logic of capital's self-reproduction).

When John Rosenthal claims that "Marx made the curious discovery of an object domain in which the inverted relation between the universal and the particular which constitutes the distinctive principle of Hegelian metaphysics *in fact* obtains," he thereby provides the most concise formulation of the notion of "Hegel's logic as the logic of capital": the very fact that Hegel's logic can be applied to capitalism means that capitalism is a perverted order of alienation: "The whole riddle of the 'Marx-Hegel relation' consists in nothing other than this: ... it is precisely and paradoxically the *mystical* formulae of Hegelian 'logic' for which Marx finds a rational scientific application."[17] In short, while, in his early critique of Hegel, Marx rejected Hegel's thought as a crazy speculative reversal of actual state of things, he was then struck by the realization that there is a domain which behaves in a Hegelian way, namely the domain of the circulation of Capital.

Recall the classic Marxian motive of the speculative inversion of the relationship between the Universal and the Particular. The Universal is just a property of particular objects which really exist, but when we are victims of commodity fetishism it appears as if the concrete content of a commodity (its use-value) is an expression of its abstract universality (its exchange-value)—the abstract Universal, the Value, appears as a real Substance which successively incarnates itself in a series of concrete objects. That is Marx's basic thesis: it is already the effective world of commodities which behaves like a Hegelian subject-substance, like a Universal going through a series of particular embodiments—this is why Marx speaks of the "commodity metaphysics," of the "religion of everyday life." The roots of philosophical speculative idealism are in the social reality of the world of commodities; it is this world which behaves "idealistically"—or, as Marx puts it in the appendix "Wertform" to the first chapter of the first edition of *Capital*:

> This *inversion* (*Verkehrung*) by which the sensibly-concrete counts only as the form of appearance of the abstractly general and not, on the contrary, the abstractly general as property of the concrete, characterises the expression of value. At the same time, it makes understanding it difficult. If I say: Roman Law and German Law are both laws, that is obvious. But if I say: Law (*Das Recht*), this abstraction (*Abstraktum*) *realizes itself* in Roman Law and in German Law, in these concrete laws, the interconnection becomes mystical.[18]

We should be very careful in reading these lines: Marx is not simply criticizing the "inversion" that characterizes Hegelian idealism (in the style of his youthful writings, especially *German Ideology*); his point is not that, while "effectively" Roman Law and German Law are two kinds of law, in the idealist dialectics, the Law itself is the active agent—the subject of the entire process—which "realizes itself" in Roman Law and German Law. Marx's thesis is that this "inversion" characterizes capitalist social reality itself, which means that *both positions—the alienated inversion as well as the presupposed "normal" state of things—belong to the space of ideological mystification.* That is to say, the "normal" state of things in which Roman Law and German Law are simply both laws is the everyday form of appearance of the alienated society, of its speculatve truth. The desire to fully actualize this »normal« state is therefore ideology at its purest and cannot but end in a catastrophe. In order to see this, we have to draw another key distinction: the one between the »alienated« situation in which we, living subjects, are under the control of a virtual Monster/Master (Capital), and the more elementary »alienation,« a situation in which (we do NOT directly control objective processes, so that they become transparent, but in which), to put it in a somewhat simplifed way, no one is in control: not only we, the »objective« process is also »decentered,« inconsistent—or, to repeat Hegel's formula, in which the secret of the Egyptians are also the secrets for the Egyptians themselves.

The question to ask is thus: where is the illusion here? As numerous analyses have demonstrated, Law (in the sense of a legal order) is in itself a contradictory notion, it has to rely on illegal violence—already in our everyday understanding, »law is law« means its opposite, the coincidence of law with the arbitrary violence: »What can you do, even if it is unjust and arbitrary, law is law, you have to obey it!« Multiple forms of law are ultimately nothing but just so many attempts to resolve the tension that inhabits law as such. This movement from one to another particular form is the core of dialectical process.

We thus have three different levels in a dialectical process of inversions which produce a fetishist effect. To remain with our example of Roman law and German law, first, there is our everyday common-sense nominalist notion of Roman law and German law as the two kinds of law. Then, there is the fetishist inversion: The Law, this abstraction, realizes itself in Roman law and German law. Finally, there is what one cannot but call the historical real: the immanent "contradiction" inscribed into the very universal notion of the law, which pushes the movement from one to another particular form.

The lesson of Marx is thus that fetishization is necessarily redoubled: a capitalist subject does not directly live in magic world of fetishes, he considers himself a utilitarian rationalist who knows very well that money is just a piece of paper giving me right to a part of a social product, etc.—fetishism is in social reality, in how he acts, not in how he thinks. Analysis thus has to proceed in two steps: first, to bring out the "theological subtleties" which lie beneath and sustain our everyday common-sense awareness; then, to discern the actual movement obfuscated by the theology of commodities—and there is no trace of common sense in this actual movement.

In today's global capitalism, this redoubling of the fetishist inversion is more prevalent than ever. At the level of our direct self-awareness, we are subjectivized (interpellated) as free agents permanently making decisions and choices, and thus responsible for our own fate. The ideology of free choice is everywhere, it is the air we breathe: we are bombarded by choices, freedom of choice appears as the basic form of freedom. Since, in our society, free choice is elevated into a supreme value, social control and domination can no longer appear as infringing on the subject's freedom—it has to appear as (and be sustained by) the very self-experience of individuals as free. There is a multitude of forms of this un-freedom appearing in the guise of its opposite: when we are deprived of universal healthcare, we are told that we are given a new freedom of choice (to choose our healthcare provider); when we can no longer rely on long-term employment and are compelled to search for a new precarious position every couple of years, we are told that we are given the opportunity to re-invent ourselves and discover new unexpected creative potentials that lurked in our personality; when we have to pay for the education of our children, we are told that we become "entrepreneurs of the self," acting like capitalists who have to choose freely how we will invest the resources we possess (or have borrowed)—in education, health, travel . . . Constantly bombarded by imposed "free choices," forced to make decisions for which we are mostly not even properly qualified (or possess enough information about), we increasingly experience our freedom as what it effectively is—a burden that deprives us of the true choice of change. Bourgeois society generally obliterates castes and other hierarchies, equalizing all individuals as market subjects divided only by class difference, but today's late capitalism, with its "spontaneous" ideology, endeavors to obliterate the class division itself by way of proclaiming us all "self-entrepreneurs," the differences among us being merely quantitative (a big capitalist borrows hundreds of millions for his investment, a poor worker borrows a couple of thousands for his supplementary education).

However, this feature tends to be accompanied by its opposite: the basic characteristic of today's subjectivity is the weird combination of the free subject who experiences himself as ultimately responsible for his fate and the subject who grounds the authority of his speech on his status of a victim of circumstances beyond his control. Every contact with another human being is experienced as a potential threat—if the other smokes, if he casts a covetous glance at me, he already hurts me); this logic of victimization is today universalized, reaching well beyond the standard cases of sexual or racist harassment—recall the growing financial industry of paying damage claims, from the tobacco industry deal in the US and the financial claims of holocaust victims and forced laborers in the Nazi Germany, up to the idea that the US should pay the African-Americans hundreds of billions of dollars for all they have been deprived of due to their past slavery ... The notion of subject as a victim involves the extreme Narcissistic perspective: every encounter with the Other appears as a potential threat to the subject's precarious imaginary balance. This notion is not the opposite but, rather, the inherent supplement of the liberal free subject: in today's predominant form of individuality, the self-centered assertion of the psychological subject paradoxically overlaps with the perception of oneself as a victim of circumstances.

What rules the universe of our phenomenal self-experience is thus a mixture of freedom (of choice) and utter contingency: our success depends on us, on our initiative, but we simultaneously need luck. The two richest people in Slovenia today are a couple of programmers who devised an application and sold it to a Chinese company for almost a billion US dollars—they showed initiative but at the same time they were lucky, they found themselves in the right place at the right moment ... However, what lurks beneath this tension between initiative and luck is the obscure domain of Fate whose well-known example was the financial meltdown of 2008—it took nearly all economists by surprise. "Fate" appears today as the mysterious global circulation of Capital full of theological subtleties and which can always strike in an unpredictable way.

Back to our main line: the self-engendering speculative movement of Capital can also be said to indicate a limit to the Hegelian dialectical process, something that eludes Hegel's grasp. It is in this sense that Gerard Lebrun mentions the "fascinating image" of Capital presented by Marx (especially in his *Grundrisse*): "a monstrous mixture of the good infinity and the bad infinity, the good infinity which creates its presuppositions and the conditions of its growth, the bad infinity which never ceases to surmount its crises, and which finds its limit in its own nature."[19] Actually, it is in *Capital* itself where in the description of the circulation of capital Hegelian references abound: with capitalism, value is not a mere abstract "mute" universality, a substantial link between the multiplicity of commodities; from the passive medium of exchange, it turns into the "active factor" of the entire process. Instead of only passively assuming the two different forms of its actual existence (money—commodity), it appears as the subject "endowed with a motion of its own, passing through a life-process of its own": it differentiates itself from itself, positing its otherness, and then again overcomes this difference—the entire movement is *its own* movement. In this precise sense, "instead of simply representing the relations of commodities, it enters . . . into private relations with itself": the "truth" of its relating to its otherness is its self-relating, i.e., in its self-movement, capital retroactively "sublates" its own material conditions, changing them into subordinate moments of its own "spontaneous expansion"—in pure Hegelese, it posits its own presuppositions.

Along these lines, Rebecca Carson deployed the "intrinsic externality" of money with regard to the circulation of capital: "Money as money only appears formally as an interruption to capital's life process as a process moving towards the accumulation of capital, its valorisation (that always relies on circulating through production and extracting abstract labor). In contrast, when money is money as capital it is constantly in motion. It becomes money as money when at rest from its movement towards valorisation."[20] Although, once the circulation of capital is here, money is one of its moments, it also remains external with regard to it in its direct material existence: I can keep it at home or deposit it in a safe, where it is "at rest". . . The question is here: what will happen with full virtualization of money when it will be just a note in digital space? Will there still be a place for it to be at rest?

Crucial is here the expression "an automatically active character," an inadequate translation of the German words used by Marx to characterize capital as "*automatischem Subjekt*," an "automatic subject," the oxymoron uniting living subjectivity and dead automatism. This is what capital is: a subject, but an automatic one, not a living one—and, again, can Hegel think this "monstrous mixture," a process of subjective self-mediation and retroactive positing of presuppositions which as it were gets caught in a substantial "spurious infinity," a subject which itself becomes an alienated substance?

This, perhaps, is also the reason why Marx's reference to Hegel's dialectics in his "critique of political economy" is ambiguous, oscillating between taking it as the mystified expression of the logic of Capital and taking it as the model for the revolutionary process of emancipation. Which of these two positions then is the correct one? Did Marx rely on Hegelian dialectics as a mystified formulation of the revolutionary process of emancipation, or did he use it as the idealistic formulation of the very logic of capitalist domination? The first thing to note is that the reading of Hegel's dialectic as an idealistic formulation of the logic of capitalist domination doesn't go all the way: what, in this view, Hegel deploys is the mystified expression of the *mystification* immanent to the circulation of capital, or, in Lacanian terms, of its "objectively-social" fantasy—to put it in somewhat naïve terms, for Marx, capital is not "really" a subject-substance which reproduces itself by way of positing its own presuppositions, etc.; what this Hegelian fantasy of capital's self-generating reproduction obliterates is workers' exploitation, i.e., how the circle of capital's self-reproduction draws its energy from the external (or, rather, "ex-timate") source of value, how it has to parasitize on workers. So why not pass directly to the description of workers' exploitation, why bother with fantasies which sustain the functioning of capital? It is crucial for Marx to include in the description of capital this intermediary level of "objective fantasy" which is neither the way capitalism is experienced by its subjects (they are good empirical nominalists unaware of the "theological niceties" of capital), nor the "real state of things" (workers exploited by capital).

Actual Life versus Substanceless Subjectivity

But the problem is how to think of the Hegelian circulation of capital and its de-centered cause (the labor force) together, i.e., how to think of the causality of a productive subject external to the circulation of capital without resorting to the Aristotelian positivity of workers' productive potentials. For Marx, the starting point is precisely such a positivity (the productive force of human labor), and he accepts this starting point as unsurpassable, rejecting the logic of the dialectical process which, as Hegel put it, progresses "from nothing through nothing to nothing." In accordance with post-Hegelian realism, Marx conceives "actual life" as a positive process external to the movement of capital, as its substantial presupposition: the "life" of capital is a spectral pseudo-life that parasitizes on actual life, a kind of vampire sucking life from actual life. The reign of Capital is thus the reign of a monstrous Subject which arises out of actual life and subordinates it to its own movement: capital's self-positing parasitizes on Life (external to capital) like a vampire, a living dead. This passage from Substance (of actual life) to (Capital as) Subject is the truth of Hegel's premise that we should conceive the Absolute not only as substance but also as subject . . .

However, a closer look compels us to reject such a reference to positive Life as the ground which is perverted in alienation: there is no actual life external to alienation which serves as its positive foundation. The true fetish is not the fetishist reversal of the "natural" hierarchy (instead of actual productive life serving as the foundation of the spectral life of capital, actual life itself is reduced to a subordinate moment of the mad dance of speculative capital); *the true fetish is the very notion of direct positive life preceding alienation, an organic life whose balance was destroyed by capitalist alienation.* Such a notion is a fetish, since it disavows the antagonisms that traverse the very heart of actual life.

From a strict Hegelian standpoint, subject itself is a "pathological" inversion of substance out of which it arises: in a violent move of abstraction, what is at the beginning a subordinated element of substance self-posits itself and retroactively posits its substantial presuppositions, thereby establishing itself as universal. In other words, the movement that defines subjectivity is not subject's alienation and then re-appropriation of the alienated content: subject returns-to-itself from externality, but this return produces what it returns to—subject emerges THROUGH alienation.

In the Hegelian passage from substance to subject, subject is the truth of substance, subjective freedom is the truth of substantial necessity. But here Marx complicates things: insofar as capital is a Subject that arises out of the substance of social life, the retroactive integration of substance/life into subject/capital fails, the substance of productive life remains external to the life of capital. This implies not only that the substance of life cannot be reduced to a moment of self-mediation of subject-capital, but that there also must be a subjectivity in life-substance itself as opposed to the subjectivity of capital. The life of capital is blindly repetitive, capital as subject is a mechanically self-reproducing life, which means that the passage of necessity into freedom doesn't work here: capital is not free, the true potential of freedom must reside in life substance external to capital. We thus have two modes of subjectivity: the spectral subjectivity of capital and the pure proletarian subjectivity which is what remains when all substantial content is appropriated by Capital. The paradox is that, in the opposition between substantial Life and the spectral subjectivity of Capital, true subject is on the side of substantial Life—the opposition between Life and Capital implies that Life is in itself already antagonistic, split between substantial Life and the void of pure subjectivity.

Is then the subject-substance of our world capital or proletariat? We should follow Hegel's lesson closely here: substance becomes subject through the movement of alienation, i.e., the proletariat emerges as pure subject when substance is sucked out of its Life. That's why there are two main references to Hegel in Hegelian Marxism: Hegel's logic as the mystified form of the logic of emancipation, and Hegel's logic as the mystified form of the logic of capital. The truth of this duality is, of course, the hidden identity of the two poles: the logic of capital is in itself (potentially) the logic of emancipation. However, this hidden identity can only be conceived if we introduce another reading of Hegel's dialectical process, not the one reducing Hegel to the model of "subject alienates itself in substance and then re-appropriates its substantial content."[21] Already decades ago, in the early years of modern ecology, some intelligent readers of Hegel perceived that Hegelian idealist speculation does not imply an absolute appropriation of nature—in contrast to productive appropriation, speculation lets its Other be, and doesn't intervene in it.

This brings us to the topic of fictions: does this gesture of releasing reality, of letting-it-be and stand on its own, mean that we accept reality as it is in itself, outside the network of symbolic fictions? Here things get more complex. For Hegel, the form of this "letting-it-be" is knowledge, scientific knowledge (in his sense of the word) which doesn't mess with its object but merely observes its self-movement. What scientific knowledge observes is not its object in itself but the interaction between in-itself and our fictions, where fictions are an immanent part of in-itself—and it is the same with Marx for whom, if we subtract fictions, social reality itself disintegrates. Today's experimental science, however, displays a stance towards its object which is the opposite of Hegel's: not a stance of impassive observing of the object's self-movement in its interplay with fictions but the stance of active intervention in its object and its technological manipulation, even the creation of new objects (through biogenetic mutations), which simultaneously aims at how this object is in itself, independently of our interaction with it. Let's take the exemplary case of today's science, brain science: neurobiologists and cognitive scientists like to undermine our common sense of being autonomous free agents with the claim that subjective freedom is a fiction—in reality, in itself, our brain processes are fully determined by neural mechanisms. The Hegelian answer to this is that yes, freedom is immanently linked to fiction, but in a more subtle way—to quote a well-known passage from the "Preface" to Hegel's *Phenomenology of Spirit*:

> The activity of dissolution is the power and work of the *Understanding*, the most astonishing and mightiest of powers, or rather the absolute power. The circle that remains self-enclosed and, like substance, holds its moments together, is an immediate relationship, one therefore which has nothing astonishing about it. But that an accident as such, detached from what circumscribes it, what is bound and is actual only in its context with others, should attain an existence of its own and a separate freedom—that is the tremendous power of the negative; it is the energy of thought, of the pure I.[22]

The power of the Understanding is the power of tearing apart in one's mind what in reality belongs together—in short, the power to create fictions. One should be attentive to a key detail in the quote from Hegel: this power is not just the basic form of human freedom, it is the power of "separate freedom" acquired by an object itself when it is torn out of its living context and thus obtains a separate existence of its own. But is this power only active in our mind while reality remains the same in itself? In other words, are we dealing with a new version of Sartre's opposition between the reality of being-in-itself and consciousness as the vortex of being-for-itself? We should recall here Marx's definition of human labor from Chapter 7 of *Capital I*:

> A spider conducts operations that resemble those of a weaver, and a bee puts to shame many an architect in the construction of her cells. But what distinguishes the worst architect from the best of bees is this, that the architect raises his structure in imagination before he erects it in reality. At the end of every labor-process, we get a result that already existed in the imagination of the labourer at its commencement.[23]

These imaginations—fictions—are, of course, not just in the worker's head, they emerge out of the socio-symbolic interaction of workers which presupposes the "big Other," the order of symbolic fictions. So how does the "big Other" relate to (what we experience as) external reality? This is the basic philosophical question with which we dealt elsewhere, so let's return to Saito who sticks to the standard version of "subject alienates itself in substance and then re-appropriates its substantial content," rejecting it as unfit to deal with ecology. However, Saito doesn't choose the opposite of Western Marxism, the general ontology of dialectical materialism: his starting point is not nature as such, but human labor as the process of metabolism between humanity (as part of nature) and its natural environs, a process which is, of course, part of the universal metabolism (exchange of matter) within nature itself. At its most basic, labor is a material process of exchange which locates humanity in a much wider context of natural processes and, as such, cannot be reduced to any form of Hegelian self-mediation: the externality of nature is irreducible. This apparently abstract point has crucial consequences for how we deal with our ecological predicament. Saito sees the root of the ecological crisis in the rift between the material metabolism of our life-process and the autonomous logic of the reproduction of capital which poses a threat to this metabolism. In the course of the book, Saito admits there were previous rifts:

despite the appearance of long-term sustainable production in precapitalist societies there was always a certain tension between nature and humans. Capitalism alone does not create the problem of desertification ex nihilo, ... it transforms and deepens the transhistorical contradiction by radically reorganizing the universal metabolism of nature from the perspective of capital's valorization. (250)[24]

But the overall scheme remains one of linear progress in the alienation. That's why Marx was also in his late years more and more interested in "unconscious socialist tendency" in the persisting remainders of pre-capitalist forms of communal life and speculated that they can directly pass into a post-capitalist society (for example, in his famous letter to Vera Zasulich, Marx plays with the idea that, maybe, Russian village communes could function as places of resistance against capital and establish socialism without going through capitalism)—these pre-capitalist forms maintain more of the intimate ties of man with the earth. Along these lines, the title of the first chapter of Saito's book—"Alienation of Nature as the Emergence of the Modern" (25)—clearly locates the "rift" in capitalist modernity: "After the historical dissolution of the original unity between humans and the earth, production can only relate to the conditions of production as an alien property" (26). And Marx's Communist project is expected to heal this rift:

> Only if one comprehends the estrangement in capitalist society as a dissolution of humans' original unity with the earth does it become evident that Marx's communist project consistently aims at a conscious rehabilitation of the unity between humans and nature. (42)

The ultimate ground of this rift is that, in capitalism, the labor process does not serve our needs, its goal is to expanded reproduction of capital itself irrespective of the damage this does to our environment—products count only insofar as they are valorized, and the consequences for the environment literally do not count. The actual metabolism of our life process is thus subordinated to the artificial "life" of the reproduction of capital, there is a rift between the two, and the ultimate goal of the

Communist revolution is not so much to abolish exploitation as to abolish this rift by way of abolishing the valorization of labor.

Eco-proletarians and the Limits of Valorization

In capitalism, exploitation as unequal exchange (the appropriation of the surplus produced by workers) takes place in the form of valorization (the reduction of the labor force to a commodity). As David Harvey pointed out, the fundamental divide that characterizes capitalism is the divide between valorized and non-valorized work: women's housework doesn't count because it is not valorized, not bought and paid as a commodity. This, of course, doesn't mean that women are not exploited: their uncounted labor is what renders the exploitation proper (say, of her husband) possible, and what provides for future workers to be exploited. This non-valorized part of work is not just a reminder of the pre-capitalist past: every epoch of capitalism necessitates a proper measure of balance between labor formally reduced to a commodity and uncounted labor, labor which is necessary although it appears as non-productive (since it is not valorized). The solution is not to valorize all labor in global commodification, but to socially acknowledge work that contributes to social reproduction although it is not included in the process of valorization.

The barely concealed irrationality of the predominance of exchange-value was best formulated two centuries ago by James Maitland, Eighth Earl of Lauderdale, known in France as "Citizen Maitland" (he was in Paris during the French Revolution, was a personal friend of Jean-Paul Marat, and had helped to found the British Society of the Friends of the People in 1792). He is known as the author of the so-called "Lauderdale paradox" which asserts an inverse correlation between public wealth and private riches such that an increase in the latter often served to diminish the former. "Public wealth," he wrote, "may be accurately defined—to consist of all that man desires, as useful or delightful to him." Such goods have use value and thus constitute wealth. But private riches, as opposed to wealth, require something additional (i.e., have an added limitation), consisting "of all that man desires as useful or delightful to him; which exists in a degree of scarcity." Scarcity, in other words, is a necessary requirement for something to have value in exchange, and to augment private riches. But this is not the case for public wealth, which encompasses all value in use, and thus includes not only what is scarce but also what is abundant. This paradox led Lauderdale to argue that increases in scarcity in such formerly abundant but necessary elements of life as air, water, and food would, if exchange values were then attached to them, enhance individual private riches, and indeed the riches of the country—conceived of as "the sum-total of individual riches"—but only at the expense of the common wealth. For example, if one could monopolize water that had previously been freely available by placing a fee on wells, the measured riches of the nation would be increased at the expense of the growing thirst of the population.

The last example gains an additional actuality today when the privatization of water is on the neoliberal agenda: the owners of water-supply companies get richer while the mass of those who need water gets poorer ... The underlying logic of this paradox is clear: for something to count on the market, it has to have value, and value is an attribute only of those objects that are scarce—if they are freely and abundantly available, they cannot be sold and have no value. The most precious wealth of a society consists precisely of objects which are freely available, like water or air, but they do not count as values which can make you rich. If water is easily available, nobody gets rich by it; if its supply is controlled by private companies, those who own these companies get rich, so in a technical sense of wealth as embodied in values, there is more wealth in society since freely available water doesn't count as wealth ...

One should nonetheless be careful not to ignore here the libidinal logic that sustains this irrationality: the role of envy and comparative advantage. If a resource like water or air is commonly available as a free gift of nature, it doesn't count as wealth—it only counts as such when it differentiates me (who owns or controls it) from others, when it gives me superiority over them. In other words, wealth counts as wealth only if there are those who are NOT wealthy. We encounter here a properly Hegelian paradox formulated already by Epicurus: "Poverty, if measured by the natural end, is great wealth; but wealth, if not limited, is great poverty." If water is freely available, we are all equally poor on account of our great wealth; if only some people possess and control water, their excessive (illimited) wealth results in poverty for others.

More generally, the great insight of the new Marxist eco-socialism is to dispel the myth of exploitation of wage-workers (based on free exchange) as the "true" and "pure" form of capitalism, and to analyze how this "pure" exploitation of wage-workers always and for necessary structural reasons operates in dialectical tension with forms of direct brutal expropriation. There are three main forms of such expropriation: the theft of natural resources and destruction of the environment; expropriation of and domination over other races (direct slavery or more refined racism); women's work (reproduction and household). These forms are *not* part of a value-relationship: a slave or a woman doing household chores doesn't get a wage and is not exploited in the same way as a salaried worker. (To this, we should add digital expropriation, the way we are "robbed" of our data by digital machines which control us.) The conclusion is that capitalism is structurally *never* pure; the wage-exploitation always has to be sustained by these other modes of expropriation. What Jason Moore claims is true: "Value does not work unless most work is not valued."[25] But we should not draw from this insight a universal claim that value should be attributed to all processes, human, animal, or natural, i.e., that value is created wherever and whenever energy is spent, so that not only workers are exploited but also animals (horses, cows . . .), and we are even "exploiting" natural resources when we burn coal or use oil . . .

In today's global situation, we should thus place in the foreground what some analysts call eco-proletarians: the Third World poor who suffer ecological expropriation and economic poverty, even if they are not exploited in the classic capitalist sense. Their environment is destroyed through the plundering of its natural resources for foreign markets, and their traditional way of life is gradually replaced by a fragile existence of becoming homeless refugees in their own land. The liberal-capitalist mantra according to which rich countries are dealing better with all problems so that the solution is for the poor to get richer is a model of what Hegel called abstract thinking: in today's global world, developed and less developed are interconnected, rich are rich also because of their interaction with the poor (exploiting their resources, using their cheap labor, etc.), so that rich are rich also because poor are poor.

What is interesting here is how the colonization of the environment can be justified in the terms of the rights of working people. John Locke, the great Enlightenment philosopher and advocate of human rights, justified the white settlers who were grabbing land from native Americans with a strange Left-sounding argument against excessive private property. His premise was that an individual should be allowed to own only as much land as he is able to use productively, not large tracts of land that he is not able to use (and then eventually give it to others to use it and get rent for it). In North America, natives claim that vast tracts of land were theirs, although they were not able to use them productively but mostly just for hunting of non-domesticated animals, so their land was unproductively wasted and the white settlers who wanted to use it for intensive agriculture had the right to seize it for the benefit of humanity ...

We should maintain the rift and tension between the material metabolism of life-processes and the circulation of capital in which value creates more value: in order for exploitation in the strict sense of surplus-value appropriation to function, there has to be a lot of work done which is not "valued" in the capitalist sense. The temptation to be resisted here is to re-adjust the injustice of direct appropriation invisible from within the horizon of value by a radical global commodification or valuation (women's reproductive domestic should also be paid, value of natural elements, air, water ...). Instead of trying to include everything that contributes to wealth in the domain of value, we should strive to liberate more and more spheres from the domain of value.

However, this in no way implies that we should simply exclude more and more domains from the sphere of valorization. Valorization could and should also be exploded "from within," by way of exploiting the paradoxes and unexpected results of the inclusion of new spheres in the process of capitalist valuation. Paolo Virno's critique of capitalism is based on the distinction between potentiality and actuality—say, language spoken by people is a potentiality, it sustains the possibility to produce an infinite set of enunciations. This potentiality is never exhausted by all actually made propositions, and these propositions do not just actualize the potentiality, they in some sense negate it—what every actual enunciation negates is the surplus of potentiality over actuality since in it, the infinite potentiality evaporates and all we have is an enunciation (or a set of enunciations) as a determinate positive entity. Virno's point is that the same holds for Marx's notion of the labor force: it is a potentiality actualized in labor which produced commodities, and what Marx calls "alienation" is not primarily the appropriation by capital of the surplus-value but the appropriation by capital of the infinite potentiality of the labor force—when labor force is bought as a commodity, its infinite potentiality is reduced to a finite object, i.e., the gap that separates potentiality and actuality disappears in a short-circuit between the two dimensions. Here, however, we should take a further step: the true short-circuit occurs not just when the workforce itself becomes a commodity, but when it is directly produced as a commodity. There are thus three (and not just two) steps of commodification: first, individual owners (or collective of producers) sell their products on the market; then, the workforce itself (used in producing commodities) becomes a commodity sold on the market; finally, the production of the commodity "the workforce" becomes a field of capitalist investment. Only at this point do we reach what Balibar calls "the total subsumption" of the productive process under capital:[26]

Whereas Marx explained that "capital" ultimately could be reduced to (productive) labour or was nothing other than labour in a different form, appropriated by a different class, the theory of human capital explains that labour—more precisely "labouring capacity" (Arbeitsvermögen)—can be reduced to capital or become analysed in terms of capitalist operations of credit, investment and profitability. This is, of course, what underlies the ideology of the individual as a "self-entrepreneur", or an "entrepreneur of oneself."[27] The issue is here "not so much to describe a growth of markets for existing products; it is much more to push the range of the market beyond the limits of the "production sphere" in the traditional sense, therefore to add new sources of permanent "extra surplus-value" that can become integrated into valorization, overcoming its limitations, because capital is valorized both on the "objective" side of labour and production, and on the "subjective" side of consumption and use.[28]

So it's not just about making the workforce more productive; it is to conceive of the workforce itself directly as another field of capitalist investment: all aspects of its "subjective" life itself (health, education, sexual life, psychic state . . .) are considered not only as important for the productivity of the workers themselves but as fields of investment which can generate additional surplus-value. Health services do not just serve the interests of capital by way of making workers more productive; they are themselves an incredibly powerful field of investment, not only for capital (health services are the single strongest branch of the US economy, much stronger than defense), but for the workers themselves (who treat paying health insurance as an investment in their future). The same goes for education: it does not just get you ready for productive work—it is in itself a profitable field of investment for institutions as well for individuals who invest in their future. It is as if, in this way, the commodification not only becomes total but also gets caught in a kind of self-referential loop: working power as the ultimate "source of (capitalist) wealth," the origin of surplus-value, becomes itself a moment of capitalist investment. Nowhere is this loop more clearly expressed than in the idea of the worker as "self-entrepreneur," a capitalist who decides freely where to invest his (meager) surplus resources (or, mostly, resources acquired through loans): in education, health, housing property . . . Does this process have a limit? When, in the very last paragraph of his essay, Balibar approaches this question, he strangely resorts to a Lacanian reference, to Lacan's logic of non-All (from his "formulas of sexuation"):

> This is what I call a total subsumption (after "formal" and "real" subsumption) because it leaves nothing outside (no reservation for "natural" life). Or, anything that is left outside must appear as a residue, and a field for further incorporation. Or must it? That is of course the whole question, ethical as much as political: are there limits to commodification? Are there internal and external

obstacles? A Lacanian might want to say: every such totalization includes an element of impossibility which belongs to the "real"; it must be pas tout, or not whole. If that were the case, the heterogeneous elements, the intrinsic remainders of the total subsumption, could appear in many different forms, some apparently individualistic, such as pathologies or anarchist resistances, others common or even public. Or they may become manifest in certain difficulties in implementing the neoliberal agenda, such as the difficulty of dismantling a Medicare system once it has been legalized.[29]

What Balibar says here is, for a Lacanian, very strange: he condenses (or, rather, simply confuses) the two sides of Lacan's formulas of sexuation, and simply reads exception as non-All: the totality of subsumption is non-all since there are exceptions which resist being subsumed to Capital. But Lacan precisely opposes non-All and exception: every universality is based on an exception, and when there are no exceptions, the set is non-All, it cannot be totalized. (An interesting exception to the politically correct control of public speech are rap lyrics: there you can say it all, celebrate rape and murder, etc. etc. Why this exception? The reason is easy to guess: blacks are considered the privileged image of victimhood, and rap the expression of the misery of the black youth, so the brutality of rap lyrics is absolved in advance as the authentic expression of black suffering and frustration.) This opposition should also be applied to the topic of subsumption: one should pass from the search for exception, for those who resist (universal) subsumption and are as such the "site of resistance," to endorsing subsumption without exception and count on its non-All. The subsumption of individual lives to which Balibar refers cannot be reduced to a particular case of the universal capitalist subsumption; they remain a particular case which, on account of its self-relating nature (the workforce itself becomes capital), redoubles the production of surplus-value.

In Marx's critique of political economy there are two main cases of universality through exception: money and the workforce. The field of commodities can only be totalized through a special commodity which functions as a general equivalent of all commodities but is as such deprived of use value; the field of the exchange of commodities only gets totalized when individual producers not only sell their products on the market, but when the workforce (as a commodity whose use-value is to generate surplus value) is also sold on the market as a commodity. So maybe here a third case: when this commodity which produces surplus-value itself becomes an object of capital investment bringing surplus-value, so that we get two types of surplus-value, the "normal" surplus value generated by the products of the workforce, and the surplus generated by the production of the workforce itself. A nice example of Hegel's insight into how the Absolute always involves self-splitting and is in this sense non-All: with the production of the workforce itself as a field of capital investment, the subsumption under capital becomes total—but, precisely as such, it becomes non-All, it cannot be totalized, the self-referential element of the workforce itself as a capital investment introduces a gap which introduces imbalance into the entire field. For example, what do the enormous investments in education actually amount to? Many empirical studies demonstrate that most higher education is not really of use for the reproduction of capital—even business schools actually do very little to train individuals to become effective managers. Consequently, although we are bombarded by the media's message that education is crucial for a successful economy, most college studies are irrelevant for business purposes. This is why state and business institutions complain all the time about how humanities serve no purpose, and how universities should be made to serve the needs of actual life (i.e., of capital). But what if this, precisely, is what makes our enormous educational system so precious? It serves no clearly defined goal, it just multiplies "useless" culture, refined thinking, sensitivity for art, etc.? Consequently, we find ourselves in a paradoxical situation: at the very moment when, formally, even education becomes increasingly subsumed under capital as a field of investment, the actual result of this subsumption is that enormous amounts of money are spent on the cultivation of knowledge and art as its own aim … We thus get hundreds of thousands of highly educated individuals who are of no use to capital (who cannot find jobs), and instead of protesting against this meaningless spending of financial resources, should we not celebrate this result as an unexpected sign of the expansion of the "realm of freedom"?

No Capitalism—And No Way Out of it—Without Science

To account for the rift between actual life and the life of capital it is not enough to evoke the fact that, in capitalism, the metabolic process between humans and nature is subordinated to the valorization of capital. What made this rift explode was the intimate link between capitalism and modern science: capitalist technology which triggered radical changes in rational environs cannot be imagined without science, which is why some ecologists already proposed to change the term for the new epoch we are entering from Anthropocene to capitalocene. Apparatuses based on science enable humans not only to get to know the real which is outside the scope of their experiential reality (like quantum waves); they also enable them to construct new "unnatural" (inhuman) objects which cannot but appear to our experience as freaks of nature (gadgets, genetically modified organisms, cyborgs, etc.). The power of human culture is not only to build an autonomous symbolic universe beyond what we experience as nature, but to produce new "unnatural" natural objects which materialize human knowledge. We not only "symbolize nature," we as it were denaturalize it from within.

Today, this denaturalization of nature is openly palpable, part of our daily lives, which is why radical emancipatory politics should aim neither at complete mastery over nature, nor at the humanity's humble acceptance of the predominance of Mother-Earth. Rather, nature should be exposed in all its catastrophic contingency and indeterminacy, and human agency should assume the whole unpredictability of the consequences of its activity. In spite of the infinite adaptability of capitalism which, in the case of an acute ecological catastrophe or crisis, can easily turn ecology into a new field of capitalist investment and competition, the very nature of the risk involved fundamentally precludes a market solution—why?

Capitalism only works in precise social conditions: it implies trust in the objectivized/"reified" mechanism of the market's "invisible hand" which, as a kind of Cunning of Reason, guarantees that the competition of individual egotisms works for the common good. However, we are in the midst of a radical change. Until now, historical Substance played its role as the medium and foundation of all subjective interventions: whatever social and political subjects did, it was mediated and ultimately dominated, overdetermined, by the historical Substance. What looms on the horizon today is the unheard-of possibility that a subjective intervention will intervene directly into the historical Substance, catastrophically disturbing its run by way of triggering an ecological catastrophe, a fateful biogenetic mutation, a nuclear or similar military-social catastrophe, etc. No longer can we rely on the safeguarding role of the limited scope of our acts: it no longer holds that, whatever we do, history will go on. For the first time in human history, the act of a single socio-political agent effectively can alter and even interrupt the global historical process, so that, ironically, it is only today that we can say that the historical process should effectively be conceived "not only as Substance, but also as Subject."

Marx's famous claim that, with capitalism, "all that is solid melts into air, all that is holy is profaned," today takes on a new meaning: with the latest biogenetic developments, we are entering a new phase in which it is simply *nature itself* which melts into air: the main consequence of the scientific breakthroughs in biogenetics is the end of nature. Once we know the rules of its construction, natural organisms are transformed into objects susceptible to manipulation. Nature, human and inhuman, is thus "desubstantialized," deprived of its impenetrable density, of what Heidegger called "earth." This compels us to give a new twist to Freud's title *Unbehagen in der Kultur*—discontent, uneasiness, in culture. With the latest developments, the discontent shifts from culture to nature itself: nature is no longer "natural," the reliable "dense" background of our lives; it now appears as a fragile mechanism which, at any point, can explode in a catastrophic direction.

Crucial here is the interdependence of man and nature: by reducing man to just another natural object whose properties can be manipulated, what we lose is not (only) humanity but *nature itself*. There is no firm foundation, a place of retreat, on which one can safely count. It means fully accepting that "nature doesn't exist," i.e., fully consummating the gap that separates the life-world notion of nature and the scientific notion of natural reality: "nature" *qua* the domain of balanced reproduction, of organic deployment into which humanity intervenes with its *hubris*, brutally throwing off the rails its circular motion, is man's fantasy; nature is already in itself "second nature," its balance is always secondary, an attempt to negotiate a "habit" that would restore some order after catastrophic interruptions. This is what it means that humanity has nowhere to retreat: not only "there is no big Other" (self-contained symbolic order as the ultimate guarantee of Meaning); there is also no *Nature qua* balanced order of self-reproduction whose homeostasis is disturbed—thrown off the rails, by imbalanced human interventions. Not only is the big Other "barred," but Nature is also barred. Indeed, what we need is *ecology without nature*: the ultimate obstacle to protecting nature is the very notion of nature we rely on.[30] The true source of problems is not "the most significant event to affect Western culture during recent centuries," namely the "breakdown of the relationship between man and nature,"[31] the retreat of the relation of confidence. On the contrary, this very "relationship of faith with reality itself" is the main obstacle that prevents us from confronting the ecological crisis at its most radical.[32]

Since the operator of this denaturalization of nature is modern science, the fact that we should fully endorse denaturalization means that we should not reduce science to its role in capitalism: the mutual implication, complicity even, of science and capitalism is not seamless, it implies an immanent tension in each of the two terms. Science offers itself to capitalism insofar as it is in itself blind to a key dimension of its existence signalled by Lacan in a couple of co-dependent formulations: science forecloses the dimension of the subject: science operates at the level of knowledge and ignores truth; science has no memory. Let's begin with this last feature:

the fact is that science, if one looks at it closely, has no memory. Once constituted, it forges the circuitous path by which it came into being; otherwise stated, it forgets a dimension of truth that psychoanalysis seriously puts to work. I must, however, be more precise. It is widely known that theoretical physics and mathematics—after every crisis that is resolved in a form for which the term "generalized theory" can in no way be taken to mean "a shift to generality"—often maintain what they generalize in its position in the preceding structure. That is not my point here. My concern is the toll [drame], the subjective toll that each of these crises takes on the learned. The tragedy [drame] has its victims, and nothing allows us to say that their destiny can be inscribed in the Oedipal myth. Let us say that the subject has not been studied to any great extent. J.R. Mayer, Cantor—well I am not going to furnish a list of first-rate tragedies, leading at times to the point of madness; the names of certain of our contemporaries, in whose cases I consider exemplary the tragedy of what is happening in psychoanalysis, would soon have to be added to the list.[33]

What Lacan aims at here goes far beyond the psychic tragedies of great scientific inventors (he mentions Cantor whose revolutionizing of the notion of infinity triggered an inner turmoil which pushed him to the limit of madness and even led him to practice coprophagia)—from the scientific standpoint, such tragedies are irrelevant private-life details which in no way affect the status of a scientific discovery. Such details *must* be ignored if we want to comprehend a scientific theory—this ignorance is not a weakness of the scientific theory but its strength. A scientific theory is "objective": it suspends its position of enunciation—it doesn't matter who enounces it; all that matters is its content. In this sense, the discourse of science forecloses its subject. Lacan, however, who tries to think the subject of modern science, brings out such "psychological" details—not in order to relativize the validity of scientific theories but to answer the question: what shifts have to happen in the subjectivity of a scientist so that such a theory can be formulated? A theory may be "objectively valid," but its enunciation can nonetheless rely on traumatic subjective shifts—there is no pre-established harmony between subject and object.

What Lacan aims at also goes beyond the so-called "ethical responsibility" of scientists for the (mis)use of their scientific achievements—on a couple of occasions Lacan mentions J.R. Oppenheimer, the wartime head of the Los Alamos Laboratory, often credited with being the "father of the atomic bomb." When the first atomic bomb was successfully detonated on July 16 1945, he remarked that it brought to mind words from the *Bhagavad Gita*: "Now I became Death, the destroyer of worlds." Beset by ethical qualms, he expressed his doubts publicly and, as a consequence, he suffered the revocation of his security clearance and was effectively stripped of direct political influence ... Commendable as it is, such a critical stance is not enough, it remains at the level of "ethical committees" which proliferate today and try to constrain scientific progress into the straight-jacket of predominant "norms" (how far should we go with biogenetic manipulation, etc.). This is not enough—it only amounts to secondary control over a machine which, if allowed to run its immanent course, would have engendered catastrophic results.

The trap to be avoided here is double. On the one side, it is not enough to locate the danger to particular misuses of science due to corruption (like the scientists who support climate change denial) or something similar—the danger resides at a much more general level; it concerns the very mode of functioning of science. On the other side, we should also reject the over-hasty generalization of danger into what Adorno and Horkheimer called "instrumental reason"—the idea that modern science is in its very basic structure directed to dominate, manipulate and exploit nature, plus the concomitant idea that modern science is ultimately just a radicalization of a basic anthropological tendency (for Adorno and Horkheimer in their *Dialectic of Enlightenment*, there is a straight line from primitive use of magic to influence natural processes to modern technology). The danger resides in the specific conjunction between science and capital.

To get the basic dimension of what Lacan is aiming at in the passage quoted above, we have to return to the difference between knowledge and truth, where "truth" acquires all its specific weight—to indicate this weight, recall how, today, anti-immigrant populists deal with the "problem" of refugees: they approach it in an atmosphere of fear, of the approaching struggle against the Islamization of Europe, and they get caught in a series of obvious absurdities. For them, the refugees who flee terror are equated with the terrorist they are escaping from, oblivious to the obvious fact that, while there are among the refugees also terrorists, rapists, criminals, etc., the large majority are desperate people looking for a better life. The cause of the problems that are immanent to today's global capitalism is projected onto an external intruder. We find here "fake news" which cannot be reduced to a simple inexactitude— if they (partially, at least) correctly render (some of) the facts, they are all the more dangerously a "fake." Anti-immigrant racism and sexism is not dangerous because it lies, it is at its most dangerous when its lie is presented in the form of a (partial) factual truth.

It is this dimension of truth that eludes science: in the same way that my jealousy is "untrue" even if its suspicions are confirmed by objective knowledge, in the same way that our fear of refugees is false with regard to the subjective position of enunciation it implies even if some facts can confirm it, modern science is "untrue" insofar as it is blind to the way it is integrated into the circulation of capital, for its link to technology and its capitalist use, i.e., for what in old Marxist terms was called the "social mediation" of its activity. It is important to bear in mind that this "social mediation" is not an empirical fact external to the immanent scientific procedure: it is a kind of transcendental a priori which structures from within the scientific procedure. So it is not only that scientists "don't care" about the eventual misuse of their work (if this were the case, more "socially conscious" scientists would be enough), this "not-caring" is inscribed into its structure, it colors the very "desire" that motivates scientific activity (which is what Lacan aims at with his claim that science doesn't have a memory)—how?

In the conditions of developed capitalism, a strict division prevails between those who do the labor (workers) and those who plan and coordinate it—the latter are on the side of capital, their job is to maximize capital's valorization, and when science is used to enhance productivity, it is also constrained to the task of facilitating the process of capital's valorization. Science is thus firmly entrenched on the side of capital, it is the ultimate figure of knowledge which is taken away from laborers and appropriated by capital and its executors. Scientists who work are also paid, but their work is not at the same level as laborers' work: they as it were work for the other (opposite) side, they are in some sense the strike-breakers of the production process … This, of course, doesn't mean that modern natural science is inexorably on the side of capital: today, science is needed more than ever in any resistance against capitalism. The point is just that science itself is not enough to do this job since it "has no memory," since it ignores the dimension of truth.

We should thus distinguish two levels of what makes science problematic. First, there is, at a general level, the fact that science "has no memory," a fact that is part of its strength, that is constitutive of science. Then, there is the specific conjunction of science and capitalism—here, "no memory" relates to a specific blindness for its own social mediation. However, Greta Thunberg is right when she claims that politicians should listen to science—Wagner's *Die Wunde schliest der Speer nur, der Sie schlug* ("The wound can only be healed by the spear that made it") thus acquires a new actuality. Today's threats are not primarily external (natural) but self-generated by the human activity permeated by science (the ecological consequences of our industry, the psychic consequences of uncontrolled biogenetics, etc.), so that sciences are simultaneously (one of) the source(s) of risks, the sole medium we have to grasp and define the threats (even if we blame scientific-technological civilization for global warming, we need the same science not only to define the scope of the threat, but often even to perceive the threat. What we need is not science that re-discovers its grounding in premodern wisdom—traditional wisdom is precisely something that prevents us from perceiving the real threat of ecological catastrophes. Wisdom "intuitively" tells us to trust mother-nature which is the stable ground of our being—but it is precisely this stable ground which is undermined by modern science and technology. So we need a science that is decoupled from both poles, from the autonomous circuit of capital as well as from traditional wisdom, a science which could finally stand on its own. What this means is that there is no return to authentic feeling of our unity with nature: the only way to confront ecological challenges is to fully accept the radical denaturalization of nature.

Is Abstract Labor Universal?

In passing in silence over this key role of modern science, Saito thinks abstractly (in the Hegelian sense of abstracting from or ignoring concrete circumstances), and the implications and consequences of this abstraction are far reaching. Like Marx, Saito sees human labor as a transhistorical feature of all societies, as a natural-historical base for different social organizations of labor. But—in a way which, at first sight, at least, cannot but appear enigmatic—he goes a step further and also asserts the transhistorical character of abstract labor: he insists that abstract labor is already there in premodern societies, that it is not—like value—a purely social form that emerges only through exchange of commodities; he quotes Marx to prove that "abstract labor is also a material element of the labor process"(109): "All labor is an expenditure of human labor-power, in the physiological sense, and it is in this quality of being equal, or abstract, human labor that it forms the value of commodities." But does it really follow from this that abstract labor is "a certain material aspect of human activity, in this case labor's pure physiological expenditure" (109)? Is it not that, as Marx has shown in his Introduction to *Grundrisse*, abstraction itself is a social fact, the result of a social process of abstracting?

> although the simpler category may have existed historically before the more concrete, it can achieve its full (intensive and extensive) development precisely in a combined form of society, while the more concrete category was more fully developed in a less developed form of society. Labour seems a quite simple category. The conception of labor in this general form—as labour as such—is also immeasurably old. Nevertheless, when it is economically conceived in this simplicity, "labour" is as modern a category as are the relations which create this simple abstraction.[34]

Does the same not hold for abstract labor? When Marx writes that "by equating their different products to each other in exchange as values," men "equate their different kinds of labor as human labor," does he not indicate that different kinds of labor are equated only through market exchange? Only in a society whose metabolism is regulated by commodity exchange "abstract labour" posited as such, for itself. In a capitalist society, its "abstraction" is a social fact (a worker receives a wage for his labor measured in its abstraction).

Saito argues that abstract labor refers to what all human labor has in common, a purely physiological expenditure of human energy in time. However, does this not remain a "mute universality," not an actual abstraction that marks labor in an immanent way, making the gap between abstract and concrete part of the very identity of labor? Furthermore, following Marx's definition of labor which Saito endorses, labor is not just physiological expenditure but also a mental activity of planning and continuous attention, and this aspect is here ignored by Saito.

Saito's main argument for his reading is that abstract labor is physiological "because it plays a social role in a transhistorical fashion in any society" (108): the total quantity of labor is inevitably limited to a certain amount of time, and this is why its allocation is crucial for the reproduction of society—abstract labor is operative in any social division of labor. But does this argument hold? It immediately strikes the eye that Saito's definition of labor as physiological expenditure is itself historically specific, rooted in nineteenth-century anti-Hegelian space—only within this space can one conceive "simple average labor" as a zero-level standard to which all its more complex forms can be reduced:

> More complex labour counts only as *intensified*, or rather *multiplied* simple labour, so that a smaller quantity of complex labour is considered equal to a larger quantity of simple labour. Experience shows that this reduction is constantly being made. A commodity may be the outcome of the most complicated labour, but through its value it is posited as equal to the product of simple labour, hence it represents only a specific quantity of simple labour. The various proportions in which different kinds of labour are reduced to simple labour as their unit of measurement are established by a social process that goes on behind the backs of the producers; these proportions therefore appear to the producers to have been handed down by tradition.[35]

The key enigmatic term is here "experience"—as David Harvey noted in his classic commentary, "Marx never explains what 'experience' he has in mind, making this passage highly controversial."[36] The least one can add is that this "experience" has to be conceived as referring to a specific historical situation: not only what counts as simple labor but *the very practice of reducing complex to simple labor* is something historically specific and not a universal feature of human productivity, limited not only to capitalism but to classic industrial capitalism. As Anson Rabinbach demonstrated, it is operative only within the nineteenth-century break with Hegel, the assertion of thermodynamic engine as a paradigm of how labor force operates, the paradigm which replaces the Hegelian paradigm of labor as the expressive deployment of human subjectivity still operative in the texts of the young Marx:

> The thermodynamic engine was the servant of a powerful nature conceived as a reservoir of undiminished and inexhaustible motivating power. The laboring body, the steam engine and the cosmos were connected by a single and unbroken chain, by an indestructible energy, omnipresent in the universe and capable of infinite mutation, yet immutable and invariant … This discovery also had a profound, game changing effect on Marx's thinking about labor. After 1859, Marx increasingly regarded the distinction between concrete and abstract labor in the language of labor power, as an act of *conversion* rather than *generation* … Put in another way, Marx superimposed a thermodynamic model of labor onto the ontological model of labor he inherited from Hegel. As a result, for Marx labor power became quantifiable and equivalent to all other forms of labor power (in nature or in machines) … Marx became a "productivist," when he no longer considered labor to be simply an anthropologically "paradigmatic" mode of activity, and when, in harmony with the new physics, he saw labor power as an abstract magnitude (a measure of labor-time) and a natural force (a specific set of energy equivalents located in the body).[37]

A question arises here: is this paradigm which relies on the mechanic linear flow of time (of labor) as measure of value still actual in our late-capitalist post-industrial societies? This question has to be answered precisely to avoid the attempts of the ruling ideology to dismiss Marx's critique of political economy as belonging to another era and to celebrate the potential of today's post-Fordist capitalism to use the labor force in a much more creative and co-operative way:

An intellectually vigorous new discourse of "antidisciplinarity" has found a niche in the boardrooms of corporations and on the editorial pages of influential newspapers and periodicals. Take for example that journal of post-Marxist studies, *The Wall Street Journal*, which in the 1990s campaigned against the lingering consequences of the Taylorist-Fordist workplace, e.g. firms sticking to an outdated model in which management distrusts the autonomy of workers, prescribes dull routinized tasks, curbs creativity, and creates a workplace ill-suited to "literate, independent-minded workers."[38]

Back to Marx and Saito, within his conceptual frame of the universality of abstract labor, Communism is not just the restored unity of man and nature but simultaneously the fulfilment of their rift: in capitalism, social production remains "irrational," not regulated by social planning (which characterizes humanity) and in this sense pre-human, part of "natural history." The underlying problem is here a philosophical one: Saito misses *this* rift because he unquestionably accepts Marx's definition (from *Capital*) of human specificity: while every living species is involved in metabolism, the exchange of matter between its own organism and its natural environs, only the human species performs this metabolism through labor in the sense of a consciously regulated activity—recall the already-quoted passage from Chapter 7 of *Capital I* on the difference between spider and man. The obviousness of this distinction should not seduce us.[39]

The obviousness of this definition should not seduce us. The question persists: conscious planning of a work process requires some kind of distance from one's own natural immediacy, and the form of this distance is language, so there is no labor in specific human sense without language. This implies a lot: language is not just an instrument of communication, it forms what Lacan calls "big Other," the substance of our social being, the thick social network of written and unwritten rules and patterns. Consequently, Marx goes too fast in his definition of labor—he obfuscates or ignores another break. Preceding the quoted passage, he writes:

> We are not now dealing with those primitive instinctive forms
> of labour that remind us of the mere animal. An immeasurable

interval of time separates the state of things in which a man brings his labour-power to market for sale as a commodity, from that state in which human labour was still in its first instinctive stage. We pre-suppose labour in a form that stamps it as exclusively human.[40]

The limitation shared by Marx and Saito is clear here: they both posit a progressive line from animality to humans, from instinctual to planned/conscious, so that premodern phases are perceived as "primitive instinctive forms of labour that remind us of the mere animal." However, these "primitive instinctive forms of labour that remind us of the mere animal" already involve a radical break with nature—the "metabolic rift" is already there, the "metabolism" of ancient societies is always grounded in a symbolic big Other of regulated exchanges. Suffice it to recall the ancient Aztecs and Incas whose social metabolism was regulated by an enormous symbolic apparatus whose activity culminated in sacrificial rituals: we have to perform human sacrifices so that the most "natural" circulation of nature will go on (so that sun will rise again, etc.), and sacrifice is by definition a disruption of the smooth metabolism. In short, the metabolic rift with (animal) Life is *culture itself*, even if—or especially when—it is grounded in natural rhythms of seasons, when it projects meaning into nature. When, in his "anthropological" writings, Freud inquires into the origins of such rituals, his ultimate result is that the true metabolic rift (the cut between nature and culture) is sexuality itself: human sexuality is immanently self-sabotaging, it involves paradoxes of desire, it imposes its own violent rhythm on "natural" rhythms—Freud's name for these paradoxes is, of course, death drive. Ludovic Tezier (a great baritone) said in an interview: "We need music to live. It's kind of a drug, and a very healthy one."[41] A properly human life needs such a drug which disturbs the biological rhythm of life, healthy or unhealthy … In short, capitalism is NOT the source of the asymmetries and imbalances in the world, which means that our goal should NOT be to restore the "natural" balance and symmetry. Such a project of restoring the pre-capitalist balance not only ignores (or underestimates, at least) the rift which is already at work in pre-capitalist societies: it also ignores the emancipatory dimension of the rise of modern subjectivity which leaves behind the traditional sexualized cosmology of mother earth (and father heaven), of our roots in the substantial "maternal" order of nature.

Marx's metaphor for capital is that of a vampire—the living dead—that sucks the blood of the living—in the topsy-turvy world of capital, the dead rule over the living and are more alive than the living. The implicit premise of this metaphor is that the aim of the revolution is to return to normality in which the living rule over the dead. Lacan, however, teaches us that a certain reversal of the relationship between the living and the dead defines the very being-human: the "barred" subject is the living dead, at a distance from its biological substance, since it is caught in the symbolic big Other which is a kind of parasite living off humans who serve it. Enjoyment itself is something that parasitizes upon human pleasures, perverting them so that a subject can draw a surplus-enjoyment from displeasure itself.

We should even go a step further (or, rather, backward) here. It is not only that a metabolic rift happens with humanity, a rift operates already in pre-human nature itself—just think about our main sources of energy, oil and coal, what kind of rifts had to happen to create these reserves. So we have to accept the paradox: if humanity is ever to reach a kind of harmonious metabolism (exchange with nature), it will be imposed by humanity as a kind of "second nature." Different ideas for regulating the entire metabolism on earth to prevent ecological catastrophes already circulate, and some of them involve radical interventions in natural cycles (like spraying our atmosphere with chemicals which would diminish the quantity of the sun's rays hitting earth).

Marx writes: "It is not the *unity* of living and active humanity with the natural, inorganic conditions of their metabolic interaction with nature ... which requires explanation ... but rather the *separation* between the inorganic conditions of human existence and this active existence" (66). However, what if a certain disunity or rift is constitutive of humanity as such, and, in this sense, transhistorical? So what requires explanation are precisely different historically-specific constructs of unity that try to obfuscate the basic disunity. Saito is in search of a pre-capitalist foundation of human life, and he posits the process of metabolism between nature and humans as the ground on which the process of Capital is based: this metabolism was distorted by Capital which parasitizes on it, so that the basic "contradiction" of capitalism is that between natural metabolism and capital—nature resists capital, it poses a limit to capital's self-valorization. The task of Communists is thus to invent a new form of social metabolism which will no longer be market-mediated but organized in a human (rationally planned) way. That's why Saito is profoundly anti-Hegelian: his axiom is that Hegelian dialectics cannot think the natural limits of Capital, the fact that the self-movement of Capital cannot ever fully "sublate"/integrate its presupposed natural base. Our rejoinder is here that Saito proceeds too fast in conceiving the transhistorical metabolism of human and natural life as the base on which capitalism parasitizes: there is a third term between these two, the symbolic order itself, the universe of symbolic fictions, the symbolic substance of our social lives—capitalism is not only destroying our natural habitat, it is simultaneously destroying our shared symbolic substance. Let's quote Carson's resume of the "Hegel's logic as the logic of capital" position:

> in Hegel, an ontological prerequisite is completely internal to the concept and therefore becomes its own form of transition from exteriority to interiority. This leads not to a "resilient" contradiction but to a reconciliation. In contrast, in Marx, the ontological perquisite of concrete life remains conflictual and produces permanent interruptions and obstacles to the concept-subject-capital, which has acquired an autonomous life. In the former reconciliation is achieved making this analysis true to Hegel's system by deploying the final moment of the absolute idea, and in the latter there is no moment of reconciliation and therefore cannot be ontologically understood from the point of view of Hegel's philosophy.[42]

One should just add two points to this. First, does this impossibility of reconciliation (between reproduction of human life and reproduction of capital) not brings us back to the Hegelian logic of essence, so that human productive ability becomes the "essence" of the movement of capital? Second, for Marx, Communism is a true reconciliation—so can it be conceived in Hegelian terms or not?

Furthermore, the expression I find problematic here is "material, which includes human life and nature in their historical modes": can the symbolic substance of our lives into which we are always-already thrown and alienated, Lacan's "big Other," really be reduced to a "material" dimension? Is it not the domain of symbolic fictions *par excellence*? Furthermore, we should be very careful when we oppose nature and culture, since the two terms fully overlap, although not in a symmetrical way. Nature is "everything there is," so that culture is ultimately a part of nature, and even when we are destroying nature, nature is destroying itself through us, its part. Conversely (what we understand by) "nature" is always a social-cultural category: what appears to us as "natural" is always overdetermined by the predominant ideological frame.

Workers or Worker?

Saito thus proceeds too fast in conceiving the trans-historical metabolism of human and natural life as the base on which capitalism parasitizes: there is a third term between these two, the symbolic order itself, the universe of symbolic fictions, the symbolic substance of our social lives, and capitalism is not only destroying our natural habitat, it is simultaneously destroying our shared symbolic substance, what Hegel called *Sitten*. This ignorance of the symbolic order also affects Marx's notion of Communism. When, towards the end of Chapter I of *Capital*, Marx deploys the matrix of four modes of production/exchange, he begins and ends with the imagined example of Robinson—and what I find important is that, at the end, he returns to it as the model for transparent Communist society with no fetishist inversion—this long passage is worth quoting in full:

> Since Robinson Crusoe's experiences are a favourite theme with political economists, let us take a look at him on his island. Moderate though he be, yet some few wants he has to satisfy, and must therefore do a little useful work of various sorts, such as making tools and furniture, taming goats, fishing and hunting. Of his prayers and the like we take no account, since they are a

source of pleasure to him, and he looks upon them as so much recreation. In spite of the variety of his work, he knows that his labour, whatever its form, is but the activity of one and the same Robinson, and consequently, that it consists of nothing but different modes of human labour. Necessity itself compels him to apportion his time accurately between his different kinds of work. Whether one kind occupies a greater space in his general activity than another, depends on the difficulties, greater or less as the case may be, to be overcome in attaining the useful effect aimed at. This our friend Robinson soon learns by experience, and having rescued a watch, ledger, and pen and ink from the wreck, commences, like a true-born Briton, to keep a set of books. His stock-book contains a list of the objects of utility that belong to him, of the operations necessary for their production; and lastly, of the labour time that definite quantities of those objects have, on an average, cost him. All the relations between Robinson and the objects that form this wealth of his own creation, are here so simple and clear as to be intelligible without exertion, even to Mr. Sedley Taylor. And yet those relations contain all that is essential to the determination of value.

Let us now transport ourselves from Robinson's island bathed in light to the European middle ages shrouded in darkness. Here, instead of the independent man, we find everyone dependent, serfs and lords, vassals and suzerains, laymen and clergy. Personal dependence here characterises the social relations of production just as much as it does the other spheres of life organised on the basis of that production. But for the very reason that personal dependence forms the ground-work of society, there is no necessity for labour and its products to assume a fantastic form different from their reality. They take the shape, in the transactions of society, of services in kind and payments in kind. Here the particular and natural form of labour, and not, as in a society based on production of commodities, its general abstract form is the immediate social form of labour. Compulsory labour is just as properly measured by time, as commodity-producing labour; but every serf knows that what he expends in the service of his lord, is a definite quantity of his own personal labour power. The tithe to be rendered to the priest is more matter of fact than his blessing. No matter, then, what we may think of the parts played by the different classes of people themselves in this society, the social relations between individuals in the performance of their labour, appear at all events as their own mutual personal relations, and are not disguised under the shape of social relations between the products of labour.

For an example of labour in common or directly associated labour, we have no occasion to go back to that spontaneously developed form which we find on the threshold of the history of all civilised races. We have one close at hand in the patriarchal industries of a peasant family that produces corn, cattle, yarn, linen, and clothing for home use. These different articles are, as regards the family, so many products of its labour, but as between themselves, they are not commodities. The different kinds of labour, such as tillage, cattle tending, spinning, weaving and making clothes, which result in the various products, are in themselves, and such as they are, direct social functions, because functions of the family, which, just as much as a society based on the production of commodities, possesses a spontaneously developed system of division of labour. The distribution of the work within the family, and the regulation of the labour time of the several members, depend as well upon differences of age and sex as upon natural conditions varying with the seasons. The labour power of each individual, by its very nature, operates in this case merely as a definite portion of the whole labour power of the family, and therefore, the measure of the expenditure of individual labour power by its duration, appears here by its very nature as a social character of their labour.

Let us now picture to ourselves, by way of change, a community of free individuals, carrying on their work with the means of production in common, in which the labour power of all the different individuals is consciously applied as the combined labour power of the community. All the characteristics of Robinson's labour are here repeated, but with this difference, that they are social, instead of individual. Everything produced by him was exclusively the result of his own personal labour, and therefore simply an object of use for himself. The total product of our community is a social product. One portion serves as fresh means of production and remains social. But another portion is consumed by the members as means of subsistence. A distribution of this portion amongst them is consequently necessary. The mode of this distribution will vary with the productive organisation of the community, and the degree of historical development attained by the producers. We will assume, but merely for the sake of a parallel with the production of commodities, that the share of each individual producer in the means of subsistence is determined by his labour time. Labour time would, in that case, play a double part. Its apportionment in accordance with a definite social plan maintains the proper proportion between the different kinds of work to be done and the various wants of the community. On the other hand, it also serves as a measure of the portion of the common labour borne by each individual, and of his share in the part of the total product destined for individual consumption. The social relations of the individual producers, with regard both to their labour and to its products, are in this case perfectly simple and intelligible, and that with regard not only to production but also to distribution.[43]

This series of four modes of production—Robinson alone, medieval domination, family collective, Communism—is surprising and counter-intuitive. The first mystery that strikes the eye is: why do we get family where we would expect capitalism as the mode which follows medieval direct domination? Should family not be at the beginning, as a mode that characterizes pre-class "primitive" societies? Instead of family, Marx begins with the example of Robinson (a sole producer)—why is Robinson the starting point when (as Marx knew very well), Robinson is not a historical starting point but a bourgeois myth? Is it not that Marx has to begin with Robinson so that, in a (pseudo-)Hegelian dialectical circle, at the end he can get back to a collective Robinson as an imagined model of Communist society? The parallel with Robinson enables Marx to imagine Communism as a self-transparent society in which relations between individuals are not mediated by an opaque substantial big Other—and our task today is to think Communism outside this horizon. In his vision of a Communist society in which production is regulated in a collective-Robinson way, Marx echoes the famous passage from his *Grundrisse* manuscripts in which he imagines Communism as a society in which the production-process is dominated by the "general intellect." This passage is worth quoting *in extenso* since in it, Marx deploys a logic of the self-overcoming of capitalism which totally ignores active revolutionary struggle—it is formulated in purely economic terms: "Capital itself is the moving contradiction, [in] that it presses to reduce labor time to a minimum, while it posits labor time, on the other side, as sole measure and source of wealth."[44] The "contradiction" which will ruin capitalism is thus the contradiction between the capitalist exploitation which relies on labor time as the sole source of value (and thus the sole source of surplus-value), and between the scientific-technological progress which leads to quantitative and qualitative reduction of the role of direct labor.

> To the degree that large industry develops, the creation of real wealth comes to depend less on labor time and on the amount of labor employed than on the power of the agencies set in motion during labor time, whose "powerful effectiveness" is itself in turn out of all proportion to the direct labor time spent on their production, but depends rather on the general state of science and on the progress of technology, or the application of this science to production.[45]

Marx's vision is here that of a fully automated production process in which the human being (worker) "comes to relate more as watchman and regulator to the production process itself":

> No longer does the worker insert a modified natural thing [*Naturgegenstand*] as middle link between the object and himself; rather, he inserts the process of nature, transformed into an industrial process, as a means between himself and inorganic nature, mastering it. He steps to the side of the production process instead of being its chief actor. In this transformation, it is neither the direct human labor he himself performs, nor the time during which he works, but rather the appropriation of his own general productive power, his

understanding of nature and his mastery over it by virtue of his presence as a social body—it is, in a word, the development of the social individual which appears as the great foundation-stone of production and of wealth. The theft of alien labor time, on which the present wealth is based, appears a miserable foundation in face of this new one, created by large-scale industry itself. As soon as labor in the direct form has ceased to be the great well-spring of wealth, labor time ceases and must cease to be its measure.[46]

Marx's systematic use of singular ("man," "worker") is a key indicator of how "general intellect" is not intersubjective—it is "monological." Recall the conclusion of Marx's description of the abstract labor process, its symptomatic "illogical" exclusion of the social dimension: "It was, therefore, not necessary to represent our laborer in connection with other laborers; man and his labor on one side, Nature and its materials on the other, sufficed." It is as if in Communism, with its rule of "general intellect," this a-social character of labor is directly realized … What this means is that, *pace* Negri, in Marx's vision of "general intellect," the objects of the production process are precisely *not* social relations themselves: the "administration of things" (control of and domination over nature) is here separated from relations between people, it constitutes a domain of the "administration of things" which no longer has to rely on domination over people. (One should here bear in mind that the entire development of "general intellect" from *Grundrisse* belongs to an unpublished fragmentary manuscript—it is an experimental line of development which Marx immediately afterwards discarded. However, the link of this passage with Marx's asocial definition of labor in general as well as with the Robinson-passage in *Capital* clearly signals that such a vision is immanent to Marx's edifice.) Today, this vision has been resuscitated by (among others) Aaron Bastani[47] for whom "the most pressing crisis of all" that we are facing today, more pressing than ecological threats, is "an absence of collective imagination":

The plummeting cost of information and advances in technology are providing the ground for a collective future of freedom and luxury for all. Automation, robotics and machine learning will

... substantially shrink the workforce, creating widespread technological unemployment. But that's only a problem if you think work—as a cashier, driver or construction worker—is something to be cherished. For many, work is drudgery. And automation could set us free from it.

Gene editing and sequencing could revolutionize medical practice, moving it from reactive to predictive. Hereditary diseases could be eliminated, including Huntington's disease, cystic fibrosis and sickle cell anemia, and cancer cured before it reaches Stage 1 ... What's more, renewable energy, which has been experiencing steep annual falls in cost for half a century, could meet global energy needs and make possible the vital shift away from fossil fuels. More speculatively, asteroid mining—whose technical barriers are presently being surmounted—could provide us with not only more energy than we can ever imagine but also more iron, gold, platinum and nickel. Resource scarcity would be a thing of the past. The consequences are far-reaching and potentially transformative. For the crises that confront our world today—technological unemployment, global poverty, societal aging, climate change, resource scarcity—we can already glimpse the remedy.

But there's a catch. It's called capitalism. It has created the newly emerging abundance, but it is unable to share round the fruits of technological development. A system where things are produced only for profit, capitalism seeks to ration resources to ensure returns. Just like today's, companies of the future will form monopolies and seek rents. The result will be imposed scarcity—where there's not enough food, health care or energy to go around.

So we have to go beyond capitalism ... We can see the contours of something new, a society as distinct from our own as that of the 20th century from feudalism, or urban civilization from the life of the hunter-gatherer. It builds on technologies whose development has been accelerating for decades and that only now are set to undermine the key features of what we had previously taken for granted as the natural order of things.

To grasp it, however, will require a new politics. One where technological change serves people, not profit. Where the pursuit of tangible policies—rapid decarbonization, full automation and socialized care—are preferred to present fantasies. This politics, which is utopian in horizon and everyday in application, has a name: Fully Automated Luxury Communism.[48]

It is easy to explode in sceptical laughter at this vision—but before we do this, we should take note of the common-sense evidence that seems to support it. With today's explosive development of new technologies, a society of abundance for everybody is, for the first time in human history, if not within our reach at least clearly discernible as a possibility. The growing "contradiction" on which Bastani dwells—capitalism created abundance that it has to contain—seems to support his argument that, while Marx was right, his vision of Communism just came too early: it is only today that abundance became objectively possible.

There are, however, problems with this technological vision of Communism. The same processes that open up the prospect of new abundance also open up new unheard-of possibilities of control and regulation of our lives. The root of this problems i: even if the production process is largely automated, who will regulate this process and how? And how will social life itself be organized in this society of abundance? There is a strong possibility that, in the absence of market mechanisms, the overcoming of capitalism will lead to the return of direct relations of domination and servitude, and this possibility is grounded in Marx's ignorance of the dimension of the big Other.

We can see now the background of Saito's decision to assert the transhistorical character of *abstract* labor: it is not against the spirit of Marx, but a feature which just brought to its logical conclusion a certain notion present in Marx himself: in spite of all his insistence of the social character of labor, Marx does some surprising things when, in *Capital*, he tries to define labor as such, independently of its particular forms. First, he says that we have only a worker on one side and objects of work on the other side—the social dimension disappears. The same abstraction from the social dimension reappears when Marx tries to imagine the basic coordinates of a future non-alienated Communist society, the worker in singular is here again.

Fiction and/In Reality

However, there are in Marx's *Capital* elements which indicate how to overcome this ignorance—passages in which he deals with the necessary role of fiction in capitalist reproduction, from commodity fetishism as a fiction which is part of social reality itself to the topic of fictitious capital introduced in *Capital II* and elaborated in *Capital III*. The three volumes of *Capital* reproduce the triad of the universal, the particular, and the individual: *Capital* I articulates the abstract-universal matrix (concept) of capital; *Capital II* shifts to particularity, to the actual life of capital in all its contingent complexity; *Capital III* deploys the individuality of the total process of capital. In recent years, the most productive studies of Marx's critique of political economy have focused on *Capital II*—why? In a letter sent to Engels on 30 April 1868 Marx wrote:

> In Book 1 […] we content ourselves with the assumption that if in the self-expansion process £100 becomes £110, the latter will find *already in existence in the market* the elements into which it will change once more. But now we investigate the conditions under which these elements are found at hand, namely the social intertwining of the different capitals, of the component parts of capital and of revenue (= s).[49]

Two features are crucial here, which are two sides of the same coin. On the one hand, Marx passes from the pure notional structure of capital's reproduction (described in Volume I) to reality in which capital's reproduction involves temporal gaps, dead time, etc. There are dead times that interrupt smooth reproduction, and the ultimate cause of these dead times is that we are not dealing with a single reproductive cycle but with an intertwinement of multiple circles of reproduction which are never fully coordinates. These dead periods are not just an empirical complication but an immanent necessity, they are necessary for reproduction, they complicate the actual life of capital.[50] On the other hand, fiction intervenes here (in the guise of fictitious capital whose notion is further elaborated in Volume III of *Capital*); fiction is needed to overcome the destructive potential of complications, delays, dead periods, so that when we pass from pure logical matrix to actual life, to reality, fiction has to intervene.

To understand this difference between *Capital I* and *Capital II*, we have to introduce another concept, that of *exemplum* as opposed to simple example. Examples are empirical events or things which illustrate a universal notion, and because of the complex texture of reality they never fully fit the simplicity of a notion.[51] Among Bayard's examples of exemplum, there is the nicely provocative case of Hannah Arendt's thesis of the "banality of evil" illustrated by Adolph Eichmann. Bayard demonstrates that, although Arendt proposed a relevant concept, the reality of Eichmann doesn't fit it: the real Eichmann was far from a non-thinking bureaucrat just following orders, he was a fanatical anti-Semite fully aware of what he was doing—he just played a figure of the banality of evil for the court in Israel. Another of Bayard's very pertinent examples is the case of Kitty Genovese who was murdered in front of her apartment block in Queens at 3:00 a.m. in 1964. The murderer followed her and stabbed her with a knife for over half an hour, her desperate cries for help were heard all around, but although at least 38 neighbors turned on their lights and observed the event, not even one called the police, a simple anonymous act which would have saved her life . . . This event found a wide echo, books were written about it and researches confirmed the thesis that people didn't call the police because they were aware that others were also looking, so they reasoned that someone else would call. Repeated experiments proved that the more people witness a traumatic event (fire, crime . . .), the less likely it is that one of them will call the police . . . Looking into the original data, Bayard shows that the reality of Kitty Genovese's murder didn't fit the popular description: there were three observers at most, and even these three didn't see anything clearly, and one of them *did* call the police. We get here another case of how an exemplum is imagined in order to illustrate a thesis which is in itself correct and important. Bayard argues that this fiction predominated over facts because it served perfectly as an apologue with a moral lesson which makes us (the public) feel better: we are disgusted by the story, presupposing that if we were among the observers we would definitely called the police.[52]

It is easy to see how this distinction between example and exemplum perfectly exemplifies the Hegelian triad of the universal, the particular, and the individual: the universal is the abstract notion, particularities are its (always imperfect) examples, and the individual is exemplum, a singularity in which the domain of contingent reality unites with the universal. It is thus not enough to insist that universality is always mediated by its particular examples; one should add to this multiplicity of examples the exemplum in which a universality returns to itself. Is the ultimate exemplum not Christ himself? We, ordinary humans, are imperfect examples of God, made in his image, while Christ is (for us, materialists, at least) a fiction and as such the exemplum in which the divine universality returns to itself.

In *Capital I*, Marx often uses an imagined exemplum to illustrate the exchange between a worker and a capitalist or the process of the circulation of capital. Here is his famous description of how, when a capitalist and a worker depart after signing a work contract, the signature causes "a change in the physiognomy of our dramatis personae": "He, who before was the money-owner, now strides in front as capitalist; the possessor of labour-power follows as his labourer. The one with an air of importance, smirking, intent on business; the other, timid and holding back, like one who is bringing his own hide to market and has nothing to expect but—a hiding."[53] Such cases are imagined cases of a "pure" situation which cannot ever take place in the thick texture of reality where different moments reproduce themselves in different rhythms which cannot directly follow demands of the market (the workforce needs decades to reproduce itself, etc.). The paradox of exemplum is thus that, although it is empirically a fiction (it never "really happened exactly like that"), it is in some sense "closer to truth" since it perfectly renders (gives body to) the inner notional structure of a phenomenon—yet another way to understand Lacan's claim that truth has the structure of a fiction. We thus have to distinguish between fiction of exemplum which illustrates the abstract notional truth and fiction which enables capital to function and reproduce itself in reality.

So Volume II of *Capital* focuses on the problem of realising surplus value, disrupted first and foremost by time and distance. As Marx put it, during its circulation time, capital does not function as productive capital, and therefore produces neither commodities nor surplus-value: capital's circulation generally restricts its production time, and hence its valorization process. This is why industry is increasingly clustered outside urban centres, close to motorways and airports in order to streamline circulation.

Another implication is the growing role for a credit system that enables production to continue throughout the circulation process. Credit can be used to bridge the gap in situations where surplus value has not yet been realised and under conditions where capitalists expect future consumption of their goods and services. This may seem like rather a banal point, but it has real consequences for how the economy functions, illuminating a systemic reliance on fictitious capital (although Marx introduced this term later, in *Capital*, Volume III). Money values backed by yet unproduced or sold goods and services are thus the essential lifeblood of capitalism, rather than an eccentric or irregular consequence of an otherwise self-reliant system: in order to function as capital, money must circulate, it must again employ labor-power and again realise itself in expanded value. Let's take an industrialist who has enough money in his bank account to retire and live off interest: the bank must *loan* his capital to another industrialist. The industrialist who has borrowed the money must service the loan, i.e., pay interest, out of the profits he makes. The sum of money on the market is thus redoubled: the retired capitalist still owns his money, and the other capitalist also disposes of the money he has borrowed. But as the class of speculators, bankers, brokers, financiers, and so on, grows, as is inevitably the case wherever the mass of capital in a country reaches a sufficient scale, the bank finds that it is able to loan out *far more* than it has deposited in its vaults; speculators can sell products that they do not possess, "the right kind of person" is good for credit even when they have nothing. Note how trust (i.e., interpersonal relations), re-enters the scene here, at the level of what appear to be completely impersonal financial speculations: the ability of the bank to make unsecured loans is dependent on "confidence":

In this way, the money form produces not only impersonal relations of domination but at the same time produces interpersonal forms of domination as fictitious capital exists as a form of appearance of value not on the basis of the substance of abstract labour that produces the subject-object inversion, but through interpersonal forms of domination that promise future production of value as substance. Therefore, there is a different kind of subjection working on the bearers of fictitious capital which is on the basis of an interpersonal relation forged through a contract.[54]

Thus one and the same unit of productive capital may have to support not just the one retired industrialist who deposited his savings with the bank, but *multiple* claims on one and the same capital. If the bank accepts one million from our retiree, but loans out ten million, each of those ten million has *equal* claim to that same value—this is how *ficitious capital* comes about. At times of expansion and boom, the mass of *fictitious capital* grows rapidly; when the period of contraction arrives, the bank finds itself under pressure and calls in its loans, defaults occur, bankruptcies, closures, share prices fall, and things go back to reality—fictitious value is wiped out. This brings us to a formal definition of fictitious capital: it is *that proportion of capital which cannot be simultaneously converted into existing use-values*. It is an *invention* which is absolutely necessary for the growth of real capital, it is a fiction which constitutes the symbol of confidence in the future. Or, as Rebecca Carson resumes this entire movement: "non-capitalist variables become formally subsumed through circulation, making them necessary for the reproduction of capital, yet they are variables nonetheless necessarily exterior, described by Marx as 'interruptions' within the movement of capital."[55]

What this means in socio-economic terms is that we should unconditionally avoid any notion of Communism as an order in which fictions no longer reign over actual life, i.e., in which we return to actual life: as Hardt and Negri repeatedly insisted, there is an unexpected emancipatory potential in the craziest speculations with fictive capital. Since valorization of the workforce is the key aspect of capitalist reproduction, we should never forget that in the sphere of fictitious capital there is no valorization, no market exchange of commodities and no labor that produces new value—and because in a capitalist society personal freedom is grounded in the "free" exchange of commodities, inclusive of the labor power as a commodity, the sphere of fictitious capital no longer demands personal freedom and autonomy: direct interpersonal relations of subordination and domination return in it. It may appear that this reasoning is too formal, but one can elaborate this in a more precise way: fictitious capital involves debt, and being indebted limits personal freedom; for the workers, debt is involved in the (re) production of their workforce itself, and this debt limits their freedom to bargain for a work contract.

The Emancipatory Potential of Capitalist Madness

So where is there any emancipatory potential? Elon Musk proposed a mega-algorithm program that would manage our investments better than any stockbroker company, allowing ordinary people to invest small sums under equal conditions as billionaires—the idea is that, when this program is freely available, it will lead to a more fair distribution of wealth . . . Although the idea is problematic and ambiguous, it does indicate the ultimate nonsense of stock exchange games: if a mega-algorithm can do the work better than humans, stock exchanges could become an automated machine—and if this works, private ownership of stocks will also become useless since all we'll need will be a gigantic AI machine for the optimal allocation of resources . . . this is how the extreme of financial capitalism can open up an unexpected path to Communism.

Musk's idea became a reality in one of the few flashes of spirit in our dark time, although not exactly in the way he imagined it. This flash is condensed in the memes, "WallStreetBets/Robinhood/ GameStop"—for a couple of days, news about it overshadowed the usual Big Bad news (the pandemic, Trump . . .). The story is well-known, so let's recapitulate the main points in a Wikipedia style. WallStreetBets (WSB) is a subreddit where millions of participants discuss stock and options trading; it is notable for its profane nature and the promotion of aggressive trading strategies. Most of the members of the subreddit are young retail traders and investors or simply young amateurs who ignore fundamental investment practices and risk management techniques, so their activity is considered gambling. Many members of the subreddit use the amateur platform Robinhood, a popular app to trade stocks and options—Robinhood's original product was a program enabling commission-free trades of stocks and exchange-traded funds. In their operations, WSB members also rely on the low price of money (low interest rates for loans) today. The space for WSB was obviously opened up by the unprecedented uncertainty of our lives brought about by the pandemic: a threat of death, chaos and social protests, but at the same time a lot of free time due to quarantines.

Their best-known operation was the unexpected massive investment in the stocks of GameStop (a company slowly losing value on the market) which drove their price up and caused further panic and oscillations on the market. The decision to invest in GameStop was not grounded in anything that was going on with the company (like knowledge that GameStop was developing a new lucrative product)—it was made just to raise the value of its stocks temporarily and then play with its oscillations. What this means is that there is a kind of self-reflexivity that characterizes WSB: what goes on in the companies in whose stocks the participants invest is of secondary importance, they primarily count on the effects of their own activity (of massively buying or selling the stocks of a company) on the market.

Critics of WSB see in such a stance a clear sign of nihilism, of reducing stock-trade to gambling—as one of the WSB participants put it: "I went from a rational investor to some sick irrational desperate gambler." This nihilism is best exemplified by the term "yolo" (You Only Live Once) used in the WSB community to characterize people who risk their entire portfolio on a single stock or options trade. But it's not simple nihilism that motivates the WSB participants: their nihilism signals indifference towards the final result—or, as Jeremy Blackburn wrote: "It's not even the ends that matter. It's the means. It's the fact that you're placing this bet, that's where the value in all this is. Sure, you may get money, or you may end up broke, but you played the game, and you did it in some crazy way."[56] Is this not a kind of des-alienation, an act of stepping out of the game—how? Lacan distinguishes between direct pleasure (enjoying the object we want) and surplus-enjoyment. His elementary example is a child sucking the mother's breast: the child does it first to satisfy his/her hunger, but then s/he begins to enjoy the act of sucking itself, and continues to do it even when there is no hunger. It's the same with shopping (many people enjoy the activity of shopping more than what they actually buy), or, basically, with sexuality itself. WSB participants bring this surplus-enjoyment of stock-exchange gambling out into the open.

How does this work in our political space? WBG is a politically ambiguous populist rebellion. When Robinhood ceded to pressures and blocked retail investors from purchasing stock, Alexandria Ocasio-Cortez opposed this move for the right reason: "This is unacceptable. We now need to know more about @RobinhoodApp's decision to block retail investors from purchasing stock while hedge funds are freely able to trade the stock as they see fit."[57] (Robinhood later restored trading.) AOC was supported by Ted Cruz from the alt-Right populist standpoint of opposing big banks and Wall Street. (She was right to refuse collaboration.)

One can imagine the horror WSB had gave rise to in Wall Street (and state apparatuses): the massive intervention on the stock market of "amateurs" who don't follow (and don't even want to know) the rules and laws of the game, and who consequently appear from the standpoint of professional investors as "irrational" lunatics spoiling the game. The key feature of the WSB community is precisely the positive function of this not-knowing: they generate shattering effects in the reality of market exchanges by ignoring the "rational" knowledge of laws and rules of investing allegedly practiced by "professional" stock-traders.

The popular appeal of WSB means that millions of ordinary people, not just exclusive trade-dealers, participate in it. A new front in America's class war opened up—Robert Reich tweeted: "So let me get this straight: Redditors rallying GameStop is market manipulation, but hedge fund billionaires shorting a stock is just an investment strategy?"[58] Who would have expected this—a class war transposed into a conflict among stock investors and dealers themselves?

So it's kill the normies again, to repeat the title of Angela Nagle's book: "For WallStreetBets, the normie culture it stands in opposition to is one of 'safe' mainstream investing: focusing on long-term gains, maxing out your 401(k)s, buying index funds."[59] But this time the normies should really be "killed" (eliminated)—why? The irony is that Wall Street, the model of corrupt speculation and insider-trading, always by definition resisting state intervention and regulation, now opposes unfair competition and calls for state regulation . . . As for the accusation from Wall Street that what goes on in Robinhood is gambling, suffice it to recall that Elizabeth Warren repeatedly accused hedge funds of using the stock market "like their personal casino." In short, WSB is doing openly and in a legal way what Wall Street is doing in secret and illegally . . . it's as if a big criminal were to accuse a small guy who is copying his secret practices of stealth.

WSB's utopia of populist capitalism—the ideal of millions who are during the day ordinary workers or students and in the evening play with investments—is, of course, impossible to realize, it can only end in a self-destructive chaos. But is it not in the very nature of capitalism to be periodically in crisis—the Big One of 1928, the financial meltdown of 2008 (created by "rational" hedge funds!), to mention just the two best-known cases—and to come out of them stronger? However, in both of these cases, as with the WBG crisis, it was (and is) impossible to restore balance through immanent market mechanisms. The price is too high, so a massive external (state) intervention is needed. Can the state then control the game again, restore the old normality ruined by WSB? The model here is China with its tight state control over stock exchange—however, doing this in the West would have meant a radical change in economic politics and this could only be have been achieved through a global socio-political transformation.

Does this mean that we should sustain so-called accelerationism, i.e., the idea that capitalism, together with technological change that it instigates, should be "accelerated" and drastically intensified to create radical social change? Yes, in principle the end of capitalism can be brought about only by its acceleration— the popular view, especially in some Third World countries, that the key role in opposing capitalism should be played by so-called "sites of resistance," local pockets of premodern traditional forms of life with greater social solidarity, is a blind alley (the Taliban in Afghanistan are definitely such a site of resistance!). However, it is not acceleration as such that produces social change: acceleration just makes us openly confront the basic deadlock of the global capitalist system.

What then is the solution? There is only one simple answer: the "excess" of the WSB brought into the open the latent "irrationality" of the stock exchange itself—it's the moment of its truth. WSB is not a rebellion against Wall Street, but something potentially much more subversive: it subverts the system by over-identifying with it or, rather, by universalizing it and thereby bringing out its latent absurdity. It's like what a Croatian outsider (a theatre actor) did when he proposed himself as a candidate in the last presidential elections there—the main point of his program was: "Corruption for everybody! I promise that not only the elite will be able to profit from corruption, you will all be able to profit from it!" When placards with this slogan appeared all around Zagreb, it was the talk of the town; people reacted enthusiastically, even though they knew it was a joke ... Yes, what the WSB participants are doing is nihilist, but it is nihilism immanent to stock exchange itself, nihilism already at work in Wall Street. To overcome this nihilism, we will somehow have to move *out* of the game of stock exchange. The moment of Socialism is lurking in the background, waiting to be seized—the very centre of global capitalism is beginning to fall apart. The opposite of WSB is, as we have already seen, Musk's idea of an investment algorithm. This idea, we should add, has already been developed and made freely available by two young programmers in the US: on average, it does the job of stock-exchange trading, of telling you what and when to buy or sell there, better than the big Wall Street traders. The unity of stock trading (carried out by experts who bring knowledge and experience with a personal touch) is thus divided into its two extremes: an objective algorithm which runs by itself and subjective gambling which breaks the rules and operates at a totally different level of manipulations.

Will this falling apart really happen? Almost certainly not, but what should worry us is that the WSB crisis is another unexpected threat to the system already under attack from multiple sides (pandemic, global warming, social protests ...), and this threat comes from the very heart of the system, not from outside. An explosive mixture is in the making, and the longer the explosion is postponed, the more devastating it could be.

Ecology with Alienation

There is a fundamental difference between subject's alienation in the symbolic order and the worker's alienation in capitalist social relations. We have to avoid the two symmetrical traps which open up if we insist on the homology between the two alienations: the idea that capitalist social alienation is irreducible since the signifying alienation is constitutive of subjectivity, as well as the opposite idea that the signifying alienation could be abolished in the same way Marx imagined the overcoming of capitalist alienation. The point is not just that the signifying alienation is more fundamental and will persist even if we abolish capitalist alienation—it is a more refined one. The very figure of a subject that would overcome the signifying alienation and become a free agent who is master of the symbolic universe, i.e., who is no longer embedded in a symbolic substance, can only arise within the space of capitalist alienation, the space in which free individuals interact. Let's indicate the domain of this symbolic alienation with regard to Brandom's attempt to elaborate "the way to a postmodern form of recognition that overcomes ironic alienation. This is the recollective-recognitive structure of trust."[60] For Brandom, this:

> may be the part of Hegel's thought that is of the most contemporary philosophical interest and value. That is partly because he attributes deep political significance to the replacement of a semantic model of atomistic representation by one of holistic expression ... It is to lead to a new form of mutual recognition and usher in the third stage in the development of Geist: the age of trust.[61]

"Trust" is here trust in the ethical substance (the "big Other" the set of established norms) which doesn't limit but sustains the space of our freedom, the assurance that if we approach the world rationally, the world will react to our inquiry and appear rational.[62] Referring to Chomsky, Brandom gives his own reading to the classic distinction between negative freedom and positive freedom: negative freedom is the freedom from predominant norms and obligations which can lead only to universalized ironic distance towards all positive regulations (we shouldn't trust them, they are illusions masking particular interests), while positive freedom is the freedom whose space is opened up and sustained by our adherence to a set of norms. As Chomsky has proven, language enables an individual who inhabits it to generate an infinite number of sentences—this is the positive freedom of expression provided by our acceptance of the rules of language, while negative freedom can only lead to ironic alienation:

> When institutions entail the proper recognitive relations both upward (from individuals to institution) and downward (from institution to individuals), they enable freedom, in the negative sense of releasing individuals from "the debilitating burden of constant reflection and negotiation of every norm" (Heikki Ikäheimo) of interaction, as well as in the positive sense of offering and promoting meaningful social goals, activities, and roles.[63]

The "positive sense" is what Brandom is aiming at in his notion of ethical substance as the foundation of our freedoms, but one should add to it the "negative sense" noted by Ikaheimo: "the debilitating burden of constant reflection and negotiation of every norm"— here, one encounters what one cannot but call a minimum of alienation as a condition of freedom. The only way to think and interact freely implies not only that we rely on shared rules of language and manners but also that we accept these rules as something given of which we are not reflectively aware—if we were to reflect on and negotiate these rules all the time, our freedom would be self-destroyed by its very excess.

But is the freedom of irony, of ironic distance, also not a form of positive freedom grounded in a deep acquaintance with the rules? Is something like ironic alienation not inherent to those who really inhabit a language? Let's take patriotism: a true patriot is not a fanatical zealot but somebody who can quite often make ironic remarks about his nation, and this irony paradoxically vouches for his true love of his country (when things get serious, he is ready to fight for it). To be able to practice this kind of irony, I have to master the rules of my language much more deeply than those who speak it in a flawless non-ironic way. One can even say that to really inhabit a language implies not just to know the rules but to know the meta-rules which tell me how to violate the explicit rules: it doesn't imply to making no mistakes but making the right kind of mistakes. And the same goes for manners that held together a given closed community—this is why, in former times when there were still schools to teach ordinary people how to behave in a high-class society, these were generally a terrible failure: no matter how much they did teach you the rules of behavior, they were not able to teach you the meta-rules that regulate the subtle transgressions of the rulers. And, speaking of expressive subjectivity, one can also say that subjectivity appears in a speech only through such regulated violations—without them, we get flat impersonal speech.

And what if we imagine Communism in a similar way: as a new ethical substance (a framework of rules) that enables positive freedom? Maybe this is how we should reread Marx's opposition of the kingdom of necessity and kingdom of freedom: Communism is not freedom itself but the structure of a kingdom of necessity that sustains freedom. This is also how I should have replied to Tyler Cowen who, in a debate in Bergen, asked me why I continue to stick to the ridiculously outdated notion of Communism, why I do not drop it and just enjoy writing my provocative anti-PC comments? My reply should have been that I need Communism precisely as the background, the firm ethical standard, the principal commitment to a Cause which makes all my transgressive pleasures possible. In other words, we shouldn't imagine Communism as a self-transparent order with no alienation, but as an order of "good" alienation, of our reliance on thick invisible cobweb of regulations which sustains the space of our freedom. In Communism, I should be led to "trust" this cobweb *and ignore it*, focusing on what makes my life meaningful.

This constitutive alienation in the symbolic substance is missing in Saito due to his focus on metabolism of the labor process. That's why Saito is profoundly anti-Hegelian: his axiom is that Hegelian dialectics cannot think the natural limits of Capital, the fact that the self-movement of Capital cannot ever fully "sublate"/integrate its presupposed natural base:

> Marx's ecology deals with the synthesis of the historical and transhistorical aspects of social metabolism in explaining how the physical and material dimensions of the "universal metabolism

of nature" and the "metabolism between humans and nature" are modified and eventually disrupted by the valorization of capital. Marx's analysis aims at revealing the limits of the appropriation of nature through its subsumption by capital. (68)

Marx does not talk about subsumption under capital in abstract formal terms; he is interested in how this subsumption is not just a formal one but gradually transforms the material base itself: air becomes polluted, deforestation occurs, land is exhausted and rendered less fertile, etc. There are three reproaches to be made to this otherwise correct reading of Marx. While Saito writes a lot on the material consequences of the form of capital, how it changes not only material productive forces but nature itself, he strangely doesn't mention two most obvious cases. First, the vast numbers of animals which are not only in their present form as a result of human production, but can also only survive as part of the human productive cycle (cows, pigs ... they cannot survive alone in nature). Second, the absolutely central role of the workforce resides in its unique mixture of value and use-value: the use-value of the workforce—labor itself—is that of producing value.

The second reproach runs in an almost opposite direction. Saito locates the limit of the classic "bourgeois" political economy in the fact that they focus exclusively on the (value-)form, ignoring content, the way form interacts with its material base (115). However, in a crucial passage of *Capital*, Marx says almost the exact opposite: the bourgeois classics focused on the content (the source) of value, and what they neglected was the value-form itself, i.e., why does the content (value) assume this form:

> Whence, then, arises the enigmatical character of the product of labor, so soon as it assumes the form of commodities? Clearly from this form itself ... Political Economy has indeed analysed, however incompletely, value and its magnitude, and has discovered what lies beneath these forms. But it has never once asked the question why labor is represented by the value of its product and labor time by the magnitude of that value.[64]

Marx here—in a properly Hegelian way—turns around the usual notion of a form concealing some mysterious content: the true mystery is in the form itself. With regard to ecology, this means that it is not enough to keep the capitalist form of production and regulate it with ecological standards so that it will not pollute our environment too much—the ultimate threat resides in the capitalist form which is in itself indifferent towards its material content. Saito is right to see in this rift the basic "contradiction" of capitalism: once social production is subsumed under the form of the self-valorization process of capital, the goal of the process becomes capital's extended self-reproduction, the growth of accumulated value, and since the environment ultimately counts just as an externality, destructive environmental consequences are ignored, they don't count:

> capital contradicts the fundamental limitedness of natural forces and resources because of its drive toward infinite self-valorization. This is the central contradiction of the capitalist mode of production, and Marx's analysis aims at discerning the limits to this measureless drive for capital accumulation within a material world. (259)

When he talks about the "contradiction" between capitalism and nature, Saito remains within the confines of the opposition between the exploding demands of humanity and the obvious limitations of the finite world in which we dwell: the entire world simply cannot rejoin the consumerism of the highly developed countries since natural resources at our disposal are limited and non-renewable . . . What such a common-sense approach ignores is the opposite, the other side, of exhaustion, of the growing *shortage* of natural resources: the excess, the exploding *abundance*, of waste in all its forms, from millions of tons of plastic waste circulating in the oceans to air pollution. (These directly man-made pollutions are accompanied by something that should worry us even more—we could call it natural pollution. In May 2021, millions of mice invaded Australian farms; in June 2021, massive amounts alien-like slime washed up on the Turkish coast, disturbing the entire reproductive cycle in the coastal sea etc.[65] Although these phenomena are probably linked to human causes, the link remains unclear.) The name for this surplus is "emissions"—what is emitted is a surplus which cannot be "recycled," reintegrated into the circulation of nature, a surplus which persists as an "unnatural" remainder growing ad infinitum and thereby destabilizing the "finitude" of nature and its resourced. This "waste" is the material counterpart of homeless refugees which form a kind of "human waste" (waste, of course, from the standpoint of capital's global circulation).[66]

Ecology is thus at the very centre of Marx's critique of political economy, and this is why, in the final decades of his life, Marx was extensively reading books on the chemistry and physiology of agriculture. (The reason why Marx turned to the physiology and chemistry of agriculture is clear: he wanted to study the life process of metabolism without falling into the trap of conceiving life that precedes capital in the terms of a Romantic "vital force.") Saito's central premise is that *this* "contradiction" cannot be grasped in Hegelian terms—this is why he mockingly mentions that Western Marxism "primarily deals with social forms (sometimes with an extreme fetishism of Hegel's *Science of Logic*)" (262). But we cannot get rid of Hegel so easily. When Marx wrote that the ultimate barrier of capital is capital itself (in *Capital*, Volume III, Chapter 15 entitled "Exposition of the Internal Contradictions of the Law")— "The *real barrier* of capitalist production is *capital itself*" ("*Die wahre Schranke der kapitalistischen Produktion ist das Kapital selbst*")—we should be precise in the Hegelian sense and clearly distinguish *Schranke* from *Grenze*: *Grenze* designates an external limitation while *Schranke* stands for the immanent barrier of an entity, for its internal contradiction. Say, in the classic case of freedom, the external limitation of my freedom is the freedom of others, but its true "barrier" is the insufficiency of this notion of freedom which opposes my freedom to the freedom of others—as Hegel would have put it, this freedom is not yet true freedom. And the whole point of Marx is that capital is not just externally limited (by nature which cannot be exploited indefinitely) but immanently limited, limited in its very concept.

Which mode of relating to Hegel then should an ecologically-oriented Marxism assume today? Should it treat Hegel's logic as a mystified/idealist model of revolutionary process (*Grundrisse*, young Lukacs), of the logic of Capital, of a new universal ontology? When Chris Arthur says that "it is precisely the applicability of

Hegel's logic that condemns the object as an inverted reality systematically alienated from its bearers,"[67] he thereby provides the most concise formulation of "Hegel's logic as the logic of capital": the very fact that Hegel's logic can be applied to capitalism means that capitalism is a perverted order of alienation . . . However, as we have already seen, in Marx's reading, the self-engendering speculative movement of Capital also indicates a fateful limitation of the Hegelian dialectical process, something that eludes Hegel's grasp. "a monstrous mixture of the good infinity and the bad infinity."[68] This, perhaps, is also the reason why Marx's reference to Hegel's dialectics in his "critique of political economy" is ambiguous, oscillating between taking it as the mystified expression of the logic of Capital and taking it as the model for the revolutionary process of emancipation. First, there is dialectic as the "logic of the capital": the development of the commodity-form and the passage from money to capital are clearly formulated in Hegelian terms (capital is a money-substance turning into a self-mediating process of its own reproduction, etc.). Then, there is the Hegelian notion of the proletariat as "substance-less subjectivity," i.e., the grandiose Hegelian scheme of the historical process from pre-class society to capitalism as the gradual separation of the subject from its objective conditions, so that the overcoming of capitalism means that the (collective) subject re-appropriates its alienated substance. The Hegelian dialectical matrix thus serves as the model of the logic of capital as well as the model of its revolutionary overcoming.

So, again, what mode of relating to Hegel should an ecologically oriented Marxism assume today? Hegelian dialectics as the mystified expression of the revolutionary process, as the philosophical expression of the perverted logic of Capital; as the idealist version of a new dialectical-materialist ontology; or should we simply claim (as Althusser did) that Marx only "flirted" with Hegelian dialectics, that his thinking was totally foreign to Hegel? There is another possibility: a different reading of Hegel's dialectical process itself, not the model of "subject appropriates substance." As Frank Ruda pointed out,[69] Hegel's Absolute Knowing is not a total *Aufhebung*—a seamless integration of all reality into the Notion's self-mediation; it is much more an act of radical *Aufgeben*—of giving up, of renouncing the violent effort to grab reality. Absolute Knowing is a gesture of

Entlassen, of releasing reality, of letting-it-be and stand on its own, and, in this sense, it breaks with the endless effort of labor to appropriate its Otherness, the stuff that forever resists its grasp. Labor (and technological domination in general) is an exemplary case of what Hegel calls "spurious infinity," it is a pursuit which is never accomplished because it presupposes an Other to be mastered, while philosophical speculation is at ease, no longer troubled by its Other.

What such a reading of Hegel implies is that Hegel's dialectics cannot be reduced to a total sublation of all contingency in the self-mediation of the concept. This brings us back to ecology. Saito opposes Hegel, since Hegel is for him the very model of the negation of the autonomy of nature—does Hegel's Idea not stand for a productive process which no longer needs to rely on a metabolic exchange with an Otherness but reduces every Otherness to a subordinate moment of the Idea's self-mediation? But if we accept our reading of Hegel then Hegel not only tolerates but demands that we should allow the irreducible Otherness of nature. This respect for the contingency of nature means that we should avoid the trap of reading ecological catastrophes as signs that point in an unambiguous linear way towards a final catastrophe. Precisely insofar as we should take ecological threats extremely seriously, we should also be fully aware of how uncertain analyses and projections are in this domain—we will know for sure what is going on only when it is too late. Fast extrapolations only give arguments to global warming deniers, so we should at all costs avoid the trap of "ecology of fear," a hasty morbid fascination of a dooming catastrophe. Only a thin line separates the correct perception of real dangers from the fantasy scenarios about a global catastrophe that awaits us. There is a specific enjoyment of living in the end time, living in the shadow of a catastrophe, and the paradox is that such a fixation on the forthcoming catastrophe is precisely one of the ways to avoid really confronting it. To maintain a minimum of credibility, such a vision has to cling on to any bad news that comes along: a melting glacier here, a tornado there, a heat wave somewhere else—they are all read as signs of a forthcoming catastrophe ... Even extensive fires that were devastating south-eastern Australia in late 2019 and early 2020 should not be read in such a simplified way. In a recent comment in *Spectator*, Tim Blair opened up a new perspective on this catastrophe:

> Controlled burns of overgrown flora were once standard practice in rural Australia, but now a kind of ecological religious fundamentalism has taken the place of common sense. There are many examples of recent legal rulings that punished those who cleared land around their properties. "We've been burning less than 1 per cent of our bushfire-prone land for the past 20 years," says fire brigade captain Brian Williams, "that means every year the fuel load continues to build." Well-meaning but ignorant attempts to protect animals' natural ecosystems are, in part, the reason those ecosystems are now nothing but cinders and ash.[70]

The bias of this comment is clear, it is directed against the presumption of global warming; as such, it should be rejected, but what we should learn from it is the ambiguity of signs. Here a turn to theology may be helpful since ecologists are often accused of harboring a quasi-religious zeal. Instead of rejecting this accusation, we should proudly accept it—and qualify it. The beginning of St. John's Gospel contains a whole theory of signs (or miracles): God produces miracles (or, signs, as we would say today, when shocking things happen which disturb our common sense of reality like the fires in Australia), but "if we see miracles without believing we will only be hardened in our sin."[71] Signs are here to convince believers, but when they occur, they simultaneously strengthen the opposition to Jesus in those who do not believe in Him—this opposition "grows harsher and more belligerent, more open in its attempt to silence him; and each time he feels a deeper threat from the powers that were arrayed against him."[72] Blair's comment should be read along these theological lines—although it was definitely meant to make us "be hardened in our sin" (of global warming denial), it should not be dismissed as a corrupt lie but as a welcome opportunity to analyze the complexity of the situation in order to make it clear how this complexity makes our ecological predicament all the more dangerous. In nature, this domain of contingency where the Idea exists in the externality with regard to itself, we are by definition in the domain of ambiguous signs and the "spurious infinity" of complex interactions where each occurrence can be a sign of its opposite, so that every human intervention aimed at restoring some kind of natural balance can trigger an unexpected catastrophe, and every catastrophe can be a harbinger of good news.

Last Exit for Communism

The latest data make it clear that, even after the (very uneven) spread of vaccination, we cannot afford to relax and return to the old normal. Not only is the pandemic not over (infection numbers are rising again, new lockdowns are awaiting us), other catastrophes are on the horizon. At the end of June 2021, a "heat dome"—a weather phenomenon where a ridge of high pressure traps and compresses warm air, driving up temperatures and baking the region—over the northwest of the US and the southwest of Canada caused temperatures to approach 50 degrees Celsius, so that Vancouver was hotter than the Middle East. This weather pathology is just the climax of a much wider process: in recent years, northern Scandinavia and Siberia have regularly seen temperatures of over 30 degrees Celsius. The World Meteorological Organization is seeking to verify the highest-ever temperature north of the Arctic Circle since records there began, after a weather station in Siberia's Verkhoyansk recorded a 38-degree day on June 20. The town of Oymyakon in Russia, considered to be the coldest inhabited place on Earth, was hotter (31.6 degrees Celsius) than it has ever been in June. And, as the cream on the top of the cake: "Smoke from Siberia wildfires reaches north pole in historic first"[73] In short: "climate change is frying the Northern Hemisphere."[74]

True, the "heat dome" was a local phenomenon, but it was the result of a global disturbance of patterns which are clearly a result of human interventions in natural cycles. The catastrophic consequences of this heatwave for life in the ocean are already palpable: "'Heat dome' probably killed 1bn marine animals on Canada coast, experts say. British Columbia scientist says heat essentially cooked mussels:'The shore doesn't usually crunch when you walk.'"[75] While weather is generally getting hotter, this process reaches a climax in local extremes, and these local extremes will sooner or later coalesce in a series of global tipping points. The catastrophic floods in Germany and Belgium in July 2021 are another of these tipping points, and who knows what will follow. Here is a similar observation from Chile:

> In the southwest Pacific Ocean, there's a huge region of unusually warm water covering an area about the size of Australia, known as "the Southern Blob." Several thousand miles away, the South American nation of Chile has been experiencing a megadrought for more than a decade, with dwindling rain and water supplies. On the surface, these two events have nothing to do with each other—but, a new study found, they are linked by invisible forces of global atmospheric pressure and circulation.[76]

We can expect many more news items like this in near future—the catastrophe is not something that will begin in the near future; it is here, and it is also not in some distant African or Asian country but right here, in the heart of the "developed West." To put it bluntly, we will have to get used to living with multiple simultaneous crises. The contours of possible global catastrophes are already visible: "Climate scientists have detected warning signs of the collapse of the Gulf Stream, one of the planet's main potential tipping points"[77]—if this happens, it will affect the lives of billions.

Not only is a heat wave at least partially conditioned by reckless industrial exploitation of nature, its effects also depend on social organization. At the beginning of July 2021, in Southern Iraq temperatures swelled to over 50 degrees Celsius, and what occurred simultaneously was a total collapse of the electricity supply (no air-conditioning, no refrigerators, no light) which made the place a living hell. This catastrophic impact was clearly caused by the enormous state corruption in Iraq, with billions of oil money disappearing into private pockets.

If we access this (and numerous other) data soberly, there is one simple conclusion to be drawn from them: "nothing short of transforming society will avert catastrophe."[78] For every living entity, collective or individual, the final exit is death (which is why Derek Humphry was right to entitle his 1992 suicide self-help book *Final Exit*). The ecological crises which have recently exploded open up a quite realistic prospect of the final exit (i.e. collective suicide) of humanity itself. On a recent local flight in Italy, the pre-recorded warning said that, in case of an emergency, passengers should locate the nearest exit and then follow the *"sentiero luminoso"* (shining path—or, in Spanish, *sendero luminoso*) on the floor that leads to it. We are all now on a flight that got caught in an emergency, so what is our shining path out of it? Is there a last exit from the road to our perdition or is it already too late, so that all we can do is find a way to make suicide more painless?

So what should we do in such an unbearable situation— unbearable because we have to accept that we are one among the species on the earth, but we are at the same time burdened by the impossible task of acting as universal managers of life on earth? Since we failed to take other, perhaps easier, exits (global temperatures are rising, oceans are more and more polluted . . .), it looks more and more that the last exit before the final one (the collective suicide of humanity) will be some version of what was once called War Communism. But the talk of war is deceiving here: we are not fighting an enemy—the only enemy is ourselves, the destructive consequences of capitalist productivity. Recall that, after the fall of the Soviet Union, Cuba proclaimed a "Special Period in Time of Peace" (*"periodo especial* en tiempos de paz"): wartime conditions in a time of peace. Maybe this is the term we should use for our predicament today: we are entering a very special period in a time of peace. Orson Welles was quite right in his acerbic comment on the duty to work for your country: "Ask not what you can do for your country. Ask what's for lunch." Hundreds of millions today have the full right to do this—the problem is just that sometimes you can get the lunch you want only if you change your country.

What I have in mind here is not any kind of rehabilitation of or continuity with twentieth century "really existing Socialism," even less the global adoption of the Chinese model, but a series of measures which are imposed by the situation itself. When (not just a country but) all of us are facing a threat to our survival, we enter a warlike emergency state which will last for decades at least. To simply guarantee the minimal conditions of our survival, mobilizing all our resources is inevitable to deal with unheard-of challenges, inclusive displacements of dozens, maybe hundreds, of millions of people due to global warming. The answer to the "heat dome" in the US and Canada is not just to help the affected areas, but to attack its global causes. And, as the ongoing catastrophe in southern Iraq makes clear, a state apparatus capable of maintaining minimal welfare of the people in catastrophic conditions will be needed to prevent social explosions.

All these things can—hopefully—be achieved only through strong and obligatory international cooperation, social control and regulation of agriculture and industry, changes in our basic eating habits—less beef—global healthcare, etc. Upon a closer look, it is clear that representative political democracy alone will not be sufficient for this task. A much stronger executive power capable of enforcing long-term commitments will have to be combined with local self-organizations of people, as well as with a strong international body capable of overriding the will of dissenting nation-states.

Badiou's thesis, which is "scandalous" for liberals, is more current than ever: "Today the enemy is not called Empire or Capital. It's called Democracy."[79] What, today, prevents the radical questioning of capitalism itself is precisely *the belief in the democratic form of the struggle against capitalism.* Lenin's stance against "economism," as well as against "pure" politics is crucial today: yes, the economy is the key domain—the battle will be decided there, one has to break the spell of the global capitalism—BUT the intervention should be properly POLITICAL, not economic. Today, when everyone is "anticapitalist," up to the Hollywood "socio-critical" conspiracy movies (from *The Enemy of the State* to *The Insider*) in which the enemy are the big corporations with their ruthless pursuit of profit, the signifier "anticapitalism" has lost its subversive sting. What one should problematize is the self-evident opposite of this "anticapitalism": trust in the democratic substance of the honest Americans to break up the conspiracy. THIS is the hard kernel of today's global capitalist universe, its true Master-Signifier: democracy. That's what makes the popular term "democratic Socialism" problematic: when I am asked if I am a democratic Socialist, my instant answer is: "No, I am a non-democratic Communist!"

What this implies is that we should also gather the strength to dispel the myth of non-violence as an effective means of radical political change. Andreas Malm[80] convincingly demonstrated that the well-known thesis about the non-violent nature of successful liberation movements is mistaken: from the movement against slavery, to the suffragettes, to the movement for Indian independence, to the Civil Rights Movement and the ANC in South Africa, the use of direct action involving property damage was an important part of the tactical arsenal. Malm refers here to the notion of "radical flank effect" elaborated by Herbert H. Haines:[81] a radical wing of a movement pushes the authorities to negotiate with and meet the demands of a more moderate wing. Malm draws the inevitable conclusion in the direction of "ecological Leninism": since, as data abundantly show, non-violent calls for lower emissions are largely ignored, the climate change movement should consider targeted property destruction and sabotage (CO_2 emitting devices that cause "luxury emissions"—such as luxury yachts and private planes, fossil fuel infrastructure . . .). The more conventional non-violent methods of protests will not do the necessary job, and the desperate calls for action are more or less just the cover for business as usual. Greta Thunberg was right when she mockingly dismissed pro-green warnings and promises of politicians as just a blah-blah-blah: we are dealing with ritualized complaints whose function is to ensure that nothing will really change.

So how would this global cooperation look? I am not talking here about a new world government—such an entity would provide an opportunity for immense corruption. And I am not talking about Communism in the sense of abolishing markets—market competition should play a role, although a role regulated and controlled by state and society. But is China now not doing exactly what has to be done? It is imposing state control and regulation of markets, selectively allowing and limiting competition; it is now striving for more egalitarian distribution of wealth and for limits on big corporations . . . The problem is that without proper feedback from the public, without the open public space in which this feedback can be formulated, the measures advocated now by the Chinese leadership are doomed to fail. How can workers' welfare be elevated when any attempt of the workers to self-organize is met by brutal repression? How can the threat of environmental catastrophes be dealt with when independent investigations are prohibited? Yes, until now China has dealt successfully with the COVID-19 pandemic, but there are good reasons to believe that if the authorities had not ignored and even suppressed the first independent warnings, what became a global pandemic could have been limited to a local level.

Why then use the term "Communism"? Because what we will have to do contains four aspects of every truly radical regime. First, there is voluntarism: changes that will be needed are not grounded in any historical necessity, they will be carried out against the spontaneous tendency of history—as Walter Benjamin put it, we have to pull the emergency brake on the train of history. Then, there is egalitarianism: global solidarity, healthcare and a minimum of decent life for all. Then, there are elements of what cannot but appear to die-hard liberals as "terror," a taste of which we got with measures to cope with the ongoing pandemic: limits on many personal freedoms, new modes of control and regulation. The unspeakable option is already mentioned here and there: among others, the actress "Joanna Lumley has suggested that a system of rationing similar to that seen during wartime, under which people would have a limited number of points to spend on holidays or lavish consumer goods, could eventually help to tackle the climate crisis."[82] The sooner we accept that this is our only rational choice, the better for all of us. Finally, there is trust in the people: everything will be lost without the active participation of ordinary people.

All this is not a morbid dystopian vision but the result of a simple realistic assessment of our predicament. If we don't take this path, what will happen is the totally crazy situation which is already taking place in the US and Russia: the power elite is preparing for its survival in gigantic underground bunkers in which thousands can survive for months, with the excuse that the government should function even in such conditions ... in short, government should continue to work even when there are no people alive on the earth over whom it should exert its authority. Our government and business elites are already preparing for this scenario, which means that they know the alarm bells are ringing.

Although the prospect of the mega-rich living somewhere in space outside of our earth is not realistic, one cannot avoid the conclusion that the attempts of some mega-rich individuals (Musk, Bezos, Branson) to organize private flights into space also express the fantasy of escaping the catastrophe that threatens our survival on the earth. So what awaits us who have nowhere to escape?

2
A Non-binary Difference?
Psychoanalysis, Politics, and Philosophy

Critique of Critique

The reading of Hegel we need today is not so much a direct reading of his texts but an imagined reading: the anachronistic practice of imagining how Hegel would have answered to new theories proposed to replace the supposedly outdated Hegelian approach. This also holds for Lacan who was in a constant critical dialogue with Hegel. In his first great *écrit* "Le rapport de Rome," Lacan (under the influence of Jean Hyppolite) relies on the parallel between the gradual symbolization (integration into the symbolic order) of symptoms that occurs in the analytic process and the Hegelian dialectical process; he even compares the end of the analytic process with Hegel's Absolute Knowing. Later, he increasingly distances himself from Hegel, rejecting the dialectical "synthesis" as the denial of the Impossible-Real, and dismisses Hegel as the ultimate philosopher of self-consciousness.

Instead of directly defending Hegel, I will rather try to outline a way back to him through the inconsistencies of Lacan's theory itself. Lacanians regularly reproach me for rejecting Lacan's critical dismissal of philosophy—and they are right: from the very beginning I openly proclaimed that I remain a philosopher and maintain a distance towards the analytic clinic. Even more, I claim that Lacan himself misses a key feature of philosophy, and that this ignorance signals a serious limitation of his project . . . How can I advocate something like this and nonetheless in some sense remain a Lacanian? I will try to elaborate this point through a dialogue with Gabriel Tupinamba, with his Lacanian critique of Lacan.

Tupinamba's *The Desire of Psychoanalysis* is a ground-breaking masterpiece: it is a surprise, but a surprise in the sense in which the second murder in Hitchcock's *Psycho* (the slaughter of the private detective Arbogast on the stairs of the mother's house) surprises the viewer much more than the notorious shower killing: the effect of surprise comes from the fact that what happens is what we expected to happen. Not only does Tupinamba's book spoil the ideological game that predominated in Lacanian circles for decades; not only is a certain innocence lost forever; much more important, Tupinamba compels us to confront in a new critical way the philosophical implications of psychoanalysis.

The topic of critique, especially of a critique of Lacan himself, is for me a very sensitive one since I am usually identified as a Lacanian Hegelian, and Hegel's basic lesson is that a critique should always be a critique of critique itself (or, as Marx and Engels put it with acerbic irony in the subtitle of their early work *The Holy Family*, a "critique of critical criticism"). When one criticizes a phenomenon, one should always be careful to note the extent to which the critique shares the basic premises of the object of critique and, far from posing a threat to it, enables it to function smoothly. Let's take a case known to everybody today: the protest against social oppression practiced by so-called Political Correctness in all its versions. (Although PC has lately been losing some of its steam, it still predominates in some academic and public circles.) Mainstream-liberal and conservative critics of PC like to make fun of its so-called "excesses" (ridiculous prohibitions of certain expressions, demands to censor classical literary texts, etc.), claiming that, in the guise of fighting patriarchy and domination, PC imposes new totalitarian rules. Partisans of PC return the blow, pointing out how, with their focus on PC "excesses," on the prohibitive aspect of cancel- and woke culture, conservative and liberal critics ignore a much graver censorship going on against those considered dangerous for the establishment: just in the UK we have MI6 vetting employments by all state and education agencies, trade unions under secret police control, secret regulation about what gets published in the media and appears on TV, underage children from Muslim families questioned for terrorist links, up to single events like the continuing illegal imprisonment of Julian Assange . . . While I agree with this assessment that such grave censorship is much worse than the "sins" of cancel culture, I think it provides the ultimate argument against woke culture and PC regulations: why does the PC Left focus on regulating details of how we speak etc. instead of bringing out the above-mentioned much bigger issues? No wonder Assange was also attacked by some PC feminists (not only) from Sweden who did not support him because they took seriously the accusations about his sexual misconduct (which were later dismissed by the Swedish authorities). An infraction of PC rules obviously outweighs the fact of being a victim of state terror . . . But when the woke stance touches on a really important aspect of the reproduction of hegemonic ideology, the reaction of the establishment changes from ridiculing the opponent for its excesses to a panicky attempt at violent legal suppression. We often read in our media complaints about the "excesses" of critical gender and race studies which try to reassess the hegemonic narrative of the American past. However, we should always bear in mind that,

alongside this reassessment, another American tradition re-emerged: a reactionary movement bent on reasserting a whitewashed American myth. These reactionary forces have taken aim at efforts to tell an honest version of American history and speak openly about racism by proposing laws in statehouses across the country that would ban the teaching of "critical race theory," the *New York Times's* 1619 Project, and, euphemistically, "divisive concepts." The movement is characterized by a childish insistence that children should be taught a false version of the founding of the United States that better resembles a mythic virgin birth than the bloody, painful reality. Legislation seeking to limit how teachers talk about race has been considered by at least 15 states . . . In Idaho, Governor Bill Little signed into law a measure banning public schools from teaching critical race theory, which it claimed will "exacerbate and inflame divisions on the basis of sex, race, ethnicity, religion, colour, national origin, or other criteria in ways contrary to the unity of the nation and the wellbeing of the state of Idaho and its citizens." The state's lieutenant governor, Janice McGeachin, also established a taskforce to "examine indoctrination in Idaho education and to protect our young people from the scourge of critical race theory, socialism, communism, and Marxism."[1]

Are the prohibited theories really divisive? Yes, but only in the sense that they oppose (divide themselves from) the hegemonic official myth which *is already in itself divisive*: it excludes some groups or stances, putting them in a subordinate position. Furthermore, it is clear that to the partisans of the official myth truth does not matter here but only the "stability" of the founding myths—these partisans, not those dismissed by them as "historicist relativists," are effectively practicing the "post-truth" stance: they evoke "alternate facts," but they exclude alternate founding myths.

A true Hegelian should always practice such a double critical approach: in criticizing a phenomenon (racist and sexist domination). This approach should simultaneously criticize the predominant form of its critique (Political Correctness), as well as the counter-attack of establishment forces. Even when we are dealing with phenomena as repellent as sexism and racism, things are thus never simple—why? Because, as Lacan put it, there is no metalanguage: when we are making a choice (in our case, between hegemonic ideology and its PC critique), the choice is never made from a neutral terrain, the act of choice changes the choice. Let's take the case of the pandemic we are still caught in—what choices are we facing here? In answering this question, Jean-Pierre Dupuy refers to counterfactual situations as something that are immanent to reality itself: things are not just what they are, their actuality is accompanied by the shadow of what might have happened if a different course of action had been taken. For example, when we decide to impose a quarantine to curb the spreading of the COVID-19 pandemic, we do this to reduce infections and deaths. However, there is a key distinction to be made here:

> I have a choice of two actions, A and B. I choose A. I estimate that I am in a better situation in the option A than in the option B, as far as I can appreciate it *after I have chosen A*. However, I have no guarantee that if I were to choose B, my situation would have been the same as the one that I envisage for B after having

chosen A. In other words, the presupposition of the economic calculus is that the "actual" (i.e., real) choice of B puts me into the same world as the "counterfactual" (i.e., virtual, "against the facts") choice of B if I've chosen A. Even more simply, the hidden hypothesis is that the "alternate" worlds have the same reality as the world in which we really find ourselves.[2]

We should abandon this hypothesis, not just for obvious empirical reasons (our counterfactual estimation of what would have happened if we were to choose A could simply turn out to be wrong—remember how, in the summer of 2020, when the UK authorities prohibited access to beaches, but when this prohibition was largely ignored and the beaches were packed, this led to almost no increase in infections). The main reason is that *A is not the same after I've chosen B*—after I've chosen B, A is measured by the standards which made me choose B. In other words, the reasons we make a choice do not preexist our choice: we only know the reasons why we chose A (or B) *once we made the choice*. Let's take a decision in fighting the pandemic when we confront a choice between A and B: A prioritizes the economy, B prioritizes health. Advocates of A claim that, if we choose B, we may first save some lives but, in the long term, the costs to the economy will generate more poverty and even more health problems. (The problem with this reasoning is that it automatically assumes that the same economic system will persist.) Advocates of B claim that, if we choose A, not only there will be more suffering and more deaths, but due to the prolonged health crisis, even the economy will suffer more in the long term. There is no neutral way to compare the two options, so, maybe, after making a choice (say, of B), the solution is to *look at B itself from the imagined standpoint of A*—in our case, *how prioritizing health appears from the standpoint of economy*. This brings us to the true problem: since, obviously, the existing economic system cannot stomach such prioritizing of health, *how should we change our economic life so that we can avoid the debilitating dilemma "lives or economy"*? And the same goes for sexual difference: for a man it is not enough just to take women's side—he should ask himself: how do I choose to be a man so that, as a man, I can avoid oppressing women?

"They are Both Worse!"

Such a critique of critique is urgently needed in all struggles that animate our social reality. In the Fall of 2021, a new *Historikerstreit*—struggle between historians—exploded in Europe. On the one side, Achille Mbembe, Dirk Moses and some others argue that distinguishing the Holocaust from other violent crimes in human history is Eurocentric and neglects the horror of colonialist crimes. On the other side, there are Saul Friedlander, Juergen Habermas, and others who insist on the unique character of the Holocaust. I think that both sides are in some sense right and wrong—one cannot but repeat here Stalin's answer to the question which deviation is worse, Leftist or Rightist: "They are both worse."

It is simply true that the wider public in the developed West is not fully aware of the breath-taking horrors of colonialism and its by-products. Just remember the horror of the two Opium Wars fought (not only) by the British Empire against China. Statistics show that, until 1820, China was the strongest economy in the world. From the late eighteenth century, the British were exporting enormous amounts of opium into China, turning millions of people there into addicts and causing great damage. The Chinese Emperor tried to prevent this, prohibiting the import of opium, and the British (together with other Western forces) intervened militarily. The result was catastrophic: soon after, China's economy shrank by half. But what should interest us is the legitimization of this brutal military intervention: free trade is the basis of civilization, and the Chinese prohibition of opium imports is thus a barbarian threat to civilization . . . One cannot avoid imagining a similar act today: Mexico and Colombia acting to defend their drug cartels and declaring war on the US for behaving in an uncivilized way by preventing a free trade in opium . . . And the list is long, very long: the Belgian Congo, regular famines with millions of dead in British India, the devastation in both Americas. The cruel irony is that, with European modernization, slavery reemerged at the very moment when, in our ideology, the central topic was freedom, the fight against the slavery of women, of workers, of citizens in authoritarian regimes . . . slavery was discovered everywhere, in all metaphorical senses, but ignored where it existed in its literal sense.

Colonialism brings out what one cannot but designate as the catastrophe of modernity: the often terrifying impact of modernization on premodern communal life. Suffice it to recall the fate of Attawapiskat, a remote aboriginal community in northern Ontario, which drew the attention of the media in early 2016, exemplifies the way Canadian aborigines remain a broken nation unable to find the minimal stability of a life pattern:

> Since autumn there have been more than 100 suicide attempts in Attawapiskat, which has a population of just 2,000. The youngest person to attempt suicide was 11 years old, the oldest 71. After 11 people tried to take their own lives on Saturday evening, exhausted leaders declared a state of emergency. On Monday, as officials scrambled to send crisis counsellors to the community, 20 people—including a nine-year-old—were taken to hospital after they were overheard making a suicide pact. "We're crying out for help," said Attawapiskat chief Bruce Shisheesh. "Just about every night there is a suicide attempt."[3]

In searching out the reasons for this toll, one should look beyond the obvious (overcrowded houses riddled with mould, drug abuse and alcoholism, etc.). Principal among the systemic reasons is the devastating legacy of the residential school system which has disrupted continuity between generations:

> for decades, more than 150,000 aboriginal children were carted off in an attempt to forcibly assimilate them into Canadian society. Rife with abuse, the schools aimed to "kill the Indian in the child", as documented by a recent truth commission. Thousands of children died at these schools—the absence of dietary standards in the schools left many undernourished and vulnerable to diseases such as smallpox, measles and tuberculosis—with hundreds of them hastily buried in unmarked graves next to the institutions. In nearly a third of the deaths, the government and schools did not even record the names of the students who had died.[4]

No wonder, then, that we are slowly learning the true story of the residential schools—almost every week we get news like the following: "A Canadian Indigenous group said Wednesday that a search using ground-penetrating radar has found 182 human remains in unmarked graves at a site near a former Catholic Church-run residential school that housed Indigenous children taken from their families."[5] To this, we should add massive sexual exploitation in residential schools run by the Church—in some cases, up to 80 percent of the children were abused. What adds insult to injury is that the very institution that pretends to embody morality has perpetrated such crimes, as is the case also in France: "Members of the Catholic clergy in France sexually abused an estimated 216,000 minors over the past seven decades, according to a damning report published Tuesday, October 5 2021, that said the Church had prioritized the protection of the institution over victims who were urged to stay silent."[6] The truly shocking aspect is here that, since most of these crimes concern paedophilic homosexuality, the very institution responsible for them is the same institution which presents itself as the guardian of morality and leads public campaigns against homosexuality. And the sad thing is that there is no return to premodern normality: it is easy to discover in premodern societies what cannot but appear to our modern sensitivity as brutal abuses of human rights, of the rights of women and children, etc.

While admitting all this, the other side emphasizes the uniqueness of the Holocaust: its goal was not just the submission of the Jews but their total annihilation, carried out in a well-planned, modern, industrial way. Jews were not a lower race in a hierarchy of races, they were the absolute Other, the principle of corruption embodied. They were not an external threat; they were—to use Lacan's neologism—ex-timate, a foreign intruder in the very heart of our civilization. That's why they had to be annihilated if the aim was to re-establish the proper order of civilizations . . . Here comes my first hesitation: years ago, Etienne Balibar pointed out that, in today's global world, the distinction inner/external gets blurred, which is why all racisms more and more resemble anti-Semitism. Half a century ago, Huey Newton, the founder and theorist of the Black Panther Party, saw clearly the limitation of local (national) resistance to the global reign of capital. He even went a key step further and rejected the term "decolonization" as inappropriate— one cannot fight global capitalism from the position of national unities. Here are his statements from a unique dialogue with the Freudian psychoanalyst Erik Erikson from 1972:

> We in the Black Panther Party saw that the United States was no longer a nation. It was something else; it was more than a nation. It had not only expanded its territorial boundaries, but it had expanded all of its controls as well. We called it an empire. We believe that there are no more colonies or neocolonies. If a people is colonized, it must be possible for them to decolonize and become what they formerly were. But what happens when the raw materials are extracted and labor is exploited within a territory dispersed over the entire globe? When the riches of the whole earth are depleted and used to feed a gigantic industrial machine in the imperialists' home? Then the people and the economy are so integrated into the imperialist empire that it's impossible to "decolonize," to return to the former conditions of existence. If colonies cannot "decolonize" and return to their original existence as nations, then nations no longer exist. Nor, we believe, will they ever exist again.[7]

Is this not our predicament today, much more than in Newton's time? Furthermore, the difference between justified critique of Israel and anti-Semitism is very ambiguous and open to manipulation. Bernard Henri-Levy claimed that the anti-Semitism of the twenty-first century will be "progressive" or there will be none. Brought to the end, this thesis compels us to turn around the old Marxist interpretation of anti-Semitism as a mystified/displaced anti-capitalism (instead of blaming the capitalist system, the rage is focused on a specific ethnic group accused of corrupting the system): for Henri-Levy and his partisans, today's anti-capitalism is a disguised form of anti-Semitism. Can one imagine a more dangerous way of inciting anti-Semitism among today's critics of capitalism?

But what we are witnessing today is a weird reversal of not-anti-Semitic critique of Israel: anti-Semitic support of Israel. Some Rightist anti-Semites support the State of Israel for three obvious reasons: if Jews go to Israel there will be fewer Jews here in the West; in Israel, Jews will no longer be a homeless foreign group whom we cannot fully trust, they will become a normal nation-state grounded in their earth; and, last but not least, they will function there as representatives of highly developed Western values against oriental barbarism—in short, with regard to the local Palestinian population, they will do the work of colonization. In order to win the support of Western states, Zionists sometimes presented themselves as colonizers. Derek Penslar points out that there are multiple—sometimes contradictory—ideological and political issues embedded within Zionism and Israel: "The Zionist project combines colonialism, anti-colonialism, and postcolonial state-building. The entire twentieth century, wrapped up in one small state."[8]

Theodor Herzl wrote in his *Der Judenstaat* (1896), the founding text of Zionism, "For Europe, we will build there (in Palestine) a part of the wall against Asia, we will provide ramparts against barbarism." Even the term "colonization" was used by early Zionists. Unfortunately, this stance chimes strangely with a series of European anti-Semites, from Reinhard Heydrich to Breivik and Trump. The clear division between the uniqueness of Jews and European colonialism thus gets complicated: Zionists themselves flirted with colonialism to gain support in the West, and the anti-colonial struggle itself sometimes comes dangerously close to anti-Semitism. Enough is being written about anti-Semitism in Arab countries and among Muslims—although I support Palestinian resistance on the West Bank, I am fully aware of this fact. One should also be careful about dismissing every call to throw the Muslims out of one's country as a case of racist Islamophobia. In my own country, Slovenia, many of the surviving folk songs talk about the horrors inflicted by Turkish invasions, and throwing the Turks out seems to me a quite legitimate endeavor.

For all these reasons, the entire debate about Holocaust versus colonialism should be rejected as something profoundly obscene. The Holocaust was a uniquely terrifying mega-crime; colonialism caused unimaginable suffering and huge numbers of deaths. The only correct way to approach these two horrors is to see the fight against anti-Semitism and against colonialism as two aspects of one and the same struggle. Those who dismiss colonialism as a lesser evil insult the victims of the Holocaust themselves, reducing an unheard-of horror into a bargaining chip for geopolitical games.

Those who relativize the uniqueness of the Holocaust insult the victims of colonization themselves. The Holocaust is not one in a series of crimes, it was unique in its own way, in the same way that modern colonization was a unique breath-taking horror carried out on behalf of civilizing others. They are incomparable monstrosities that cannot and should not be reduced to mere examples.

A Critique of Lacanian Ideology

What, then, does such a critique of critique amount to with regard to Lacan's work? When Lacan was excommunicated from the IPA in 1963 and decided to set up his own new psychoanalytic organization, this decision had radical consequences aptly described by Tupinamba:

> just as the clinic would have to be reformulated, after 1963, in accordance with the principle that the "unconscious is outside", so would the analytic community have to come to terms with the idea that *it is a community composed only of its own exterior*, that is, a community whose esoteric center coincides with its most exoteric material, the speech of those who seek analysis on account of their suffering.[9]

Although the formula proposed by Tupinamba is wonderful—"a community composed only of its own exterior"—it begs some questions. The "exterior" is the Unconscious itself, but since we are dealing with a community of individual subjects, this exterior has to be represented within the community by a subject who stands for knowing the Unconscious, the analyst as the subject supposed to know (SStK, *sujet suppose savoir*), predestined to occupy the position of a Master.[10] What this means is that the community of analysts can be operative only if it is held together by a figure of transference (thus conflicting with the definition of the end of analysis as the fall of the SStK)—membership in the analytic community de facto reduces analysts to analysands. For this reason, I find the idea of the "community" of analysts and analysands united by their care and concern for the Unconscious problematic—the asymmetry between the two is simply too strong. Yes, for Lacan, the true end of the analytic treatment occurs only when the analysand becomes analyst, but this is like saying that in a true Communist party all workers will become party intellectuals. While one can at least imagine this as the ideal goal of a political process thwarted only by empirical obstacles, the analytic treatment precludes this option for a formal and not just empirical reason: the radical irreversibility of the positions of the analyst and the analysand.

Sympathetically "democratic" as it may appear, the practice of Sandor Ferenczi (who, according to some witness reports, sometimes interrupted his patient in the middle of the latter's flow of free associations, took his place on the divan and began to pour out his own associations) simply does not make analytic sense since it ruins the position of the analyst as the subject supposed to know. In short, who will predominate in this community? If analysands (as in the case enacted by Ferenczi), then analysts will lose their status of SStK and will simply no longer be analysts. If analysts, then the transferential subordination of analysands to analysts will remain in full force—which is also frequently the case in Lacanian society where we regularly have not only those who are only analysts and those who are only analysands but also the crucial third category, something like foot-soldier analysts: analysts (receiving patients of their own) who are simultaneously in analysis with "higher" analysts (who are themselves no longer in analysis). I even knew a couple of cases of analysts who found themselves in a really difficult predicament: they were in an endless analysis with the "pure" analyst (quite often for the simple reason of safeguarding their status in the analytic community—ending their analysis could entail the rage of the "pure" analyst who was their de facto master), and they sometimes worked themselves as analysts just to earn money to pay for their own analysis.

To paraphrase Lacan's famous statement that a madman is not only a beggar who thinks he is a king but also a king who thinks he is a king: a madman is also an analyst who thinks he is an analyst— and this is how analysts act in their organization. One should go to the end in this direction: are there analysts at all? Is an analyst not a subject/analysand who, within the analytic clinical setting, acts as if he is an analyst or even plays the role of an analyst? The moment we substantialize the analyst, the moment we conceive him as a subject who is an analyst in itself, outside of the clinical setting, analysts become a new group of people of a special mold, made of special stuff (as Stalin put it apropos Bolsheviks), and all the deadlocks of how to deal with a Master reappear.

In the short text that announces his dissolution, Lacan addresses himself to "those who love me (*a ceux qui m'aiment*)," which unambiguously implies that in his school, transference on him remains in full force—there is no "fall of the subject supposed to know" taking place ... The topology is here that of the Moebius strip: in the work of analysis, you gradually progress towards its concluding moment, the traversing of identifications, but at that very point when you are finally recognized as belonging to the group of analysts, you find yourself back in a rather primitive form of group identification. In a recent text dealing with the rise of the trans culture and obsession with victimhood, Miller himself claims not only that he was the victim of "unspeakable and incessant abuse of authority" by Lacan, but that he even consented to this abuse, finding pleasure in it:

> Fifty years after the fact, it is time for *Me Too* to confess. *Horresco referens*, it's awful to say, but I was, for years, a victim of unspeakable and incessaant abuse of authority by my father-in-law, in both public and private, constituting a true crime of moral and spiritual incest. I gave in to something stronger than myself. I even consented—*Shame!* as Adèle Haenel would say—to take some pleasure in it, a certain pleasure. I remained divided forever. The monster having passed away forty years ago, the lawsuits I would come to initiate would only have a symbolic but nevertheless decisive impact on healing the wounds in my soul and repairing the damage done to my self-esteem.[11]

How are these lines to be read? It is obvious that they contain a heavy dose of irony: Miller's point is how, from today's Politically Correct culture, his relationship with Lacan, the pivot of his life, a supreme case of how an authentic master can change the life of his pupil, can only appear as a case of unspeakable abuse. But there is a further (and certainly unintentional) irony in the quoted lines:

whatever Lacan was, he certainly was not a liberal advocating mutual recognition and respect, so how is it that in the last years Miller proposed a reading of the late Lacan as a liberal, as somebody who elaborated a liberal critique of the 1968 student protests? If ever there was a brutal Master fully exerting his power and not caring about how this would affect others it was Lacan—the basic liberal motto of mutual respect, of "I do to you only what you can also do to me," was totally foreign to Lacan. The numerous anecdotes that circulated about Lacan clearly bring out his disregard and disrespect towards others: he belched loudly and was flatulent when close to others; if, in a restaurant, after the dishes were ordered and arrived, he preferred the dish his neighbor had ordered, he simply exchanged plates, etc. But my basic reaction to Miller's quoted lines is that they are ultimately irrelevant, of no interest whatsoever—their only interest is that they indicate how (since Lacan also acted also in his way in his school) he certainly failed in organizing his school so that it would enable the members to exit the transferential relationship to him. In his school, he was not a symbolic Master (a dead father who rules through his name), but much closer to the mythic primordial father.

There is one particular feature that demonstrates how Lacan remains a subject supposed to know: in the Millerian regime of his school, all new discoveries had to be presented as insights into what Lacan himself discovered and articulated, although in a murky way, in his last years—in short, as insights into Lacan's last secret, what he saw his before he died. What we get here is a new version of Althusser's struggle to locate Marx's "epistemological break": first he firmly located it in German Ideology, but at the end of his career as a philosopher, he claimed that Marx really saw the contours of his discovery only in a passage from his critical notes on Adolph Wagner . . . In a similar way, Catherine Millot, Lacan's last "official" mistress, was present when he was dying, and there was a rumor in Millerian circles that just before his last breath, Lacan whispered words to her which contained his ultimate insight into the mystery of our world . . .

There is another aspect of this persisting transferential relationship with Lacan: when one formulated a small critical point about Lacan, the critique is not only rejected as based on a misunderstanding of Lacan, but is (or, at least, was when I moved in Lacanian circles) often directly clinicized, treated as a symptom to be interpreted analytically. This happened to me when I formulated some small critical remarks about Miller: the reaction of his followers was: "What's your problem with Miller? Why do you resist him? Do you have some unresolved traumas?" Things get even more complicated here when we take into account Lacan's claim that, in his seminars, he is in the position of the analysand and his public his analyst: it is as if the split between analysand and analyst cuts across Lacans' own work, so that in his spoken seminars he is the analysand, freely associating on theoretical topics, returning to the same points and changing course, while in his opaque writings he is the analyst supposed to know, uttering obscure formulas destined to provoke our (the analysand-reader's) interpretation.

The transferential group dynamics that characterizes the Lacanian schools leads to what cannot but be designated as a true ethical fiasco: when a conflict between different groups (or, rather, factions) explodes, the analysts that head one group regularly mobilize their analysands to publicly support them and attack the others, thus violating what I see as the basic ethical rule by way of exploiting the attachment to themselves grounded in transference, i.e., the dependency of the analysands on them, for the political purpose of power struggles in the analytical community. Can one even imagine the personal crises such a combination of clinics and politics can unleash?

One should also mention a feature which shocked me (for the simple reason that my desire was to publish a book): when, three decades or so ago, Miller was not writing a lot but just made many spoken interventions, an unspoken prohibition became operative in his school: you don't write books proper—the most that you are allowed to do is to collect a slim volume of transcriptions of written interventions. Many of his followers were brought close to despair in this way, as they wanted to publish their theses, and to publish outside the Millerian circle was a very risky move ...

This does not mean that one should deny the extraordinary productive power of the transferential relationship to a Master figure also in the field of theory. The basic function of a Master is not to serve as the model of rational reasoning, providing the ultimate arguments for adopting a certain position, but, on the contrary, to surprise us by uttering statements which run against our (and the Master's own) hitherto *doxa*, i.e., by performing gestures which cannot but appear as willful arbitrariness. I remember how, at a congress of the school decades ago, Miller improvised on how, with regard to the opposition between S1 (master-signifier) and S2 (the chain of knowledge), superego is not on the side of the master but on the side of the chain of knowledge. All of us present there were shocked by this claim since we accepted as an obvious fact that the superego injunction is precisely a master's gesture at its purest, an arbitrary imposition not grounded in a chain of reasoning. However, after some thinking, I not only endorsed Miller's claim but found it extraordinarily productive: it served as the basis of my entire theorization of Stalinism as the exemplary case of the university discourse, as well as of my reading of the role of bureaucracy in Kafka's universe.

Apropos Freud's analysis of Dora, Tupinamba proposes an apt clarification of how the transference in the treatment (i.e., the elevation of the analyst into a subject-supposed-to-know) is linked to the hysterical question. The hysterical question is "What for an object am I for the Other?," and *a subject-supposed-to-know is supposed to know precisely the answer to this question*: "Dora cannot directly think the object that she is for some Other, but she could delegate this thought to another." The crucial role of transference in the analytic treatment is nicely rendered by Tupinamba: "psychoanalysis found out that, as far as psychic suffering is concerned, the subject who is supposed to know—supposed to recognize the signs, supposed to tell the patient 'you have such and such disease', supposed to include the suffering into a causal chain connecting an early trauma to a current symptom, and supposed to expect the patient to adjust itself to a certain normative criteria of happiness or health—this subject is part of the pathology." Karl Kraus's ironic claim that psychoanalysis is itself the disease it tries to cure is thus fully true, but Kraus missed the point of its truth: this coincidence (between disease and its treatment) is not a reproach against psychoanalysis but the very premise of its treatment in which transference repeats/re-enacts the illness.

We should thus abandon the view that a Master as the figure of authority just enforces old wisdoms and the established views while change comes "from below," from those who doubt the Master's wisdom. We theorists are hysterics and, as such, we need a Master. There is no democracy in theoretical development: something new does not emerge through better reasoning etc., but mostly through desperate attempts to discover the meaning of the Master's "arbitrary" statements which reverse the shared theoretical *doxa*. Such "arbitrary" statements are, of course, not without risks of their own: they can misfire, not set in motion new theoretical inventions but simply remain irrelevant arbitrary claims—but it is crucial to bear in mind that it depends on us, his hysterical pupils, how the master's claim will turn out. The Master is not a genius in himself, he only becomes a genius through our hard work. What this means is that, after he has done his work, the Master should be ruthlessly abandoned, left for what he is: an illusory point of transference whose misery is finally revealed. Does this mean that it's all over for the (one who was) Master? No, but the only space open to him in order to stay alive is to hystericize himself again, to start to work as an analysand—what Lacan himself was doing constantly in his seminars . . . If, in his seminars, Lacan was acting as an analysand, this doesn't mean that his public was his collective analyst: the single figure of the analyst as the point of transference is replaced here by the "enlightened" collective of those supposed to share the same desire of psychoanalysis.

A (Malevolent) Political Neutrality of the Analyst

In political matters, however, Miller did not display these features of a true master but all too often regressed to liberal banalities. For example, in the last decades, he interpreted Lacan's critical remarks about the '68 student rebellion as a liberal critique of the Left (not to mention how he shocked the public at his seminar with his high appraisal of Sarkozy). The quite vulgar roots of this unfortunate turn became obvious in the patent absurdity of the Millerian argumentation against any radical political upheaval—the syllogism that sustains it is as follows: (1) psychoanalytic clinic can only thrive in a stable civic order with no public unrest; (2) Left radicals by definition want to unsettle the stable social order; (3) psychoanalysts should oppose Left radicals because they pose a threat to the stability of the social order. (There is also a Zionist version of this argument: in times of instability anti-Semitism increases, and since the radical Left causes instability one should oppose it.) Tupinamba is fully justified here in pointing out the obscene falsity of the Millerian mobilization against the threat of Marine le Pen in the last French presidential elections. Although the official reason for the mobilization organized by Miller (whose first electoral choice was Sarkozy!) was to prevent the victory of the racist-populist Right, it immediately became clear that its true target was the part of the Left which did not succumb to the blackmail "if you don't vote for Macron, you objectively support le Pen"—Miller even coined the term "lepeno-trotskysts" for those who refused to engage for Macron. Tupinamba hits the target when he points out how Miller's mobilization against le Pen conceals the fact that the psychoanalytic business would have gone on unperturbed in the case of her victory: his mobilization was an act against the Left masked as anti-Fascist resistance.

I witnessed a similar incident at a Lacanian congress in Paris a year or so before the Malvinas/Falkland war, i.e., when Argentina was still a military dictatorship. To the consternation of many of those present, Miller proposed that the next congress be held in Buenos Aires, and his proposal was supported by those Argentinians who came from Argentina and claimed that, if the congress were not held in Buenos Aires, they (representatives of the strongest analytic community) would be de facto kept in a subordinated place—why should they travel to another country to attend it? The numerous exiled Argentinians (most of whom had to flee Argentina to save their lives) immediately pointed out that those who continued to live in Argentina at least could go to another country to attend the congress while they were de facto excluded from attending it (they would be arrested); but Miller didn't budge and imposed his decision. (Happily, a year later the military regime collapsed and democracy was restored.) Obviously, military rule was OK for Miller provided it tolerated analytic business . . .

Unfortunately, the same sad choice was made in 1934 in Austria by the analytic community when Dolfuss dissolved democratic institutions and imposed a "soft" Fascist dictatorship: when Social Democrats resisted and street fights exploded in Vienna, the psychoanalytic organization ordered its members to abstain from every engagement in the struggle and carry on as normal— essentially a decision in favor of business as usual, even if it meant silently accepting a Fascist dictatorship. Obviously, the thing that matters is not democratic politics, but business as usual ...

Tupinamba is right to point out that, although psychoanalytic treatment is in principle open to everybody, the economy enters here in a most brutal way: there is a vast group of people who simply cannot afford not only the full treatment (which ends up in the transformation of the analysand into the analyst), but any treatment at all. When Lacanians deal with the problem of money, they as a rule limit themselves to the role played by the payment for the sessions in the treatment: by way of paying the analyst, the analysand makes sure that the analyst maintains the proper distance towards the analysand—that the analyst remains outside the circle of symbolic debt and exchanges. The first big example that imposes itself here is Freud's treatment of Wolfman: when Wolfman's family lost its wealth after the October Revolution, and Wolfman was no longer able to pay Freud for his treatment, Freud not only decided to pursue the treatment for free but even financially supported Wolfman, with an easily predictable result— Wolfman reacted to Freud's "goodness" with paranoiac symptoms. He began to ask himself why Freud was doing this; what obscure plans he had for him—did he want Wolfman to marry his daughter? Only the later continuation of Wolfman's analysis with Muriel Gardiner set things straight and enabled Wolfman to lead a more or less normal life. So why is the analyst paid? The exchange between the analyst and the analysand is a very strange market exchange, since in the usual market exchange I demand from the seller an object that I need and I am ready to pay for —but "the job of the analyst is not to answer to the patient's demand."

A similar thing also happened to me: when, at a certain point in my analysis, I could no longer avoid the fact that I was unable to afford the continuation of my analysis—I had to support my unemployed wife and a son, and continuing my analysis would have meant seriously depriving them of a very basic standard of living, which I found unacceptable—and proposed to my analyst that we should stop, he immediately interpreted my proposal "immanently," as a form of my resistance to the progress of my analysis. He told me that we could continue the analysis: I would not have to pay him immediately, but my payment for each session would accumulate into a debt which I would pay later, when I had enough money. I rather stupidly accepted this proposal and, luckily, an unexpected big honorarium enabled me to repay my debt ... What I failed to do is to take a step further and acknowledge the analysand's lack of money as a feature that is external to the immanent logic of the analytic treatment, as a piece of meaningless social reality which should not be simply and directly integrated into the immanent logic of the analytic process.

When Tupinamba describes the supposition of belief that sustains the role of money in the exchange of commodities, he is right to emphasize the non-psychic status of this belief: when we act on the market, we do not suppose that other persons naively believe in commodity fetishism, we just suppose that, as it were, the system itself believes, i.e., that commodities "behave" as if they believe in the market. This is why commodity fetishism is not a psychoanalytic category, it does not designate a phenomenon that could and should be reduced to libidinal dynamics, but is strictly a category of political economy, of "objective" social relations. Linked to this is Tupinamba's distinction between the two levels of desire: the desire of a determinate subject (psychoanalyst, mathematician ...) and the desire that sustains the field in question itself (the desire of psychoanalysis, of mathematics). Tupinamba claims that Lacan reduces the second to the first: "the lack of resources to distinguish between the mathematician's desire and the desire of mathematics—the desire for the 'maximality of thinking' striving towards the consistency of as many mathematical structures as a formalism can uphold—also prevents him from distinguishing the desire of the analyst, which only concerns a finite analytic sequence, from the desire which participates in the institution of the idea of psychoanalysis." This distinction is fully pertinent: the desire that sustains an analyst as a member of an analytic community is not the same as the enigma of the "analyst's desire" which traumatizes the analyzand and pushes it to work, it is a desire to participate in a collective work of theory and clinic, in a space where in principle no one should be allowed to occupy the privileged point of transference.

Back to the ambiguous role of money in the analytic treatment, the standard answer of the "socially conscious" analysts (which, when I moved in their circles, I heard again and again) is first to admit the problem, and then to propose (and practice) a "humanitarian" solution: I knew quite a few wealthy and successful analysts who proudly boasted that, once or twice a week, they would reserve their afternoons to receive patients from the lower classes and treated them for free . . . Tupinamba is right to point out that, with this "humanitarian" solution, the class distinction reemerges in a brutal and direct way, in the guise of the distinction between two types of analysands: the "full" analysands who are able to regularly pay the analyst and can also continue their analysis to its "logical" conclusion, to the point at which they become analysts, and the non-paying analysands who are given only short-term treatment with no chance of bringing it to the point of becoming analysts.

How, then, does politics enter the analytic process? Tupinamba follows Althusser who condemned Lacan's dissolution of his school: Lacan presented his act of dissolution as an analytic act, a concluding gesture of a psychoanalytic treatment, but since his gesture affected a community it was a political act which denied itself as such, non-democratic. I was in Paris at that time and I remember that, when those members of the school who didn't agree with the dissolution (they thought that Lacan was too senile to decide and that the letter of dissolution was written by Miller), the court agreed with them that a single individual does not have the right to dissolve an organization, so that the circle around Miller had to mobilize its members and (barely) obtained the signatures of more than half of the members who agreed with the dissolution, thereby "democratically" confirming Lacan's act. My position was (and is) that, in the dissolution of Lacan's school, one should not pretend that we were dealing with a community whose life (or death) is regulated by democratic rules: Lacan's school was grounded on the unconditional transference to Lacan as a person.

And (up to a point), the same holds for political organizations: what holds such an organization together can also be the figure of a Master who provides the "surplus" over the inert reproduction of the established order. One should turn around here the standard notion of an oppressive Master who sustains the existing order while individuals tend to rebel against this order—what if, left to themselves, individuals are prone to inertia, so that they have to be awakened from its spell by an authentic Master whose message to them is: "Yes, you can … (reach beyond yourself, change things)!" Maybe—an unfashionable hypothesis—the party form (as embodied in the Leninist party) provides a third way here, resisting both the democratic temptation and the subordination to authority, insofar as this party form of organization unites the unshakable "dogmatic" fidelity to a Cause with the stance of questioning everything inclusive of the form of this Cause.

Brecht gives us a clue here. In what is for some the most problematic song of *The Measure Taken*, the celebration of the Party, Brecht proposes something much more unique and precise than may at first appear. That is to say, what appears is that Brecht is simply elevating the Party into the incarnation of Absolute Knowledge, a historical agent which has complete and perfect insight into the historical situation, a subject supposed to know if there ever was one: "You have two eyes, but the Party has a thousand eyes!" However, a close reading of this poem makes it clear that something different is the case: in his reprimand of the young Communist, the chorus says that the Party does *not* know all, that the young Communist may be *right* in his disagreement with the predominant Party line: "Show us the way which we should take, and we / shall follow it like you, but / do not take the right way without us. / Without us, this way is / the falsest one. / Do not separate yourself from us." What this means is that the authority of the Party is *not* that of determinate positive knowledge, but that of the *form* of knowledge, of a new type of knowledge linked to a collective political subject. The crucial point on which the Chorus insists is only that, if the young comrade thinks that he is right, he should fight for his position *within* the collective form of the Party, not outside it—to put it in a somewhat pathetic way, if the young comrade is right, then the Party needs him even more than its other members. What the Party demands is that one accepts grounding one's "I" in the "WE" of the Party's collective identity: fight with us, fight for us, fight for your truth against the Party line, *just don't do it alone*, outside the Party. Exactly as in Lacan's formula of the discourse of the analyst, what matters with the Party's knowledge is not its content, but the fact that it occupies the place of Truth.

Perhaps, one should read Tupinamba's reflections on what happens in the analytic process after the final moment of the treatment (the analysand's traversal of the fantasy) against this "Leninist" background. Taking literally (and much more seriously than most Lacanians) Lacan's claim that the final moment of the analytic process is the transformation of the analysand into the analyst, and combining this claim with Lacan's idea of *la passe*, the procedure of "passage" which makes a subject the analyst of the school, Tupinamba fearlessly draws out its consequences. Lacan proclaimed that an analyst authorizes himself only by himself—but, as he then added with a little bit of sarcasm, others have to confirm that he actually authorized himself (otherwise any idiot could proclaim himself an analyst). A new dimension of collectivity enters here: we are no longer in the intimacy of the relationship between analysand and analyst. The analysand who makes public his intention to become analyst is first asked to give a testimony of what he learned about himself in his treatment in the guise of a narrative about himself he is expected to tell to two other average members of the school (his "passeurs") who are selected by lot—in short, after the fall of (the analyst as) the subject supposed to know, the analysand has to become his own subject supposed to know.

The big change here is that the analysand who is a candidate for the title of the analyst has to formulate his testimony in such a way that all traces of authentic subjective truth are erased from it (or, rather, become irrelevant): his subjective position of enunciation disappears; all that matters is the enunciated content. The analysand has to formulate his testimony in such a way that the two average and neutral "passeurs" (who know nothing about the analysand's subjective struggles) will be able to get it … to do what with it? Simply to transmit it further to the jury (composed of three analysts of the school) which will then confirm (or not) that the candidate is an analyst of the school. So why is the candidate not allowed to render his testimony directly to the jury? Why is there no direct contact between him and the jury? In order to prevent any initiatic closure, to prevent the jury serving as an initiatic body with special access to truth and deep personal contact with the candidate—everything has to happen at the level of public knowledge which can be fully transmitted by two average idiots. (One cannot but note a certain similarity with judicial judgment in a society of free subjects where, as Hegel pointed out, those who decide on innocence or guilt are not the judges but a jury selected by lot and composed of the accused's peers, not of those who possess some special abilities or qualifications.)

Tupinamba further points out that the aim of the analysand's testimony is not just to prove to the jury that it fits the established theoretical doxa, i.e., that the analysand is able to interpret himself in the terms of Lacanian theory. Theory and (clinical) practice are intertwined so that theory is never just the theory of the practice but also theory of the limitations of the practice; and practice never just offers "examples" of theory, but produces examples that displace and transform theoretical insights. What this means is that the candidate's testimony harbors the potential to contribute to and transform the field of theory itself—to paraphrase T.S. Eliot's famous dictum, every new theoretical insight changes the entire past edifice. Here we pass from the desire of the analyst to the desire of psychoanalysis itself to expand, to gain new insights—and this desire can only be operative in a "Leninist" collective of the members of the party (school) dedicated to the same Cause.

So how did this subversive core of the "passage" get lost in the actual functioning of the Lacanian school? The source of the difficulties in which the Lacanian movement got caught up is "Lacanian ideology": a double move, described by Tupinamba, as (1) conferring on the analysts a radical epistemological privilege: due to its roots in the unique clinical constellation, psychoanalysis can see the "constitutive lack" or blindness of science (which forecloses the subject), of philosophy (which is ultimately a *Weltanchsauung* covering up the crack of impossibility) and politics (which remains constrained to the domain of imaginary and symbolic identifications and group formations); and simultaneously (2) silently cutting off psychoanalytic theory from its specific roots in the clinical setting, ideologically elevating it into a universal status by definition wiser than all other discourses (the logic of the signifier or the theory of discourses de facto became a new ontology). The exemplary case of this double move is Miller's politicization of psychoanalysis in his political movement, Zadig, where a liberal-democratic choice is directly legitimized in Lacanian terms.

Does Tupinamba not do for Lacan what, at the end of his book, he so admirably describes as the concluding moments of the analytic treatment: traversing the fantasy plus naming and narrating in the testimony the non-symbolizable obstacle which sustained transference? He enables us to get rid of our transference on Lacan by way of nominating Lacan's fatal limitation: we are no longer caught in the endless process of grasping the ultimate mystery of Lacan, we get the formula of how Lacan himself got caught in the space in which this eluding excess emerges. We don't resolve the mystery, we formulate how—to paraphrase Hegel's dictum on the secrets of the ancient Egyptians—the mystery that Lacan presents to us, the mystery we are trying to get at in interpreting him, was a mystery for Lacan himself, and how this mystery emerged out of a precise theoretical deadlock.

In order to break the enclosure of "Lacanian ideology," Tupinamba mobilizes the notion of parallax elaborated by Kojin Karatani. Let's take the example of a naked human body: we can approach it as an erotic object, which means that we forcefully abstract from all facts about it accessible to a biological or medical approach (the glands and their excretions beneath the surface, the smooth running of inner organs). In order to notice this, we have to de-eroticize the body … These approaches are mutually exclusive; there is no higher synthesis between the two of them. And it's the same with psychoanalytic treatment: the artificial isolation of the couple analysand-analyst creates its own reality, but there are aspects of it (like the role of money) which cannot be accounted for in the immanent terms of the transference dynamics. Consequently, in dealing with psychoanalysis, one should treat its three dimensions (theory, clinical practice, analytic organizations) like a Borromean knot of three irreducible dimensions: "we do not privilege any of its components as the one which overdetermines the model as a whole." And the same applies to how psychoanalysis in all its dimensions relates to social life: Lacanians are deep in muddy ideological waters when they de facto elevate analytic theory into a universal clue enabling them to have the last word on political and economic phenomena—in this way, they overlook even the political dynamics at work in their own organization.

My critical point here is that the formula of the Borromean knot of the three dimensions doesn't fully work: the whole IS always overdetermined by one of its parts, and to think this overdetermination, a specific theory is needed, analytic theory doesn't suffice here. I think—in a very traditional sway, I have to admit—that therein resides the role of philosophy, so the formula of the Borromean knot should be extended to another dimension, to 3 plus 1. The triad of science (theory)—clinic—organization should be supplemented by philosophy. Philosophy is not the old *metaphysica universalis*, a general view of the universe, it knows very well that there is no neutral universality, that every universality is overdetermined by a specific domain within which it can only be formulated—this is the classic Marxist topic of historical specification of ideological universals ("human rights are effectively the rights of . . ."). But philosophy also knows that every specific situation has to be accounted for in terms of a more universal dimension within which it emerged: historical relativization cannot relativize itself; it presupposes itself as universally valid.

Let's tackle the topic of the difficult relationship between analytic clinics (the artificial analytic situation) and the universal theory that emerges out from these (theory of signifier, four discourses . . .). Yes, Freudian theory is rooted in artificial clinical experience, but the task of analytic theory is not just to relativize itself in this way but to account for the very possibility of something like clinical experience in terms of universal human predicament: how is our symbolic space structured so that a couple of analysand and analyst can operate the way it does, contravening the standard form of intersubjective exchanges? This abyssal circle is the proper topic of philosophical reflection. What Freud saw along these lines is clearly indicated by his inclusion of psychoanalysis in the list of "impossible professions": psychoanalytic theory is not just the theoretical grounding of clinical practice, it also explains why this practice ultimately has to fail—as Freud put it succinctly, psychoanalysis would only be possible in the conditions where it would no longer be needed.

The Limits of Historicization

A philosophical approach also enables us to formulate in an adequate way the implications of the historicization of the analytic clinic. Tupinamba aptly refers here to the Kantian distinction between negative judgments (judgments that negate a predicate, like "he is not dead") and infinite judgments (judgments that assert a non-predicate, like "he is undead"). Along the same lines, Tupinamba proposes the distinction between the negation of positive universals and affirmation of negative universals:

> Considered only in its structural aspect, Freud's investigation could simply seem like a negation of positive universals—a movement that unproblematically binds clinical practice and metapsychological theory—and therefore appear as a rather static process, concerning solely the analyst and his subversive position. But what this picture is missing is the essential dynamism through which the contradiction of previously held universal claims enriches our understanding of how to listen to new patients: a transformation of what is considered invariant in the space of the possible, and therefore an affirmation of negative universals—more may vary in the space of subjective solutions to sexuation than we previously imagined.

Here we encounter the crux of the problem: while fully endorsing this line of thought, I would just give it a slightly different reading. "Negation of positive universals" remains caught in what Hegel called "bad infinity": it is "static" in its over-dynamization itself, a process that reached its peak in "postmodern" historicist relativism. Every positive universality is "deconstructed," it is demonstrated how its universality is biased, how it secretly privileges and eternalizes a content which is a contingent historical variable. But we should always bear in mind that historicization can also be ideology, not only because it applies a procedure of historicization clearly grounded in our time to all epochs, but, more importantly, when it reduces to a historical variable a basic feature of a certain domain.

Along these lines, Fredric Jameson rejected the (once fashionable) notion of "alternate modernities," i.e., the claim that our Western liberal-capitalist modernity is just one of the paths to modernization, and that other paths are possible which could avoid the deadlocks and antagonism of our modernity: once we realize that "modernity" is ultimately a code name for capitalism, it is easy to see that such historicist relativization of our modernity is sustained by the ideological dream of a capitalism which would avoid its constitutive antagonisms—was Fascism not the exemplary case of alternate modernity? In a strictly homologous way, the reduction of the impasses of sexuality to a specific historical constellation (say, of Western patriarchy) opens up the space for the utopia of a full sexuality without its impasses and perversions which, as Freud demonstrated, inhabit its very notion.

Let's take the well-known case of the ending of *Casablanca*: Rick lets Ilsa, his great love, go to Lisbon with her husband and, together with Captain Renault, decides to join the resistance against the Nazis … This ending can be read as the portrait of an ethical decision in times of trouble: one has to sacrifice the prospect of the personal when a collective struggle against Fascism is needed. However, one can here also mobilize Lacan's motto *il n'y pas de rapport sexuel* and propose a different reading: sexual relationship is such a mess that the only way to get out of its deadlock is to form an exclusively male group of combatants. The irony of this solution strikes the eye: men can only elude the "war" (antagonism) between sexes by way of escaping into warfare proper …

The way out of this ideological deadlock is to supplement the negation of positive universals with the assertion of negative universals, i.e., with an impossibility constitutive of the entire domain: yes, all positive universals are relative, unstable, they can be transformed, but not simply because of the dynamic and changeable form of reality. Positive formations are so many attempts to deal with the same underlying antagonism, and what triggers change is the ultimate failure of every attempt to resolve this antagonism. One of Lacan's negative universals is "there is no sexual relationship," which means that it is not enough to point out the immanent instability and historical character of the traditional gender binary—one should also add that every determinate form of gender relationship, no matter how open and flexible it is, will fail to overcome the impossibility constitutive of human sexuality.

Maybe, there is some kind of sexual relationship among bees. A drone is a male honey bee which, unlike the female worker bee, does not have stingers: they gather neither nectar nor pollen and are unable to feed without assistance from worker bees. A drone's only role is to mate with an unfertilized queen. Mating occurs in flight; should a drone succeed in mating, the first thing that happens is all of the blood in the drone's body rushes to his endophallus which causes him to lose control over his entire body. His body falls away, leaving a portion of his endophallus attached to the queen which helps guide the next drone to the queen ... Does this not seem to be a pretty high price for a full sexual relationship? No wonder that the Latin word for male bee drone is *fucus*, which also means "pretence, disguise, sham," and that *fūcum facere* means (not "to fuck" but) to play a trick." And no wonder that the term "drone" is today widely used for a remotely controlled aircraft (unmanned aerial vehicle)[12]—are drones not some kind of phalluses detached from human bodies and thus remotely controlled?

It is thus crucial to keep in view how ideological limitation works in two opposed directions. Ideology is not only the eternalization of a specific historical situation, it is also the reduction to a specific contingent property of something that is constitutive of the entire field. Ideology is not just the elevation of capitalism into the most appropriate and rational economic order; it is also the dismissal of crises and antagonisms that characterize capitalism into a deviation due to particular contingent circumstances, and the accompanying idea that another capitalism is possible which would avoid crises ant antagonisms.

With regard to this amphibian status of ideological limitation, I find problematic Tupinamba's critique of "structural dialectics" which is based on his attempt to historicize the real: the "logic of the signifier," the core of structural dialectics, ontologizes into a universal frame the differential structure caught in a self-referential movement circulating around its constitutive impossibility, and the real appears within this frame as the "impossible" of this structure and, as such, as an ahistorical limit—as the elusive excess that defines the structure itself. However, this ontologization of the logic of the signifier is based on ignoring the fact that it is rooted in the artificially produced analytic situation, produced by the "enclosure of the clinical space" (analyst-analysand): the real is the "impossible" excluded from and by this situation, and as such a historical variable which can be analyzed as part of another wider reality.

We can now understand in what sense, for Tupinamba, what is ultimately to blame for Lacan's limitations are his "philosophical commitments" as they are discernible in his elevation of the logic of the signifier into an ontological a priori. The logic of the signifier, the ultimate frame of our access to reality, is, of course, not a homogeneous logical frame, it is self-reflectively twisted, thwarted, structured around its immanent impossibility; however, since it provides a kind of transcendental frame to our access to reality, what eludes it cannot be conceptualized in itself as another reality but can only appear as a limit-phenomenon, an elusive virtual point of reference ultimately defined only by our failure to reach it. Out of fear of regressing into a naïve realism of a presupposed external reality that our symbolic frame cannot ever fully capture, Lacan thus proposes his own version of Wittgenstein's motto "the limits of our language are the limits of our reality": the fact that our symbolic space circulates around an elusive point impossible to grasp should not be reduced merely to a sign of our cognitive limitation, this impossibility must also hold for reality itself. The real is not just impossible for us to grasp, it is impossible in itself, it fully coincides in its own impossibility, and Tupinamba rather dismissively refers to this redoubling of impossibility, to Lacan's claim that we only touch the real through the failure of our attempts to grasp it, as a "proof by impotence": "The impotence of the model counts as the potency of the proof."

It is here that I disagree with Tupinamba: I think that he all too easily gets rid of the subversive power of the "proof by impotence" which indicates the pivotal point at which Lacan's motif of the overlapping of two lacks (subject's lack and the lack in the Other) echoes the basic Hegelian motif of the problem/deadlock as its own solution. In my past work, I obsessively kept returning to this motif, enumerating examples, say, of Adorno's well-known analysis of the antagonistic character of the notion of society. In a first approach, the split between the two notions of society (the Anglo-Saxon individualistic-nominalistic and the Durkheimian organicist notion of society as a totality which preexists individuals) seems irreducible, we seem to be dealing with a true Kantian antinomy which cannot be resolved via a higher "dialectical synthesis," and which elevates society into an inaccessible Thing-in-itself. However, in a second approach, one should merely talk not of how this radical antinomy which seems to preclude our access to the Thing ALREADY IS THE THING ITSELF—the fundamental feature of today's society IS the irreconciliable antagonism between Totality and the individual. What this means is that, ultimately, the status of the Real is purely parallactic and, as such, non-substantial: it has no substantial density in itself; it is just a gap between two points of perspective, perceptible only in the shift from the one to the other. The parallax Real is thus opposed to the standard (Lacanian) notion of the Real as that which "always returns at its place," i.e., as that which remains the same in all possible (symbolic) universes: the parallax Real is rather that which accounts for the very *multiplicity* of appearances of the same underlying Real—it is not the hard core which persists as the Same, but the hard bone of contention which pulverizes the sameness into the multitude of appearances.

For Tupinamba, this refusal to think the Real in itself, this reduction of the Real to a mark of its own impossibility, is, insofar as the Unconscious is one of the names of the Real, also, "in the last instance, the reason why for Lacan the unconscious must be conceived of as an 'ethical' instance, and not as a psychoanalytic concept." But I see this as a wrong alternative: "ethical" is here a psychoanalytic concept, it designates the dimension of Ought in Freud's formula "*wo es war soll ich werden* (where it was I shall become)" which points towards Lacan's refusal to ontologize the Unconscious into a substantial base of the subject's psychic life. Here we encounter a "proof by impotence" at its most trenchant: the inaccessibility of the Unconscious is not just a sign of our epistemological limitation, of our inability to reach another site where the Unconscious "fully exists"—the Unconscious "in itself" does not fully exist, since it dwells in the domain of neither-being-nor-not-being.

Formulas of Sexuation

Tupinamba's critique of Lacan's relying on "proof by impotence" also motivates his reading of Lacan's formulas of sexuation: he claims that

> Lacan silently reintroduces here the difference between the real of psychic space—the 'other-in-the other' that functions as a cause of desire's structural dissatisfaction—and the real that Freud marked with an 'x' in his theory of ideals—the radical alterity of the 'thing' beyond its representational apprehension—a difference which the grammar of 'structural dialectics' had a hard time maintaining without implying a 'pre-symbolic' referent.

Really? Let me return here for the twentieth time to one of my eternal examples: Claude Levi-Strauss's exemplary analysis, from his *Structural Anthropology*, of the spatial disposition of buildings in the Winnebago, one of the Great Lake tribes, might be of some help here. The tribe is divided into two sub-groups ("moieties"), "those who are from above" and "those who are from below"; when we ask an individual to draw on a piece of paper, or on sand, the ground-plan of his/her village (the spatial disposition of cottages), we obtain two quite different answers, depending on his/her belonging to one or the other sub-group. Both perceive the village as a circle; but for one sub-group, there is within this circle another circle of central houses, so that we have two concentric circles, while for the other sub-group, the circle is split into two by a clear dividing line. In other words, a member of the first sub-group (let us call it "conservative-corporatist") perceives the ground-plan of the village as a ring of houses more or less symmetrically disposed around the central temple, whereas a member of the second ("revolutionary-antagonistic") sub-group perceives his/her village as two distinct groups of houses separated by an invisible frontier ...[13]

The point Levi-Strauss wants to make is that this example should in no way entice us into cultural relativism, according to which the perception of social space depends on the observer's group-belonging: the very splitting into the two "relative" perceptions implies a hidden reference to a constant—not the objective, "actual" disposition of buildings but a traumatic kernel, a fundamental antagonism the inhabitants of the village were unable to symbolize, to account for, to "internalize," to come to terms with—an imbalance in social relations that prevented the community from stabilizing itself into a harmonious whole. The two perceptions of the ground-plan are simply two mutually exclusive endeavors to cope with this traumatic antagonism, to heal its wound via the imposition of a balanced symbolic structure.

We get here a clear distinction between the external reality—the "actual," "objective," arrangement of the houses—and the Real that announces itself in the clash of the two different symbolizations which both distort in an anamorphic way the actual arrangement. The "real" is here not the actual arrangement, but the traumatic core of some social antagonism which distorts the tribe members' view of the actual arrangement of the houses in their village. And it would be easy to add numerous similar examples from contemporary political life—say, if one were to ask a partisan of Trump or of the liberal center-Left to describe the basic coordinates of the US political scene, we would each time get a fundamentally different description (Trump would have presented himself as the voice of hard-working people against the corrupt non-patriotic "enemies of the people," and a liberal Leftist would have presented themselves as the last bulwark of human rights and freedom against Fascist demagoguery), and the Real of this opposition is not provided by the description of social reality as it is but by the antagonism that both poles of the opposition obfuscate, each in its own way.[14]

So I think that not only what Tupinamba critically refers to as "structural dialectics" can differentiate between the real of psychic space and the external real, their difference is the basic feature of "structural dialectics": it is easy for Lacan to "differentiate between what is inaccessible from a finite standpoint and the infinity of the external world." So when Tupinamba claims that, "within structural

dialectics, the infinite can only be thought of as the inaccessible—
as being absolutely other to the finite, and therefore present only
virtually, as an indirect supplement," he seems to forget the lesson
of Hegel, THE philosopher of actual infinity: true infinity is not a
transcendent outside with regard to the finite, it is nothing but the
immanent self-mediation/self-mediation of the finite itself.

Now we reach the next central motif of Tupinamba's critique of
Lacan: the way he extends the reproach that Lacan's "structural
dialectics" cannot think the actual infinite positively, in itself, but
only from a finite standpoint, as a forever eluding limit-point, to a
critical reading of Lacan's formulas of sexuation. To somewhat
simplify the line of argumentation, Tupinamba equates "phallicism"
(the masculine side of the formulas of sexuation) as the logic of
enclosure (totalization of a finite set) which generates what it
excludes as a non-existing virtual excess that escapes language, and
although Lacan deploys the feminine side of the formulas as
escaping this logic of enclosure, he ultimately still conceives the
feminine side (of the infinite *jouissance feminine*) the way it appears
from the masculine side, as an excess with no positive reality of its
own since it is outside language (signifier). But since Lacan's
"structural dialectics" (whose core is the logic of the signifier) is
ultimately an illegitimate universalization of the way speech
functions in analysis, one should not conceive feminine enjoyment
as "structurally inaccessible" but only as "currently outside of our
reach": if we define the analytic setting in a new way, supplementing
it with axioms which reach beyond the enclosure of the logic of the
signifier, we can also produce "the articulation between 'feminine
enjoyment' and the axiomatic transformation of the domain of
psychoanalysis itself." Tupinamba is well aware that the founding
experience of psychoanalysis came to Freud through listening to
feminine (hysterical) subjects, to how they undermine "phallic"
authority, but he simultaneously constrained the full scope of this
experience:

If the "field" of which phallicism is the "function" is language as
such, then this infinite supplement, which cannot be arrived at
neither by Φ nor by its negation, can only be outside of language
itself—hence a contradiction with the very principle of

psychoanalysis. If, however, the field at stake here concerns only speech in analysis, as we have repeatedly argued throughout this investigation, then to posit the existence of an indeterminate extension that we cannot arrive at simply by running the course of free association, does not need to point to something that is structurally inaccessible—it could also mean that it is currently outside of our reach, but which could become accessible to clinical work through an axiomatic institution. In short: by recognizing the regional status of speech in analysis, we would be able to equally recognize the articulation between "feminine enjoyment" and the axiomatic transformation of the domain of psychoanalysis itself—an articulation that is, in fact, more than documented in the history of psychoanalytic thinking.

The epistemological implications of the phallic logic are thereby clear: since it can only conceive radical otherness external to the symbolic space as an immanent excess of this space itself, with no status of its own, and since this immanent excess is part of our libidinal (psychic) reality, it has to "generalize the properties of the psychic real over those of indifferent otherness": "'what is not the signifier' exists only insofar as it remains marked within the signifying chain as a stumbling block that is then displaced to a fantasmatic exception with no actual existence." The logic of feminine enjoyment (of the non-all) seems to circumvent this deadlock: it "gives precedence to the 'external x' of Freud's schema, submerging the enclosed space of signification itself into the world's exteriority to signification: since we are, here, always already on the outside, there is no place to deposit an exception to signification, but there is also no way to affirm the consistent closure of the space under this function." However, this attempt to break out of the phallic domain is fatally constrained: the fateful limitation of Lacan's formulas of sexuation is

a consequence of not thinking the infinite in its own terms, that is, of not accepting that actual infinity is more than the limit-point of the finite, but the opening to a whole group of functions other than Φ which delimit possible transformations over both countable and uncountable infinite sets.

Does this hold? It is true that some formulations in Lacan's *Encore* are somewhat ambiguous (he does characterize feminine enjoyment as an excess outside language), but the main thrust of his argumentation is clear: there is no need for a "function other than Φ" to conceptualize femininity as it is "in itself" and not just as something in excess of the phallic function—to see this one should only read Lacan closely and literally. It is patently not true that feminine enjoyment "cannot be arrived at neither by Φ nor by its negation," since this is precisely the way Lacan arrives at it: in the formulas of sexuation, femininity is defined precisely by its full immersion in the phallic function (there is no exception to it), which is why, paradoxically, the feminine position is *more* (*not less*) immersed in the "field of phallicism." In my reading of the formulas of sexuation, I am thus tempted to reach exactly the opposite conclusion: do Lacan's formulas of feminine sexuation not enact precisely the overcoming of any kind of "commitment to the primitive status of otherness"? Is the externalization of "what is not closed under phallicism" into an unfathomable Otherness not part of the masculine formulas? Or, to put it in more conventional terms, is the very idea of a substantial Woman that eludes the masculine symbolic grasp not part and parcel of masculine ideology?

Tupinamba of course sees that, far from being limited to the relation between sexes, Lacan's formulas of sexuation are extraordinarily productive as a means to clarify other relations. For example, the couple of (whatever remains of the classic) proletariat and precariat functions exactly as the masculine and feminine side of Lacan's formulas: working class is clearly an All (of the fully employed and exploited) based on an exception (the permanent threat of unemployment), while members of the precariat integrate this external limit: they are unemployed (with no permanent job) in search of short-term contracts and, in this sense, non-all (dispersed in multiple temporary identities).[15] Plus, insofar as Tupinamba insists so much on historicity, we should point out that the very difference that separates historicity proper from mere historicism can also be captured by the formulas of sexuation.

Historicism is clearly masculine: all social reality is ultimately contingent, constructed in historically specific circumstances, there are no trans-historical essentials, the basic form of ideology is the eternalization of some historically specific content...—however, such a historicist approach exempts from the domain of historical relativism its own stance which is silently universalized, i.e., historicism applies the same notion of history to all historical epochs. We can discern this exception when we raise a simple question apropos the anti-essentialist thesis that all forms of social identity are contingent constructs: say, when proponents of gender theory claim that every gender identity is a contingent historical construct, does this apply in the same way to our late-capitalist societies as well as to pre-historic tribal or hunter societies? If the answer is yes, then we have to surmise that we live in a privileged era when the historical contingency of every identity became obvious, i.e., we are caught privileging our own epoch.

The basic feature of authentic historicity is that, on the contrary, it is feminine in the sense of Lacan's formulas of sexuation: it abolishes this exception, i.e., it relativizes its own position and thus historicizes its own notion of historicity. It is in this sense that Hegel is a radical historicist: for him, with every historical epoch, the universal notion of history also changes. Such an approach thus allows for no exception to historicity and is for this reason "non-all": there is no single universal notion of historicity since this notion is itself caught in the process of historical change. Historicism is not radical enough because it does not take into account how each historical break is not simply a break within history but changes the very notion of history. This is why we shouldn't dismiss as ridiculous Fukuyama's talk about the end of history in 1990: after the victory of global capitalism, the sense of history changed. And, in some properly metaphysical sense, our total immersion in the global digital network which makes our entire tradition instantly accessible, signals the end of historical experience as we knew it. We already "feel" how, in some sense, cyberspace is "more real"—more real than external physical reality: it is a complex version of the Platonic realm of Ideas where all that has happened and that happens now is inscribed into an atemporal synchronous order. In our physical reality that we relate to through our senses, things always change, everything is set to disappear, reality comes to fully exist only when it is registered in cyberspace.

The Vagaries of Truth

We see now clearly that Hegel is not a historicist relativist just describing different truth-discourses: there is a crucial difference between Hegel and a historicist relativist like Michel Foucault. For Hegel, each discourse implies its own notion of truth, but each discourse is inconsistent, caught in immanent antagonisms, and the dialectical movement deploys how, through its immanent "contradictions," a discourse passes into another discourse. For Foucault, however, different discourses just co-exist in mutual indifference. Foucault's notion of truth can be summed up in the claim that truth/untruth is not a direct property of our statements but that, in different historical conditions, different discourses each produce their own specific truth-effect, i.e., they imply their own criteria of what values are "true":

> The problem does not consist in drawing the line between that in discourse which falls under the category of scientificity or truth, and that which comes under some other category, but in seeing historically how effects of truth are produced within discourses which are neither true nor false.[16]

Science defines truth in its own terms: the truth of a proposition (which should be formulated in clear explicit and preferably formalized terms) is established by experimental procedures which can be repeated by anyone. Religious discourse operates in a different way: its "truth" is established in complex rhetorical ways which generate the experience of inhabiting a meaningful world benevolently controlled by a higher power. (In his last book, Peter Sloterdijk[17] analyses different modes of theo-poetry, complex forms of rhetoric which "bring gods to speak.") Then there are other discourses: traditional mythologies, art, everyday life, each with its own truth-effect ... but what does it mean that discourses themselves are "neither true nor false"? In what sense can the field of discourses be a neutral background with regard to truth? Obviously, a meta-theory is needed here: what is the status of Foucault's theory (of the truth-effects of discourses) itself? In some (which?) sense, it is obviously meant to be true: he argues for it, provides arguments and examples ...

Also, science is not simply one of discourses; it touches the real in a different way (based on scientific knowledge we can make biogenetic changes, we can use nuclear energy ...), so it's not enough to say it is one of the discourses with a specific truth-effect. And this brings us to the ambiguous relationship between science and psychoanalysis. Freud himself remained a scientist. He thought that his psychoanalysis would be just a temporary solution which would be left behind when neurobiology was finally able to account for the functioning of our mind.

For Lacan, however, psychoanalysis is not science (in the modern sense of a formalized natural science, at least)—to clarify its status, he refers to Aristotle's distinction of four modes of causality: material cause, formal cause, final cause and efficient cause. If a carpenter makes a table, the wood out of which he makes is its material cause, the idea of the table which he realizes in the wood is ideal cause, his work is its efficient cause, and the use of the table is its final cause, the reason we are making tables. Lacan applies these four aspects of causality to the notion of truth. As Hegel pointed out, truth as adequacy of our notion/judgment to object should be supplemented by a higher mode of truth: truth as the adequacy of the object itself to its notion. Not only is my notion of a table in the next room adequate if there really is a table in the next room, this table itself is also "truly a table" if it is a useful table. Therein resides the true content of Hegel's much-maligned claim that, if facts do not fit theory "so much worse for the facts"—if a table doesn't fit the notion of a table so much worse for the table). Maybe this couple fits the Aristotelian opposition of material cause and formal cause: truth as material cause is at work when we verify a statement with a reference to material reality which makes it true, while the fact that an empirical object fits its notion concerns formal cause: a material table is "a true table" when it fits its form/notion. Sciences operate between these two extremes of empiricism and construction of notions—with the exception of mathematics, of course. Let's take quantum physics: notional as it is, it ultimately hinges on the results of measurements (although we must be more precise here, distinguishing between the real and reality: the reality of empirical measurements is not the same as the Real of the unrepresentable quantum universe which is, from our standpoint, also a construct).

In contrast to science, psychoanalysis mobilizes truth as efficient cause—but is the direct causal efficiency of truth not the feature that characterizes magic thinking? In magic thinking, you pronounce a formula (a prayer, a curse), and something happens in reality (rain, health . . . or the death of your enemy). The shamanizing subject acts within structures and signifiers: "it is in the form of signifiers that what must be mobilized in nature appears: thunder and rain, meteors and miracles." In magic the idea of the truth as cause thus only appears in the guise of efficient causality—the symbolic directly falls into the real. In religion, the causality is different: "Truth in religion is relegated to so-called 'eschatological' ends, which is to say that truth appears only as final cause, in the sense that it is deferred to an end-of-the-world judgment."[18] That's why religion is faith and not knowledge: faith that there is another place, inaccessible to us, that of God in Himself, where full knowledge can be articulated.

How, then, do things stand in psychoanalysis? One should note here that, while the early Freud naively believed in a direct causal power of truth (if the analyst gives a patient the correct interpretation of his/her symptoms, these symptoms will automatically disappear or dissolve), he soon encountered a nasty surprise: even if correct, an interpretation remains inefficient, symptoms don't disappear. This insight brought Freud to the topics of transference and temporality: to become efficient, truth must be told at the right moment, not only after transference of the patient to the analyst is established but when transference brings the patient into the right psychic state of experiencing the antagonisms that ravage his/her subjectivity. Later, Freud added two further complications: the subject's free decision (a "successful" psychoanalysis doesn't restore the patient to a conflictless life, it just brings him to a point where, aware of what goes on in his psychic life, he can decide what course to choose), plus the so-called "negative therapeutic reaction" (since the patient enjoyed his symptoms, their dissolution may trigger a catastrophic depression).

All these complications just confirm that the truth of interpretation is judged on its effect on the subject, so that we are not dealing with a truth-effect—*truth itself is the cause which produces effects*. This is not simply a pragmatic view ("it doesn't matter if the analyst's interpretation of a symptom is true, what matters is only that it works")—not because Lacan presumes that the truth of a symptom is already there in the depths of the unconscious, waiting to be discovered, but because, as Lacan put it, a symptom precedes what it is a symptom of, it doesn't have a determined meaning before its interpretation. Lacan evokes here the science-fiction motif of travel from the future: the symptom is like a message sent from the patient's future when its meaning will be determined.

It is crucial that, in order to explain this specific role of truth in psychoanalysis, Lacan draws a parallel with Marxism: modern science derives its power from the fact that it "does-not-want-to-know-anything about the truth as cause"[19]—or, as Lacan put it, science forecloses the subject: in a scientific text, the subjective position of enunciation is totally neutralized, it doesn't matter who said it, anyone can repeat the experiment and verify its truth. Psychoanalysis introduces here the dimension of subjective truth. An example:

> Feigang Fei, who runs Aunt Dai Chinese restaurant in Montreal, has taken a different approach, with a menu offering bracingly honest descriptions of the dishes on offer. "Comparing to our general tao chicken, this one is not THAT good," reads the entry for orange beef. Under "mouth-watering chicken", Fei writes: "We are not 100% satisfied with the flavour now and it will get better really soon. PS: I am surprised that some customers still order this plate."[20]

Such a way of "telling the truth" is, of course, the ultimate lie: truth becomes here the most efficient form of self-publicity. We are here back at the opposition between subjective truth and factual exactitude: the greatest lie occurs when all the data in our statements are factually true. And, in clear contrast to the scientific neutralization, Marxism, along with psychoanalysis, "seriously puts to work" a dimension of subjective truth that science has to forget, since science, once it has been constituted, ignores "the circuitous path by which it came into being."[21] (Note that Lacan's text on science and truth appeared in 1965, soon after the French translation of Lukacs' *History and Class Consciousness* was published in 1960.) This dimension of truth gets lost in the orthodox Marxism that reduces its own teaching to objective science—or, to quote Stalin from his "On Dialectical and Historical Materialism":

> In the eighties of the past century, in the period of the struggle between the Marxists and the Narodniks, the proletariat in Russia constituted an insignificant minority of the population, whereas the individual peasants constituted the vast majority of the population. But the proletariat was developing as a class, whereas the peasantry as a class was disintegrating. And just because the proletariat was developing as a class the Marxists based their orientation on the proletariat. And they were not mistaken; for, as we know, the proletariat subsequently grew from an insignificant force into a first-rate historical and political force.[22]

In this view, Marxists first objectively analyze social processes and discover the move in the direction of Communism when the working class will take power; after establishing this as an objective scientific fact, they engage themselves on the side of the working class, thus backing the winning horse . . . This is why they distinguish between Marxist science and Marxist ideology: first, Marxism as an objective science establishes the truth; then, this truth is transposed into ideology which mobilizes the masses, explaining how they should act if they want to win. For authentic Marxism this gap has to fall: Marxist theory implies a subjectively engaged position—the path to universal truth leads through an engaged partial position. Lacan quotes here Lenin:

> In writing that "Marx's theory is omnipotent because it is true," Lenin says nothing of the enormity of the question his speech raises: If one assumes the truth of materialism in its two guises— dialectic and history, which are, in fact, one and the same—to mute, how could theorizing this increase its power? To answer with proletarian consciousness and the action of Marxist politics seems inadequate to me.[23]

True, Lenin is ambiguous here: his claim can be read as "Marxism is based on true scientific knowledge of society, so it is omnipotent," in the same way as modern physics can build nuclear devices. But Lacan's critical question—"how could theorizing this increase its power"—is easy to answer: proletarian self-consciousness changes what it gets to know, its object (which is itself), into a revolutionary subject, and is, in this sense, precisely *not* "mute." Lacan (and Lenin) miss this point theorized by Lukacs: Marxism is "universally true" not in spite of its partiality but *because* it is "partial," accessible only from a particular subjective position—and the same holds for psychoanalysis.

Trans versus Cis

Where does Tupinamba stand here? He enjoins us "to treat the 'real' in historical as well as structural terms, since thinking the domain of a given operation is also to relativize the concept of the inaccessible—it can function as a limit-point, but this does not require us to maintain it as an ahistorical 'impasse of formalization.'" I think that, in this critique of Lacan's alleged "phallicism," Tupinamba gets all too close to Judith Butler's critique of the Lacan's Real, i.e., to evoking the wealth of external reality which always undermines every fixed symbolic structure. What I find problematic here is the central claim that what eludes the phallic domain "does not need to point to something that is structurally inaccessible—it could also mean that it is currently outside of our reach."

So when, in the very last paragraph of (the manuscript of) his book—the fact which cannot but confer on his plea the status of the final declaration of the path to be taken—Tupinamba pleads for "a new compossibility between transgender and feminist critiques, on the one side, and psychoanalysis, on the other," as a way to articulate positively, not just as a limit-case, "what is not closed under phallicism," I am tempted to propose a counter-claim: in the same way that Tupinamba tries to separate "Lacanian ideology" from the radical core of Lacan's teaching, our task today is to separate the transgender and feminist ideology from the radical core of this movement—only in this way can the movement be redeemed, and only Lacanian psychoanalysis (combined with Marxist social analysis) can do this job. This brings us back to the distinction between the negation of positive universals and the assertion of negative universals: in its ferocious negation of positive universals (emphasizing how the gender binary is a historical variable, not a transcendental a priori of human sexuality), the predominant form of transgender and feminist ideology forgets to assert a negative universal, the impossibility/antagonism that characterizes human sexuality as such, proposing an ideological vision of sexuality which, freed from patriarchal/binary constraints, becomes a joyful expression of our true selves, a practice of non-binary plasticity where a subject permanently experiments with itself and reconstructs itself, playing with different identities, from hetero to gay, from bisexual to asexual?

To refer here briefly to the well-known joke from Ernst Lubitsch's *Ninotchka*, the status of "coffee without milk" is not the same as that of "coffee without cream," and they both differ from "plain coffee," although materially all three are same. This fact enables us to throw a new light on the conflict among feminists which has recently exploded, triggered by the transgender movement: cis (biological women who also perceive themselves in their socio-symbolic identity as women) versus trans (biological men who experience their psychic identity as feminine and sometimes even undergo a painful chirurgic procedure to bring their bodily features in line with their psychic femininity). For some cis, trans are drag performers, women with penises, men dressing and acting like women, i.e., agents of cultural appropriation like white artists performing black art. Trans reacted to this dismissal in a no less violent backlash, accusing cis of biological essentialism ("anatomy is destiny") and designating them as TERFs ("trans-exclusionary radical feminists"). However, they are also no less immune to essentialism: for some of them, being a woman is a profound innate form of gender-identity independent of bodily features or social practices. The socio-political stakes of this conflict are high, because cis do not want to allow trans to participate in feminist meetings and in other forms of women's activities—they perceive trans as foreign intruders. On the other hand, not all trans want to be identified with real women: some of them insist on their specific identity.

Trans want to enact their psychic gender identity at a distance from their biological bodily features, not just dressing and acting like women but also conforming their bodily features to their true identity, but when they do this, a distance remains that separates their rearranged bodies from "natural" feminine bodies, so that calling their surgically reconstructed organs directly by their biological names makes them uneasy. Their solution is to replace the usual names with more neutral ones: vagina becomes "front hole," breastfeeding becomes "chest-feeding" ... In this way, they want to make the point that cis is just a species of trans, that we are ultimately all trans. However, the suspicion persists that their "front hole" is just a miserable artificial remake of the vagina. However, cis have a point to make here: there is a real weight to the feminine body, of motherhood, that affects feminine self-experience, with all the details this involves (periods, pregnancy ...), and it is doubtful this dimension can be recuperated by the trans.

So what are we to do here? All the obvious options are wrong. It is wrong to advocate a vague synthesis, preaching solidarity of all forms of feminine struggle—this just sidesteps the real problem. It is wrong to side with trans, insisting that all forms of gender identity are contingent social constructs—this also sidesteps the real problem. But it is also wrong to endlessly ponder on the problem. The only correct stance is to realize that this tension itself—the tension between cis and trans—is specifically feminine. It is important to note that we do not encounter the same conflict among men, between "real" men and trans-men—why? Because masculine identity is already in itself, as such, in some sense "trans," grounded in an exception. We are referring here, of course, to Lacan's formulas of sexuation where the masculine position is defined as a conjunction of universality with its constitutive exception, and the feminine position as the conjunction of non-all with no exception. So while man's identity is grounded in an exception which negates the universal order, the implication of the split between cis and trans is that there is no exception here (as trans point out, trans and cis are all women, nothing is excluded here), but women are also not-all (as cis insist, not all women are women). The solution is thus a kind of speculative identity of the two sides: women are not-all, and there is no constitutive exception to being-woman.

This brings us back to our example of coffee without milk: if men are like coffee with milk/penis, trans-women are in some sense "castrated men," women who are not men, without milk/penis, but this does not make cis "natural" real women. This is what Lacan aims at with his claim that *la femme n'existe pas*: although a woman is not defined by the negation of being-man, there is no substantial feminine identity. In his seminar on feminine sexuality, Lacan claims that, while man can be defined differentially, as not-woman, the obverse does not hold: woman cannot be defined as not-man. This does not mean that women possess a substantial identity outside relation to man: what characterizes a woman prior to the relation to man is rather a NO as such, a self-relating negativity, and man as not-woman means man, in its very being, denies the NO itself that defines feminine subjectivity, not that it negates some substantial feminine essence. In a homologous way, the status of "coffee without milk" implies that there is no simple positive "plain coffee" lacking nothing: "plain coffee" without a without is already in itself marked by negation, it is just that this negation is not yet a determinate negation.

How do transgender subjects fit into this frame? The multiple shades of the meaning of "transgender" form a clear Hegelian triad of a gradually radicalized negation of the starting point. At the zero level of feminism, we remain fully within the standard opposition between masculine and feminine, the task is just to refashion it in a more just way (more power and equality for women, rejection of all forms of domination and exploitation). Then, in the first move, we focus on all those stances (and practices) which deviate from standard heterosexuality—in this sense, gays and lesbians are also transgender. While the standard sexual opposition of men and women remains here also in power, it is just that men couple with men and women with women (which, exactly, fully relies on this opposition). Second, there are individuals who actually transgress (pass over) the line of division: men who became women and women who became men (in whatever way, from just cross-dressing to enduring the surgery to change their sexual organs). Note that here also the sexual opposition remains fully in power (you are either a man or a woman), it is just that you can cross the line to the other pole. Finally, there is the true transgender: individuals who adopt an identity that fits neither of the two poles, i.e., who are neither men nor women. And, in a proper Hegelian sense, it is only at the end, through this triple (or, rather, quadruple) negation, that we arrive at what the starting point (sexual difference) effectively is as an impossible-real, beneath its predominant heterosexual form. Far from abolishing sexual difference, the true transgender stands for difference as such: a difference from difference itself (as the established difference of two sexual identities). For those identified with a given gender role, transgender doesn't fit any identity, it sticks out, it is difference as such.

Sexual Difference is Not Binary

This is how the Hegelian "reconciliation" looks: the reconciliation with difference itself in its traumatic dimension of an impossible/real. And this is why sexual difference does not work as a "binary" couple, but precisely as that which subverts any binary identity. In the domain of sexuality, the exemplary case of the struggle against "binary" logic is the perception of a sexual *couple* as a form of oppressive limitation. The title of Sasha Roseneil's comment—"It's time to end the tyranny of coupledom"—tells it all: although a lot has been done in recent decades to "spread ideals of equality, freedom and self-actualization throughout the population" (divorce has become easier, equality legislation has enabled more women to live autonomously, same-sex marriage has been legalized),

> one unchanging aspect of the cultural ordering of intimacy becomes ever clearer: our lives remain profoundly shaped by the couple norm. This is the powerful and ubiquitous force—at once both social and psychological—which maintains that being in a couple is the natural and best way of living ... It has remained largely unchallenged by the social movements that have changed so much about gender and sexuality; and, in fact, it is becoming more visible and potent as other norms of intimate and family life have been withering. The couple norm mandates that the intimate/sexual dyad is the basic unit of social life. It operates through laws and policies that assume and privilege coupledom, with myriad economic impacts in terms of access to welfare benefits, pensions, inheritance and housing. It works through

the injunctions, expectations and informal social sanctions of family, friends and colleagues who encourage and cajole the uncoupled towards coupledom. And it is perpetuated through cultural representations of the good life as the coupled life that make it hard to imagine the possibility of contentment beyond the conventional pairing. The couple norm is also internalised, and becomes woven into our sense of self. It forms part of our "normative unconscious", so that non-conformity all too often produces feelings of shame, guilt, disappointment and anxiety for uncoupled people. But there is an increasingly vocal and confident cohort of people who are actively challenging the couple norm ... The question to ask is, what it would mean for societies to cease promoting coupledom above all else, and to work instead to reduce the negative impacts of the couple norm? We propose a rethinking of the welfare state to be more "single-person friendly", and to start thinking about how international human rights conventions might be extended to place the right to a fulfilling single life alongside the right to family life.[24]

Remember how Marx ironically celebrated the "free" contract between a capitalist and a worker as "in fact a very Eden of the innate rights of man. There alone rule Freedom, Equality, Property and Bentham." "Bentham" is the element which stands out from the series, signalling the utilitarian egotism which gives the capitalist spin to freedom and equality—and it is exactly the same with the triad of "equality, freedom and self-actualization" with which Roseneil's comment begins. "Self-actualization" evokes the liberal-individualist notion of human being not as a subject but as an entity whose ultimate aim is to express and actualize its inner potentials, and it is the external social circumstances which prevent the realization of these potentials—there is no space here for the inconsistencies and tensions in what the individual wants. If the individual feels guilty for not living as part of a couple, it is the consequence of the "tyranny" of social order; if the individual feels this tension as internal, it indicates an internalized social pressure, not an immanent reversal in which the individual can find pleasure its very feeling of guilt.

But what I want to argue for here is something more radical: the notion of an individual that wishes to realize its potentials ultimately excludes LOVE—the true target of the polemics against the tyranny of coupledom is simply love in its radical character. If, in our erotic life, we just seek to realize our potentials, our strivings which are as a rule multiple and even inconsistent, this, of course, opens the path to polyamory: the limitation to one partner cannot satisfy all our needs, and forming a couple has to appear as a "tyranny" that represses a strong part of our libidinal strivings. But love is something else: love is in its very notion exclusive. When I am really in love, the limitation to One (the beloved) is experienced as its opposite—as a true liberation. When I fall in love, it is not because the beloved is the one who best satisfies my needs—the fall into love redefines who I am, it redefines my needs and potentials. In this sense, love is beyond transferential repetition: it cannot be explained by my previous secret fantasies to which the beloved fits (in the vulgar pseudo-Freudian sense of "I fell in love with her because she echoes the unconscious features of my mother").

The critique of ideology compels us to raise here a simple question: from which ideological standpoint is coupledom experienced as "tyranny"? The answer is clear: from the "post-modern" notion of free individuality which is hegemonic in today's developed countries and which emphasizes fluidity against fixations, permanent re-discovery of new forms against identity, etc. People today truly "feel guilty" if they are "stuck" with the same partner—even some psychoanalysts categorize permanent coupledom as a case of "pathological" fixation . . . The true "tyranny" is today the tyranny of permanent re-discovery of new identities, so that it is a passionate love link which is the true transgression, and some theorists have made this step and argued that love is the last obstacle to truly free sex.[25] All the conservative-fundamentalist campaigns against contemporary hedonist egotism are therefore fakes—a reactive phenomenon which is already contaminated ("mediated") by what it opposes. Is not the ultimate proof here Donald Trump himself, a ruthless hedonist posing as a partisan of conservative values? Along these lines, in a column in *The Guardian*, Suzanne Moore praised Judith Butler's reduction of sex to gender:

> Butler writes: "If the immutable character of sex is contested, perhaps this construct called 'sex' is as culturally constructed as

gender; indeed, perhaps it was always already gender, with the consequence that the distinction between sex and gender turns out to be no distinction at all." No distinction at all. How immensely freeing that it is. As Jeanette Winterson writes in her book *Frankissstein: A Love Story*: "I'm a woman. And I'm a man. That's how it is for me. I am in a body that I prefer."[26]

For Moore, the notion of "sex" designates an immutable, stable binary identity (masculine or feminine); it is a contingent social construct, but this contingency is obfuscated by a reference to biology (sex is part of our natural identity) or justified by ideology. "Gender" (gender identity) is, in contrast, a contingent social construct, and the experience of this contingency is "immensely freeing: it opens up the space for freely shifting between different identities—a permanent shifting which runs smoothly, involving no antagonisms and tensions. So the idea is that antagonism and tension emerge when the open space of gender games is subordinated to the tyranny of "sex," to the patriarchal order of binary opposites. Patriarchal order is about power, about the exercise of power and domination, and power is what sustains the passage from gender to sex … In short, *gender identities* move in the liberal space of the freedom of choice, a space which is inherently "safe" (nobody controls me there, nobody tries to impose on me an identity which is not mine), while sex (or sexuality as such) involves abuse, violence, domination, and is as such the space of antagonisms—"there is no sexual relationship" (Lacan), but there is a freely negotiated relationship between gender identities. Sex is stable, clearly structured, but simultaneously antagonistic, full of tensions, because the order of sex is an imposed order which constrains the open space of gender identities.

What gets lost in this dissolution of sex in gender is not the fact that there is something basic, natural, etc., in sexual difference, some stable ground which resists being dissolved in the game of social construction; what gets lost is a basic impossibility, antagonism, rift, constitutive of sexuality. Sexuality is not just traversed by antagonisms, it is in itself the name of an antagonism, of a non-relationship. There is a basic discontent/unease in sexuality, and the passage from traditional patriarchal order to today's multiple gender identities is ultimately just a passage from one to another mode of obfuscating this discontent. Traditional patriarchy elevates sexual difference into a stable natural order and attempts to obliterate its antagonistic nature by dismissing tensions as deviations from the natural order: in itself. Sexual difference is the creative tension between the two poles, masculine and feminine, which supplement each other and form a harmonious Whole; when one of the poles oversteps the boundaries of its proper role (say, when a woman behaves like an aggressive man), catastrophe occurs. Gender theory locates antagonism and violence in sexual difference as such and endeavors to create a space of identities outside this difference.

What multiple gender identities exclude is not sexual difference as a stable hierarchical order but the antagonism, unease, impossibility, that define this difference. Traditional heterosexual binary order admits the potential aggressiveness and tension that pertains to sexual difference, and it tries to contain it through the ideological notion of a harmonious relationship between the two sexes. Sexual antagonism is here repressed, but it remains as a potential threat. In the space of multiple gender identities, what is repressed returns with a vengeance, all sexual perversions, all violations of heterosexual normativity, are not only permitted but even solicited. However, the paradox is that repression gets much stronger in this return of the repressed: what is much more repressed than before (in traditional heterosexuality) is the immanent antagonism of sexuality. So we should agree with those who claim that every sexual identity is socially constructed, that there is no natural sexual identity, but what one should add is that multiple constructs are attempts to cope with the Real of an impossibility that cuts across the domain of sexuality. Multiple gender identities are not the starting point, they are endeavors to stabilize the antagonism/impossibility of sex.[27] Sexual difference as real/impossible thus has the structure of a failed negation: it is not a differential relation between two terms, each of them with its own identity which negates the opposite's identity; each term rather gives body to the failure of negating its opposite. This is why the only problem I had when I heard of Katherine Angel's *Tomorrow Sex Will Be Good Again*[28] was its title which seems to imply that sex was once good (not-antagonistic) and will be that again. (After I began to read the book, I of course immedaitely saw that the title is an explicit and ironic invocation of Foucault.) I've rarely read a book with whose basic premise I agreed so fully—since this premise is formulated concisely in the publicity paragraph for the book, I will shamelessly quote it:

> Women are in a bind. In the name of consent and empowerment, they must proclaim their desires clearly and confidently. Yet sex researchers suggest that women's desire is often slow to emerge. And men are keen to insist that they know what women—and their bodies—want. Meanwhile, sexual violence abounds. How can women, in this environment, possibly know what they want? *And why do we expect them to?* Katherine Angel challenges our assumptions about women's desire. Why, she asks, should they be expected to know their desires? And how do we take sexual violence seriously, when *not knowing what we want is key to both eroticism and personhood*?[29]

From my standpoint, the parts in italics are crucial: any feminist theory should take into account not-knowing as a key feature of sexuality and ground its opposition to violence in sexual relationship not in the usual terms of "yes means yes" but evoking this not knowing. This is why the motto that women "must proclaim their desires clearly and confidently" is not just a violent imposition on sexuality but literally de-sexualizing/a promotion of "sex without sex." This is why feminism, in some instances, enforces precisely the same "shaming and silencing" of women's sexuality that it seeks to oppose. What makes male sexual advances violent is not just direct physical (or psychic) violence, but the very presumption that *he knows* what the "confused" woman doesn't know (and is thereby legitimized to act upon this knowledge). A man is thus violent even if he treats a woman respectfully (while patronizingly assuming that he knows . . .). This is no way implies that women's desires are in some sense deficient with regard to those of men (who are supposed to know what they want): for Lacan, the divided subject means precisely a constitutive gap between what I (know that I) want and what I desire. Brecht was right to write in 1929 (in *Individual and Mass*): "The divisibility of the individual is to be emphasized (as the belonging to several collectives)." One should only add to this that the proper name for the divided individual (the "dividual") is subject. The difference between subject and individual is easy enough to explain: an individual is, as the term itself indicates, indivisible, a One, a unity which cannot be further divided into parts (if we do it, we no longer have an individual), while a subject is divided—not into two or more parts but into the minimal dyad of something and nothing. The exemplary case of subject's division is the gap that separates desire from want. This division has two versions. A subject not only desires something but often wants to get it without explicitly asking for it, as if I don't want it, as if it was imposed on me—demanding it directly would ruin it all. And inversely, a subject wants something, dreams about it, but doesn't desire to get it—its desire is for his want to remain unfulfilled because its entire subjective consistency depends on this not-getting-it: directly getting-it would lead to a collapse of subjectivity. We should always bear in mind that one of the most brutal forms of violence occurs when something that we secretly desire or fantasize about (but are not ready to do in real life) is imposed on us from outside.

If PC advocates nonetheless admit the fact of a divided subject, they do it in their own way, elevating sexual experience into the ultimate trauma, talking about "sexual assault survivors who hide their trauma—even from themselves." How, then, can such a brutal act as rape be unacknowledged, i.e., not experienced as what it is? It happens when, during a sexual encounter, "deep down I knew that what had happened had felt violating, degrading and not what I signed up for. Yet it took me a whole decade to realise what had really happened: I had been sexually assaulted." Why did it take such a long time (till the rise of MeToo) for me to get it? "My limited understanding of consent and sexual violence at that time, and my overall sexual inexperience, meant I believed I was to blame for what had happened, that perhaps I just didn't know 'how sex usually is.'" Only when, more than a decade later, my therapist told me "That's trauma," hearing these words "gave me permission to feel the weight of what I had endured at 19, to understand why anxiety lurked close to the surface of my body. A voice inside my head finally said: "That was sexual assault." At 33, I know that now." So "it can take years—sometimes decades—for some survivors to realise or accept that their experience amounts to sexual assault or rape."[30]

Such things definitely happen: it is easy to imagine a young woman who feels uneasy and abused in sex, but dismisses this experience as resulting from her naïve notion of what sex is—under the influence of prevailing ideology, she decides to endure her suffering ... So we should not denounce the idea that a trauma can be recognized a decade later as a ridiculous PC retroactive projection. With new higher standards of what women's rights and freedoms are, we have a full right to read past events through this new frame—one should absolutely reject false historicism here, the idea that, in previous eras, the oppression of women, racism and slavery were considered normal and we should not judge them by today's standards.

There are nonetheless two further observations to be added here. First, the case described above is not a case of repression in the strict Freudian sense: it is a (fully conscious) feeling of disgust and humiliation kept at bay because of (male chauvinist) social values. So what would (or could) be really repressed and traumatic here? One option is: the exact opposite, i.e., the true trauma was that the woman secretly enjoyed being mistreated, and was absolutely not ready to admit it. Her being disgusted and feeling humiliated was already a fake, a cover destined to obfuscate this disavowed enjoyment, a fact much more traumatic than her mistreatment by the sexual partner. To avoid any misunderstanding: this in no way implies that the man's mishandling was justified (since the woman enjoyed it, so "she got what she wanted")—quite the opposite. As we have already pointed out, we all have secret dirty fantasies, and perhaps the most humiliating experience is to get what we secretly dream about brutally imposed from outside. This is why—an extreme example—a woman who secretly dreams about being raped will be much more traumatized when raped in reality than a strong autonomous woman.

The second observation: one cannot but be struck by the surprising similarity between the PC vision of women threatened by male aggressiveness which can cause lifelong delayed traumas even if they were not directly experienced as traumatic, and the Taliban stance on protecting women from male aggressiveness. On August 24 2021, the Taliban suddenly changed its stance towards women in public and working places: their spokesperson Zabiullah Mujahid said at a news conference that women should not go to work for their own safety, undermining the group's efforts to convince international observers that it would be more tolerant towards women than when they were last in power. Mujahid said the guidance to stay at home would be temporary, and would allow the group to find ways to ensure that women are not "treated in a disrespectful way" or "God forbid, hurt." He admitted the measure was necessary because the Taliban's soldiers "keep changing and are not trained." This is why the new government has asked women "to take time off from work until the situation gets back to a normal order and women related procedures are in place, then they can return to their jobs once it's announced."[31]

The predictable Western reaction to this statement was that we now see how falsity and hypocrisy of the Taliban's assurance that the entitlement of women to education and work will be respected: now they are showing their true colours . . . But the reality is more complex. We don't need direct accusations of lies and hypocrisy to understand the shift in the Taliban's position. The soft attitude towards rape in Muslim countries seems based on the premise that a man who rapes a woman was secretly seduced (provoked) by her into doing it—such a reading of male rape as the result of a woman's provocation is often reported by the media. Here we stumble upon what I take the risk of calling the *ideological unconscious*: an ideological edifice implies and relies on a set of claims which are necessary for its functioning, but which should not be stated publicly. In the Fall of 2006, Sheik Taj Din al-Hilali, Australia's most senior Muslim cleric, caused a scandal when, after a group of Muslim men had been jailed for gang rape, he said: "If you take uncovered meat and place it outside on the street . . . and the cats come and eat it. . . whose fault is it—the cats' or the uncovered meat? The uncovered meat is the problem." The explosively scandalous nature of this comparison between a woman who is not veiled and raw, uncovered meat distracted attention from another, much more surprising premise underlying al-Hilali's argument: if women are held responsible for the sexual conduct of men, does this not imply that men are totally helpless when faced with what they perceive as a sexual provocation, that they are simply unable to resist it, that they are totally enslaved to their sexual hunger, precisely like a cat when it sees raw meat? In contrast to this presumption of the complete lack of male responsibility for their own sexual conduct, the emphasis on public female eroticism in the West relies on the premise that men *are* capable of sexual restraint, that they are not blind slaves to their sexual drives.

In a debate years ago, an Australian Muslim woman emphatically claimed that Islam is the most feminist of all religions—now we can understand why: Islam—in its fundamentalist version, at least—is obsessed with the idea of protecting women ... but protecting them *from what*? From aggressive men? Beneath this public justification it is easy to discover its (mostly) hidden truth: not from men—the true fear is that a woman might *enjoy* being sexually "mistreated"/used by men ... Beneath the desire to protect and control women, there is thus lurking a much more ambiguous mixture of panicky fear and of the deep distrust of the moral composure of men themselves.

Is all this simply a remainder of the oppressive Muslim tradition? Reading about life in Kabul these days one should take a minute to look at some of the images from Kabul in the 1960s that are easy to find on YouTube.[32] What we see there is not a Muslim city with women covered etc. but a city of young women walking around in miniskirts, modern record stores, dance clubs, university halls full of women, etc. Yes, there were conservative Muslim communities in the countryside, but they peacefully coexisted with other religions and with elements of contemporary secular culture. There is no direct continuity between this past and the Taliban: precisely in what appear as its most "archaic" features (the very narrow interpretation of sharia, using state power to prohibit modern secular life like playing music in public), the Taliban is a product of modernity, a reaction to enforced modernization first by Soviet occupation and then by the Western occupation.

These paradoxes already indicate the route emancipation should take. Men should not be portrayed as brutal oppressors but as weak beings whose macho exterior covers up their frailty and impotence. And women should learn to treat men like that. A strong man is the only true feminist—he doesn't need to oppress women in order to assert himself.

There is no sexuality without antagonism, so the choice is not that between the "alienated" antagonist sex and the non-antagonist harmonious sex—in other words, the choice is not that between the utopian-optimist vision of a harmonious sexuality and the pessimist vision of sexuality condemned to end up in a deadlock. Antagonism remains, but it can be reformulated, its status can be radically changed, in a way which is vaguely parallel with what happened with the imaginary number (root square of −1) in the course of nineteenth century (the imaginary number i is defined solely by the property that its square is −1; with i defined in this way, it follows directly from algebra that i and $−i$ are both square roots of −1 − i is indifferent to the opposition of positive or negative). Its status passed from nonsense to something that can be operationalized: houses are built on calculations which involve imaginary numbers ... Is it not similar with capitalism? The impossibility of achieving a state of balance, the permanent self-revolutionizing, is its condition of existence. And is it not similar with democracy? The moment which was for other political orders the most traumatic one—"the throne is empty," the place of supreme power is unoccupied—is in democracy the very resort of its regular functioning: the place of power is in principle empty, it can only temporarily be occupied the elected officials.

From Special to General Theory of Queerness

What this means is that sexuality as such is queer—in what sense? The reason I find Colin Ripley's *Stealing Home: On the Kleptogenetics of Architecture* irresistible is that it is a sublime book in the Lacanian sense of the term: Ripley elevated writing about being queer to the level of Thing, which, in this case, means universal *formal* theory. The book systematically ascends from the singularity of its topic (queer sexuality, i.e., sexuality that deviates from the heterosexual norm) through the particular social meaning (behavior that is strange, unusual, not expected, or even destined to fail—see the British colloquial expression "queer the pitch" which means "ruin the chance of success") up to the level of what one cannot but designate as general formal ontology—queerness in the sense of imbalance, deviation, broken symmetry, out-of-jointness of the reality itself, as if reality itself arises out of a kind of ruined balance or symmetry of the cosmos. The usual view is that of a balanced universe which is temporarily derailed by some excess, but then balance is reestablished when the excess is brought back to measure. From a queer viewpoint, the excess is constitutive of reality, so that the abolition of the excess entails the abolition of the very balanced state with regard to which excess is excess.

In the socio-political domain of class relations, the balanced approach is exemplified by Fascism: for a Fascist, class struggle emerges only when one of the classes disturbs class cooperation with its excessive behavior (workers demand too much from capitalists; capitalists exploit workers too much)—in both cases, the figure which introduces discord is a Jew (financially exploiting productive capitalists, instigating workers to rebel), so one should liquidate the Jew and in this way reestablish the just class balance. For a Marxist, on the contrary, the relationship between classes is by definition that of a discord and imbalance, so that the only way to abolish class antagonism is to abolish classes as such. Recently, in Germany and some other countries, a vogue has been emerging of what is called "classism": a class version of the politics of identity. Workers are taught to safeguard and promote their socio-cultural practices and self-respect, they are made aware of the crucial role they play in social reproduction ... Workers' movements thus become another element in the chain of identities, like a particular race or sexual orientation. Such a "solution" of the "workers problem" is what characterizes Fascism and populism: they respect workers and admit that they are often exploited, and they (often sincerely) want to make their position better within the coordinates of the existing system. Trump was doing this, protecting US workers from banks and the unfair Chinese competition.

Is *Nomadland* (Chloe Zhao, 2020) not the ultimate example of such "classism"? It portrays the daily lives of our "nomadic proletarians"—workers without a permanent home who live in trailers and wander around from one temporary job to another. They are shown as decent people, full of spontaneous goodness and solidarity with each other, inhabiting their own world of small customs and rituals, enjoying their modest happiness.[33] Even occasional work in an Amazon packaging center goes quite well . . . that's how our hegemonic ideology likes to see workers—no wonder the movie was a big winner at the Oscars. Although the lives depicted are rather miserable, the movie bribes us into enjoying it with the charming details of a specific way of life, so its subtitle could have been: "enjoy being a nomadic proletarian!"

It is precisely the refusal to be such an element in the chain of identities which defines authentic workers' movements. In India, I met with the representatives of the lowest group of the lowest caste of the Untouchables, the dry toilet cleaners; I asked them what is the basic premise of their program, what they want, and they instantly gave me the answer: "We don't want to be ourselves, what we are." Workers are, to quote Jacques Ranciere, a "part of no-part" of the social body, lacking a proper place in it, an antagonism embodied. Are we asking too much of Hollywood if we expect movies about lives which are a "part of no-part" of our societies? Bong Joon Ho's *Parasite* did it, Todd Phillips' *Joker* did it, Neil Burger's *Divergent* did it, and it can be done again.

Divergent (2014) is set in a futuristic dystopian Chicago where society is divided into five factions: Abnegation (the selfless), Amity (the peaceful), Candor (the honest), Dauntless (the brave), and Erudite (the intellectual). When children reach the age of 16, they undergo a serum-induced psychological aptitude test which indicates their best-suited faction, but they are allowed to choose any faction as their permanent group at the subsequent Choosing Ceremony. The film's heroine Tris was born into Abnegation, which runs the government; she takes her test and her results show equal attributes of multiple factions, which means that she is Divergent. She is warned to keep the result a secret: because Divergents can think independently and are aware of any serums injected into them, the government cannot control them and considers them to be threats to the existing social order, so they are killed . . . In this neo-Fascist new corporate order, Divergents are precisely its "part of no-part": they don't just have a special identity, they diverge from the very principle which allocates to each member of the social body its proper place.[34]

And Ripley's central claim is, of course, that the same goes for sexuality. His view is well-founded in Freudian orthodoxy. The basic premise of Freud's *Three Essays on Sexuality* (1905) is that perversions also exist in normal people, in multiple deviations of sexual aims, as well as in the tendency to linger over preparatory sexual aspects such as looking and touching. Freud formalized the distinction between the "fore-pleasures" of infantile sexuality and the "end-pleasure" of sexual intercourse; children have sexual urges, from which adult sexuality only gradually emerges via psychosexual development. So

> a disposition to perversions is an original and universal disposition of the human sexual instinct and that … this postulated constitution, containing the germs of all the perversions, will only be demonstrable in *children*.[35]

Here a step further is needed: we (some of us) arrive at the heterosexual norm only through deviations, and this path through deviations is not an organic "natural" process but a process of brutal symbolic cuts, prohibitions and impositions. This is the basic paradox of human sexuality: what appears as a "natural" sexual orientation, the way in which reproduction (the biological function of copulation) happens, is the final outcome of a complex socio-symbolic process. The "progress" from infantile sexuality to the heterosexual norm is not the process which follows a pattern of natural development. What, then, is so scandalous about infantile sexuality? It is not the sole fact that even children, presumed innocent, are already sexualized. The scandal resides in two features (which are, of course, the two sides of the same coin). First, infantile sexuality consists is a weird entity which is neither biological(ly grounded) nor part of symbolic/cultural norms. However, this excess is not sublated by adult "normal" sexuality—this latter also is always distorted, displaced:

> when it comes to sexuality, man is subject to the greatest of paradoxes: what is acquired through the drives precedes what is innate and instinctual, in such a way that, at the time it emerges, instinctual sexuality, which is adaptive, finds the seat already taken, as it were, by infantile drives, already and always present in the unconscious.[36]

The "natural" form is the outcome of a complex symbolic process: the starting point (infantile sexuality) is not yet fully "cultural," but it is also not "natural," so that perversions (whose model is infantile sexuality) do not simply disappear, they are not simply left behind in normal adult heterosexuality. They remain in the form of kissing, touching, and the eroticization of non-sexual parts of the body: "normal" sexuality erotically works only through the shadows and remainders of these elements, otherwise it is just raw coupling, like the insemination in *Handmaid's Tale*. Perverse "deviations" are thus necessary, we arrive at the norm only through them, so that (to put it in Hegelian terms) what appears as "norm" is the ultimate self-sublated perversion. We encounter here what Hegel called "absolute recoil": as deviations from the Norm, perversions presuppose the norm, the pleasure they generate resides in the transgression of the Norm; however, this Norm itself arises through deviations, as the ultimate deviation. In other words, the very process of deviation retroactively constructs what it deviates from, or, as Hegel would have put it, perversion is an act which posits its own presupposition, it is an effect which retroactively posits its cause.[37]

The hero of Chris Sheridan's TV series *Resident Alien* (2021),[38] an alien sent to earth with a secret mission and assuming the body and name of a human whom he killed, is precisely a figure who lacks customs, unwritten rules: he knows the explicit rules, but he is totally ignorant of the complex texture of exceptions, innuendos, etc., which makes the explicit rules livable—he is "inhuman" through his very perfection in his obedience of the rules. The supreme ironic case of this discord is the scene in which he makes love for the first time: he doesn't know how to take the bra off the woman he is with—he tries to tear it off, he bites it . . . Immediately after penetrating her, he reaches the climax which he accompanies with ridiculously strange sounds totally different from what we presume are the "normal" expressions of an orgasmic experience. In short, he has not had the opportunity to *learn* how to act "spontaneously" in making love.

Ripley's book is not about queer sexuality, as if there are two species of sexuality, straight and queer; it is about how *sexuality as such is queer*. Queerness changes its status from predicate to subject which is a universal ontological feature. That's why Ripley deals in his book with queerness of architecture, with special focus on the work of Jean Genet:[39] not to discover in architecture traces of queer sexuality but to discover in architecture at a more general level traces of the same queerness which "distorts" sexuality. His reading of architecture analyzes queer distortions in purely formal terms: while "normal" architecture deals with a clear division between outside and inside, with straight walls separating spaces, "queerness" articulates itself in everything that deviates from such straight space—curved walls, elliptic structures which blur clear divisions, a false outside which exists only as looked upon from the inside, an inside which, once we are within it, miraculously looks larger than seen from the outside, double walls with interstitial space in which entities like electric cables, mice, cockroaches and fantasized trolls dwell, the space of canalization in which excrement disappears from our reality after we flush the water, etc.

In a homologous way, there is a queerness that pertains to the very heart of the prohibitive Law: it discreetly solicits what it prohibits in order to maintain its rule. We find this queerness already in *The Laws of Manu*, the ancient Indian text, one of the most exemplary texts of ideology in the entire history of humanity. While its ideology encompasses the entire universe, inclusive of its mythic origins, it focuses on *everyday practices as the immediate materiality of ideology*: how (what, where, with whom, when . . .) we eat, defecate, have sex, walk, enter a building, work, make war, etc. Here, the text uses a complex panoply of tricks, displacements and compromises whose basic formula is that of universality with exceptions: in principle yes, but . . . *The Laws of Manu* demonstrates a breath-taking ingenuity in accomplishing this task, with examples often coming dangerously close to the ridiculous. For example, priests should study the Veda, not trade; in extremity, however, a priest can engage in trade, but he is not allowed to trade in certain things like sesame seed; if he does it, he can only do it in certain circumstances; finally, if he does it in the wrong circumstances, he will be reborn as a worm in dogshit . . . Is the structure here not exactly the same as that of the famous Jewish joke on the marriage-mediator who reinterprets every deficiency of the bride-to-be as a positive asset: "She is poor . . ." ". . . so she will know how to handle the family money, making most of it!" "She is ugly . . ." "So the husband will not have to worry that she will cheat on him!" "She stutters . . ." "So she will keep quiet and not annoy the husband with

incessant prattle!," and so on until the final "She really stinks!" "So
what, do you want her to be perfect, without any failings?" The
general formula of this procedure is to state one general rule, to
which the whole of the subsequent treatise constitutes nothing but
a series of increasingly specific exceptions. A specific injunction is
stronger than a general one.

In other words, the great lesson of *The Laws of Manu* is that the
true regulating power of the law does not reside in its direct
prohibitions, in the division of our acts into permitted and
prohibited, but in *regulating the very violations of prohibitions*: the
law silently accepts that the basic prohibitions are violated (or even
discreetly solicits us to violate them), and then, once we find
ourselves in this position of guilt, it tells us how to reconcile the
violation with the law by way of violating the prohibition in a
regulated way ... The whole point of law is to regulate its violations:
without violations, there would be no need for the law. These
regulations (telling us how the law can cope with its violations) are
ultimately a form of mercy: OK, you can do it (violate my general
prohibition), just do it in the way that I prescribe ... In the finale of
Mozart's *Clemenza di Tito*, we get a ridiculously sublime explosion
of mercies? Just before the final pardon, Tito himself fulminates at
the proliferation of treasons which oblige him to proliferate acts of
clemency:

> The very moment that I absolve one criminal, I discover another
> ... I believe the stars conspire to oblige me, in spite of myself, to
> become cruel. No: they shall not have this satisfaction. My virtue
> has already pledged itself to continue the contest. Let us see,
> which is more constant, the treachery of others or my mercy ...
> Let it be known to Rome that I am the same and that I know all,
> absolve everyone, and forget everything.

One can almost hear Tito complaining in the style of Figaro: "Uno
per volta, per carita!"—"Please, not so fast, one after the other, in
the line for mercy!" Living up to his task, Tito forgets everyone, but
those whom he pardons are condemned to remember it forever:

> SEXTUS: It is true, you pardon me, Emperor; but my heart will not
> absolve me; it will lament the error until it no longer has memory.

TITUS: The true repentance of which you are capable, is worth more than constant fidelity.

This couplet from the finale blurts out the obscene secret of *Clemenza*: the pardon does not really abolish the debt, it rather makes it infinite—we are forever indebted to the person who pardoned us. No wonder Tito prefers repentance to fidelity: in fidelity to the Master, I follow him out of respect, while in repentance, what attached me to the Master is the infinite indelible guilt. In this, Tito is a thoroughly Christian master. One usually opposes rigorous Jewish Justice and Christian Mercy, the inexplicable gesture of undeserved pardon: we, humans, were born in sin, we cannot ever repay our debts and redeem ourselves through our own acts—our only salvation lies in God's Mercy, in His supreme sacrifice. In this very gesture of breaking the chain of Justice through the inexplicable act of Mercy, of paying our debts, Christianity imposes on us an even stronger debt: we are forever indebted to Christ, we cannot ever repay him for what he did to us. The Freudian name for such an excessive pressure which we cannot ever remunerate is, of course, *superego*. (One should not forget that the notion of Mercy is strictly correlative to that of Sovereignty: only the bearer of sovereign power can dispense mercy.) Accordingly, it is Judaism which is conceived as the religion of the superego (of man's subordination to the jealous, mighty and severe God), in contrast to the Christian God of Mercy and Love. However, the queerness of Christianity resides in the fact that it is precisely through *not* demanding from us the price for our sins, through paying this price for us Himself, that the Christian God of Mercy establishes itself as the supreme superego agency: "I paid the highest price for your sins, and you are thus indebted to me *forever* ..."[40] If ever there was a detour that condenses the queerness of the Law, this is it.

The queerness of the Law thus reaches its apogee in Christianity in which we, humans, are a priori presumed to be fallen, to dwell in sin, so that the entire reign of the law consists of the rules of how to deal with our violations of the law: through confessions and other modes of ritualized repentance. That's why, as many perspicuous theologians knew, the Fall is *felix culpa*, the fortunate fault / the blessed fall—or, as St. Augustine put it: "For God judged it better to bring good out of evil than not to permit any evil to exist." We have to add another step to this reasoning: in order to bring good out of evil, the Good itself—God—has to bring evil out of itself. This is why we should turn around the standard the standard Christian (or more precisely Catholic) explanation of why there is evil in the world: God gave us freedom, and freedom is the freedom to choose what we freely decide, inclusive of evil . . . But is it not the other way round? God (more than just exposed us to the temptation of evil, he) *pushed us into evil so that we would discover our freedom.* There is no freedom without evil since, as Hegel knew very well, to be able to choose between good and evil one already has to be in evil.

Plato described the gradual ascent from the beauty of an individual's body through bodily beauty as such etc. up to the Idea of Beauty as such, and Ripley provides a materialist version of such ascent: from queer sexuality through more formalized architectural queerness and legal queerness up to Queerness as a universal ontological category. From this perspective, a new answer offers itself to the basic metaphysical question: why is there something instead of nothing? There is something only insofar as the universe is unbalanced, out-of-joint . . . in short: queer.

Why There is No True Love Without Betrayal

Does biochemistry open up the way out of this queerness of sexuality? The media has reported that scientists are now working on artificially creating sperms from feminine bodies, so that a lesbian couple can have their own child or a woman can even impregnate herself. Processes to create artificial wombs are also being developed, so the moment is approaching when it will be possible to totally separate procreation from sexual interaction— no sperm donors, etc. What will this procedure amount to if it becomes widely practiced, especially if it is also combined with the obvious further option of genetically manipulating embryos? Talking about "parents" will become meaningless, children will be just directly produced, and the only "parent" will be their scientific creator. Who will then be responsible for these children's education?

While some feminists celebrate this prospect as a gain for women, asserting their full independence from men, one should bear in mind that women will also be deprived of their identity. This will give rise to new conflicts among women, worse than that between trans and cis, the conflict between those gladly endorsing the disappearance of femininity and those still clinging to it. And, last but not least, how will all this affect sexuality? Will it survive as a trifling amusement or ...?

But human sexuality names a symbolic deadlock which just parasitizes on biological facts. In John Huston's *The Night of the Iguana* (1964), based on a play by Tennessee Williams, despite all the sexual tensions between Shannon (played by Richard Burton) and numerous other women in the decrepit Mexican hotel, the scene that steals the show is the chaste Hannah's (Deborah Kerr) delicate description to Shannon of what she calls her "love experience" with the Australian underwear salesman:

> I noticed that he became more and more ... / SHANNON: What? / HANNAH: Well ... agitated ... as the afterglow of the sunset faded out on the water. Well, finally, eventually, he leaned towards me ... we were vis-à-vis in the sampan ... and he looked intensely, passionately into my eyes. And he said to me: "Miss Jelkes? Will you do me a favour? Will you do something for me? "What?' said I. 'Well,' said he, 'if I turn my back, if I look the other way, will you take off some piece of your clothes and let me hold it, just hold it?' / SHANNON: Fantastic! / HANNAH: Then he said, 'It will just take a few seconds.' 'Just a few seconds for what?' I asked him. He didn't say for what, but .../ SHANNON: His satisfaction?/ HANNAH: Yes. / SHANNON: What did you do—in a situation like that? / HANNAH: I ... gratified his request, I did! And he kept his promise. He did keep his back turned till I said ready and threw him ... the part of my clothes. / SHANNON : What did he do with it? / HANNAH: He didn't move, except to seize the article he'd requested. I looked the other way while his satisfaction took place.[41]

This is how sexuality works: such a ridiculous scene in which there is no physical contact can be experienced in a much more intense way than even the most hardcore bodily interaction—what sexualizes bodily movements is their symbolic context. Does, then, sexual love do the job of immanently resolving this deadlock? Lacan claims that love supplements the inexistence of sexual relationship—does this mean that love is a fantasy formation which obfuscates this inexistence? No: in love, the gap that makes sexual relationship impossible returns at a different level, in the guise of the gap between love and Cause. Perhaps the supreme example of this gap is the destiny of some couples who came together because one of them was a spy ordered to cover the other. The most extraordinary Cold War love story was the one between Vera Lengsfeld and Knud Wollenberger who, in the now defunct German Democratic Republic, married her and had two children with her. After the fall of the Wall, when Vera, a GDR dissident, gained access to her Stasi archives, she learned that Knud, a Stasi informer codenamed Donald, married her and lived with her on the orders of his masters, so that he was able to report on her activities; upon learning this, she immediately divorced him and they have not spoken since. Afterwards, Knud sent her a letter explaining that he wanted to shield her and that his betrayal was, in fact, an act of love. Now that he is dying of a galloping form of Parkinson's, Vera said: "I have forgiven him" . . . no wonder Hollywood was considering making a film with Meryl Streep as Vera.[42] Betrayal as an act of love—the formula was already proposed by John le Carre in his masterpiece *A Perfect Spy*.

However, more often in real life, the woman is the agent. There are a couple of real-life stories from World War II where a woman seduced a man in order to spy on him, and after the war when the truth came out they remained together . . . In spy fiction, recall the last minutes of the finale of the last season of *Homeland*, which begin with a flash forward two years: it appears that Carrie Mathison (Claire Danes), the CIA agent who is the heroine of the series, has fully changed sides—turned—she is living in Russia with Yevgeny, her Russian spying counterpart, and has written a tell-all book about betraying her country. But then in one final twist, Carrie sends Saul (her CIA superior) a message using the same method of passing information that Saul and his Russian asset did—she's now a full-time spy working from inside Russia . . . Here is how *Homeland* co-creator Alex Gansa answered the question of whether Carrie's relationship with Yevgeny is real, or whether she's just playing him:

> my feeling is that it is a *real* relationship, in the way that Carrie *has* real relationships. She is, by nature, attracted to duplicitous situations. So she can have real feelings for this guy and at the same time be betraying him. These are the situations that Carrie thrives in. And this particular situation is one she can be content in. And almost happy. She's got a smile on her face at the end.[43]

True, the finale of *Homeland* is a happy ending if there ever was one. Maybe, the duplicitous relationship between Carrie and Yevgeny is the closest we can get to happiness—happiness thrives precisely in the radical duplicity of Carrie's predicament. If Carrie were to make any of the two clear choices (confess everything to Evgeny because of her love for him; just fake her love in order to cover up that she is still working for CIA) would ruin her love, the first option even more than the second one. Serving a Cause is not an external obstacle to love, it is its inner constituent—to put it brutally, no true love without betrayal.

And it is important to notice that a woman (Carrie) is traversed by this gap more radically than a man. The common idea is that a man is torn between love and his Cause, but a man is as a rule forced to decide, to make a choice, while only a woman is able to enjoy the duplicity itself. As for the masculine version of this gap, a detour through the best (or worst) of Hollywood melodrama can be of some help here. The basic lesson of King Vidor's *Rhapsody* is that, in order to gain the beloved woman's love, the man has to prove that he is able to survive without her, that he prefers his mission or profession to her. There are two immediate choices: (1) my professional career is what matters most to me, the woman is just an amusement, a distracting affair; (2) the woman is everything to me, I am ready to humiliate myself, to forsake all my public and professional dignity for her. They are both false, they lead to the man being rejected by the woman. The message of true love is thus: even if you are everything to me, I can survive without you, I am ready to forsake you for my mission or profession. The proper way for the woman to test the man's love is thus to "betray" him at the crucial moment of his career (the first public concert in the film, the key exam, the business negotiation which will decide his career)—only if he can survive the ordeal and accomplish his task successfully although deeply traumatized by her desertion, will he deserve her and will she return to him. The underlying paradox is that love, precisely as the Absolute, should not be posited as a direct goal—it should retain the status of a by-product, of something we get as an undeserved grace ... There is a double difference between the masculine and the feminine version. The man publicly chooses the Cause and (maybe) gets love as a by-product; the woman publicly chooses love and secretly remains faithful to the Cause. The man makes a painful choice; the woman chooses (and gets) both sides of the choice, enjoying division itself.

Now we come to the crux of the problem: but is the impossibility/ antagonism that pertains to sexuality not historical and as such variable? Why can't we imagine (and practice) a different sexuality no longer branded by a constitutive antagonism? A sexual relationship which is not "structurally inaccessible" but just "currently outside of our reach"? Incidentally, it is sad to see how even Badiou falls into this trap: his solution[44] for our sexual predicament is the creation of a new symbolic space for men and women, beyond traditional patriarchal hierarchy, but also beyond capitalist nihilism of the out-Law Real. Such a new symbolic space can only arise by means of a properly philosophical gesture of the creation of new basic Signifiers, of a new symbolization through which both sexes are reinvented: a new space where women are also scientists, politicians, artists, where men also deal with reproduction. From the Lacanian perspective, however, the first thing to do is not to search for the traces of some new symbolization of sexual difference but to interrogate what is in sexuality here and now more than its patriarchal traditional symbolization—without this interrogation, the dream of a new symbolic space of sexuality is just that, an empty dream, an ideological mirage that enables us to avoid the antagonism constitutive of human sexuality.

But, again, is this antagonism/impossibility an ahistorical a priori? The Lacanian answer seems easy to me: it is of course not eternal, but it is constitutive of human sexuality. We can of course imagine an asexual reproduction, or a life with a different modality of pleasures, but in this case we are simply no longer dealing with sexuality. It's exactly like with alternate modernities: one thing is to pass from one to another form of "modernity" (capitalist political power), say from liberal democracy to Fascism or authoritarian populism, which are just different ways of dealing with the underlying antagonism that defines capitalism; another thing is to break out of the very field of modernity inclusive of its constitutive antagonism. This is the point on which one should insist: if and when we enact the radical change of stepping out of the entire field defined by its constitutive impossibility/antagonism, we do not "historicize" this impossibility in the sense that we step beyond it, that "impossible becomes possible," that we see how the impossible/real was just a kind of fetish preventing us from seeing a different reality. We do something much more radical: the "impossibility" disappears because the entire field in which it operated is no longer here.

What one should avoid here, as a good vampire avoids garlic, is any form of evolutionary empiricism—any reference to the "real" external world which, in its eternal change, gradually undermines all symbolic structures. Who knows what is out there, the only thing we can be sure is that there is an infinite number of things we don't yet know, but this "infinity of the external world" is something profoundly indifferent, in itself banal, flat and even stupid. The fact that we don't know it means just that—that we don't know it, there is no mystery here, no proper dialectics of appearance, no structural illusion in the proper dialectical sense. But the impossibility of the sexual relationship is something radically different: the "mystery" of sexuality, our structural need to supplement the lack of a fixed formula of sexual relationship with fantasmatic supplements, is constitutive of sexuality—it is what transforms animal mating into human eroticism. There is no external reality to be discovered behind this specter of fantasies; the only "mystery" is here the mystery of the form itself (in exactly the same way Marx points out that the mystery of the commodity-form is the mystery of this form itself, i.e., the rise of the form of mystery).

Here we can see how the difference between the two reals, the Real of the impossible Thing and the indifferent external reality, is fundamental for Lacan: the source of metaphysical mystification resides precisely in the confusion between the two, i.e., in the identification of the libidinal "Thing from the inner space" with the ultimate mystery of reality—one could even say, in a Kantian mode, that this identification is a necessary transcendental illusion. The external universe is not a mystery, it is just whatever it is, it only appears "a mystery" when it gets caught in the deadlocks of our libidinal economy.[45] We can evoke yet again the anecdote, repeatedly mentioned by Lacan, about Zeuxis and Parrhasius, the two painters from ancient Greece, who compete to determine who can paint a more convincing illusion.[46] First, Zeuxis produced such a realistic picture of grapes that birds tried to eat them. Next, Parrhasius won by painting a curtain on the wall of his room, so that when he showed Zeuxis the painting, he asked Parrhasius: "OK, now please pull aside the veil and show me what you painted!" In Zeuxis's painting, the illusion was so convincing that the image was taken for the real thing; in Parrhasius' painting, the illusion lay in the very notion that what the viewer saw in front of him was just a veil covering up the hidden truth . . . This is how mystery functions in a symbolic space: there is no mystery behind the veil, the only "mystery" to be explained is how to convincingly paint a veil that creates the illusion of a content hidden behind.

This anecdote about Zeuxis and Parrhasius also enables us to locate the fatal weakness of the "object-oriented-ontology" which proposes a realist ontology of objects only partially accessible to us, humans, who are one among the objects in the universe: we see (and our science measures) the phenomenal surface of things, the way they appear to us, but beneath this surface there is the hidden In-itself, the way things are independently of us. When Parrhasius displays his painting and Zeuxis asks him "Ok, can you now please open the curtain covering your painting so that I can see what you painted?", the appearance here doesn't conceal-and-indicate the hidden content, it creates the appearance that there is something behind the veil of appearance (while, effectively, there is nothing behind). In Hegelian terms, this means that we are dealing with two In-itself: the way things are really (independently of us) in itself, and the way they *appear to us to be in-itself*—every appearance implies (or, rather, creates) its own in-itself, it conceals-and-indicates a dimension of substantial reality behind its veil, and, for Hegel, we pass from substance to subject when we realize that there is nothing behind the veil, just what we (the observing subjects) put (or, rather, projected) there. "Object-oriented-ontology" ignores this duality, it identifies these two in-itself; its "transcendence" (reality in itself) is therefore immanent, transcendentally constituted, i.e., what it conceives as the In-itself is subjectively constituted, it emerges within a given horizon of meaning.

So, to conclude, I agree with Tupinamba's general point about the problematic nature of Lacan's philosophical commitments, but I see this limitation of Lacan in the opposite direction: it is not that Lacan tended to subsume the indifferent external real onto the immanent psychic-libidinal Real-Thing, it is rather that, in his last years, he remained all too obsessed with how to think the Real "in itself," in its radical externality to the Imaginary/Symbolic, refusing to draw full consequences from his own insight into how the Real has no substantial reality in itself since it is an immanent self-impediment of the Symbolic itself. The basic insight of Tupinamba is that psychoanalytic theory does not provide a universal truth of others, enabling us to circumscribe what other discourses have to ignore: there are dimensions of our lives for which the psychoanalytic discourse is mute, which are not heard in it, dimensions like political economy The case of Miller is exemplary here: in order to assert the privilege of the analytic discourse, he has to reduce politics to the level of imaginary and symbolic identifications—the proper dimension of socio-political antagonism is thus (mis)perceived as a disturbance in psychic economy and its libidinal investments. Here philosophical reflection enters: philosophy explores this relation between seen and unseen/excluded of a field (for example, it shows what modern science has to ignore in order to see what it sees). What this means is that the problem of Lacan was not that he was too much of a philosopher (or, as Althusser put it, that, instead of developing psychoanalysis into a full science, he offered just a philosophy of psychoanalysis), but that he was not enough of a philosopher.

Kurc te gleda . . . Through Lubitsch's Looking Glass

Perhaps the greatest contribution of psychoanalysis to philosophy is to bring out the reflexivity that forms the very core of the

PSYCHOANALYSIS, POLITICS AND PHILOSOPHY

Unconscious—the reflexivity that leaves traces even in everyday vulgar expressions like "kurc te gleda" in Slovene. The title of this part of the chapter is printable only in (what is for the reader) a foreign language, making sure that readers will not understand it. In Slovene it is an extremely vulgar common expression, an outburst of rage which can be roughly translated as "let a prick take a look at you" (in everyday use meaning something like "up yours"). But what if we read this expression more literally: in what sense can a penis look at you? Another expression can be of some help here, the expression every average English reader knows well: "through the looking glass," the title of Lewis Carol's sequel to his *Alice in Wonderland* which designates the strange world Alice finds when she steps through a mirror, a world in which things are not as they should be. Normally, you see in a glass a mirror-image of reality (and of yourself), but it is when you step through the glass that you enter the strange world from which the mirror-image looks back at you, and here we find the point from which "a prick looks at you." (We'll see why at the end.) Lubitsch's films are like this: in them, you as it were see our (your) reality through the looking glass—the weirdness of reality, and how this reality looks at us, how we are implied in it, inscribed into it . . . So what do we see of our society through Lubitsch's looking glass?

Theodor Adorno turned around Benedetto Croce's patronizing historicist question about "what is dead and what is alive in Hegel's dialectic?" (the title of his main work). If Hegel is really alive as a thinker, then the question to be raised today is not the historicist one of "how does Hegel's work stand with regard to today's constellation? How are we to read it, so that it will still say something to us?", but: "how do *we today* stand with regard to—in the eyes of—Hegel?" Exactly the same holds for Ernst Lubitsch—the question is: "How would our contemporaneity appear in the eyes of Lubitsch?" While I've already dealt with such a reading of our contemporary topsy-turvy world with (or, rather, through) Lubitsch,[47] I propose here a different approach to this topic: a third element will intrude between Lubitsch and our contemporary society, the thought of Hegel. From the Hegelian standpoint, thought has to appropriate reality with all its horrors in the spirit of forgiving recollection, and Lubitsch would have added that this forgiving has to be done in the spirit of comedy, the same spirit in which Lubitsch deals with the topic of sexuality. Lubitsch saw clearly that what makes sexuality inherently comical is its "mediated" character—"mediated" in the sense that the couple engaged in it is never alone: a third element is always at work in it in the form of fantasy, and the comical effect arises from the confusion between reality and fantasy as well as from the gaps that separate the two. The awareness of this gap gives rise to a special kind of metaphysical relating to the world that permeates Lubitsch's entire work.

Let's take one of Lubitsch's absolute masterpieces, *To Be or Not to Be*: it is a film about the horrors of the German occupation of Poland and the Polish resistance to the Nazis, but the events are presented through the looking glass of comical forgiveness—even bad German guys can be more witty than our good guys, even Hitler is caught in a comedy of confusions ... The Nazis remain bad, the task of destroying them remains as urgent as ever, and Lubitsch is not playing the game of forgiving them because "they are also human"—the point is rather than nobody in the film is really human. What Lubitsch does is just avoiding rigid moral condemnation—a stance needed more than ever today when one of the few artists who successfully avoid this danger is Larry David.

But is all that Lubitsch is doing in his films just a playful admission of the perversions immanent to sexuality? Recall the Slovene vulgar expression with which we began: if this were to be all he does, he would remain within the domain designated by this vulgarity, just repeatedly reminding us of how "a prick is looking back at us," i.e., of how we are caught in a circular game of sexuality.

Let's take a closer look at how "kurc te gleda."[48] This Slovene expression signals a gesture of disrespect, of refusing an unwanted demand—not so much "Fuck off" or "Fuck it" as "Fuck you!", showing someone one's penis as a sign of disrespect. In a better society, one might also say "falus te okulira"—"let the phallus oculate you (oculate means having eyes, or, more precisely, having spots or holes resembling eyes—when an animal is characterized as "ocellated," it means it has eye-like markings. In his commentary of Freud's notion of drive, Lacan remarks (with a good dosage of humor) that a subject effectively sees himself in his virile member when he all of a sudden notices that his member is glad to be seen.

The dimension of refusing the other's demand is crucial here. Worldwide protests are today triggered by a particular demand which is not what it is really about, so when those in power concede to it, our reply should be "kurc te gleda" ... Rejecting demands is also at the core of so-called "F**k It Therapy," the invention of John and Gaia Parkin, a husband-and-wife pair who woke up one day in London, said "fuck it," quit their jobs, left their home, and moved to Italy to start a retreat for their kind of therapy.[49] But "kurc te gleda" is not quite the same—for "fuck it." There are other expressions in Slovene like "jebi se" or "odjebi" (more like "fuck off"). The closest to "kurc te gleda" in English is "up yours," although there is a significant difference: "up yours" is an active gesture (performed or accompanied by the elevated middle finger) while "kurc te gleda" is a passive stance, no act is performed. This vulgar Slovene outburst of annoyance perfectly reproduces the structure of an object returning the gaze, like the sardine can mentioned by Lacan in *Seminar XI*. This point at which the object returns the gaze is the point of anamorphosis (Holbein), and anamorphosis is precisely enacted in an erection of the penis: a penis "looks at you" when erect:

> One day, I was on a small boat, with a few people from a family of fishermen in a small port ... as we were waiting for the moment to pull in the nets, an individual known as Petit-Jean ... pointed out to me something floating on the surface of the waves. It was a small can, a sardine can. It floated there in the sun, a witness to the canning industry, which we, in fact, were supposed to supply. It glittered in the sun. And Petit-Jean said to me—You see that can? Do you see it? Well, it doesn't see you! ... if what Petit-Jean said to me, namely, that the can did not see me, had any meaning, it was because in a sense, it was looking at me, all the same.[50]

There is something inherently ridiculous in seeing a man walking around or just standing with his penis erect—it sticks out as an ugly protuberance, over-extended like an anamorphic stain[51]—or, to paraphrase Lacan: "You see that prick? Do you see it? Well, it doesn't see you"—which means that it is looking at you, all the same!" In this sense, the perceiving subject is inscribed into the scene of a man with an erect penis: when a woman sees a man with an erect penis in front of her, she can presume that she is the object-cause of this erection. And the erect penis nonetheless doesn't see you—it is not an intersubjective recognition when you cause the erection, you are in a sense objectivized, depersonalized at least, ignored as subject.

One should insist on the difference between penis and vagina here: even in the standard cliché scene of sexual invitation (a naked woman lying on her back and gradually spreading her legs), the vagina is not like an erect penis, it is not looking at you, although it obviously "sees" you. So we have to resist the vulgar association of a vagina with an eye: the vagina is not ocellated since, in such a scene, the woman herself is actively looking at you, she remains an agent— in contrast to a man with an erection who is reduced to a ridiculous idiot helplessly observing what a part of his body is doing. Lubitsch draws a lot of fun from situations in which the role of the erect penis is played by the subject's exalted ideal-ego, the way he wants to appear to others, but he plays this role in such a ridiculous way that, when he gets caught in the game, he himself cannot but helplessly notice that he acts as an idiot. This is the point at which my own prick is looking back at me: I cannot but helplessly observe how stupidly I act, unable as I am to break out of the constraints of my ideal-ego . . . Is it then possible to break out of this circle where we are reduced to acting like helpless idiots? When, towards the beginning of Anouilh's *Antigone*, the heroine returns home from wandering around the garden early in the morning, she answers the Nurse's query "Where were you?" with:

Nowhere. It was beautiful. The whole world was grey when I went out. And now—you wouldn't recognize it. It's like a postcard: all pink, and green, and yellow. You'll have to get up earlier, Nurse, if you want to see the world without colors . . . The garden was lovely. It was still asleep. Have you ever thought how lovely a garden is when it is not yet thinking of men? . . . The fields were wet. They were waiting for something to happen. The whole world was breathless, waiting. I can't tell you what a roaring noise I seemed to make alone on the road. It bothered me that whatever was waiting wasn't waiting for me. I took of my sandals and slipped into a field.[52]

One should read these lines closely: when Antigone sees the world in gray, before the sunshine transforms it into a postcard kitsch, her predicament is not that of the proverbial solipsist who all of a sudden turns his head around to catch how the world is before he sees it. She didn't see the world the way it was before her eyes saw it, she saw the world *before the world returned the gaze on her*. In Lacan's terms, while walking around the garden before sunlight Antigone was looking at the world before the world was returning the gaze. To return to our vulgar Slovene saying, no prick is looking back at her—nobody is waiting for her or awaiting her, and she is afraid to make a noise not because she thinks she might disturb something but because she is aware the world is not waiting for it, so that the world would not react to her disturbance. Maybe, this is what Hegel meant when he wrote that philosophy paints reality grey on grey.

To take a step further here, there is a link between Antigone before dawn and Oedipus at Colonus who paints grey on grey (to put it in Hegel's terms) at the end of his life, but this link makes clear the contrast between the two figures: Antigone's experience of life before dawn is a suspension of the phallic dimension while Oedipus's final curse on life is a majestic assertion of this dimension at its purest. We can read Oedipus' fate in *Oedipus at Colonus* as yet another variation on Beckett's motif: "Try again, fail again, fail better." In staging his death, Oedipus at Colonus "fails better" than in his incestuous and parricidal act that brought him his destruction.

Let's elaborate this point. *Oedipus at Colonus* is a unique play in which the contours of post-human subjectivity are clearly outlined for the first time. That is to say, what if the passage from humanity to post-humanity is the passage from Oedipus to Oedipus at Colonus? If the human subject is Oedipal (with all this implies: constitution through symbolic castration, regulation of desire through the symbolic Law, etc.), post-human subject is like Oedipus at Colonus, "anti-Oedipus" or, as Lacan put it, beyond Oedipus, reduced to an excremental remainder of the signifying chain.[53] As Hegel put it, guilt is the highest honor for the tragic hero—if we deprive him of his guilt, we submit him to a thorough humiliation—and Oedipus is deprived even of this honor of guilt, which means that "he is not even allowed to participate in his fate with his desire."[54] There was no "unconscious desire" in him that pushed him to his acts, which is why, after learning what he did, he refused to act as a tragic hero and to assume his quilt. As Lacan put it repeatedly, in contrast to all of us, Oedipus is the only one without an Oedipus complex. In the usual Oedipal scenario, we compromise our desire by submitting ourselves to the symbolic Law, renouncing the true (incestuous) object of desire. Oedipus at Colonus, on the contrary, remains stubborn to the end, fully faithful to his desire, *il n'a pas cede sur son desir*: Paradoxically, Oedipus at Colonus is a subject at ease with himself: he is not a wise old man who learns the vanity of desire, he only here accedes to it fully. Lacan saw this clearly in his first seminar where he wrote about Oedipus at Colonus: "So Oedipus does exist, and he fully realized his destiny. He realized it to that final point which is nothing more than something strictly identical to a striking down, a tearing apart, a laceration of himself—he is no longer, no longer anything, at all. And it is at that moment that he says the phrase I evoked last time—*Am I made man in the hour when I cease to be?*" The precise moment Oedipus says this is when, knowing that the place of his death will profit its inhabitants, dignitaries no longer treat him as an excremental outcast but are asking for his favor: "They run after him. Hearing that he is about to receive some visit, all kinds of ambassadors, wise men, politicians, enthusiasts, his son, Oedipus then says—*Am I made man in the hour when I cease to be?*" In what sense has he ceased to be? "When the oracle's prophecy *[parole] is* entirely fulfilled, when the life of Oedipus has completely passed over into his destiny, what remains of Oedipus? That is what *Oedipus at Colonus* shows us—the essential drama of destiny, the total absence of charity, of fraternity, of anything whatsoever relating to what one calls human feeling."[55]

Lacan evokes here Mr. Valdemar from Edgar Allan Poe's story who, when awakened from death by magnetism, pronounces the terrifying impossible words: "Quick! Put me back to sleep! I am already dead." But (as Terry Eagleton pointed out) precisely as such, as excluded from all human feeling and charity, Oedipus becomes a political figure, he grounds a new powerful city-state, Athens: Oedipus at Colonus

> becomes the cornerstone of a new political order. Oedipus's polluted body signifies among other things the monstrous terror at the gates in which, if it is to have a chance of rebirth, the *polis* must recognize its own hideous deformity. This profoundly political dimension of the tragedy is given short shrift in Lacan's own meditations ... In becoming nothing but the scum and refuse of the *polis*—the "shit of the earth," as St. Paul racily describes the followers of Jesus, or the "total loss of humanity" which Marx portrays as the proletariat—Oedipus is divested of his identity and authority and so can offer his lacerated body as the cornerstone of a new social order. "Am I made a man in this hour when I cease to be?" (or perhaps "Am I to be counted as something only when I am nothing / am no longer human?"), the beggar king wonders aloud.[56]

Christ, a later beggar-king, by his death as a nothing—an outcast abandoned even by his disciples—grounds a new community of believers. Both Oedipus and Christ re-emerge by way of passing through the zero-level of being reduced to an excremental remainder—in short, what comes after the gesture of "kurc te gleda" is a new socio-political order ... The key lesson here is that revolution is not an Oedipal rebellion against a paternal figure culminating in the killing of father but an event that takes place in a post-Oedipal space, triggered by an agent who passes through the zero-level of subjective destitution and assumes excremental identification. Consequently, we should add to these two a third figure, Che Guevara from the photo after his capture in Bolivia, just before he was shot dead. Guevara's position between the soldiers who captured him, the style of his hair and the expression on his face, all give birth to an unmistakable Christological dimension:

Like Christ (and, we may add, like Salvador Allende and Victor Jara in Chile), Guevara had to die a miserable death in order to become the cult figure that he is. Through his death, he became a sacred figure where the "normal" criteria of actual achievements no longer matter—Carlos Puebla (whose most popular Guevara song is "Hasta siempre") also wrote another Guevara song, "Lo eterno (The eternal one)," which directly mobilizes the Christological echoes:

> People say, Che Guevara, / that it's a lie that you're dead. / Your presence, continuous and bright, / like a shining star, / is still on alert and ready for combat, / Comandante Che Guevara. / People like you never get erased, / both from history and from time. / How could people who are eternal die! / Since you were more than a man, / since you were the light and the example, / you will live eternally / in the hearts of the people.[57]

One can even claim that, like Christ, Guevara knowingly or unknowingly strived for death, and that he knew that his cause in Bolivia was lost. In his review of the Guevara-film *The Motorcycle Diaries*, Paul Berman critically claimed that

> the entire movie, in its concept and tone, exudes a Christological cult of martyrdom, a cult of adoration for the spiritually superior

person who is veering toward death—precisely the kind of adoration that Latin America's Catholic Church promoted for several centuries, with miserable consequences. The rebellion against reactionary Catholicism in this movie is itself an expression of reactionary Catholicism. The traditional churches of Latin America are full of statues of gruesome bleeding saints. And the masochistic allure of those statues is precisely what you see in the movie's many depictions of young Che coughing out his lungs from asthma and testing himself by swimming in cold water.[58]

To this, one should simply answer: true, but—so what? Why should revolutionary politics not take over the Catholic cult of martyrdom? The parallel with Oedipus at Colonus and Guevara makes it clear that what matters is not the pain of martyrdom as such but the step outside the symbolic circuit which defines our identity. Here we encounter the unique moment where history and eternity meet: far from being a mere withdrawal from history into the abyss of inner life, the excremental identification is necessary for a radical historical change, it renders visible the high subjective price of an authentic revolutionary act. Of course, we should be careful to note that the reversal from miserable death to glory is not direct: there is a gap between the two—it might have been the case that the death of Jesus (to use a well-known example!) would have remained an insignificant forgotten detail. An extreme expression of this can be found in the Christological content of the lyrics (written by Joan Baez to Ennio Morricone's music) of "Here's to you," which describes the final agony experienced by Christ on the cross as a "triumph." These lyrics make use of a statement attributed to Vanzetti by Philip D. Strong, a reporter for the North American Newspaper Alliance: "If it had not been for these things, I might have lived out my life talking at street corners to scorning men. I might have died, unmarked, unknown, a failure. Now we are not a failure. This is our career and our triumph. Never in our full life could we have hoped to do such work for tolerance, for justice, for man's understanding of man as we now do by accident. Our words—our lives—our pains—nothing! The taking of our lives—lives of a good shoemaker and a poor fish peddler—all! That last moment belongs to us—that agony is our triumph."[59] What one should resist here is the perverse reading of these lines: Vanzetti has consciously chosen agony (death) to achieve triumph. Such manipulation doesn't work; the passage through the zero-point counts as the new beginning only if the subject effectively assumes its excremental status—the triumph takes place later as a kind of "collateral damage." In the case of Christ, without Paul who interpreted his death on the cross as a triumph, he would remain just one in a series of largely forgotten sectarian martyrs . . .

No wonder, then, that, in a unique moment in the history of art, the dying Christ himself was portrayed in a similar way, giving an "Up yours!" to God-the-Father himself. Wolfram Hogrebe proposed such a reading of Michelangelo's unfinished drawing of Christ on the Cross which he first gave to Vittoria Colonna, his passionate intimate friend, and then inexplicably asked her to return it to him. She refused, as she was enthusiastic about the drawing, and is reported as studying it in detail with mirror and magnifying glass— as if the drawing contained some forbidden half-hidden detail Michelangelo was afraid would be discovered.[60] The drawing renders the "critical" moment of Christ's doubt and despair, of "My God, my God why have you forsaken me?"—for the first time in the history of painting, an artist tried to capture Christ's abandonment by God the Father. While Christ's eyes are turned upwards, his face does not express devoted acceptance of suffering, but desperate suffering combined with—here, some unsettling details indicate an underlying attitude of angry rebellion—defiance. The two legs are not parallel, one is slightly raised above the other, as if Christ is caught in the middle of an attempt to liberate and rise himself; but the truly shocking detail is the right hand: there are no nails to be seen, and the hand's forefinger is stretched out—a vulgar gesture which, according to Quintillian's rhetoric of gestures probably known to Michelangelo, functions as a sign of the devil's rebellious challenge. Christ's "Why?" is not resigned, but aggressive, accusatory. More precisely, there is, in the drawing, an implicit tension between the expression on Christ's face (despair and suffering) and of his hand (rebellion, defiance)—as if the hand articulates the attitude the face doesn't dare to express. Recall Goethe's formula *Nemo contra deum nisi deus ipse*—no one but god himself can stand against god, so what we get in Michelangelo's drawing is God-the-Son giving an "up yours" to his father. This, of course, is not Christ's final word: just before collapsing, he says "It is finished!" and then "Father, into thy hands I commend my spirit" (hands again!), and they should be read as a move from the aggressive "Up yours!"—not to a devoted resignation but—to an even more defiant "Kurc te gleda!" ...

This religious dimension of a radical political act is founded in a very precise fact: the triumph of a revolution is the moment when we step out of the existing economic and social order by way of suspending its main written and unwritten rules—we (try to) do what, within this order, appears impossible. We do things to which the hegemonic ideology reacts with "But you can't just do this!", we do what Brecht, in his praise of Communism, called "simple things that are hard to do"—nationalizing banks and large corporations, expanding free education and health services, providing housing for the poor, legalizing gay and LGBT+ rights, etc. Remember the first year of Allende government in Chile in 1970—they provided free meals in schools, nationalized copper mines, engaged in the construction of workers' housing, "simple things" like that ... and, we have to go to the end, in the specific conditions of that time. With brutal resistance from the local bourgeoisie supported by the US, they *had* to fail, inflation soared, etc. They had to fail not only because of the resistance of the forces of the established order but also due to an immanent reason: their failure (exemplified by the violent death of a leader) provides the point of excremental identification which gives a new force to the movement. It is meaningless to deplore the fact that revolutionaries were not pragmatic enough—this, precisely, was the point of their acts once they took over, namely to violate the existing "pragmatic rules." Whatever the new problems, the Allende government changed Chile into a "liberated territory" where, in some sense, even the air the people were breathing was different, and the problems it faced just prove the fact that, within the existing order, even doing "simple things" like providing free meals and housing for workers is impossible. Later, revolutionaries should become pragmatic, of course, but they *have* to begin with crazy simple acts. This is why Robespierre was completely correct when, in his final speech on 8

Thermidor, he pointed out that, seeing a revolution just as a series of actual events, without taking note of the sublime Idea that sustains it (or, as Badiou would have put it, of its dimension of an Event), means this revolution becomes just a "noisy crime" that destroys another crime:

> But there do exist, I can assure you, souls that are feeling and pure; it exists, that tender, imperious and irresistible passion, the torment and delight of magnanimous hearts; that deep horror of tyranny, that compassionate zeal for the oppressed, that sacred love for the homeland, that even more sublime and holy love for humanity, without which a great revolution is just a noisy crime that destroys another crime; it does exist, that generous ambition to establish here on earth the world's first Republic.[61]

We can now see how the abstract moral view—the stance of "forget about all the ideological stuff, about dreams that reverberate in a revolution, bear in mind just what effectively took place in it, and judge these facts morally"—covers up its opposite, an utter cynical indifference. So how does this look in Lubitsch? There are moments in many of Lubitsch's movies in which one can discern a similar stance. They are not moments of some mystical inner peace which signals our disengagement from reality—let's read Anouilh's key lines again: the wet fields "were waiting for something to happen. The whole world was breathless, waiting. I can't tell you what a roaring noise I seemed to make alone on the road. It bothered me that whatever was waiting wasn't waiting for me." So there IS something the world is waiting for, *it's just not me it is waiting for*. This is why Antigone doesn't want to make a noise: not in order to disturb some inner peace of the world but because her noise would not resonate . . . Remember Gandhi's famous motto: "Be the change that you wish to see in the world." The moments we are now dealing with are precisely the moments when we realize that we cannot be that change: we just have to accept the painful fact that we are not part of the Event reality is calling for.

Furthermore, recall a famous moment of discord in *Trouble in Paradise* when Gaston loses his smooth manners and explodes in anger at Marietta (who is ready to prosecute a small crook like him but not her manager for stealing her money since they both belong to the same class): at this moment, reality is rendered grey, it is deprived of all its erotic colors, there is no "Lubitsch touch" here. Gaston's anger is not directed just at Marietta but also at himself: the noise the world is waiting for, the change needed to abolish the corruption he is decrying, is the noise of a social revolution, but he knows that, due to the way he earns his living (he is a crook and thief), he only parasitizes on the existing social order. Similar discordant moments arrive in *Ninotchka*, in *To Be or Not to Be*, and especially in Lubitsch's last finished film, *Cluny Brown*, which in its entirety strikes a discordant note in Lubitsch's universe. It tells the story of Adam Belinski, a Czech refugee to England before World War II who tries to mobilize public opinion against the Fascist threat. A rich English friend invites him to his country estate where Belinski meets Cluny Brown, an ordinary girl fascinated by plumbing, and finds her spontaneity intoxicating and refreshing ... To cut a long story short, at the end, they get married and move to America where Belinski publishes a bestselling detective novel making them both rich—the struggle against Fascism simply disappears from the story, i.e., the two lovers make all the noise in order for them (and for us, viewers) NOT to hear what the world is waiting for: war against Fascism.

And, maybe, erotic love itself is something the world is not waiting for, something which makes noise only for the lovers and doesn't resonate in social reality. The illusion of love is that all reality should resonate with it—that the world returns the gaze and looks back at happy lovers; however, social reality goes on and remains grey, unaffected by the colors of love. Maybe, therein resides the hidden lesson of Lubitsch's—films, especially of *Ninotchka* which directly deals with this topic. And therein also resides the lesson of Freud: *everything is not sexual(ized), there is a space for a-sexual universal causes*—where we should read "asexual" with Lacan: what stands outside the sexual domain is *a*, the object-cause of desire that sustains our cause.

3
Surplus-Enjoyment, Or, Why We Enjoy our Oppression

Vikings, Solaris, Katla: The Big Other and its Vicissitudes

What Lacan calls "the big Other" designates a dimension beyond (or, rather, beneath) the sphere of reality and the pleasure-principle of hedonism as well as of the perfidious calculations and manipulations applied to ruthlessly reach a goal—a dimension that is also, in some sense, beyond good and evil. But this dimension can also appear in the guise of a "superficial" link of respectful friendship which cannot be reduced to egotist calculation. Let's take a perhaps unexpected but perfect example. In the TV series *Vikings*, Ragnar Lothbrok tells the Seer, an old half-blind Viking who predicts the future: "I don't believe in the gods' existence. Man is the master of his own fate, not the gods. The gods are man's creation, to give answers that men are too afraid to give themselves." The supreme case of how Ragnar acts as a master of his own fate is his plotting of his own death, turning it into his greatest victory. In season 4, Ragnar is tired and defeated: after losing battles in England and France, he returns home, bereft of his aura—he is despised and ignored, even his sons no longer believe in him. He becomes obsessed by his own death: upon his return, he challenges his sons to stab him to death and take the crown from him, which they refuse to do. Later he tries to hang himself from a tree but fails (the rope is somewhat magically bitten through by a raven who descends on the tree). At this lowest point, he elaborates a complex plan to use his own death to set his enemies up for defeat, and his sons for victory and fame. Since no volunteers are ready to join him when he announces his plan to raid England again, as revenge for the Viking community being slaughtered there, he digs out his secret treasure and bribes a group of old warriors to join him, together with his crippled son Ivar the Boneless, the only volunteer. However, soon upon landing there, Ragnar and Ivar kill all the other Vikings, and Ragnar goes with Ivar to the castle (the Roma villa) of the Wessex king Ecbert, surrendering himself to him—why?

In England, Ragnar has two main enemies, Ecbert and king Aella of Northumbria. He plundered both of their lands, but with Ecbert the situation is more complex. Ragnar made a pact with him, which obliged Ecbert to give some fertile land for a Viking settlement to Northmen who wanted to farm there; but soon after Ragnar returned to Norway, Ecbert organized the slaughter of all Viking settlers, making Ragnar look an impotent ruler in the eyes of his people. So Ragnar has to take revenge. However, since he is an old and exhausted man who cannot mobilize the Vikings for another invasion of England, he makes a cold calculation: the only thing that can mobilize the Vikings to take revenge is his horrible death there. So he surrenders to Ecbert with his son Ivar, knowing that he will be killed and that his crippled son will not be hurt but will return home with reports of his terrible death, which will mobilize all his sons and even all Vikings to invade England. He tricks Ecbert into believing that his crime—slaughtering the Viking settlers—is forgiven and offers him a deal: Ecbert would hand him over to Aella for execution and let Ivar go free, so that the Viking invasion will leave Wessex in peace and focus just on destroying Aella. (Since Aella really hates Ragnar, it is also clear that he will put Ragnar to death in a horrible way that will enrage the Vikings.) However, when he is saying goodbye to Ivar, he whispers him that the Vikings should take revenge not only on Aella but even more on Ecbert, which is exactly what happens. (But there are signs that Ecbert did not really believe Ragnar's lie: he knows the Vikings will take revenge on him too—that's why he awaits them alone in his Villa when they arrive, ready to die like Ragnar.) The basic goal of Ragnar's death—the destruction of both Ecbert and Aella as well as the establishment of a large Viking settlement in England—is thus achieved.[1]

However, their similar personalities and their shared love for Athelstan, a monk torn between the Viking paganism and Christianity, mean that Ragnar and Ecbert have a great deal of respect for each other. There is between the two a bond of friendship and genuine intellectual exchange—after Ragnar's surrender to Ecbert, the two spend long hours drinking and engaged in existential debates where, among other things, Ragnar admits that he is an atheist. The mystery is not only why Ragnar returned to Ecbert and surrendered himself to him (this can be explained by Ragnar's plot of revenge), but why Ecbert receives him without surprise: "Why did it take you so long to come?" Ecbert does not refer here to return as an act of revenge—he expected Ragnar to come back to him alone. So it is too easy to say that Ragnar just faked friendship with Ecbert to pursue his plot: the joy of their encounter is genuine.[2]

There is another excess in Ragnar which cannot be accounted for in the terms of a cunning plot: his wish to die (twice before, he has attempted to kill himself). And, again, after Ragnar's death, Ecbert displays the same excess. He is present at Ragnar's final moments, anonymous in a crowd of observers and deeply shaken. When, after defeating and killing Aella, the Viking forces approach the Wessex seat of power (the "Villa")—all residents are evacuated to a safe terrain beyond the reach of the Vikings, except Ecbert who remains in the palace alone, waiting for Ragnar's sons to arrive and exact revenge on him. (As a special favour, they don't subject him to blood eagle, as Ivar wants, but allow him to choose his own death—he cuts his wrists in his Roman pool—but in exchange he has to designate a Viking as his royal successor.) Why did he surrender to the Vikings alone (exactly as Ragnar surrendered alone to him), when he could have escaped them with the others?

While Ragnar's plot of planning his spectacular death can be read as a pagan appropriation of the Christian sacrifice, the two excesses over cunning manipulation of one's opponent point to another dimension. Although they appear unrelated to one another (what could a wish to die have to do with genuine intellectual exchange and friendship?), there is a link between the two: they are both located beyond the pleasure principle and its supplement, the reality principle, i.e., neither can be accounted for in terms of a pursuit of political or social goals of power and domination. The point is not that beyond their mutual manipulation Ragnar and Ecbert really loved each other, the point is that the very *form* of their interaction is irreducible to its content (revenge, etc.): although for both of them their polite interaction is just a form, a mask for the ruthless realization of their interests (which include the destruction of the partner), there is more truth in this form (mask) than in the raw egotist content beneath it.[3]

This form, which contains its own truth prior to and independent of the content transmitted by it, is what Lacan called the "big Other"—say, if I address my partner respectfully, the respectful form establishes a certain intersubjective relation which persists even if my address serves just to deceive my partner. The big Other is as such a purely virtual identity: it doesn't contain any deeper truth of mine, its truth is its form itself. However, as Lacan insists, "there is no big Other," which means not only that the big Other is virtual, with no substantial reality of its own, but that it is in itself inconsistent/incomplete, perforated by gaps. These gaps are filled by another version of the big Other: a fantasmatic apparition of the big Other as a real Thing in the guise of the so-called Id-machine, a mechanism that directly materializes our unacknowledged fantasies. This possesses a long, if not always respectable, pedigree. In cinema, it all began with Fred Wilcox's *The Forbidden Planet* (1956), which transposed onto a distant planet the story-skeleton of Shakespeare's *The Tempest*: a mad-genius scientist living alone with his daughter (who had never met another man) on an island. Their peace is disturbed by the arrival of a group of space-travelers. Strange attacks of an invisible monster soon start to occur, and, at the film's end, it becomes clear that this monster is nothing but the materialization of the father's destructive impulses against the intruders who disturbed his incestuous peace. The Id-machine that, unbeknownst to the father, generates the destructive monster is a gigantic mechanism beneath the surface of this distant planet, the mysterious remnants of some past civilization that succeeded in developing such a machine for the direct materialization of one's thoughts and thus destroyed itself . . . Here, the Id-machine is firmly set in a Freudian libidinal context: the monsters it generates are the realizations of the primordial father's incestuous destructive impulses against other men who threaten his symbiosis with the daughter.[4]

The ultimate variation of the Id-machine is arguably Andrei Tarkovsky's *Solaris*, based on Stanislaw Lem's novel, in which this

Thing is also related to the deadlocks of sexual relationship.[5] *Solaris* is the story of a space agency psychologist Kelvin, sent to a half-abandoned spaceship above a newly discovered planet Solaris, where strange things have recently been taking place (scientists going mad, hallucinating and killing themselves). Solaris is a planet with an oceanic fluid surface which moves incessantly and, from time to time, imitates recognizable forms, not only elaborate geometric structures, but also gigantic child bodies or human buildings; although all attempts to communicate with the planet fail, scientists entertain the hypothesis that Solaris is a gigantic brain which somehow reads our minds. Soon after his arrival, Kelvin finds his dead wife, Harey, at his side in his bed. Harey had killed herself years ago on Earth after he had abandoned her. He is unable to shake Harey off. All attempts to get rid of her fail miserably (after he sends her into space in a rocket, she rematerializes the next day); analysis of her tissue demonstrates that she is not composed of atoms like normal human beings—beneath a certain micro-level, there is nothing, just void. Finally, Kelvin grasps that Harey is a materialization of his own innermost traumatic fantasies. This accounts for the enigma of strange gaps in Harey's memory— of course she doesn't know everything a real person is supposed to know, because she is not such a person, but a mere materialization of *his* fantasmatic image of her in all its inconsistency. The problem is that, precisely because Harey has no substantial identity of her own, she acquires the status of the Real that forever insists and returns to its place: like fire in Lynch's films, she forever "walks with the hero," sticks to him, never lets him go. Harey, this fragile specter, pure semblance, *cannot ever be erased*—she is "undead," eternally recurring in the space between the two deaths. Are we thus not back at the standard Weiningerian anti-feminist notion of the woman as a symptom of man, a materialization of his guilt (his fall into sin) who can only deliver him (and herself) by her suicide? *Solaris* thus relies on science-fiction rules to enact in reality itself, to present as a material fact, the notion that woman merely materializes a male fantasy: the tragic position of Harey is that she becomes aware that she is deprived of all substantial identity, that she is Nothing in herself, since she only exists as the Other's dream—it is this predicament that imposes suicide as her ultimate ethical act: becoming aware of how Kelvin suffers on account of her permanent presence, Harey finally destroys herself by swallowing a chemical that will prevent her recomposition. (The ultimate horror scene of the movie takes place when the spectral Harey reawakens from her first failed suicide attempt on Solaris: after ingesting liquid oxygen, she lies on the floor, deeply frozen; then, suddenly, she starts to move, her body twitching in a mixture of erotic beauty and abject horror, enduring unbearable pain. Is there anything more tragic than such a scene of failed self-erasure, when we are reduced to the obscene slime which, against our will, persists in the picture?) The Weiningerian ontological denigration of woman as a mere "symptom" of man—as the embodiment of male fantasy, as the hysterical imitation of the true male subjectivity—is, when openly admitted and fully assumed, far more subversive that the false direct assertion of feminine autonomy; perhaps, the ultimate feminist statement is to proclaim openly "I do not exist in myself, I am merely the Other's fantasy embodied" . . .

What we have in *Solaris* are thus Harey's *two* suicides: the first (in her earlier earthly "real" existence, as Kelvin's wife), and then her second suicide, the heroic act of the self-erasure of her very spectral undead existence: while the first suicidal act was a simple escape from the burden of life, the second is a proper ethical act. In other words, if the first Harey, before her suicide on Earth, was a "normal" human being, the second is a Subject in the most radical sense of the term, precisely insofar as she is deprived of the last vestiges of her substantial identity (as she says in the film: "No, it's not me . . . It's not me . . . I'm not Harey . . . Tell me . . . tell me . . . Do you find me disgusting because of what I am?"). The difference between Harey who appears to Kelvin and the "monstrous Aphrodite" who appears to Gibarian, one of Kelvin's colleagues on the spaceship (in the novel, not in the film: in the film, Tarkovsky replaced her with a small innocent blonde girl), is that Gibarian's apparition does not come from "real life" memory, but from pure fantasy: "A giant Negress was coming silently towards me with a smooth, rolling gait. I caught a gleam from the whites of her eyes and heard the soft slapping of her bare feet. She was wearing nothing but a yellow skirt of plaited straw; her enormous breasts swung freely and her black arms were as thick as thighs."[6] Unable to sustain confrontation with his primordial fantasmatic apparition, Gibarian dies of shame.

Is the planet around which the story turns, composed of the mysterious matter which seems to think, i.e. which in a way is the direct materialization of Thought itself, not again an exemplary case of the Lacanian Thing as the "Obscene Jelly,"[7] the traumatic Real, the point at which symbolic distance collapses, the point at which there is no need for speech, for signs, since, in it, thought directly intervenes in the Real? This gigantic Brain, this Other-Thing, involves a kind of psychotic short-circuit: in short-circuiting the dialectic of question and answer, of demand and its satisfaction, it provides—or, rather, imposes on us—the answer before we even raise the question, directly materializing our innermost fantasies which support our desire. Solaris is a machine that generates/materializes in reality itself my ultimate fantasmatic objectal supplement/partner that I would never be ready to accept in reality, although my entire psychic life turns around it.

Jacques-Alain Miller[8] draws the distinction between the woman who assumes her non-existence, her constitutive lack, i.e. the void of subjectivity in her very heart, and what he calls *la femme a postiche*, the fake, phony woman. This *femme a postiche* is not what common sense conservative wisdom would tell us (a woman who distrusts her natural charm and abandons her vocation of rearing children, serving her husband, taking care of the household, etc., and indulges in the extravagances of fashionable dressing and make-up, of decadent promiscuity, of career, etc.), but almost its exact opposite: the woman who takes refuge from the void in the very heart of her subjectivity, from the "not-having-it" which marks her being, in the phony certitude of "having it" (of serving as the stable support of family life, of rearing children, her true possession, etc.)—this woman gives the impression (and has the false satisfaction) of a firmly anchored being, of a self-enclosed life, satisfied in the circuit of everyday life (her man has to run around wildly, while she leads a calm life and serves as the safe protective rock or safe haven to which her man can always return . . .). (The most elementary form of "having it" for a woman is, of course, having a child, which is why, for Lacan, there is an ultimate antagonism between Woman and Mother: in contrast to woman who "n'existe pas," mother definitely *does* exist.) The interesting feature to be noted here is that, contrary to the commonsensical expectation, it is the woman who "has it," the self-satisfied *femme a postiche* disavowing her lack, who not only does not pose any threat to the patriarchal male identity, but even serves as its protective shield and support, while, in contrast to her, it is the woman who flaunts her lack ("castration"), i.e., who functions as a hysterical composite of semblances covering a Void, that poses the serious threat to male identity. In other words, the paradox is that the more the woman is denigrated, reduced to an inconsistent and insubstantial composite of semblances around a Void, the more she threatens the firm male substantial self-identity (Otto Weininger's entire work centers on this paradox); and, on the other hand, the more the woman is a firm, self-enclosed Substance, the more she supports male identity.

Solaris supplements this standard, although disavowed, male scenario with a key feature: this structure of woman as a symptom of man can be operative only insofar as the man is confronted with his Other Thing, a decentered opaque machine which "reads" his deepest dreams and returns them to him as his symptom, as his own message in its true form that the subject is not ready to acknowledge. It is here that one should reject the Jungian reading of *Solaris*: the point of Solaris is not simply projection, materialization of the (male) subject's disavowed inner impetuses; what is much more crucial is that, if this "projection" is to take place, the impenetrable Other Thing must already be here—the true enigma is the presence of this Thing. The problem with Tarkovsky is that he himself obviously opts for the Jungian reading according to which the external journey is merely the externalization and/or projection of the initiatic journey into the depth of one's psyche. Apropos of *Solaris*, he stated in an interview:

> Maybe, effectively, the mission of Kelvin on Solaris has only one goal: to show that love of the other is indispensable to all life. A man without love is no longer a man. The aim of the entire "solaristic" is to show humanity must be love.[9]

In clear contrast to this, Lem's novel focuses on the inert external presence of the planet Solaris, of this "Thing which thinks" (to use

Kant's expression, which fully fits here): the point of the novel is precisely that Solaris remains an impenetrable Other with no possible communication with us—true, it returns us our innermost disavowed fantasies, but the "Que vuoi?" beneath this act remains thoroughly impenetrable (Why does It do it? As a purely mechanical response? To play demonic games with us? To help us—or compel us—to confront our disavowed truth?). Nowhere is this gap between the novel and the film more perceptible than in their different endings: at the novel's end, we see Kelvin alone on the spaceship, staring into the mysterious surface of the Solaris ocean, while the film ends with the archetypal Tarkovskian fantasy of combining within the same shot the Otherness into which the hero is thrown (the chaotic surface of Solaris) and the object of his nostalgic longing, the home *dacha* (Russian wooden country house) to which he longs to return, the house whose contours are encircled by the malleable slime of Solaris' surface—within the radical Otherness, we discover the lost object of our innermost longing.

The latest endeavor in portraying the Id-machine is *Katla*,[10] an Icelandic television series which complicates the logic of Id-machine, making it morally much more ambiguous. *Katla* is set in Vik, a small Icelandic town located on the precipice of Katla, an active volcano which has been active for over a year, so Vik is covered by constantly raining ash. Most of the villagers have already migrated out of the place, leaving behind some stubborn folks. The story sets in motion when people who were presumed dead suddenly start returning from somewhere near the volcano, covered in a mixture of ash and clay—how and why? In episode 7 Darri—a geologist from Reykyavik—heads beneath the glacier to investigate the meteorite in the volcano; after collecting some rock samples, he deduces that this meteorite which crashed down to Earth a long time ago has a strange, alien, life-giving element within it. This element enables the meteorite to detect the most intense emotional feelings that each of the townsfolk has and uses them to recreate the people that are missing. These replicas are molded by the thoughts people have about them: they are a more exaggerated version of their real counterparts, clinging to the main trait that made them come into being, as a kind of more direct realization of the Platonic idea of a person. The reason for their return is provided by local folklore according to which a changeling appears for a purpose, and vanishes once its purpose is served.

Here are the main cases that take place in the first season of the series. Police Chief Gisli's wife who lies bedridden in a hospital creates her own changeling: she makes the humanoid out of the memories of her past when she was not bedridden; this brings the estranged couple back together again . . . To Grima, the protagonist of the series, a changeling of her deceased sister Asa appears. Following Asa's death, Grima had lived in a state of permanent depression, obsessed by the memory of Asa's sad fate, so she created Asa's changeling to help her cope with her disappearance (death)—this was the purpose for which Asa reappeared . . . But then a changeling of Grima herself appeared, created by her husband Kjartan who wanted to feel the warmth of Grima again. Out of his memories, he made Grima's changeling the way Grima was before the disappearance of Asa. Hence, Grima's changeling was much more happy and affectionate because the tragedy never struck her. The real Grima is conscious enough to realize this, so she confronts her changeling and challenges her to a game of Russian roulette. The real Grima doesn't survive the game, so her changeling takes her place with affection, warmth, and gentleness without anyone noticing the difference. The original Grima's dead body is covered with ash and buried outside their house.

A 20 years younger changeling of Gunhild is created by Gunhild herself who blamed herself for her son's (Bjorn's) genetic disability—she wanted to go back in time (the time she was pregnant twenty years before) and to reverse the pain she caused to her child due to her carelessness and her thoughts of abortion. In the end, her husband Thor tells her it wasn't her fault: the syndrome was genetic, and therefore Gunhild had little to contribute to Bjorn's defect. In her final visit to the hospital to see Bjorn, after learning about the disappearance of the changeling, Gunhild looks in a mirror and smiles—she finally comes out of her remorse; the purpose for which the changeling was created has been fulfilled.

So why does Mikael, the son of Darri and Rakel, reappear? Since the meteorite creates mutants based on the thoughts and feelings of those closest to them, Mikael can only remember things that Darri and Rakel remember about him. Darri always believed that his son Mikael was a dangerous madman, and the changeling is more in line with Darri's interpretation than with the real Mikael. Both parents agree that their real son is dead and that this specter in front of them is just an aberration, so they lead him by the hand into the sea and drown him while he begs them not to ... The action brings them closer together, which indirectly fulfills Darri's thoughts, as he had blamed Mikael for his divorce.

So what returns from Katla in the guise of changelings? Recall Ragnar saying to Ecbert: *"The gods are man's creation, to give answers that men are too afraid to give themselves."* In this sense (and in this sense only) Katla is divine: it is returning to individuals who remain in Vik what they are "too afraid to give themselves." In other words, Katla rather brings out the dark side of the divine: when a changeling appears to a subject, the subject doesn't get a sublime confrontation with its inner truth; this appearance is rather grounded in a brutal egotist calculation. In the case of Darri and Rakel, the two parents kill a changeling who nonetheless exists as a self-conscious living being—they conveniently ignore this fact and commit a cold-blooded murder just to re-establish their relationship. In the same vein, Kjartan coldly accepts the changeling as his old-new wife: she better suits his purposes since, she is just his imagination materialized.

Does this mean that I have to learn to distinguish between the reality of my partner and my fantasy of him/her, so that I can deal with my partner's reality without projecting my fantasies on him/ her? What complicates things is that each of us IS also what others think/dream he/she is. In other words, it is not enough to say that the split between my partner and his/her changeling is the split between the reality of my partner and my idea/projection of him/ her: this distinction is immanent to my partner him/herself. In a key scene of *Katla*, Kjartan moves around his house having conversations with both versions of Grima (the real Grima who, after twenty years, returns from Sweden, and her changeling who looks like she did twenty years earlier) without realizing that there are actually two of them—is this not what happens to us all the time? When an ordinary anti-Semite talks to a Jew, is he not doing exactly the same thing? In his perception and interaction, the reality of the Jew in front of him is inextricably mixed with his fantasies about Jews (say, if the Jew counts some money to return it to me, I will perceive this as an expression of an intense Jewish stance towards money...). However—and this is the crucial point—we cannot simply distinguish between "real" Jews and the way they are perceived by others: thousands of years of the exclusion and persecution of the Jews, and all the fantasies projected onto Jews, have inevitably also affected their identity which is formed in reaction to the fantasies grounding their persecution.

The general point to be made here is that the gap between me and my symbolic identity is not external to me—this means that I am symbolically castrated. And one should be careful not to dismiss this image of what I am for others just as a form of alienation, of something that I should abandon in order to arrive at my true self: it is easy to imagine a situation in which others trust in me and see me as a hero while I am full of doubts and weaknesses, so it takes a great effort for me to overcome my weaknesses and act at the level of what others see in and expect from me.

The moral ambiguity of changelings in *Katla* resides in the fact that they don't simply serve a precise purpose or goal: the Thing-Katla is a machine which just blindly realizes our fantasy, and we humans opportunistically use it to suit our egotist purposes—what we ignore is the subjectivity that pertains to changeling itself. Here, we should read *Katla* through *Solaris* and focus on the moment of subjectivation of the changeling who has no autonomy since its psyche contains only what others thought about it. In the Millerian distinction between *femme a postiche* (the fake) and the woman who assumes the void of her inexistence, it is only the changeling who, at the point of assuming its non-existence, emerges as a pure subject deprived of its substance, while the "real" woman remains a fake. In other words, the authentic position is that of a changeling who becomes aware that it only materializes another's fantasy, that it only exists insofar as an another fantasizes about it. Can one imagine a more anxiety-provoking existential situation than that of being aware that my being has no substantial support, that I exist only insofar as I am part of another's dream—as Deleuze wrote decades ago, if you are caught in another's dream, you are fucked.

Are changelings, therefore, beings who fit the criteria of Berkeley's subjective idealism—they exist only insofar as they are in the thoughts of another mind? We have to introduce here a further key complication: what if existence as such implies a certain non-knowledge? This paradoxical relation between being and knowing introduces a third term in the standard opposition between ordinary materialism for which things exist independently of our knowledge of them, and subjectivist idealism with its *esse = percipi* (things exist only insofar as they are known or perceived by a mind): things that only exist insofar as they are NOT known. The most uncanny case of this link between being and not-knowing is provided by one of the best known Freudian dreams, the one about the apparition of a "father who didn't know he is dead"—for Freud, the full formula of the dream is thus: "Father doesn't know *(that I wish)* that he is dead." The elision of the signifier *(that I wish)* registers the subject's (dreamer's) desire. However, what gets lost in such a standard reading is the uncanny effect of the scene of a father who doesn't know he is dead—of an entity which is alive only because it is not aware of being dead.

So what if we read this dream following Lacan's re-reading of the Freudian dream about the dead son who appears to his father, uttering a terrifying reproach: "Father, can't you see that I am burning?" What if we interpret the wish for the father to be dead not as the repressed unconscious wish, but as the pre-conscious problem that bothered the dreamer? The dynamic of the dream is thus the following: the dreamer invents the dream to quell his (preconscious) guilt-feeling for wishing his father dead while he was nursing him; but what he encounters in the dream is something much more traumatic than his preconscious death-wish, the figure of a father who is still alive because he doesn't know that he is dead, the obscene specter of the undead father. Lacan shifts the focus from the fascinating figure of the father who "doesn't know he is dead" to the question that lurks in the background: to the *other* subject (the dreamer to whom the father appears, in this case) who *does* know that the father is dead, and, paradoxically, in this way *keeps him alive by not telling him that he is dead*. Recall the archetypal scene from cartoons: a cat walks floating in the air above the precipice, and it falls only after it looks down and becomes aware of how it has no support beneath its feet—the dreamer is like a person who draws the cat's attention to the abyss beneath its feet, so that when father learns he is dead, he actually drops dead. This outcome is, of course, experienced by the dreamer as the ultimate catastrophe, so his entire strategy is directed at protecting the other/father from knowledge— the protection that goes up to self-sacrifice: "Oh! may that never happen! May I die rather than have him know." This brings us to one of the fundamental functions of sacrifice: one sacrifices oneself to prevent the Other from knowing. Is this not Roberto Benigni's *La vita e bella* is about? The father sacrifices himself so that his son would not know (that they are in a death camp), i.e., the father's reasoning can be rendered again by Lacan's words: "May I die rather than have him know that we are in a death camp!"

The psychoanalytic notion of symptom designates such a reality which subsists only insofar as something remains unsaid, insofar as its truth is not articulated in the symbolic order—which is why the proper psychoanalytic interpretation has effects in the real, i.e., it can dissolve the symptom … While such a notion of reality may appear to be an exemplary case of idealist madness, one should not miss its materialist core: reality is not simply external to thought/ speech, to the symbolic space. Reality thwarts this space from within, making it incomplete and inconsistent—the limit that separates the real from the symbolic is simultaneously external and internal to the symbolic.

The question is: how are we to think the structure (the Other) so that a subject emerges from it? Lacan's answer is: as an inconsistent, non-All, symbolic structure articulated around a constitutive void/impossibility. More precisely, subject emerges through the structure's reflective self-relating which inscribes into the structure itself its constitutive lack—this inscription *within* the structure of what is constitutively *excluded* from it is "the signifier which represents the subject for other signifiers."

But aren't we here caught in a contradiction? I exist only insofar as I am another's fantasy, AND I exist only insofar as I elude others' grasp? The solution: a stone exists when nobody thinks about it— but a stone is just indifferent towards being-thought-about or not; in the case of a subject, its existence is correlated to being-thought, but being-thought incompletely. I am a lack in Other's thought, a lack which is immanent to the thought. One has to take this claim literally: I am not a substantial entity that the big Other (the symbolic order) cannot fully integrate/symbolize, this impossibility of the big Other to integrate me IS myself (that's why Lacan talks about the barred subject, $). There is a subject insofar as the Other doesn't know it, and subject is inscribed into the Other through S_1, the master-signifier which reflexively marks in it the lack of a signifier. What this means is that subject is not the real person behind the symbolic mask but the self-awareness of the mask itself in its distance towards the real person.

This also accounts for why the minimal number in an intersubjective communication is not two but three: when two meet, they are BOTH divided into their self-experience and their symbolic identity, and this redoubling can only function if a third moment is operative, the big Other which is not reducible to the two. Recall the old Alphonse Allais's story of Raoul and Marguerite who arrange to meet at a masked ball: when they recognize each other's mask they withdraw to a hidden corner, pull off their masks, and—surprise—he discovers she is not Marguerite and she that he is not Raoul ... such a double missed encounter is, of course, a logical nonsense: if he is not Raoul, how could he have expected to see Marguerite and then be surprised by not seeing her real face, and vice versa? The surprise only works when only one of the partners is deceived in this way. Does something like a double deception not happen in real life, however? I arrange to meet a person whom I know and who knows me, and, in an intense exchange, I discover that he is not the one I thought him to be and he discovers that I am not the one he thought me to be ... The real surprise is here my own: the fact that the other doesn't recognize me means that I am not myself.

But we still recognize each other because the mask I am wearing for others (the mask embodying what others think of me) and the mask the other is wearing for me (embodying what I think of him) are in some senses more truthful than what is behind the mask. How can this be? Here the dimension of the big Other enters: the mutual "what do others think of me" (what do I think of him, what does he think of me) is replaced by (or sublated in) "what does the big Other (a virtual entity presupposed by both of us) think of me and him."

Back to *Katla*, we can thus say that, in the case of an Id-machine, a changeling represents (not an other but) me (its creator) for the others—although it is the image on an other, it stands for me, for my fantasy universe. As such, a changeling signals a malfunctioning of the symbolic big Other: the big Other is no longer a virtual symbolic space, it is a real Thing, a mega-object which no longer possesses its own truth as form, it just materializes our repressed content. This is why the Id-machine is more real that the big Other (it is part of reality) and simultaneously more subjective than the intersubjective space proper of the big Other (the Thing mirrors/realizes our subjective fantasies). The Id-machine is a first step towards the prospect of a wired brain, an Other which fully exists and desubjectivizes me since in it, the very limit of external reality falls.

The best-known project in this direction is Neuralink, a neurotechnology company founded by Elon Musk and eight others, and dedicated to developing implantable brain-computer interfaces (BCIs), also called a neural-control interface (NCIs), mind-machine interface (MMIs), or direct neural interface (DNIs)—all these terms indicate the same idea of a direct communication pathway, first between an enhanced or wired brain and an external device, and then between brains themselves. What kind of apocalypse announces itself by the prospect of so-called "post-humanity" opened up by a direct link between our brain and a digital machine, what the New Age obscurantists call Singularity, the divine-like global space of shared awareness? One should resist the temptation to proclaim the prospect of a wired brain an illusion, something that we are still far away from and that cannot really be actualized: such a view is itself an escape from the threat, from the fact that something New and unheard-of is effectively emerging. One should approach this threat coldly and raise the question: is there a dimension which will elude its grasp. Ranciere's term "the paradigm of the dreaming cogito"[11] nicely brings together the two dimensions that escape the total objectivization of neuralink: cogito and the domain of dreams where the unconscious persists. When Lacan famously claimed that cogito is the subject of the unconscious, he meant precisely such a "dreaming cogito" as the hidden obverse of the rational self-transparent cogito.[12]

One thing is certain: we should not underestimate the shattering impact of collectively shared experience—even if it will be realized in a much more modest way than today's grandiose visions of Singularity, everything will change with it.[13] Why? Because with neuralink, the big Other is no longer an enigmatic Thing outside us (like Solaris or Katla): we are directly IN the Thing, we float in it, we lose the distance that separates us from external reality.

This, then, is what *Katla* is about: a community (of a small town) is in crisis due to a natural disaster, only a few residents remain there whose symbolic links are deeply disturbed; they can no longer rely on the big Other as the neutral space of symbolic exchanges, and, to supplement this failure, they become increasingly caught up in the cobweb of mutual fantasies which intrude into their reality, so that this reality is losing its consistency. Id-machine is a fiction, of course, but it is a fiction with real effects, and we can observe and measure these effects in how many people react to the pandemic or to heat domes and floods: in conspiracy theories and other paranoiac constructs, changeling-like entities are treated like part of reality. The potentially liberating aspect of the appearance of changelings is that what is in our usual experience conflated (a person in front of us and our fantasy projections onto her/him) gets clearly separated, which makes the job of critique somewhat easier.

The fact that Id-machine signals the failure of virtual big Other does not mean that it appears only exceptionally: the big Other is in itself failed, inconsistent, which means that, in one form or another, it always engenders the Id-machine as its supplement. When the big Other fails, the Id-machine is a kind of defense-pathology, a pathological formation which prevents full regression into psychosis. In this sense, the relationship between the big Other and the Id-machine is homologous to that between the symbolic Law and superego: superego is also a structural imperfection of the Law, a pathological formation which prevents the dissolution of the Law.

The Birth of the Superego Out of the Breakage of the Law

When Freud elaborated the complex interaction between Ego, Superego and Id (to which one should add I as different from Ego, and a moral Law as different from Superego), his starting point is the strange phenomenon of the "unconscious sense of guilt" which

> sets us fresh problems, especially when we gradually come to see that in a great number of neuroses an unconscious sense of guilt of this kind plays a decisive economic part and puts the most powerful obstacles in the way of recovery. If we come back once more to our scale of values, we shall have to say that not only what is lowest but also what is highest in the ego can be unconscious.[14]

Or, as Freud puts it later in the same text: "If anyone were to put forward the paradoxical proposition that normal man is not only far more immoral than he believes but also far more moral than he knows, Psycho-analysis, on whose findings the first half of the assertion rests, would have no objection to raise against the second half."[15] (One should note here the use of the opposition between belief and knowledge: a normal man is more immoral than he *believes* and more moral than he *knows*.) It is not that Superego is the agent of morality and Id the reservoir of dark "evil" drives, but it is also not that Superegop stands for internalized social oppression and Id for drives that should be liberated. Freud always insisted on the dark hidden link between Superego and Id: not only is the unbearable pressure of the Superego sustained by the energy from the Id, we can also be more moral than we know. Imagine a typical postmodern permissive individual who perceives himself as a tolerant egotist searching for all kind of pleasures: a closer look quickly reveals that his activity is regulated by taboos and prohibitions he is not aware of.

However, this unconscious morality is not limited to pathological inhibitions of which my Ego is not aware; it also includes ethical miracles such as a resistance to commit an act I consider unacceptable even if I will pay the ultimate price for my refusal. Think of Antigone—and remember that Lacan, in his reading of her figure, does NOT do what one would expect from an analyst (looking for some pathological fixation, traces of incestuous desire, etc.), but precisely tries to save the ethical purity of her NO to Creon. Or think of an irrepressible commandment one feels to do something suicidally heroic—one does it simply because one cannot not do it (risk one's life in public protests, joining resistance against a dictatorship or occupation, helping others in natural catastrophes). Here, again, one should resist the obvious pseudo-psychoanalytic temptation to search for some "deeper" pathological motivation that would explain such acts (say, a combination of death-drive with narcissism). Think, today, of thousands of underpaid health-care people who help the infected, well aware that they are risking their lives, and of volunteers who offer their help—they are much more numerous than those who submitted themselves to brutal tyrants. This is also the reason why Lacan claims that the status of the Freudian unconscious is ethical: for Lacan, Kant's moral Law is desire at its purest.

It is against this background that we can answer the question: how does the a-sexual social space come to distinguish itself from the domain of libidinally cathexed interactions? One should locate this question in the context of Freud's reactions to the Great War. Today, one tends to forget the traumatic impact of this war which shattered the very foundations of European trust in progress and gave birth to phenomena such as Communism and Fascism. Even Freud, whose theory of the unconscious libidinal processes seemed to prepare him well for the explosion of "irrational" violence, felt the need to radically reformulate his basic theoretical premises. He dealt with the problem in three steps. First, in his "Beyond the Pleasure Principle" (1920), he introduced the notion of death-drive to account for dreams and acts which generate no pleasure but only pain. Then, in *Crowd Psychology and the Analysis of the Ego* (1921), he analyzed the formation of social groups which bring individuals to forsake their "rational" behavior and surrender to self-destructive violence. Hans Kelsen, the leading Austrian legal philosopher, reproached Freud that his theory of crowd-formation cannot account for social formations held together by normative structures, and, in reaction to Kelsen's critique, Freud wrote "The Ego and the Id" (1923) where he directly addresses our question: the operator of the a-sexualization of social space is superego.

In his superb essay "The Invention of the Superego,"[16] Etienne Balibar deals with the dialogue between Freud and Hans Kelsen. The irony is that the title *The Ego and the Id* is in some sense deceiving: the crucial new term introduced in the booklet is superego which forms a triad with Ego and Id, and the main point of Freud's detailed analysis is how superego, the instance of our psychic life that acts as a self-critical conscience, internalizing social standards mostly learned from parents and teachers, draws its libidinal energy from the darkest sadistic and masochistic depths of the Id. However, Lacan has convincingly shown that there is a confusion in Freud: the title of the third chapter of *The Ego and the Id* is "The Ego and the Super-Ego (Ego-Ideal)", so Freud tends to use these two terms as synonyms (conceiving the Ego-Ideal as a forerunner of the Superego), plus he also uses Ego-Ideal and ideal ego as interchangeable terms. The premise of Lacan's clarification is the equation between *jouissance* and superego: to enjoy is not a matter of following one's spontaneous tendencies; it is rather something we do as a kind of weird and twisted ethical duty.

Based on this equation, Lacan introduces a precise distinction between the three terms: the "ideal ego" stands for the idealized self-image of the subject (the way I would like to be, I would like others to see me); the Ego-Ideal is the agency whose gaze I try to impress with my ego image, the big Other who watches over me and propels me to give my best, the ideal I try to follow and actualize; and the superego is this same agency in its revengeful, sadistic, punishing, aspect. The underlying structuring principle of these three terms is clearly Lacan's triad Imaginary-Symbolic-Real: ideal ego is imaginary, what Lacan calls the "small other," the idealized double-image of my ego; Ego-Ideal is symbolic, the point of my symbolic identification, the point in the big Other from which I observe (and judge) myself; superego is real, the cruel and insatiable agency which bombards me with impossible demands and which mocks my failed attempts to meet them, the agency in the eyes of which I am all the more guilty, the more I try to suppress my "sinful" strivings and meet its demands. The old cynical Stalinist motto about the accused at the show trials who professed their innocence ("the more they are innocent, the more they deserve to be shot") is superego at its purest. So for Lacan superego "has nothing to do with moral conscience as far as its most obligatory demands are concerned":[17] superego is, on the contrary, the anti-ethical agency, the stigmatization of our ethical betrayal.[18]

In his critique of Freud's notion of the crowd, Kelsen as a neo-Kantian implicitly relies on the distinction between Ego-Ideal (the anonymous big Other, the symbolic order the status of which is non-psychic, i.e., which cannot be reduced to empirical psychic processes) and superego (the product of empirical psychic dynamic in an individual's interaction with others).[19] The reproach to Freud is, to simplify it, that he only provides the empirical psychic genesis of a crowd held together by a Leader—there is no space in his theory for the big Other, for the ideal symbolic order which sustains individual subjects, for the public space of institutional state authority which makes us subjects in the double meaning of the term (autonomous subject and an individual subjected to the Law). More precisely, what Freud describes is the pathological distortion of the Law, is regression into mythic crowd-psychological level: Freud describes crowd pathology (constituted through the short-circuit of I and *a*, in Lacanese), and since he lacked the notion of the Symbolic, he misses the normal-normative big Other. That's also why, from Lacan's standpoint, there is no space in Freud's triad of Ego-Superego-Id for the "pure"/barred subject ($), subject of the signifier, for the subject which is not psychic-empirical but equal to the Cartesian *cogito* or Kant's transcendental apperception: the Lacanian subject is not ego (which, for Lacan, is defined by imaginary identifications).

At this point, Balibar returns to Freud and defends him: superego as a psychic process is not just as accidental pathological distortion, it is the process which enables the subject to internalize the law, to integrate it into its psychic life as an agency which exerts an authority over him/her. As such, superego is a "pathological" supplement which necessarily accompanies the law, since the public law exists ONLY as internalized by subjects. What this means is that a subject is the subject of law only insofar as s/he remains caught in the unresolved Oedipal tensions which are the form of the interpersonal politics of power and subordination. These persisting tensions open up the subject to the authority of the Law—they push the subject to accept authority of the Law as the external (non-psychic) agency, the stable point of reference which can ease the inner-psychic tensions.

The tensions described by Freud are, of course, not simply internal to the subject but are part of the interpersonal (family) politics, power struggle—this is why Balibar points out that, in his description of the formation of a crowd and the genesis of the superego, Freud doesn't provide a "psychoanalysis of politics" (an explanation of the political dynamic of crowds through libidinal processes which are in themselves apolitical), but rather its opposite, the politics of psychoanalysis (the explanation of the rise of the triadic structure of Ego-Id-Superego through the familial "political" power struggles)—or, as Lacan put it, the Freudian Unconscious is political.

But, as Lacan repeatedly points out, the big Other of the symbolic Law must already be here if a subject is to refer to it as the neutral external space—so here we should take one step further: how can the public authority itself, in its non-psychic status, emerge? Lacan's answer is: the big Other cannot be reduced to a psychic agency, but it exists only if it is "externalized" by subjects—the "internalization" of the Law is effectively its externalization, its (presup)position as a non-psychic symbolic space. The Law is non-psychic, but it exists only if there are subjects who take it as existing. One has to be very precise here: Lacan is not providing the genesis of the big Other from psychic dynamics, his thesis is rather that the subject is constitutively divided in itself, that its psychic intimacy exists only if there is a big Other, a space alienated from the subject to which it relates. (Only in psychosis is this alienation suspended.) The subjective correlate of the big Other is the empty "barred" subject ($) which is more "intimate" than all the intimacy of even the deepest psychic processes. So we should turn around the usual notion that the "pure" abstract subject (the Cartesian *cogito*) is a kind of ideological illusion whose reality is the actual concrete individual caught and torn in psychic antagonisms: all the wealth of the individual's "inner life" is a content which ultimately just fills in the void of the pure subject—in this sense, Lacan said that the ego is the "stuff of the I".

Today, however, fathers behave more and more as ideal-egos, engaged in narcissistic competition with children—they no longer dare to assume the "authority" of a father—and, paradoxically, this process poses a serious obstacle to the emancipatory process. Let's take the case of Chile: the difficulties in the ongoing struggle there are not the legacy of Pinochet's oppressive dictatorship as such but the legacy of the gradual (fake) opening of his dictatorial regime. Particularly, through the 1990s, Chilean society underwent what we may call a fast post-modernization: an explosion of consumerist hedonism, superficial sexual permissiveness, competitive individualism, etc. Those in power realized that such atomized social space is much more effective than direct state oppression against radical Leftist projects which rely on social solidarity: classes continue to exist "in themselves" but not "for themselves," I see others from my class more as competitors than as members of a same group with solidary interests. Direct state oppression tends to unite opposition and promote organized forms of resistance, while in "postmodern" societies even extreme dissatisfaction assumes the form of chaotic revolts (from Occupy Wall Street to the gilets jaunes) which soon run out of steam, unable to reach the "Leninist" stage of an organized force with a clear program.[20]

At a more general level, this means that, if the symbolic Law (God-the-Father) loses its authority—i.e., if there is no prohibition—desire itself (sustained by the prospect of transgressing it) vanishes—this is why permissiveness kills desire. Along these lines, Pierre Legendre and some other Lacanians claim that the problem today is the decline of the God-the-Father, of the paternal symbolic authority: in its absence, pathological narcissism explodes, evoking the specter of the primordial Real Father. Consequently, we should try to restore some kind of Law as the agent of prohibition.

Although this idea is to be rejected, it correctly points out how the decline of the Master in no way automatically guarantees emancipation but can well engender much more oppressive figures of domination. Is, however, the return to Prohibition sustained by Law the only way out? It seems that the very last Lacan, aware of this problem, proposed another solution which Miller, in his reading of Lacan, calls "cynical"— we cannot return to the authority of the Law, but what we can do is act as if we sustain the Law. We should maintain its authority as necessary although we know it is not true. Adrian Johnston[21] brought out the intricacies and ambiguities of this solution:

Passage through a concluding experience of "subjective destitution", in which ego-level identifications as well as points of reference such as big Others and subjects supposed to know vacillate or vanish altogether, indeed is an essential, punctuating moment of the Lacanian analytic process. Nevertheless, Lacan does not consider it possible or desirable to dwell permanently in such an analysis-terminating destitute state. He sees it as both appropriate and inevitable that egos, big Others, subjects supposed to know, and the like will reconstitute themselves for the analysand in the aftermath of his/her analysis. Hopefully, the versions of these reconstituted in the wake of and in response to analysis will be better, more livable versions for the analysand.

What we get here is some kind of "postmodern" Lacan: we can confront the Real only in rare moments of lucidity, but this extreme experience cannot last, we have to return to our ordinary life of dwelling in semblances, in symbolic fictions … So instead of erasing god from the picture, the only way is learn to how "'make use of' *Dieu comme le Nom-du-Père*." In what precise sense, then, are *les non-dupes errent*, i.e., those who pretend not to be duped by the religious illusion, in the wrong? Johnston indicates how:

> Lacan's paraphrase of Dostoyevsky, according to which "if God is dead, then nothing is permitted", seems to convey the sense that permanent radical atheism is undesirable as per the strict Lacanian definition of desire. De Kesel claims that, for Lacan, religion enjoys the virtue of sustaining desire. If so, does Lacan's version of analysis really seek to do away with theism, religiosity, and the like? … The libidinal economy of the unconscious, centered on desire with its fundamental fantasies involving *objet petit a*, is sustained by the Law of God as the dead father and/or Name of-the-Father. If this God dies, then the entire economy He supports collapses (i.e., 'nothing is permitted'). In *Télévision*, Lacan, speaking of matters Oedipal, remarks, "Even if the memories of familial suppression weren't true, they would have to be invented, and that is certainly done." Paraphrasing this remark, one might say that, by Lacan's lights, if God is dead, then, at least for libidinal reasons, he would have to be resurrected—and that has certainly been done.[22]

This is also how one can read Agamben's idea that if there is no god then reason itself disappears. Does "if god doesn't exist, then everything is prohibited" not mean that, in order to avoid the deadlock of everything being prohibited, there has to be a big Prohibition which calls for exceptions, i.e., which opens up the space for transgressions which generate *jouissance*? Or that, in order to sustain our desire, we need something like god (even if it is only in its more neutral irreligious form, as subject supposed to know)? How to combine this with Lacan's claim that atheism is the pinnacle of psychoanalytic experience? Is Lacan's line that God-the-Father should not be abolished but make use of the only way out? Miller has fearlessly spelt out the political implications of this stance: psychoanalysis "reveals social ideals in their nature of semblances, and we can add, of semblances with regard to a real which is the real of enjoyment. This is the cynical position, which resides in saying that enjoyment is *the only thing that is true*."[23] What this means is that a psychoanalyst

> acts so that semblances remain at their places while making sure that the subjects under his care do not take them as *real* ... one should somehow bring oneself to remain *taken in by them* (fooled by them). Lacan could say that "those who are not taken in err": if one doesn't act as if semblances are real, if one doesn't leave their efficacy undisturbed, things take a turn for the worse. Those who think that all signs of power are mere semblances and rely on the arbitrariness of the discourse of the master are the bad boys: they are even more alienated.[24]

The axiom of this cynical wisdom is that "one should protect the semblances of power for the good reason that one should be able to continue to *enjoy*. The point is not to attach oneself to the semblances of the existing power, but to consider them necessary. 'This defines a cynicism in the mode of Voltaire who let it be understood that God is our invention which is necessary to maintain people in a proper decorum.' Society is kept together only by semblances, 'which means: there is no society without repression, without identification, and above all without routine.'"[25] But is this cynical stance the only way out? It raises a series of questions.

First, what if God, the divine authority, only really functions when the believer is aware that "God is our invention which is necessary to maintain people in a proper decorum"? Baudelaire saw this well—he wrote: "God is the only being who, in order to rule, doesn't even need to exist" (*Dieu est le seul être qui, pour régner, n'ait même pas besoin d'exister*).[26] Consequently, one should reject the obscene reasoning according to which, ultimately, I act ethically because I feel the threat of divine punishment—if I see a child drowning and decide to jump into the water to save him only because I fear I'll go to hell if I don't do it, this is a case of immoral calculation at its worst. An ethical person acts in the way prescribed by religion even if he knows there is no god—the moment god enters the equation, we are not dealing with faith but with calculation. That's why we have to accept the paradox that only atheists have true faith.

If a believer directly "really believes," we slide into fundamentalism—every authentic religion is aware that its authority is a fetishist fake: I know it is not really true, but I believe in it. The opposite of fundamentalism is the awareness that the authority we refer to has no real fundament but is self-referentially grounded on an abyss. Let's take a perhaps surprising example: the finale of Wagner's *Rhinegold* which ends with the contrast between Rhinemaidens' bemoaning lost innocence and the majestic entrance of the Gods into Valhalla, a powerful assertion of the rule of Law. It is customary to claim that the sincere and authentic complaint of the Rhinemaidens makes clear how the triumphant entrance of the Gods into Valhalla is a fake, a hollow spectacle; however, what if it is precisely the saddening background of the Rhinemaidens' song which gives to the entry into Valhalla its authentic greatness? Gods know they are doomed, but nonetheless they heroically perform their ceremonial act. This is why we are not dealing here with the usual fetishist disavowal but with a courageous act of taking a risk and ignoring my limitations, along the lines of Kant's *Du kannst, denn du sollst!*—I know I am too weak to do it, but I'll do nonetheless do it—a gesture which is the very opposite of cynicism.

Let's ground this conclusion from another starting point. Authority has the effect of symbolic castration on its bearer: if, say, I am a king, I have to accept that the ritual of investiture makes me a king, that my authority is embodied in the insignia I wear, so that my authority is in some sense external to me as a person in my miserable reality. As Lacan put it, a psychotic is a king who thinks he is as king (or a father who is a father) by his nature, as he is, without the processes of symbolic investiture. This is why being-a-father is by definition a failure: no "empirical" father can live up to his symbolic function—to his title. How can I, if I am invested with such authority, live with this gap without obfuscating it through psychotic direct identification of my symbolic status with my reality? Miller's solution is cynical distance: I am aware that symbolic titles are just semblances, illusion, but I act AS IF they are true in order not to disturb not only the social order but also my own ability to desire.

Aaron Schuster adds three modes to deal with the impossibility of acting with authority (it is because of this impossibility that Freud counted exercise of power as one of the three impossible professions): "to pretend as if there were no Other; to make oneself the mouthpiece of the Other; to identify the Other with one's charismatic persona"(191). The example of the first option is that of a postmodern friendly boss who acts as if he is one of us, part of the team, ready to share dirty jokes with us, joining us in a drink, etc.—but while doing this, he retains his full symbolic authority and can treat us in an even more ruthless way. The second option is personified in the figure of an expert, a medium through which the authority of impersonal science (or law) speaks; such a figure avoids the position of authority by pretending that he is not giving orders, just saying what says science should be done (like an economist who claims market mechanisms should not be disturbed). The third option is exemplified by an obscene charismatic leader like Donald Trump who takes himself, with all his personal quirks, as a direct embodiment of the big Other—his authority is not based on his knowledge but on his will: "It is so because I say so." At this point, Schuster makes a crucial observation:

The leader of competence and calculation, disappearing behind and speaking in the name of the big Other, finds its uncanny counterpart in the overpresent leader whose authority is based on his own will and who openly disdains knowledge—it is this rebellious, anti-systemic theater that serves as the point of identification for the people." (234)

The obscene charismatic leader is thus the "return of the repressed" of the expert knowledge which pretends to act without support in a figure of the master: the repressed Master (authority which personifies the Law) returns in its (almost, not quite) psychotic form, as a lawless obscene Master. The Master is here "overpresent": he is not reduced to his symbolic dignity, he stands for authority with all his idiosyncrasies. And what happens to knowledge with the rise of the obscene Master? As we can see it abundantly, neutral expert knowledge is transformed into its (immanent) opposite, the "special" knowledge of conspiracy theories accessible only to the initiated (global warming is a scam, the COVID-19 pandemic was invented by state apparatuses and medical corporations . . .).

So is there a way out of this deadlock? The obvious one would have been for the bearer of authority to admit openly to those subjected to him that he is not qualified to exert authority and to simply step down, leaving his subjects to confront reality as they can—Schuster quotes Hannah Arendt who outlines this gesture apropos parental authority:

> Modern man could find no clearer expression for his dissatisfaction with the world, for his disgust with things as they are, than by his refusal to assume, in respect to his children, responsibility for all this. It is as though parents daily said: "In this world even we are not very securely at home; how to move about in it, what to know, what skills to master, are mysteries to us too. You must try to make out as best you can; in any case you are not entitled to call us to account. We are innocent, we wash our hands of you."[27]

Although this imagined answer of the parents is factually more or less true, it is nonetheless existentially false: a parent cannot wash his/her hands in this way. (The same goes for saying: "I have no free will, my decisions are the product of my brain signals, so I wash my hands, I have no responsibility for crimes that I committed!" Even if this is factually true, it is false as my subjective stance.) This means that "the ethical lesson is that the parents should pretend (to know what to do and how the world works), for there is no way out of the problem of authority other than to assume it, in its very fictionality, with all the difficulties and discontents this entails" (219).

But, again, how does this differ from Miller's cynical solution? Paradoxically, it is that that the subject, although fully aware of his/her incompetence to exert authority, assumes it not with a cynical distance but with fully sincerity, ready even to sacrifice his/her life for it if needed. To grasp this difference, one should also bring into view libidinal economy, different modes of *jouissance*. Politics does not happen primarily at the level of semblances and identifications (imaginary and symbolic), it always involves also the real of *jouissance*. Political semblances and identifications are profoundly impregnated by different modes of *jouissance*—can one even imagine a racism or anti-feminism which does not mobilize *jouissance* (*jouissance* attributed to another race or women, *jouissance* I find in attacking and humiliating them . . .). That's why, in his detailed analysis of the Petainist discourse in the Vichy France, Gerard Miller[28] speaks of Petain's "pushes-to-enjoy (even pushes-to-come)"—and, in a homologous way, can one even hope to understand Trump without taking into account his "pushes-to-enjoy"?

The same also goes for societies with emancipatory goals. Let's take Lacan's own psychoanalytic society (which he dissolved, thereby admitting it was a failure): was it also a society "kept together only by semblances"? Is the only step out of the domain of semblances only the individual moment of "traversing the fantasy" in the analytic process? It certainly wasn't meant to be this: was Lacan's attempt to organize a society not a "Leninist" attempt to constitute a society which is NOT kept together "only by semblances" but by the Real of a Cause. (This is why, after dissolving his school, Lacan formed a new one called *École de la Cause freudienne*—a school of the Cause itself—which, it is true, failed again.)

Does it help to introduce some order in this confusion if we turn Lacan's anti-Dostoyevsky formula around: if god DOES exist then NOTHING is prohibited? It is clear that this holds only for so-called "fundamentalists" who can do anything they want since they act as direct instruments of god—of his will. We can see how PC rigorism and religious fundamentalism are two sides of the same coin: in both cases, there is no exception—either nothing is prohibited or everything is prohibited . . . To bring some clarity into this picture, we should perhaps bring into the play Lacan's so-called formulas of sexuation. The two couples of universality grounded in exception and non-universality ("non-all") which implies there is no exception.

From Authority to Permissiveness . . . and Back

So what is the status of the postmodern permissiveness in which everything turns out to be prohibited by infinite PC regulations? Are they masculine (everything is permitted except . . .) or feminine (there is nothing which is not prohibited)? It looks as though the second version is the right one: in a permissive society, violations of the regulations (which allegedly guarantee sexual permissiveness) are themselves really prohibited and not secretly tolerated. This means that we should transpose Lacan's claim into feminine form: if god doesn't exist then there is nothing which is not prohibited, which means that not-all is prohibited, and this not-all exists in the guise of a universal permissiveness: in principle, everything is permitted (all different form of sexuality), but every particular case is prohibited. At a political level, Chapter 15 of the Khmer Rouge constitution of Kampuchea stated: "Every citizen of Kampuchea has the right to worship according to any religion and the right not to worship according to any religion. Reactionary religions which are detrimental to Democratic Kampuchea and Kampuchean people are absolutely forbidden."[29] So, any religion is permitted but every particular existing religion (Buddhism, Christianity . . .) is "absolutely forbidden" as reactionary.[30] There is another version of how the shift from prohibition to permissive regulation works in cinema, as described by Duane Rouselle:

> In the 1930s the "Hays Code" provided a set of prohibitions or rules within cinema. There was the explicit prohibition of displays or representations of sexuality on screen. But what do we see today? With the latest rules set out by the Oscars, there has been an obvious shift: it is no longer a universal prohibition of sexuality but rather the particular or selective affirmation (quota system, ultimately) of sexuality: you must include particular representations of sexualities on the screen. This is

why I have been stressing the importance of the new cultural logic that imposes the particular affirmations of enjoyments.[31]

It is easy to find examples of this: one of the reactions to *Lalaland* was that there was no person depicted as gay in the story, although there is a relatively high percentage of gays in Hollywood. (The same goes for publishing today—when a reader is proposed on any topic, the first reaction of the publisher is "are there enough women, blacks, Asians, etc. among the authors?" A minimally serious approach should raise a different question: why are there not more good writers on a chosen topic among women, blacks …? Can something be changed at this level? Direct imposition of equal proportion (enough women, blacks …) is counter-productive and just breeds resentment—at the end, organization of a colloquium becomes a matter of following Politically Correct rules: find some women, a black guy, an Asian, a Latino, a gay, a trans …

The entire procedure of a balanced distribution of enjoyments that pertain to particular identities is wrong. In the conditions of the Hayes Code, we at least got codified ways to violate prohibitions: the mention of homosexuality was prohibited, but if a man in the movie is noted for using perfume this signals he is gay; dealing with prostitution is prohibited, but if a woman is characterized as coming from New Orleans … With Politically Correct "justice," the censorship is in a sense much worse because prohibitions are replaced by regulatory injunctions. To quote the title of Ben Burgis's book, the agents of cancel culture are "comedians while the world burns":[32] far from being "too radical," their imposition of new rules is one of the exemplary cases of pseudo-activity, of how to *make sure that nothing will really change by pretending to fight for the change all the time.* Along these lines, Saroj Giri[33] drew attention to so-called "woke capitalism": new forms of capital, in particular anti-Trump tech capitalists (Google, Apple, Facebook), which intertwine with anti-racist and pro-immigrant struggles. One does not really change things by prescribing measures which aim at establishing a superficial "just" balance without attacking the underlying causes of the imbalance. Here is a recent example:

California's Department of Education has announced that the gap between well-performing students and their less able peers must disappear, indicating that mere words are not enough—schools must deliver "equity" in classrooms. Such an effort would involve faculty holding well-performing students back, even while pushing their less intellectual peers forward (as if they were all indeed equal in abilities). "*We reject ideas of natural gifts and talents,*" the proposal states, insisting "*there is no cutoff determining when one child is 'gifted' and another is not.*" The proposal also wants to "*replace ideas of innate mathematics 'talent' and 'giftedness' with the recognition that every student is on a growth pathway.*"[34]

This is an exemplary case of fake egalitarianism destined to just breed envy and hatred. The obvious problem is that we need good mathematicians to do serious science, and the proposed measures certainly don't help in this regard. The solution? Why not more access to good education for everyone, better living conditions for the poor ... And it is easy to imagine the next step in the direction of the false egalitarianism: is not the fact that some individuals are much more sexually attractive than others also a case of supreme injustice? So should we not invent some kind of push towards justice here also, a way of holding the more attractive back, since *there is no cutoff determining when one person is sexually attractive and another is not*? Effectively, sexuality is a domain of terrifying injustice and imbalance ... Equity in enjoyment is the ultimate dream of false egalitarianism.

How, then, do things stand with today's pandemic regulations? Do they also solicit transgressions (private rave and parties, even violent outbursts)? But they are not the Law, they are scientifically grounded regulations, they belong to the university discourse. Scientists and health administrators gladly explain why they are demanded, they don't function as the abyssal law, as regulations which should not be questioned. Is thus the hedonism of *jouissance* the other side of the reign of the university discourse? But what if those who resist pandemic prohibitions and regulations are confusing scientifically grounded regulations with ungrounded arbitrary prohibitions (which solicit transgression)? Of course, one should add: but what if this confusion is already present in the thing itself? Is the "truth" of the university discourse not a Master, or, as we say today, is the (not even so) secret agenda of those who impose anti-pandemic prohibitions not to assert social control and domination?

To complicate things further, we should introduce here two other axes. First: permitted versus enjoined (ordered). Lacan's argument was that enjoyment, once permitted, sooner or later inevitably turns into injunction—you HAVE to enjoy, hedonism is superego at its most cruel. This is the truth of today's permissiveness: we feel guilty not when we violate prohibitions but when we cannot enjoy. That's why psychoanalysis aims not to enable the patient to fully enjoy but to limit the power of the superego, to turn enjoyment from enjoined to permitted (you can enjoy but you are not obliged to.)

The other axis is that of possibility and impossibility. Prohibition is, as Lacan repeatedly claimed, here precisely to create the illusion that enjoyment is not in itself impossible, that we can reach it through violating the prohibition. The goal of psychoanalysis is precisely to make the move from prohibition to immanent impossibility. So a prohibition primarily prohibits something that is in itself impossible . . . But is this not going too far? When a poor starving man is prohibited from grabbing a piece of food which is not his, does this prohibition not prohibit something that is in itself quite possible? In other words, is an elementary operation of ideology also not to present as in itself impossible something that is prohibited because of economic class interests and the interests of domination? (No universal healthcare because it is impossible, it would ruin economy . . .)

Further paradoxes arise here. There are prohibitions one is not only permitted to violate but obliged to violate, so that the true transgression is to stick strictly to the rule of prohibition. (This is what I called inherent transgression: if you do not participate in the secret transgressive rituals of a closed community, you are excluded faster than if you violate its explicit rules.) And then there are prohibitions that are themselves prohibited (one obeys them, but one cannot announce them publicly). The big Other of appearances enters here: you obey a prohibition, but you publicly act as if this means nothing, as if it is just a chance that you don't do that, as if, if you wanted, you could easily do it; plus the obverse, you can violate a prohibition, just not publicly, in an open way. (Trump and today's New Right populists break this rule: they violate prohibitions openly, in public.)

A further complication: what if we enjoy oppression itself, not just its violation? Is this not the elementary form of surplus-enjoyment? For example, with regard to the pandemic, Darian Leader pointed out how obeying the rules imposed by the authorities due to the pandemic can bring its own compulsive satisfaction. Similarly, Politically Correct enjoyment arises through the very process of discovering how we unknowingly violated the PC rules ("now I discovered that the phrase I used has a racist dimension . . ."). Recall the already-mentioned joke about a go-between who tries to convince a young man to marry a woman he represents; his strategy is to turn every objection into a positive feature: There is a homology between the structure of this joke and the structure exemplified by the proverbial figure of a permissive husband who, in principle, allows his wife to have lovers, but is opposed to every particular choice ("why did you have to choose precisely THIS appalling guy? Anyone BUT him . . ."). The moment of truth arrives here when the wife proposes a lover for whom the husband, in parallel with the go-between from Freud's joke, cannot find any reason why he is not appropriate, so he prohibits him for no reason—just for the sake of it. In contrast to Freud's joke, he is "imperfect" (doesn't fit the series of reasons) precisely because he is perfect . . . And, to go a step further, is not a similar stance at work with some radical practitioners of the PC struggle against sexual exploitation who are all for sex without any constraints, only provided that it is not in the service of power relations or done under pressure of power and domination. In practice this means that every concrete case of a possible sexual contact (especially if it is heterosexual) is rejected because, through their critical analysis, they discern in it traces of power relations (the man is wealthier than you, he can influence your career . . .) Hopefully, at some point, there will be a partner who is fully acceptable, so he has to be rejected not because of any of his particular properties but because sex as such is intertwined with power relations. The surplus-enjoyment of this critical operation is in the repeated joy of the discovery that every case involves power (so that sexual pleasure has to be renounced).

The worst solution here is to oppose necessary repression (renouncing the satisfaction of some of our desires as the condition of our survival) and surplus-repression done on behalf of exploitation and domination (as Herbert Marcuse did)[35]—for conceptual reasons, this distinction cannot be drawn. First, domination and exploitation are as a rule operative in the very way the renunciations necessary for our survival are libidinally cathexed. Second (and in an apparent contradiction to the first point), it is the surplus-oppression (the prohibition for which there is no apparent reason) which generates surplus-enjoyment—as Lacan says, enjoyment is something that serves nothing ... Third, one should draw another distinction here: between oppression and repression. Oppression (the brutal exercise of power) is not repression: oppression is directly experienced as such, but we are not aware of repression (in the Freudian sense). When I am oppressed, what is often repressed is the way I enjoy this oppression (with all that it involves: my complaints, etc.).

So what we get here are not just the two axes of a semiotic square (impossible-possible, prohibited-permitted), but a complex texture which includes the axis of permitted-enjoined and even a triangle of oppression-repression-depression. Miller simplifies the image here: he claims that oppression is necessary, by which he means that there is no enjoyment without oppression (obstacles, prohibitions to our desires). The opposite of oppression is not freedom to do what one wants but *depression, the loss of desire itself.* But is oppression the only way to save our desire, the only way to avoid depression? The question we should raise at this point is: where is repression here? Lacan strictly opposes the traditional Freudo-Marxist thesis that repression is the internalization into the victim's psyche of external oppression (I misperceive social oppression as a psychic force that sabotages my desires)—repression comes first (in the guise of what Freud called "primordial repression"), it designates an immanent impossibility that is constitutive of human subjectivity. This "primordial repression" is the other face of what we call "freedom": it opens up the void, a crack in the chain of natural causes, which makes us free. The figure of an external symbolic Law as the agent of Prohibition already obfuscates this immanent impossibility of desire.

That's why psychoanalysis does not aim at liberating our desires so that we can freely desire what we want (what we want is not what we desire: our innermost desire as a rule appears to us as what we don't want, what terrifies us)—more precisely, it liberates our desires only in the precise sense that we fully assume the impossibility on which our desiring capacity is grounded. Psychoanalysis endeavors to mark this impossibility out in a new way—it's premise is that we cannot get rid of a constitutive impossibility, but we can re-inscribe it in a different way.

This is why one should resolutely reject the idea that the goal of the psychoanalytic treatment is to enable the patient to move from internal psychic conflicts (between his conscious ego and unconscious desires and prohibitions) to external obstacles to his happiness which s/he can now approach without self-sabotaging inner conflicts. This idea was not foreign to Freud: already in his early *Studies on Hysteria* (1895, co-written with Breuer), he wrote, addressing an imagined reader/patient, that "much will be gained if we succeed in transforming your hysterical misery into common unhappiness. With a mental life that has been restored to health, you will be better armed against that unhappiness."[36] Later, however, the new topics of death drive and the so-called "negative therapeutic reaction"—clearly point towards an immanent conflict constitutive of our psychic life.

No Freedom Without Impossibility

The move accomplished by psychoanalysis is thus a Hegelian one: from external opposition to immanent impossibility, and this holds also for the vision of a Communist society: there is no freedom without impossibility, and this impossibility not just the limit imposed on us by external reality (the limited number of objects that satisfy our needs) but also the immanent "self-contradiction" of our desire. There is, however, another trap that lurks here: to confuse this impossibility with our finitude, so that the impossibility that grounds our freedom is the fact of our mortal life full of risks and non-transparencies—there is no freedom in immortality.

Exemplary is here Martin Hägglund who, through new readings of Hegel, Marx, Heidegger and Martin Luther King, deploys a coherent global vision which brings together materialism, existential finitude, and anti-capitalism.[37] His starting point is the rejection of the religious ideal of eternity: the only life we have is THIS life, our social and bodily existence which is irreducibly marked by mortality and incertitude. Every faith in another world or a higher being that guarantees our fate is an illusion, so faith has to be reconceived in secular terms: it expresses our practical commitment which, due to our finitude, exposes us to contingency and always involves a risk of failure. However, precisely because we are finite beings who have to decide without any higher guarantee, we are free: freedom and mortality are the two sides of the same coin.

In the second part of his book, Hägglund turns to the socio-economic and political implications of his focus on "this world" of our finite temporal existence. Since, as finite mortal beings, we don't have infinite time at our disposal (and since our eventual immortality would also make our life meaningless: choosing a life project that determines our engagement can only occur in a finite lifetime), our central preoccupation is to own our time, getting as much of it as possible disposable for the free development of our creative capacities in all their diversity. This, however, by definition cannot happen in capitalism where, in order to survive, we have to spend most of our time working for a wage, "losing time" for things we intrinsically don't care about. If we want to overcome this alienation, we should enact a new revaluation of our values, replacing the money-form of value with the value of the free time at our disposal. The only way to do this is to replace a capitalist form of life with a post-capitalist democratic socialism where private ownership of the means of production as well as the alienated state apparatuses regulating our lives will disappear; in this way, we will no longer be competing with each other for the possession of money-value but spontaneously working for the common Good—the very antagonism between the common Good and my personal interests will disappear.

Hägglund doesn't go into the specifics of how to realize this radical social change, and many critics of his work see in this vagueness the main failure of his book. One can also speculate that it is precisely this vagueness which made *This Life* susceptible to being praised not only in academic circles but also by the big media. The topic of disalienation, of people directly exerting their power, is a feature that, in spite of their radical differences, unites Hägglund and Trump.

But what I find much more problematic is that, to put it in a brutally simplified way, there is simply no place for Freud in Hägglund's universe. How can he claim that, in a post-capitalist society, people would spontaneously tend to work for the common Good—why? Where is the envy constitutive of human desire? Where are all the basic "perversions" of human desire described by Freud and concentrated in his notion of death-drive? It is his humanist trust that all the horrors humans are capable of—all the self-sabotaging, all the complex forms of search for unhappiness, of pleasure in pain and in humiliation, etc.—can be reduced to the effect of a specific alienated social form, that makes Hägglund's book so attractive for the broader public. What I try to develop is a vision of Communism compatible with all these horrors, with the "alienation" implied by the very fact of language, with all the reflexive twists of human desire (how the repression of desire necessarily turns into a desire for repression, etc.). (Kevin Bacon said: "I've been told I'm more well known for being well known than for anything I've acted in'"[38]—this is the reflexivity of language or, in Hegelese, the way, in a language, a genus can be one of its own species: being-well-known-for-something has many species, and one of them is being-well-known-for-being-well-known. The same holds not only for Kim Kardashian but also, in a more specific way, for love: you can well (and you always do) love somebody for love itself, not just due to reasons to love her/him/it.) This reflexivity is Hegel's name for actual infinity (as opposed to the spurious infinity of a series without end), and, since this reflexivity is constitutive of the Freudian death-drive, we encounter here—from my Freudo-Lacanian standpoint, at least—a fateful limitation of Hägglund's insistence on radical finitude of the human condition.

The axiom of the philosophy of finitude is that one cannot escape finitude/mortality as the unsurpassable horizon of our existence; Lacan's axiom is that, no matter how much one tries, one cannot escape immortality. But what if this choice is false—what if finitude and immortality, like lack and excess, also form a parallax couple, what if they are the same from a different point of view? What if immortality is an object that is a remainder/excess over finitude, what if finitude is an attempt to escape from the excess of immortality? What if Kierkegaard was right here, but for the wrong reason, when he also understood the claim that we, humans, are just mortal beings who disappear after their biological death as an easy way to escape the ethical responsibility that comes with the immortal soul? He was right for the wrong reason insofar as he equated immortality with the divine and ethical part of a human being—but there is another immortality. What Cantor did for infinity, we should do for immortality, and assert the multiplicity of immortalities: the Badiouian noble immortality/infinity of the deployment of an Event (as opposed to the finitude of a human animal) comes after a more basic form of immortality which resides in what Lacan calls the Sadean fundamental fantasy: the fantasy of another, ethereal body of the victim, which can be tortured indefinitely and nonetheless magically retains its beauty (recall the Sadean figure of the young girl sustaining endless humiliations and mutilations from her depraved torturer and somehow mysteriously surviving it all intact, in the same way Tom and Jerry and other cartoon heroes survive all their ridiculous ordeals intact). In this form, the comical and the disgustingly terrifying (recall different versions of the "undead"—zombies, vampires, etc.—in popular culture) are inextricably connected. The same immortality underlies the intuition of something indestructible in a truly radical Evil. This blind indestructible insistence of the libido is what Freud called "death drive," and one should bear in mind that "death drive" is, paradoxically, the Freudian name for its very opposite, for the way immortality appears within psychoanalysis: for an uncanny excess of life, for an "undead" urge which persists beyond the (biological) cycle of life and death, of generation and corruption. Freud equates the death drive with the so-called "compulsion-to-repeat," an uncanny urge to repeat painful past experiences which seems to outgrow the natural limitations of the organism affected by it and to insist even beyond the organism's death.

Matthew Flisfeder noted two features that clearly distinguish the "theoretical anti-humanism" of the 1960s from today's post-humanism: "Whereas the anti-humanists of the 1960s proclaimed the death of the subject, today we encounter a far more unnerving death of the human. While the anti-humanists sought merely to deconstruct the subject within discourse, the Posthumanists today are far more ambitious in realizing a return to matter and objectivity that they claim has been displaced by the verticality of humanity."[39] So in the 1960s, with Foucault and Althusser, the notion of subject (our self-perception as subjects) was "deconstructed" as a historically specific discursive formation (although, for Althusser, it was more a universal ideological misrecognition); plus the ultimate horizon of this deconstruction was discourse, i.e., discourse was posited as a kind of transcendental a priori, as that which is always-already here in our dealings with reality. Today's posthumanism, on the contrary, doesn't deal with the "death of the subject" but with the "death" of humans, it asserts the falsity of our self-perception of humans as free responsible beings, demonstrating that this self-perception is based not on some ignored discursive mechanisms but on our ignoring of what we really are—the "blind" neuronal processes that go on in our brain. In contrast to the anti-humanism of the 1960s, today's posthumanism relies on direct materialist reductionism: our sense of freedom and personal dignity is a "user's illusion," we are really just a complex network of bodily processes in their interaction with environment . . .

An ironic consequence of this shift from anti-humanism to post-humanism is that the remaining anti-humanists or their followers (like J.-A. Miller), when confronted with the posthumanist challenge of full naturalization of human beings, all of a sudden start to talk (almost) like humanists, emphasizing the uniqueness of human self-experience ("decentered" as it is), and the impossibility of fully reducing it to "objective" neuronal processes. A further difference is that, while discursive deconstruction doesn't directly affect our everyday life (where we continue to experience ourselves as free responsible agents), posthumanism promises (and to some extent already achieves) interventions in our reality which will radically change our self-perception: when we are submitted to total digital control and our brains are directly wired, when our DNA can be modified, when pills can change our behavior and affections, this basically affects the way we experience ourselves and act.

In July 2021, the public was shocked by a great achievement of investigative journalism: the discovery of Pegasus, a spyware developed by the Israeli cyberarms firm NSO Group, that can be covertly installed on mobile phones (and other devices) and capable of reading text messages, tracking calls, collecting passwords, location tracking, accessing the target device's microphone and camera, and harvesting information from apps. Pegasus was (and is) used by many states to control dissidents, opposition politicians, journalists, etc. We, of course, assumed that something like Pegasus is operative, so we learned what we already knew; however, it is nonetheless important that we learned concrete data—if it remains a vague general suspicion, the level of our being under control can be ignored, but now we cannot go on as if we don't know it.

Back to Flisfeder, my only difference with him is that, based on these insights, he argues for a new universal humanism that could ground the global emancipatory struggle needed today. His argumentation is ultimately a new version of transcendental reflection: when I as a neuroscientist argue that I am just a set of neuronal and biological processes, I always do this in the form of rational argumentation, trying to convince others, as a part of scientific community—the space of this community where I address others (and act as) a free rational being convinced by reasons is always-already here, operative in my activity, not as an abstract Cartesian cogito but as a human collective ... So, to simplify the image a little bit, while Flisfeder is ready to sacrifice subject but not humanity, not the basic dimensions of our being-human, I am tempted to do the exact opposite: I am ready to sacrifice (what we perceived until now as) the basic features of our being-human but not subject. "Humanity" is a notion at the same level as personality, the "inner wealth" of our soul, etc.—it is ultimately a phenomenal form, a mask, which fills in the void that "is" subject. What subject stands for is the inhuman core of being-human: what Hegel called self-relating negativity; what Freud called death drive. So in the same way that Kant distinguished the subject of transcendental apperception from a person's soul and its wealth, in the same way Freud and Lacan distinguish the subject of the unconscious from the Jungian personality full of deep passions, we should in our unique predicament stick to the inhuman core of subjectivity against the temptations of being-human. Subject is what is in a human being more than human, the immortality of the death-drive which makes it a living dead being, something that insists beyond the cycle of life and death.

The ontological implications of the notion of death-drive are paradoxical. If—as we read in *Oedipus at Colonus*—the best thing that can happen to us is not being born in the first place, then our being born is already a kind of failure, the failure of being born, the failure to achieve the optimal state of not being born at all—it is not the lack of being which is a failed being, it is our being itself which is our failure to achieve non-being.[40] In other words, our being is immanently measured by the counterfactual hypothesis of non-being. One should not be afraid to draw radical ontological consequences from this reversal. According to the standard ontological configuration, entities strive for perfection, their goal is to actualize their potential, to become fully what they are, and the lack of being signals the failure of a thing to fully realize its potentials. This configuration has to be turned around: being as such (in the sense of being a determinate entity) signals a failure, everything that is (as a particular entity) is marked by a failure, and the only way to achieve perfection is to immerse oneself into the void of no-being.

In some sense Plato himself was aware of this: all being(s) originate from the Supreme Good which is *epekeina tes ousias*, beyond being(s)—like a black hole (to apply this overused metaphor) onto which event-horizon surface we project our fantasmatic constructions of the In-itself beyond the event-horizon. We fail to reach the void that is the In-itself since, as Hegel put it clearly in his *Phenomenology*, id beyond the veil of phenomena is only what we (subject) put there—every being is also a failed approach to Non-being. The thesis that being is a failed non-being is usually read as the reversal of a radical negative act into a comic failure: "in deep despair you wanted to self-destroy, you fail even in this . . ."—with the added point that this type of negation of negation is foreign to Hegel and much closer to Freud (repression as a negation, as a negation of negation, a return of the repressed, a proof of the failure of repression/negation). Is, however, such a logic really foreign to Hegel? Does one of the most famous passages in Hegel, the dialectic of master and servant, not begin precisely with a failed non-being? If in the confrontation of the two self-consciousnesses engaged in the struggle for life and death, every side is ready to go to the end in risking its life, then the struggle ends in a blind alley—one dies, the other survives but without an other to recognize it.[41] The whole history of freedom and recognition—in short, the whole history, the whole being of culture—can take place only with this original compromise: in the eye-to-eye confrontation, one side (the future servant) "averts its eyes"—is not ready to go to the end.

Repression, Oppression, Depression

The underlying problem is here: how can we avoid depression without returning to repression, even in the form of oppressive social authority needed so that its transgressing can bring us satisfaction? In his novel *Another Now*, Yanis Varoufakis[42] applies this opposition between repression and depression to social reality itself. To simplify the plot to the utmost, a group of individuals in our present find a way to communicate with and then enter an alternate reality ("Another Now") in which, in the aftermath of the 2008 crisis, history took a different turn, and the result is a global society of democratic market socialism: there is only one central state bank which regulates money supply in a transparent way, financial speculation disappears because it becomes meaningless, ownership is dispersed since each citizen is allocated its part, healthcare and human rights are guaranteed for everyone, etc.—in short, it's a global self-management where every particular demand finds its way to be heard, so there are no antagonisms and no reasons to rebel ... The choice our group confronts is: should they remain in Another Now or return to our neo-liberal Now with all the struggles and violence we know? Varoufakis gives a series of features that spoil the perfection of Another Now. First, although economic alienation and exploitation are overcome, and the state as an alienated entity is dissolved in the transparent self-management of the society, the more fundamental repression of women survives in a more subtle way at the level of everyday practices. (Here I disagree with Varoufakis: I think that today we also face the opposite option: a postmodern multicultural society in which racism and patriarchal oppression are left behind but economic exploitation remains.) Second, market exchange and the competitive stance (the "transactional quid pro quo mentality") implied by it remain in full force:

> I am, I admit, fascinated, impressed, awestruck even, by what the rebels have achieved in the Other Now, particularly the democratization of corporations, money, land ownership and markets. Except that democratized markets still prioritize the transactional quid pro quo mentality that undermines the sovereignty of good and, ultimately, our fundamental wellbeing. Democratized market societies, freed from capitalism, are infinitely preferable to what we have here, except for one crucial thing: they entrench exchange value and thereby, I fear, make impossible a genuine revolution that leads to the final toppling of markets. (218–19)

In the terms of the Frankfurt School, something like "instrumental reason" remains in this calculating society of exchanges: there is no space for simple goodness, for acts done just for the sake of it, out of love, without expecting anything in exchange. But here one should supplement Varoufakis: what would have ruined the society imagined in Another Now is envy as constitutive of human desire. For Lacan, the fundamental impasse of human desire is that it is the other's desire in both subjective and objective genitive: desire for the other, desire to be desired by the other, and, especially, desire for what the other desires. Envy and resentment are thus a constitutive component of human desire, as already St. Augustine knew so well—recall the passage from his *Confessions*, often quoted by Lacan, the scene of a baby jealous for his brother sucking the mother's breast: "I myself have seen and known an infant to be jealous though it could not speak. It became pale, and cast bitter looks on its foster-brother."

Based on this insight, Jean-Pierre Dupuy[43] proposed a convincing critique of Rawls' theory of justice: in the Rawls' model of a just society, social inequalities are tolerated only insofar as they also help those at the bottom of the social ladder, and insofar as they are not based on inherited hierarchies, but on natural inequalities, which are considered contingent, not merits.[44] What Rawls doesn't see is how such a society would create conditions for an uncontrolled explosion of resentment: in it, I would know that my lower status is fully justified, and would thus be deprived of excusing my failure as the result of social injustice. Lacan shares with Nietzsche and Freud the idea that justice as equality is founded on envy: the envy of the other who has what we do not have, and who enjoys it. In his "American Utopia," Jameson totally rejects the predominant optimist view according to which in Communism envy will be left behind as a remainder of capitalist competition, to be replaced by solidary collaboration and pleasure in others' pleasures; dismissing this myth, he emphasizes that in Communism, precisely insofar as it will be a more just society, envy and resentment will explode—why? The demand for justice is ultimately the demand that the excessive enjoyment of the other should be curtailed, so that everyone's access to enjoyment will be equal. The necessary outcome of this demand, of course, is asceticism: since it is not possible to impose equal enjoyment, what one *can* impose is the equally shared *prohibition*. However, one should not forget that today, in our allegedly permissive society, this asceticism assumes precisely the form of its opposite, of the generalized injunction "Enjoy!" We are all under the spell of this injunction, with the outcome that our enjoyment is more hindered than ever. This, perhaps, is what Nietzsche had in mind with his notion of the Last Man—it is only today that we can really discern the contours of the Last Man, in the guise of the predominant hedonistic asceticism—Third, due to its very transparency, the society in Another Now is one of total control: my properties and activities are transparent to others, my behavior is regulated in a severe PC way, etc.—Fourth, due to its very democratic transparency and justice, there is nothing to rebel against in Another Now—this is how Iris, the old radical Leftist in the book, is described:

raging against the system was Iris's only way of being, her loneliness vaccine. The Other Now was too pleasant, too wholesome to rage against. It would have made Iris's life intolerable" (219). "Surely if there is one thing you know about me, Yango," she replied cheerfully, "it is that I am a dissident. There was nothing for me on the other side to dissent from except their political correctness and smugness at having created the perfect society" (228). "This Now, my dear Yango, is my natural habitat—it's so bloody awful that I feel alive and usefully dangerous. Having experienced the rebellion and seen the institutions it created, I am more confident over here than anyone I know when lambasting the stupidity of the ruling class and its system. It is far easier to subvert them here, let me tell you!" (229)

Would then Iris not feel quite at home in Belarus where a rebellion raged against the unpopular tyrant in 2020 and 2021? Would she not feel at home in Ukraine which resists Russian invasion in March 2022? . . . So, again, how to resolve this deadlock between repression (in our Now) and depression (in Another Now)? How to avoid the obvious but false conclusion that, since rebellion is the sense of our lives, we should first establish a force of oppression in order to be able to rebel against it? Would Iris really accept that millions will continue their needless suffering so that she can feel and act as a true rebel? The typical solution is to avoid the deadlock by way of positing that the struggle against oppression is endless, new forms of oppression always arise—this solution was already criticized by Hegel in his analysis of the contradictions that inhabit Kant's moralism of infinite task, or, to quote Findlay's concise resume: "If the highest good is taken to be a Nature which conforms to morality, morality itself vanishes from this good, since it presupposes a non-conforming Nature. Moral action, being the absolute purpose, seems to look to the elimination of moral action."[45] Is this not what Iris is complaining about? Rebellion, being the absolute purpose, seems to look forward to the elimination of rebellion . . . The only solution to this deadlock is the Hegelian one: we should abandon the very ideal of a self-transparent society where full democracy abolishes all alienated structures. Alienation is a condition of our freedom, it gives us a breathing space to exercise freedom. I am free only insofar as the big Other (social substance) in which I dwell is non-transparent to me *and to itself* (there is no secret Master who pulls the strings). Reconciliation means that we have to reconcile ourselves with alienation, not its overcoming, so the problem with Another Now is precisely that it effectively abolishes alienation.

With regard to desire and pleasures, this paradox of alienation complicates the way desire relates to its object. Recall how Iris's "raging against the system" is described as her "only way of being": "The Other Now was too pleasant, too wholesome to rage against." Iris's radical decision at the end of the novel thus exemplifies the fact that desire, at its most fundamental, is not just a desire for this (our world) or that (the Other Now)—it can also be a desire to say NO to this or that, so that the subject experiences that his/her desire is threatened when s/he is deprived of a space to just say NO. This paradox also confronts us with the minimal structure of surplus-enjoyment: the object that we desire provides pleasure, while the satisfaction provided just by saying NO to an object comes in surplus of this object, a surplus which cannot be reduced by proposing to the subject another object. In short, in the Other Now Iris would have been deprived of the surplus-enjoyment.

To put it another way, Iris intuitively grasps that the overcoming of alienation would also deprive her of enjoyment. In his "Beyond Satire,"[46] Aaron Schuster demonstrated that enjoyment is constitutively, at its most basic, *enjoyment in alienation itself*—there is no "direct" enjoyment that somehow by-passes the symbolic alienation. Let's take the most elementary form of enjoyment: sucking one's own thumb. In a mythic first time, sucking was performed to satisfy a bodily need (thirst), but then the pleasure focused on the act of sucking itself which generates surplus-enjoyment even when it is performed in an empty way (no fluid is sucked). This reflexive turn upon oneself is possible only because the need (for drink) is already "structured like a language," overdetermined by the symbolic order where demand is demand for love: I depend on a big Other embodied here in the figure of the Mother, and my demand for milk from mother is simultaneously the demand addressed at her to show her love by giving milk:

> After alienation in the symbolic order where "man's desire is the Other's desire," enjoyment entails a kind of return-to-self, an appropriation of the alienated conditions of desire as if they were one's own ("the human subject is able to take possession of the very conditions imposed upon him" and "manages to be satisfied with them").

So enjoyment is a kind of autonomization with regard to the big Other: I don't need the Other's love, satisfaction is brought by my own activity. The structure of alienation remains here, I go on doing exactly the same thing as before, I only disconnect it from the need it was intended to satisfy as well as from the Other who expressed its love for me by way of satisfying my need. In this way, my activity becomes mine, it generates my enjoyment:

> Through enjoyment I possess my dispossession, or at least I get off on it. My desire may not be mine, but nevertheless I can find some satisfaction there, in the chain of signifiers that reigns over my divided existence—this jolt of excitement from loss and estrangement is what the concept of *jouissance* designates. In other words, enjoyment is always the enjoyment of the subject's alienation, it's how the subject lives this alienation and makes it its "own". (181)

What we should be careful not to miss is that enjoyment of the alienation itself is just one side of the irreducible parallax that characterizes the relationship between desire and enjoyment. On the one hand, as Lacan put it, "desire is a defense, a defense against going beyond a limit in jouissance":[47] since desire is always non-satisfied, since it always aims at something beyond every available object which is "never that," desire protects us from the suffocating over-presence of enjoyment. But . . .

> But shouldn't we add that jouissance is also a defense against desire? Enjoyment, understood as partial satisfaction, is what renders the subject's alienation in the symbolic order livable— one's very own alienation—even though this is not pleasing or fulfilling in any straightforward manner. Enjoyment is an excess that gives bodily form to a symbolic lack. (241)

Enjoyment is thus at the same time a defense against (or an escape from) the void or pure transcendence of desire: if desire is by definition never fully satisfied, enjoyment enacts a reflexive turn by means of which, while still missing the absent Thing, we achieve satisfaction in the very act of repeatedly missing it. This duality is at the same time the duality between desire and drive: desire stands for lack, non-satisfaction, while drive's circular movement generates satisfaction. Desire and drive are co-dependent: each can be understood as a reaction to the other. Desire is metonymic, always sliding from one to another object, again and again experiencing that "this is not that," and drive resolves this endless movement of desire by way of elevating the endless circulation around a lost object into a source of satisfaction. Drive is a circular movement, caught in its closed cycle, and desire breaks out of this closure, bringing fresh air into the situation, externalizing the object and sending the subject on a quest for it. Such a situation is a parallax at its purest: neither of the two terms are more primordial than the other. The third term is not any synthesis of the two but just the pure gap itself, and desire and drive are the two reactions to this gap: desire externalizes the lack into a cause-object, drive circulates around the object. In desire, the gap appears as lack; in drive, it appears as an excess that derails the circulation of life.

The best case of the porosity of the distinction between desire and drive is the case of Antigone. In his seminar on ethics of psychoanalysis, Lacan proposed that "the only thing one can be guilty of, at least in the analytic perspective, is having given up on one's desire"(321). His motto is thus: *ne pas ceder sur son desir*—but here ambiguity enters immediately: since desire is hysteric and metonymic, since it targets the gap beyond or between demands, so what "not giving up on one's desire" amounts to is precisely the readiness to pass from one to another object because no determinate object is "that"—or, as Lacan put it in his seminar *Encore*: "*Je te demande de refuser ce que je t'offre parce que c'est pas ça*" (session of February 9 1972): "I demand from you (ask you) to reject what I offer you because it is not that." But does Antigone not function in the exactly opposite way? Her act expresses the unconditional fidelity to a deep law, not its transgression—in short, she unconditionally insists on her demand—to bury her brother properly—there is no metonymic desire here, no compromise. Now we can understand why Lacan's formula of drive is $-D, a subject attached to a demand—and this is what Antigone does. Is this also why Lacan's formula of ethics (do not compromise your desire) is pronounced only once, it never returns, in clear contrast to Lacan's other formulas to which he always returns in new variations.

The same parallax is reproduced in the position of *objet a* which is simultaneously the cause-object of desire and the object of drive:

in desire, it functions like the always-eluding surplus, what desire cannot ever attain, while in drive, it functions like the central void around which drive circulates. At an even more formal level, *objet a* is simultaneously what Schelling called the "indivisible remainder," a rest that escapes formal structure, like the proverbial piece of trash that prevents the smooth running of a machine, AND a purely formal twisted structure of the machine itself which makes it turn around itself. The two are strictly correlative: the piece of trash gives body to a contortion in the machine itself, and it is undecidable which comes first.

If subject is constitutively alienated in the big Other (symbolic order), does the reversal that characterizes enjoyment then function as the moment of separation which, for Lacan, follows alienation? No: separation means separation in the Other itself, i.e., the lack of the subject with regard to the Other is transposed into the Other itself, as a separation of the Other from itself—what the subject presupposed the Other has (the subject's object-cause of desire), the Other itself doesn't have, so what unites me with the Other is this shared lack. So where does separation enter here? Desire and enjoyment relate as lack and excess, but on the opposite sides of the Moebius track: the excess cannot be used to fill in the lack because excess is the obverse of the lack itself. Desire and enjoyment therefore cannot be united in any kind of higher synthesis or with a turn to some more fundamental dimension that grounds both poles—what comes first is only the gap itself that separates the two poles, lack and excess. Separation is to be located in this gap which separates the two versions of *objet a*, pure form and formless remainder, lack and excess: it *separates the same object from itself*, into its form without stuff and its formless stuff.

So What is Surplus-Enjoyment?

In a famous scene from Brecht/Weil's *Dreigroschenoper* (finale of Act 1) Polly expresses her wish to be happy and find a man who she can really love; her father Peachum (with a Bible in is hand) agrees with her wish—but with a twist:

> Das Recht des Menschen ist's auf dieser Erden,
> da er doch nur kurz lebt, glücklich zu sein,
> teilhaftig aller Lust der Welt zu werden,
> zum Essen Brot zu kriegen und nicht einen Stein.
> Das ist des Menschen nacktes Recht auf Erden,
> doch leider hat man bisher nie vernommen,
> dass etwas recht war und dann war's auch so!
> Wer hätte nicht gern einmal Recht bekommen?
> Doch die Verhältnisse, sie sind nicht so.

Or later, in a repetition:

> Wir wären gut anstatt so roh,
> Doch die Verhältnisse, sie sind nicht so.

Or, in English translation:

> It's the right of a man on this earth,
> since he doesn't live long, to be happy,
> to enjoy all the pleasures of this world,
> to get bread to eat, and not a stone.
> This is man's justifiable law on earth,
> but so far, regrettably, no one has ever heard
> that that, what was justifiable, came true!
> Who wouldn't want to get what he wants?
> But the circumstances, they aren't so (good).[48]

And, in the repetition:

> We would be good instead of / being so / brutal,
> But the circumstances, they aren't so.

The lyrics work here only in combination with Weil's ingenious music, in its very simplicity the true work of a genius.[49] Let's first take a look at the lyrics of Peachum's reply: the first half (comprising five lines) celebrates in a preaching religious style the way we would all like to live (a long and happy life full of earthly pleasures); then, the second half confronts this wishful thinking with the cruel reality of misery and suffering caused by objective social circumstances—"But the circumstances, they aren't so (good)." This last line, with its obvious cynical sarcasm, already points to the change in the tone of the music which goes in the direction opposite to what one would have expected—one would have expected the first half to half to be joyful, celebrating earthly pleasures, and the second part to destroy our illusions and evoke the sadness and despair of our daily life. What happens is that the first half is done in the slow preaching way of a religious sermon, while the second half is done in a joyfully cynical lively way—the obvious pleasure with which the bad news (the sad message) is delivered is surplus-enjoyment at its purest. (One should also note that Polly joins Peachum in this cynically joyful stance.) This surplus-enjoyment culminates in the almost ecstatic tone of the last two lines: "We would be good instead of / being so / brutal, / But the circumstances, they aren't so." Both in the first and the second half, the gap that separates the subjective position of enunciation from the "objective" content is mobilized: the reference to harsh circumstances is evoked with a pleasure which gives body to pure hypocrisy: "What can I do, I would love to do it in another way, but such are the circumstances!" It is the way to obfuscate one's subjective engagement, to make oneself an impassive victim of circumstances, like Valmont's famous "C'est pas ma faute!" from *Les liaisons dangereuses*. (In the song that follows, one finds the inverted version of the same cynical wisdom: "Es geht auch anders, aber so geht es auch." You can do this differently, but you can also do it like this!) It is the opposite of the usual Leftist mantra which tells us that things are not inevitably as they are, but they could also be done otherwise, that another world is possible.

Enjoying Alienation

Can one imagine a better example of how enjoyment is alienated? What the constitutive alienation of enjoyment means is that we ultimately experience enjoyment as mediated by the big Other: it is the Other's enjoyment inaccessible to us (woman's enjoyment for men, another ethnic group's enjoyment for our group . . .), or our rightful enjoyment stolen from us by an Other or threatened by an Other. Russel Sbriglia noticed how this dimension of the "theft of enjoyment" played a crucial role when Trump's supporters stormed the Capitol on January 6 2021:

Could there possibly be a better exemplification of the logic of the "theft of enjoyment" than the mantra that Trump supporters were chanting while storming the Capitol: "Stop the steal!"? The hedonistic, carnivalesque nature of the storming of the Capitol to "stop the steal" wasn't merely incidental to the attempted insurrection; insofar as it was all about taking back the enjoyment (supposedly) stolen from them by the nation's others (i.e., blacks, Mexicans, Muslims, LGBTQ+, etc.), the element of carnival was absolutely essential to it.[50]

What happened on January 6 2021 in the Capitol was not a coup attempt but a carnival. The idea that carnival can serve as the model for the progressive protest movements—such protests are carnivalesque not only in their form and atmosphere (theatrical performances, humorous chants), but also in their non-centralized organization—is deeply problematic: is late-capitalist social reality itself not already carnivalesque? Was the infamous *Kristallnacht* in 1938—this semi-organized, semi-spontaneous outburst of violent attacks on Jewish homes, synagogues, businesses, and people themselves—not a carnival if there ever was one? Furthermore, is "carnival" not also the name for the obscene underside of power—from gang rapes to mass lynchings? Let us not forget that Michail Bakhtin developed the notion of carnival in his book on Rabelais written in the 1930s, as a direct reply to the carnival of the Stalinist purges. Traditionally, in resisting those in power, one of the strategies of the "lower classes" has regularly been to use terrifying displays of brutality to disturb the middle-class sense of decency. But with the events on Capitol, carnival again lost its innocence.

Most of the Capitol protesters "flew from their affluent suburbs to the US Capitol, ready to die for the cause of white privilege"[51]—true, but many of them were also part of a lower-middle class which sees their privileges threatened by the imagined coalition of big business (new digital media corporations, banks), state administration (controlling our daily lives, imposing lockdowns, masks, gun control and other limitations on our basic freedoms), natural catastrophes (pandemic, forest fires), and "others" (the poor, other races, LGBT+ . . .) who are allegedly exhausting the state's financial resources, compelling it to raise taxes. Central is here the category of "our way of life": socializing in bars and cafeterias or in large sport events, free car movement and the right to possess guns, rejection of everything that poses a threat to these freedoms (like masks and lockdowns), and of state control (but not against controlling the "other")—everything that poses a threat to this way of life (unfair Chinese trade practices, Politically Correct "terror," global warming, pandemics . . .) is denounced as a plot. This "way of life" is clearly not class-neutral: it is the way of life of the white middle-class who perceive themselves as the true embodiment of "what America is about."

So when we hear that the agent of this conspiracy did not just steal the election but is taking from us (gradually eroding) our (way of) life, we should apply here another category, that of the *theft of enjoyment*. Jacques Lacan predicted way back in the early 1970s that capitalist globalization will give rise to a new mode of racism focused on the figure of an Other who either threatens to snatch from us our enjoyment (the deep satisfaction provided by our immersion in our way of life), and/or itself possesses and displays an excessive enjoyment that eludes our grasp (suffice it to recall the anti-Semitic fantasies about secret Jewish rituals, the white supremacist fantasies about the superior sexual prowess of black men, the perception of Mexicans as rapists and drug dealers . . .). Enjoyment is not be confused here with sexual or other pleasures: it is a deeper satisfaction in our specific way of life or paranoia about the Other's way of life—what disturbs us in the Other is usually embodied in small details of daily lives (the smell of their food, the loudness of their music or laughter . . .).

Incidentally, was not a similar mix of fascination and horror present in the Left-liberal reaction to the protesters breaking into the Capitol? "Ordinary" people breaking into the sacred seat of power, a carnival that momentarily suspended our rules of public life . . . some of my friends were totally traumatized by the shots of the mob invading the Capitol, telling me: "The crowd taking over the seat of power—we should be doing this! The wrong people are now doing it!" This, maybe, is why the populist Right so annoys the Left: the Rightists are stealing enjoyment from the Left.

When we deal with the social dimension of surplus-enjoyment, we should bear in mind that Lacan's notion of surplus-enjoyment is modeled on Marx's notion of surplus-value; however, one has to be very precise about the link between surplus-enjoyment and surplus-value. As Alenka Zupančič put it, "we are not dealing here with a parallelism between surplus-enjoyment and surplus-value, between libidinal and social economy, but with a *short circuit* between the two": with its focus on extracting surplus-value, capitalism changes the basic coordinates of how we desire. Todd MacGowan[52] provided a Lacanian explanation of the resiliency of capitalism, boldly admitting that, in some (very qualified) sense capitalism effectively does fit "human nature." In contrast to premodern social orders which obfuscate the paradox of human desire and presume that desire is structured in a straightforward teleological way (we humans strive towards some ultimate goal, be it happiness or another kind of material or spiritual fulfillment, and aim at finding peace and satisfaction in its achievement), capitalism is the first and only social order that incorporates into its functioning the basic paradox of human desire. This paradox concerns the functioning of surplus in our libidinal economy: whatever we achieve is never "that," we always want something else and more, and the ultimate aim of our desire is not to achieve some ultimate goal but to reproduce its own endless self-reproduction in an ever expanded form. This is why the imbalance of the system defines capitalism: capitalism can only thrive through its own constant self-undermining and revolutionizing. The paradox is that, because we desire the surplus that eludes every object, our very orientation towards pleasure and satisfaction compels us to permanently sacrifice available satisfactions on behalf of satisfactions to come—in capitalism, hedonism and asceticism coincide.

Does this mean that capitalist consumerism is inherently hysteric? That we are by definition disappointed after we buy a product, the mysterious ingredient is never there, "*ce n'est pas ca,*" the thing we buy is never "it," so we pass to the next object in the metonymy of desire? Not really—Zupančič perspicuously noted that in consumerism, the hysterical stance is effectively re-appropriated by a perverse libidinal economy: as consumerists, we know well in advance that we will not get what we desired, so we are never really disappointed, the properly hysterical drama of deceit fails to take place, and it is this knowledge-which-neutralizes-the-hysterical-drama that defines perversion. Hysteria is a subjective stance of questioning (what do I really desire? what does my Other see or desire in me, i.e., what am I for the Other?), while a pervert knows, he is not haunted by questions. Today's consumerist is a cynical pervert who knows—in this way, desire is neutralized, nothing happens when we achieve the object of desire, no event of a true encounter, when we love there is no FALLING in love.

Along the same lines, in capitalism we have to further distinguish between the capitalist's enjoyment and the enjoyment attributed to Capital itself. The capitalist is also in a perverse position, he enjoys observing (and actively promotes) the expanded self-reproduction of Capital. At the very end of his *Encyclopaedia*, Hegel writes that the absolute Idea enjoys its repeated self-reproduction: "The eternal Idea, in full fruition of its essence, eternally sets itself to work, engenders and enjoys itself as absolute Mind."[53] At the highpoint of absolute knowing, the philosopher is just an impassive observer of this self-enjoyment of the absolute Idea. And does the same not hold for the capitalist who observes the self-enjoyment of the Capital?

Robert Pfaller elaborated the notion of "impersonal beliefs," beliefs which function as a social fact and determine how we act although (almost) no one directly believes—the usual excuse of individuals is something like: "I know it's probably not true, but I follow the rules because they are a constituent part of my community." To be clear: this impersonal belief doesn't exist independently of subject (who believes or presupposes another to believe), it exists (or, rather, it is operative) only as presupposed by the subject who (or, rather, precisely when) they pretend not to believe. The status of this impersonal belief is thus exactly that of the big Other: "I don't believe . . . (but the big Other does, and for its sake I have to act as if I do believe)." And, relying again on Alenka Zupančič, one should posit that, in a parallel with impersonal belief, there is also something we should call *impersonal enjoyment*: enjoyment which cannot be attributed to individuals (as "subjects who directly enjoy")—this enjoyment is attributed by subject to some figure of the big Other. Such impersonal enjoyment is what characterizes perversion, which is why Lacan defines a pervert as the agent who conceives himself as the instrument of the Other's enjoyment. This is what, in the very last pages of his *Seminar XI*, Lacan alludes to when he says that

> the offering to obscure gods of an object of sacrifice is something to which few subjects can resist succumbing, as if under some monstrous spell. Ignorance, indifference, an averting of the eyes may explain beneath what veil this mystery still remains hidden. But for whoever is capable of turning a courageous gaze towards this phenomenon—and, once again, there are certainly few who do not succumb to the fascination of the sacrifice in itself—the sacrifice signifies that, in the object of our desires, we try to find evidence for the presence of the desire of this Other that I call here the dark God.[54]

A pervert who operates under this "monstrous spell" and does what he does for the enjoyment of the divine Other, is not a sleazy dirty guy who enjoys torturing his victims; he is, on the contrary, a cold professional who does his duty in an impersonal way, for the sake of duty. The shift from an ordinary sadist to a true pervert is what underlies Hannah Arendt's description of the change that occurred in the Nazi concentration camps when the SS replaced the SA as their administrators:

> Behind the blind bestiality of the SA, there often lay a deep hatred and resentment against all those who were socially, intellectually, or physically better off than themselves, and who now, as if in fulfillment of their wildest dreams, were in their power. This resentment, which never died out entirely in the camps, strikes us as *a last remnant of humanly understandable feeling*. The real horror began, however, when the SS took over the administration of the camps. The old spontaneous bestiality gave way to an absolutely cold and systematic destruction of human bodies, calculated to destroy human dignity; death was avoided or postponed indefinitely. The camps were no longer amusement parks for beasts in human form, that is, for men who really belonged in mental institutions and prisons; the reverse became true: they were turned into "drill grounds", on which perfectly normal men were trained to be full-fledged members of the SS.[55]

Eichmann was not just a bureaucrat organizing train timetables etc., he was in some sense aware of the horror he was organizing, but his distance from this horror, his pretense that he was just a bureaucrat doing his duty, was part of his enjoyment, it was what added a surplus to his enjoyment—he enjoyed, but in a purely interpassive way, through the Other, the "dark god" to whom de Sade referred as "the Supreme-Being-in-Evil" (*l'être suprême en méchanceté*). To put it in somewhat simplified terms, although an SS officer might pretend (and even sincerely believe) he worked for the Good (of his nation, in getting rid of its enemies), the very way he works for his nation (the brutality of the concentration camps) makes him a bureaucrat of Evil, an agent of what Hegel would have called the ethical substance (*Sitten*) of his nation. And it is not just that he misunderstands the true greatness of his nation: the tension between the noble greatness of the idea of a nation and its dark underside is inscribed into the very notion of a nation. The Nazi idea of the German nation as an organic community threatened by Jewish intruders is in itself false, it forecloses immanent antagonisms which then return in the figure of the Jewish plot—the necessity to get rid of the Jews is thus inscribed into the very (Nazi) notion of German identity.

Things are similar with the new Rightist populism. The contrast between Trump's official ideological message (conservative values) and the style of his public performance (saying more or less whatever comes into in his head, insulting others and violating all rules of good manners ...) tells a lot about our predicament: what world do we live in in which bombarding the public with indecent vulgarities presents itself as the last barrier to protect us from the triumph of the society in which everything is permitted and old values go down the drain—as Alenka Zupančič put it, Trump is not a relic of old moral-majority conservatism, he is to a much greater degree the caricatural inverted image of postmodern "permissive society" itself, a product of this society's own antagonisms and inner limitations. Adrian Johnston proposed "a complementary twist on Jacques Lacan's dictum according to which 'repression is always the return of the repressed': the return of the repressed sometimes is the most effective repression."[56] Is this not also a concise definition of the figure of Trump? As Freud said about perversion, in it, everything that was repressed, all repressed content, comes out in all its obscenity, but this return of the repressed only strengthens the repression—and this is also why there is nothing liberating in Trump's obscenities, they merely strengthen social oppression and mystification. Trump's obscene performances thus express the falsity of his populism: to put it with brutal simplicity, while acting as if he cares for the ordinary people, he promotes big capital.

Totalitarian masters often discreetly admit that they are aware they have to employ brutal thugs to get the job done, and that these thugs are sadists who enjoy their brutal exercise of power. But they are wrong in constraining pleasure to a "human factor" which spoils the purity of the structure: the brutal obscenity of enjoyment is immanent to the social structure, it is a sign that this structure is in itself antagonist, inconsistent. In social life also, surplus-enjoyment is needed to fill the gap ("contradiction") that traverses social structure. Zupančič proposes here the hypothesis of a two-level surplus. In contrast to other modes of production, capitalism does not try to contain its structural instability, it puts to use the surplus that destabilizes other social formations: it thrives on surplus, counting it ... However, sooner or later a second-level excess is produced, a surplus that cannot be included in capital's reproduction (workers' dissatisfaction with the system), and Rightist populism is an attempt to re-configure this excess that threatens to destabilize the smooth running of capitalist reproduction in the guise of racist enjoyment, working class resentment, anti-intellectualism ...

But who is this Other whose instrument the pervert is? It appears in two figures which are very different. There is the Valmont-type pervert (the way Valmont seduces Madame de Courvel in *Liaisons dangereuses*): a cold methodical seducer who wants additionally to humiliate his victim by not just seducing her in a moment of weakness but by making her fully aware what she succumbed to and thus making her ashamed of her enjoyment in subordination. The victim is thus not an object, she is fully subjectivized, a divided subject unable to assume her enjoyment in her own humiliation.

This aspect of the relationship between power and sexuality tends to be neglected today: if I am sexually desired by another subject, this gives me a certain amount of power over the other who loves me, the other can even enjoy his/her subordination to me, and I can ruthlessly exploit this power. Such power plays are an immanent part of the dialectics of sexual desire: when I love or desire somebody passionately, I am helplessly exposed to him/her and as such profoundly vulnerable. On the other hand, my (asexual) power over another subject enables me to sexually exploit him/her: a teacher can demand a sexual favor from his student, a boss can demand the same from his subordinates ... It is significant that the first aspect is largely ignored in contemporary debates about sex and power which focus almost exclusively on how somebody in a position of power over me can exploit me by way of demanding sexual favors from me.

But the SS executioners in Auschwitz were not doing this; their enjoyment was not externalized in their victims but in the impersonal big Other. A pervert is not an exception to how enjoyment functions—he rather brings out the basic de-centering of enjoyment with regard to subject: enjoyment is *never directly subjectivized*, assumed as "mine," subjectivation is always a reaction to the traumatic intrusion of enjoyment, a way to acquire a distance towards it—maybe, desire is the name of how enjoyment is subjectivized.

Martin Luther as a Film Noir Figure

Now we reach the core of our topic, the theologico-political dimension of enjoyment—from a materialist standpoint, "theology" signals the de-centering of enjoyment with regard to subject: "God" is the ultimate figure of the enjoying big Other, and such a figure of the big Other poses a threat to the subject's freedom, it compels us to abolish human freedom. Frank Ruda developed this topic in detail, and it is crucial that, in reading his *Abolishing Freedom*,[57] we do not take its premises (of the need to abolish freedom, etc.) as some kind of postmodern irony, as a series of paradoxes not meant quite literally but just formulated to make us aware of true freedom—Ruda's premises are to be taken literally and seriously, "freedom" IS today, as Ruda puts it, a term of disorientation, a term which, instead of enabling us to draw the line of crucial distinction, blurs this line.

The enigma that underlies Ruda's book is: if there is no freedom of will, either in the religious sense of Predestination or in the naturalist sense of brain sciences, why does it matter so much to those who deny free will to coinvince us and make us admit that we have no free will, as if this admission will make a big difference? In technical terms, we are dealing here with a pragmatic contradiction: the enunciated propositional content (full determinism) is contradicted not by other positive facts or claims but by the very process of its enunciation (subjects who argue and try to convince us there is no free will act as free agents engaged in rational argumentation). This contradiction indicates a more radical gap. The solution is: yes, free will is ultimately an appearance, not a fact waiting to be discovered by objective science—but this appearance itself has an efficiency of its own. In his reading of Tourneur's classic *Out of the Past*, Pippin notes, the finesse of the hero's predicament in *film noir*: yes, we are doomed, Fate pulls the strings, every manipulator is in his/her turn manipulated, every position of a free agent who decides his fate is illusory—but to simply endorse and assume this predicament is also an illusion, an escapist avoiding of the burden of responsibility:

> If the traditional assumptions about self-knowing, deliberation-guided, casually effective agents are becoming less credible and are under increasing pressure, *what difference should it make in how we comport ourselves?* What would it actually be to *acknowledge* "the truth" or take into practical account the uncertainty? It is difficult to imagine what *simply* acknowledging the facts would be, to *give up* all pretensions to agency . . . when Jeff refuses to accept Kathie's fatalistic characterization that both of them simply *are* "no good," implying that it is useless to fight, and he calls the police, he . . . assumes a stance, a practical point of view, that in effect concedes how limited is the room for action allowed him by this point, but which does not assume that he is simply "carried along" by the consequences of his history (his past) or his nature ("no good"). He ends up an agent, however restricted and compromised, in the only way one can be. He acts like one.[58]

We cannot escape from the clutches of Fate, but we also cannot escape from the burden of responsibility into Fate. "Many of the best *noirs* are quite good at conveying to us the sense that this, this complicated and paradoxical situation, is what could more properly be said to be our modern fate."[59] Is this not why psychoanalysis is exemplary of our predicament? Yes, we are decentered, caught in a foreign cobweb, overdetermined by unconscious mechanisms, yes, I am "spoken" more than speaking, the Other speaks through me, but simply assuming this fact (in the sense of rejecting any responsibility) is also false, a case of self-deception—psychoanalysis makes me even more responsible than traditional morality, it makes me responsible even for what is beyond my (conscious) control. Don't we get here a nice case of "negation of negation": first subjective autonomy is negated, but then this negation itself is "negated," denounced as a subjective stratagem?

Was Luther not dealing with exactly the same paradox when he deploys how only the limit-experience of our utter impotence and incapacity to fulfill god's commandments, the experience which compels us to accept that we have no free will, can bring us to true faith—here is Ruda's concise description of this paradox:

> God has willed what he willed for eternity, "even before the foundation of the world." For this reason his "love . . . and hatred [are] eternal, being prior to the creation of the world." This is why there is predestination. This is also why his commandments cannot be fulfilled by us if he does or did not will it so. They exist for us in order to allow us to have the "undeniable experience of how incapable" we are. The law thus generates knowledge of one's own incapacity and impotence, of "how great weakness there is." Commandments produce knowledge of the fact that there is no free will. (31–2)

The first thing to note here is the superego-dimension of divine commandments: for Freud, superego is a commandment coming from an obscene agent who bombards us with it with the aim of making visible our failure to comply with it—the one who enjoys here is the Other (God), and it sadistically enjoys our failure. This convoluted structure of an injunction which is fulfilled when we fail to meet it accounts for the paradox of superego noted by Freud:

the more we obey the superego commandment the more we feel guilty. This paradox also holds when we follow Lacan and read superego as an injunction to enjoy: enjoyment is an impossible-real, we cannot ever fully attain it, and this failure makes us feel guilty. (Another paradox is at work here: enjoyment as an impossible-real means that we cannot ever attain it AND that we cannot ever get rid of it since our very attempts to get rid of it generate a surplus-enjoyment of their own.)

A series of situations that characterize today's society perfectly exemplify this type of superego-individualization: ecology, Political Correctness, poverty, up to indebtedness in general. Does the predominant ecological discourse not address us as a priori guilty, indebted to Mother Nature, under the coinstant pressure of the ecological superego-agency which addresses us in our individualty: "What did you do today to repay your debt to nature? Did you put all newspapers into a proper recycling bin? And all the bottles of beer or cans of Coke? Did you use your car where you could have used a bike or some means of public transport? Did you use air conditioning instead of just opening wide the windows?"[60] The ideological stakes of such individualization are easily discernible: I get lost in my own self-examination instead of raising much more pertinent global questions about our entire industrial civilization. This is why it is in a way quite justified that I feel guilty: following the injunctions to recycle etc. ultimately means that I follow rituals which allow me to postpone doing something that would really address the causes of ecological crisis.

The same goes for the endless Politically Correct self-examination: was my glance at the flight attendant too intrusive or sexually offensive? Did I use any words with a possible sexist undertone while addressing her? etc. etc. The pleasure, thrill even, provided by such self-probing is evident—recall how self-critical regret is mixed with joy when I discover that my innocent joke was not so innocent after all, that it contained a racist undertone ... As for charity, recall how we are all the time bombarded by messages destined to make us feel guilty for our comfortable way of life while children are starving in Somalia or dying unnecessarily from easily curable diseases—messages which simultaneously offer an easy way out ("You *can* make a difference! Give $10 monthly and you will make a black orphan happy!"). Again, the ideological underpinning is easily discernible here. Lazzarato's notion of "indebted man" provides a general structure of such subjectivity for which the superego-pressure of being indebted is constitutive—to paraphrase Descartes, I am in debt, therefore I exist as a subject integrated into the social order.

And does the same not hold even for the pathological fear of some Western liberal Leftists of being guilty of islamophobia? Any critique of Islam is denounced as an expression of Western islamophobia, Salman Rushdie is denounced for unnecessarily provoking Muslims and thus (partially, at least) responsible for a *fatwa* condemning him to death, etc. etc. The result of such a stance is what one can expect in such cases: the more the Western liberal Leftists probe into their guilt, the more they are accused by Muslim fundamentalists of being hypocrites who try to conceal their hatred of Islam. This constellation again perfectly reproduces the paradox of the superego: the more you obey what the Other demands of you, the guiltier you are. It is as if the more you tolerate Islam, the stronger its pressure on you will be …

And the implicit lesson of Luther is that we should not be afraid to apply this notion of superego to God himself and to how he relates to us, humans. God not only imposes on us commandments (he knows) we are unable to fulfill, he imposes on us these commandments not in order to really test us, not with the hope that we will perhaps succeed in following the commandments, but precisely in order to bring us to despair, to make us aware of our failure—and here, at this point only, we reach the limit of Christianity proper: this awareness of our utter impotence is the act of freedom, it changes everything. It is because of our freedom that the experience of our impotence drives us to despair: without freedom, we would simply accept that we are an unfree cog in the divine machinery. (If, on the contrary, we were to find in ourselves the strength to meet the challenge and to act according to divine commandments, this would also not mean that we are free but simply that the ability to act according to divine commandments is part of our nature, of our natural dispositions and potentials.) For this insight into our despair and utter impotence, Christ is not needed—it is just the omnipotent hidden God versus us. In Ruda's words:

the affirmation of the fact that there is no common measure that relates God and mankind—there is no human-divine relationship. Erasmus falsely assumes that there is a continuity between man and God and thereby also confuses "God preached and God hidden." It is precisely this distinction (in Hegelian terms, that between God for us and God in itself) that needs to be taken into account. God is not his Word. The Word is God revealed to mankind. To think God, one needs to avoid the temptation of fusing revelation (the Word, Christ) and God as such. (32)

Here, however, we have to introduce a key Hegelian twist: if "there is a radical gap, a difference different from all other differences, that separates the revealed God (Scripture) and God in himself (the hidden or 'naked' God)" (33), then this gap is not just the gap between God-in-itself and how God appears to us, it is also a gap in God itself—the fact that god appears is an event which deeply affects god's identity. There is no human-divine relationship—but *this non-relationship exists as such, in the figure of Christ*, God who is a human being. In other words, Christ is not a figure of mediation between god and man, a proof that god relates to man with loving care; what happens with Christ is that the non-relationship between god and man is transposed into god itself—the gap that separates man from god is asserted as immanent to god. Everything changes with this move: the one who experiences utter despair (expressed in his "My God, my God, why have you forsaken me?") is god (the son) himself, Christ dying on the cross, and through my belief in Christ I identify with god in my very despair. Identity with god is not achieved through some sublime spiritual elevation but only in the passage through utter despair, by way of transposing our own incapacity and impotence to God himself.[61] When this happens, God the father is no longer an obscene superego agent, and the abyss of utter despair turns out to be the other face of my radical freedom. We should never forget that, in Luther's vision, an individual is thrown into despair when he experiences his impotence and inability to obey god's commandments, not to carry out some impossible task (in Paradise already, Adam and Eve ate the prohibited apple)—and is freedom not precisely the freedom *not* to obey commandments?

The unique role of Christ is something that escapes mysticism even at its best, which means, of course, Meister Eckhart. Eckhart was on the right track when he said that he'd rather go to hell with God than to heaven without—but his ultimate horizon of the mystical unity of man and god as the abyssal Oneness in which man and God as separate entities disappear prevents him from drawing all the consequences from his insight. Let us quote extensively from Eckhart's Sermon 87 ("Blessed are the poor in spirit") which focuses on what does true "poverty" amounts to:

> as long as a man still somehow has the will to fulfill the very dear will of God, that man does not have the poverty we are talking about; for this man still wills to satisfy God's will, and this is not true poverty. For, if a man has true poverty, then he must be as free of his own will now, as a creature, as he was before he was created. For I am telling you by the eternal truth, as long as you have the will to fulfill God's will and are longing for eternity and for God, you are not truly poor. For only one who wills nothing and desires nothing is a poor man ... Therefore we say that a man should be so poor that he neither is nor has a place in which God could accomplish his work. If this man still holds such a place within him, then he still clings to duality. I pray to God that he rids me of God; for my essential being is above God insofar as we comprehend God to be the origin of all creatures. In that divine background of which we speak, where God is above all beings and all duality, there I was myself, I willed myself and I knew myself, in order to create my present human form. And therefore I am my own source according to my timeless being, but not according to my becoming which is temporal. Therefore, I am unborn, and, in the same way as I have never been born, I shall never die. What I am according to my birth will die and be annihilated; since it is mortal it must decompose in time. In my eternal birth all things were born and I was the source of myself and of all things; and if I had so willed there would be neither I nor any things; but if I were not, then God would not be, for I am the cause of God's existence; if I were not, God would not be God. However, it is not necessary to know that.[62]

Eckhart relies here on the distinction between me as a creature, part of the realm of creatures with God (the origin of all creatures) at its apex, and between the eternal impersonal I that is one with God beyond all creaturely life ("as I stand empty of my own will, of God, of God's will, and of all His works and of God Himself, there I am above all creatures, I am neither God nor creature, rather I am that I was and will remain, now and forever").[63] But this distinction is not enough to really account for Eckhart's own claim that it is better to be in Hell with God than in Heaven without God.

One has to be precise here—Eckhart does not talk about Christ, but about God: "ich will lieber in der helle sin und daz ich got habe, denne in dem himelriche und daz ich got nit enhabe" ("I would rather be in hell and have God than be in the kingdom of heaven and not have God").[64] It is my contention that one should replace here "God" with "Christ": one cannot be without God in Heaven because God IS Heaven, and the only way God can be in Hell is in the figure of Christ. The reason we have to replace "God" with "Christ" is thus simply that this is the only way to make Eckhart's proposition meaningful in a Christian sense. (We have here a nice example of how a misquote is closer to truth than the original.) Or, to go a step further: not only is a world without God Hell, but God without Christ (i.e. God in his separation from man) is the Devil himself. The difference between God and the Devil is thus that of a parallax: they are one and the same entity, just viewed from a different perspective. The Devil is God perceived as a superego authority, as a Master enacting his caprices.

The mystical unity of my I and God in which we both dissolve is beyond Heaven and Hell, there is even no proper place for Christ in it, it is the void of eternity. Insofar as we nonetheless define Heaven as the bliss of eternity in which I am fully one with God, then Christ as an embodied individual, as a God who is simultaneously a mortal creature (dying on the Cross), definitely belongs to the domain of Hell. In their "Engel," Rammstein describe in simple but touching terms the sadness and horror of angels who dwell in Heaven afraid and alone, sad because there is no love up there— maybe the deadly-suffocating love of God which is a mask of His indifference. God-the-Father knows I don't want to be an angel, but He keeps me there. Love comes only through Christ, and Christ's place is in Hell where life is, where passions divide us. And there is a step further to be made here: if, in order to reach the abyss of the Void, I have to get rid of God himself as the supreme creature, the only place to do it is Hell where God is by definition absent. To step out of the realm of creatures one has to descend to the lowest level of creaturely life which is Hell.

In his provocative claim, Eckhart doesn't only imagine where to be with or without Christ, he proposes a real choice we have to make, the choice between God and Christ, and it is the choice between Heaven and Hell. Rimbaud wrote in his *A Season in Hell*: "I believe I am in Hell, therefore I am." One has to take this claim in its full Cartesian sense: only in Hell can I exist as a singular unique I, a finite creature which is nonetheless able to separate itself from the cosmic order of creatures and step into the primordial Void.

Eckhart progresses from the temporal order of creatures to the primordial abyss of eternity, but he avoid the key question: how do creatures arise from this primordial abyss? Not "how can we reach eternity from our temporal finite being?" but: "How can eternity itself descend into temporal finite existence?" The only answer is that, as Schelling saw it, eternity is the ultimate prison, a suffocating closure, and it is only the fall into creaturely life which introduces Opening into human (and even divine) experience. This point was made very clearly by G.K. Chesterton who wrote apropos of the fashionable claim about the "alleged spiritual identity of Buddhism and Christianity":

> Love desires personality; therefore love desires division. It is the instinct of Christianity to be glad that God has broken the universe into little pieces . . . This is the intellectual abyss between Buddhism and Christianity; that for the Buddhist or Theosophist personality is the fall of man, for the Christian it is the purpose of God . . . Christianity is a sword which separates and sets free. No other philosophy makes God actually rejoice in the separation of the universe into living souls.[65]

And Chesterton is fully aware that it is not enough for God to separate man from Himself so that mankind will love Him—this separation HAS to be reflected back into God Himself, so that God is abandoned BY HIMSELF:

When the world shook and the sun was wiped out of heaven, it was not at the crucifixion, but at the cry from the cross: the cry which confessed that God was forsaken of God. And now let the revolutionists choose a creed from all the creeds and a god from all the gods of the world, carefully weighing all the gods of inevitable recurrence and of unalterable power. They will not find another god who has himself been in revolt. Nay (the matter grows too difficult for human speech), but let the atheists themselves choose a god. They will find only one divinity who ever uttered their isolation; only one religion in which God seemed for an instant to be an atheist.[66]

Because of this overlapping between man's isolation from God and God's isolation FROM HIMSELF, Christianty is "terribly revolutionary. That a good man may have his back to the wall is no more than we knew already; but that God could have His back to the wall is a boast for all insurgents for ever. Christianity is the only religion on earth that has felt that omnipotence made God incomplete. Christianity alone has felt that God, to be wholly God, must have been a rebel as well as a king."[67] We all know Einstein's claim against quantum physics: "God doesn't play dice!" Niels Bohr aptly answered Einstein: "Don't tell God what to do!" And we should go to the end in this direction: when a theologist claims "God cannot be evil!", our reply should be: "Don't tell God what he can or cannot be!" Chesterton is fully aware that we are thereby approaching "a matter more dark and awful than it is easy to discuss . . . a matter which the greatest saints and thinkers have justly feared to approach. But in that terrific tale of the Passion there is a distinct emotional suggestion that the author of all things (in some unthinkable way) went not only through agony, but through doubt."

In the standard form of atheism, emancipated humans stop believing in God; in Christianity, God dies *for himself*—in his "My God, my God, why have you forsaken me?", Christ himself commits what is for a Christian the ultimate sin: he wavers in his Faith. And, again, this is what eludes Eckhart: for him, God "dies for himself" in the sense that God as the supreme Being, as the origin of all creaturely life, also disappears when a human being reaches its utmost poverty—at this zero-point, man and God become indistinguishable, the abyssal One. For Chesterton, however, the ultimate mystery of Christianity is the exact opposite, the DIVISION of man from God which is transposed into God himself in the figure of Christ.

Here we finally reach the ultimate paradox of Luther's theology: how does the divine self-division affect the relationship between freedom and Predestination? Predestination is not an objective fact but a matter of choice, of our own unconscious choice which precedes our temporal existence:

> This peculiar kind of choice to which we are condemned is structurally analogous to what Freud calls "the choice of neurosis"—a choice that is peculiarly "independent of experiences". This means that in a certain sense the subject is forced to choose its own unconscious: "This claim that the subject, so to speak, chooses her unconscious ... is the very condition of possibility of psychoanalysis." (162)

When Freud says that this forced choice (forced because it always-already happened: we never choose), this choice which is simultaneously impossible and necessary (unavoidable), is "independent of experiences," one should give to this formulation all its Kantian weight: the fact that the choice of neurosis is independent of experience means that it is not an empirical ("pathological," in Kant's sense) choice but a properly transcendental choice that precedes our empirical temporal existence. Kant talks about such an eternal/atemporal choice of our character, and Schelling follows him at this point: if I am evil, I cannot avoid acting in evil ways in my life, such is my character, but I am nonetheless responsible for it because I've chosen it in an atemporal act. Are we thereby not back at exemplum as different from examples? The eternal/atemporal choice is, of course, a fiction in the sense that it never takes place in our temporal reality, it is a fictional X presupposed by all our actual acts and choices—and precisely as such, it is THE exemplum of a free choice. Or, to put it in Kantian terms, all our temporal choices can be suspected of being "pathological," not free acts but conditioned by our contingent interests and determinations—only the eternal/atemporal choice is actually free.

Ruda is right to point out that such a choice explains Freud's formula "anatomy is destiny" which should be read as a Hegelian speculative statement in which subject passes into predicate. It doesn't mean "the anatomic/biological fact of having a penis or not determines our social destiny as a man or a woman"; it means (almost) the exact opposite: what we (mis)perceive as a fact of anatomy is symbolic destiny, i.e., we choose our destiny in a forced choice and this choice underlies the everyday perception of our sexual identity being based on anatomy:

> The fact that it is the female logic that makes all this visible means that, for Freud, woman is the name of this peculiar freedom that we know nothing of. But if woman is a name for this choice, this also means that within the female logic woman does not exist (as a fixed entity). Rather woman is a name for this act. (163)

The act of choice is not neutral, there is no neutral subject choosing a side in sexual difference: the act of choice is feminine, man is a chosen identity. To put it in somewhat simplified terms, sexual difference is ultimately the one between becoming and being, and this is how one can also read Lacan's claim that the woman doesn't exist: man exists, woman is becoming. Which also means: man is object, woman is subject. Is this not confirmed even at the level of anatomy? In her *Erased Pleasure*, Catherine Malabou[68] provides a philosophical investigation into the paradoxical status of the clitoris: the clitoris doesn't penetrate anything and, as such, it contains the possibility of a different way to relate to power, free from domination and will to penetrate. The clitoris is the only organ that serves nothing, i.e., just pleasure (other mammals also have it, although it is not clear if it brings orgasm). It gives the body an anarchic excess outside binary complementarity of protruding penis and vaginal hole.

It is easy to explain the clitoris in an evolutionary way as a remainder of the bisexuality of the fetus in the first weeks of pregnancy, with no function now (like male breast nipples). But, of course, what is at stake is not the evolutionary origin of the clitoris, it is its role in the symbolic space of a woman which makes it traumatic (for men), an object willfully ignored and even circumsised (cliterodectomy). However, Malabou all too quickly dismisses Lacan (and Freud) as phallogocentric. It is not that we have a "normal" phallic constellation (erect penis, vaginal hole to be penetrated, ejaculation and vaginal orgasm), and then clitoris as an element which poses a threat to this phallic constellation, challenging it, introducing a heterogeneous moment, a source of pleasure independent of phallic sexuality. This may appear to fit Lacan's formulas of sexuation: the masculine position is phallic while the feminine position is not-all caught in the phallic logic, something escapes it, and this something (the non-phallic jouissance feminine) is embodied in the clitoris … However, such a reading ignores the paradox of Lacan's formulas: the feminine position of not-all implies that there is no exception (there is nothing which eludes phallic function), while the masculine logic implies an exception. This reference to Lacan enables us to see how the phallic constellation (penis/vagina) and clitoris are moments of the same all-encompassing constellation of sexual difference as impossible.

We should thus shift the accent: it's not just that the clitoris embodies autonomous feminine enjoyment as opposed to vaginal enjoyment which is complementary to phallic. With the clitoris, sexual difference itself is integrated/reflected in the feminine body: the clitoris is a phallic remainder, its visible head is a "small penis" (but inside it is much larger, spreading down beneath vaginal lips. What if, then, what defines feminine sexuality is the distance itself between the clitoris and the vaginal hole, between non-phallic clitoral orgasm and phallic-vaginal one (recall the classical scene of a woman who masturbates herself clitorally while being penetrated by a penis). In the heterosexual masculine case, the division is external, it is penis versus vagina, while in the feminine case it is internal, it is vaginal hole versus clitoris. Here we can see clearly how "woman" stands for choosing while "man" stands for an accomplished choice (of phallus). Or, at a more abstract ontological level, "woman" stands for abyssal freedom while "man" stands for Predestination.

A Desire Not to Have a Mother

We should avoid here the pseudo-Freudian temptation: the "woman" which stands for abyssal freedom is NOT mother—the subject (inclusive of women) who dares to confront this abyss has precisely to reject mother: it is Medea who, through her rejection of motherhood (killing her children), assumes this abyss. Rammstein outlines this rejection in one of their supreme songs, "Mutter." The lyrics tell the story of a child not born from a womb but in an experiment, thus having no true father or mother; they describe his plan to kill both the mother "who never gave birth to him" and then himself. However, he fails to kill himself, instead ending up mutilated and no better off than before. The child begs and prays for strength, but his dead mother does not answer. His situation is ambiguous: was it an experimental birth out of the womb, an abortion so that he sings as dead, or, at a more general level, is it a metaphor for the situation of Germans after World War II where they found their "motherland" destroyed and thus their lives ruined? One should resist here the temptation to decide what the song "really is about"—it "really is about" the formal constellation of a motherless child who survives his suicide. And a similar ambiguity is surprisingly at work in different musical versions of the song: there is the Rammstein hard rock "original," but then there are versions for solo soprano accompanied by piano or symphonic orchestra, for a male chorus, even for a children's chorus (with lyrics in Russian), and they all sound so "natural" in spite of the extreme brutality of the event described in lyrics.

Even the (obvious) nonsenses of the lyrics (how can a child who never had a mother kill her?) are meaningful here: mother failed, she is guilty, precisely for *not* being there when needed. The children with grey hair are not just the paradox of old children—newborns can often look like old men, with grey hair and wrinkled skin; it takes a couple of days to "become a child" without hair and with smooth skin ... Is this child not like an angel stuck in a limbo, neither unborn not born? (Angels in heaven are also motherless.) But the lesson of the song is much more radical, metaphysical even—the extreme situation it describes is the universal predicament of all of us, actually existing human beings. In psychoanalytic terms, Mother is impossible/real, no actual mother is Mother, so we are all in some sense not even fully born, we are freaks not even fully thrown into the world. The problem is not that we are still stuck in the mother's body but that we were never in it—we were from the beginning aliens parasitizing in the womb. The hero's suicide had to fail because he never was fully alive, it is only through the failure of his suicide that he comes to be—the ultimate proof that being is failed non-being.

So is there a happy outcome to this deadlock? Yes—see *The Butterfly Effect* (2004, directed by Eric Bress and J. Mackye Gruber) which tells the story of Evan (played by Ashton Kutcher) who finds he can travel back in time to inhabit his former self. He repeatedly attempts to change his catastrophic present by changing his past behaviors and set things right for himself and his friends, but every time he does this and returns to the present, the situation is even worse, until he finds the only solution. He views a family film of his father's, that showed Evan's mother just before she was about to give birth to Evan. Evan travels back to that moment and strangles himself in the womb with his umbilical cord so as to prevent himself from continuing. (This ending is available only in the director's cut of the film—the version released in movie theaters has a standard happy ending.)[69] The film is right: this is the only truly happy ending we can imagine to our lives (as Sophocles knew when he wrote that the greatest happiness is not being born at all). One should raise Evan's final act to the transcendental level of a primordial atemporal decision by means of which we choose ourselves, our eternal character (of which Kant spoke): in this case, he successfully chooses his own not-being.

This, however, is not the last word to be said on this topic. Evan's mistake is that he focuses his life on happiness, on how to avoid suffering—he sacrifices even his love only so that he and others will not suffer. However, to use Badiou's terms, happiness is a category of the "human animal," of our ordinary life whose horizons are pleasure and satisfaction in all their guises, perverted as they are—this life is effectively just a postponed suicidal despair. If we are to overcome this despair, we have to enter another dimension of existence, what Badiou calls the Event in its four modes: science (philosophy included), art, politics (including politicized economy), and love. To live in fidelity to an Event does not entail happiness but a life of struggle, of risks and tensions, of the creative engagement for a Cause which surpasses our existence.

Finale
Subjective Destitution as a Political Category

Lately, after the publication of Heidegger's *Black Notes*, attempts abound to exclude him from the list of philosophers to be taken seriously on account of his anti-Semitism and his Nazi links. For this very reason, one should insist that Heidegger remains pertinent: even when he is at his worst, unexpected links open themselves up. In the mid-1930s, Heidegger said: "there are human beings and human groups (Negroes like, for example, Kaffirs) who have no history ... however, animal and plant life has a thousand year long and eventful history ... within the human region, history can be missing, as with Negroes."[1] ("Kaffir" was at the time of apartheid an ethnic slur used to refer to black Africans in South Africa.) The quoted lines are strange, even by Heidegger's standards: so animals and plants do have history, but "Negroes" do not? "Animal and plant life has a thousand year long and eventful history"—but for sure not in the strict Heidegger sense of the epochal disclosure of Being ... Plus where then do countries like China or India stand which are also not historical in Heidegger's specific sense? The true enigma which should not be dismissed as a simple case of misunderstanding is, however, the case of Grant Farred, a noted contemporary black philosopher who teaches at Cornell. His short book *Martin Heidegger Saved My Life*[2] was written in reaction to a racist encounter: in the Fall of 2013, while raking leaves outside his home. Farred experienced a racist encounter: a white woman stopped to ask him, "Would you like another job?" Farred responded, "Only if you can match my Cornell faculty salary." In order to understand what happened to him, Farred turned to

Heidegger: "Heidegger saved me because he gave me the language to write about race in such a way as I'd never written it before. Heidegger enabled me to write in this way because he has made me think about how to think."[3] What he found so useful in Heidegger was the notion of language as a "house of being": not the abstract-universal language of science and state administration but language rooted in a particular way of life, language as the medium of an always-unique life experience which discloses reality to us in a historically specific way. It is easy to imagine how such a stance enables a subject to resist being swallowed into a global universe of technological domination ... however, is this the way to fight what is often calls the "Americanization" of our lives? To answer this question, we have to think—and, as Farred repeatedly points out, this is what he learned from Heidegger, not just to think but to think about thinking.

We live in a unique moment which gives rise to the urgency to think. Ours is not a peaceful time which provides the opportunity to comfortably withdraw into reflection on the world but a time when our survival itself as humans is under threat from different directions: the prospect of total digital control which aims to invade our mind itself ("the wired brain"), uncontrollable viral infections, the effects of global warming ... In a recent interview, Brian Greene suggested that there are two opposite ways to react when we find ourselves in such a difficult predicament:

> In this moment of global crisis—when all future plans have seemingly been upended and the fragility of life illuminated with terrible clarity—there is much solace to be found in focusing on the present moment; meeting each day, each hour, each meal as it comes. But there is also a type of inner peace to be found by zooming out beyond this moment, this century, this millennium, back to the beginning of time and forward to the death of the universe.[4]

So we either withdraw into our immediate (spatial and temporal) proximity—forget about global crisis, think about the grass in front of us, the good food we are chewing ...—or into a global view of the universe which makes us an invisible tiny drop—when you think about the Big Bang and the formation of first stars, one can ignore what happens on a tiny planet in a small galaxy . . .[5] But what if such a messy time is the proper time to raise "eternal" questions in a different sense? The worst thing to do today would be to say that we should focus on solving actual problems and forget about "eternal" questions. In some sense which is far from simply metaphorical, "eternity" is what is at stake today. However, is "philosophy" still a good name for such thinking about our predicament? Are we, philosophers, not bombarded from all sides by the notion that the era of philosophy is over?

The Two Ends of Philosophy

In his short but crucial late text "The End of Philosophy and the Task of Thinking,"[6] Heidegger resumed in a succinct way his basic insight into the possibility of thinking after the culmination of Western philosophy in modern science and technology. However, the topic of the end of philosophy dominates European philosophy from Kant onwards: Kant designates his critical approach as a prolegomena to a future philosophy (metaphysics); Fichte talks about the "doctrine of science (*Wissenschaftslehre*)" instead of philosophy; Hegel saw his system as no longer just philo-sophy (love of wisdom), but knowledge itself; Marx opposed philosophy to study of actual life; etc. until Heidegger whose motto was "the end of philosophy and the task of thinking." My first thesis is that there is a deep paradox in this fact. It is only with Kant's revolution, with his notion of the transcendental, that philosophy came to itself. Is it not that, ultimately, philosophy *as such* begins with Kant, with his transcendental turn? Is it not that the entire previous philosophy can be understood properly—not as the simple description of the "entire universe," of the totality of beings, but as the description of the horizon within which entities disclose themselves to a finite human being—only if read "anachronistically," from the standpoint opened up by Kant? Is it not that it was Kant who also opened up the field within which Heidegger himself was able to formulate the notion of *Dasein* as the place in which beings appear within a historically determined/destined horizon of meaning? (I am well aware that Heidegger would never have accepted the use of the term "transcendental" for his approach, since "transcendental" is for him irreducibly branded by the notion of modern subjectivity. In spite of that, I keep this term since I think it remains the most appropriate one to indicate the idea of a horizon within which entities appear to us.)

There are, of course, numerous reactions to the claim that philosophy is over: we have in the last decades attempts to resuscitate pre-Kantian metaphysical ontology. Already the status of Deleuze's thought is ambiguous: while Derrida is the ultimate historicist deconstructionist, does Deleuze not deploy in his great works (from *Difference and Repetition* on) a kind of global vision of reality? And is Badiou's "logic of the worlds" not a kind of *a priori* of all possible realities (in a conversation with me, he characterized his "logics of the worlds" as his dialectics of nature)? Then comes Quentin Meillassoux and the "object-oriented-ontology" with its new "theory of everything" (Graham Harman) which conceives humans as one among the objects. Although, in my view, Harman simply deploys yet another transcendental vision of reality, this certainly is not his intention. New anti-transcendental realists from Harman to Markus Gabriel deploy new ontologies, new universal Theories of Everything; what we should propose is a new plurality of ontologies, a multiverse in the sense of a realist reading of Plato's *Parmenides*: different ontological models describe different worlds—there is a world in which phenomena can be reduced to an underlying stable essence, a world in which soul is an immanent principle of its body, a world in which there is no contingency since iron necessity reigns in it—a world of limitless contingent interaction of phenomena, a world totalized by God, etc.

In contrast to these returns to ontology, I think that after Heidegger such thinking is no longer possible. We also have attempts to provide a more refined version of naturalism which avoids the narrow confines of reducing everything to natural objective reality. In his "Naturalism without Representationalism,"[7] Huw Price elaborates the difference between object naturalism (ON) and subject naturalism (SN). As an ontological doctrine, ON "is the view that in some important sense, all there *is* is the world studied by science. As an epistemological doctrine, it is the view that all genuine knowledge is scientific knowledge." In contrast to this approach which directly focuses on objective reality, SN begins with "what science tells us *about ourselves*. Science tells us that we humans are natural creatures, and if the claims and ambitions of philosophy conflict with this view, then philosophy needs to give way. This is naturalism in the sense of Hume, then, and arguably Nietzsche. I'll call it subject naturalism." Although ON seems universal and SN its particular case (we, humans, as natural beings), Price demonstrated with a subtle analysis that SN has logical priority: "Subject naturalism is theoretically prior to object naturalism, because the latter depends on validation from a subject naturalist perspective." What this implies is a shift in our notion of language from its representational functioning (we use words to refer to non-linguistic external reality) to its performative functioning: language as a material practice which includes a multitude of games (orders, expressions, declarations of facts) obeying different rules. "Objective" scientific approach is always rooted in these symbolic practices—which means, in my terms, that Price's SN subtly transcendentalizes naturalism: although we are part of nature, our symbolic practice is an *a priori* which already has to be here if we are to analyze objective reality. However, from my standpoint, SN still leaves open the ultimate question: how does a subject emerge out of pre-linguistic reality?[8]

To recapitulate our first result, the gap between reality and its transcendental horizon concerns the universal structure of how reality appears to us: what conditions must be met for us to perceive something as really existing? In this way, we can avoid the reproach that philosophy is an illegitimate vision of the universe not grounded in scientific research: transcendental thought doesn't speculate about all of reality, about how reality really is in itself, it just concerns itself with how we in our actual lives accept something as really existing. "Transcendental" is the philosopher's technical term for such a frame which defines the coordinates of reality; for example, the transcendental approach makes us aware that, for a scientific naturalist, only spatio-temporal material phenomena regulated by natural laws really exist, while for a premodern traditionalist, spirits and meanings are also part of reality, not only our human projections. The ontic approach, on the other hand, is concerned with reality itself, in its emergence and deployment:

How did the universe come to be? Does it have a beginning and an end? What is our place in it?

Prior to Kantian transcendental break, philosophy was a view-notion of the totality of beings: how is all of reality structured, is there a highest Being, what is the place of humans in it? Thales is usually named as the first philosopher, and his answer was: water is the substance of everything. (Note that he says water and not earth, the usual mythic reply!) As already Hegel noted, water as the ultimate substance is not the empirical water we see and feel—a minimum of idealism is already at work here, Thales's water is an "ideal" entity. This short-circuit stands for the inaugural gesture of philosophy: one particular element stands for all.

The usual modern reproach is that this short-circuit performs an illegitimate jump into universality: in its meta-physical speculations, philosophy proposes a universalization without proper empirical study and justification. Only today, with "theories of everything" in physics, are we gradually approaching a serious scientific answer to "big" questions, and this means the end of philosophy. In recent decades, technological progress in experimental physics has opened up a new domain, unthinkable in the classical scientific universe, that of the "experimental metaphysics": "questions previously thought to be a matter solely for philosophical debate have been brought into the orbit of empirical inquiry."[9] What until now has been the topic of "mental experiments" is gradually becoming the topic of actual laboratory experiments—exemplary is here the famous Einstein-Rosen-Podolsky double split experiment, first just imagined, then actually performed by Alain Aspect. The properly "metaphysical" propositions tested are the ontological status of contingency, the locality-condition of causality, the status of reality independent of our observation, etc.

Here one should be absolutely clear: these accounts are, in spite of their imperfections, in a certain sense simply and rather obviously *true*, so one should abandon all obscurantist or spiritualist reference to some mysterious dimension that eludes science. Should we then simply endorse this prospect and abandon philosophy? In philosophy, the predominant form of resistance to the full scientific self-objectivization of humanity which nonetheless admits science's achievements is the neo-Kantian transcendental philosophy (whose exemplary case today is Habermas): our self-perception as free and responsible agents is not just a necessary illusion, but the transcendental *a priori* of every scientific knowledge. For Habermas,

> the attempt to study first-person subjective experience from the third-person, objectifying viewpoint, involves the theorist in a performative contradiction, since objectification presupposes participation in an intersubjectively instituted system of linguistic practices whose normative valence conditions the scientist's cognitive activity.[10]

Habermas characterizes this intersubjective domain of rational validity as the dimension of "objective mind" which cannot be understood in terms of the phenomenological profiles of the community of conscious selves comprised in it: it is the intrinsically intersubjective status of the normative realm that precludes any attempt to account for its operation or genesis in terms of entities or processes simpler than the system itself. (Lacan's term for this "objective mind" irreducible to the Real of raw reality as well as to the Imaginary of our self-experience is, of course, the big Other.) Neither the phenomenological (imaginary) nor neurobiological (real) profiling of participants can be cited as a constituting condition for this socially "objective mind."

Although Habermas and Heidegger are big philosophical opponents, they share the basic transcendental approach which poses a limit to scientific naturalism. One can say that Heidegger brings philosophy to its conclusion by radicalizing the transcendental approach: he strictly distinguishes between reality (entities) and the horizon within which reality appears—he calls the gap between the two "ontological difference." For example, reality appears to us, moderns, differently than to premodern people for whom reality was full of spiritual agents and deeper meanings—in modern science, there is no place for this dimension, "real" is only what science can measure and quantify.

When I was young, I remember that an old dogmatically-Marxist handbook for philosophy that was used in high schools characterized Heidegger as an "agnostic phenomenalist"—stupid but true. Heidegger is "phenomenalist" in the sense that his ultimate horizon is the transcendental mode of appearance of entities, and he is "agnostic" in the sense that he ignores the status of entities prior to or outside of their appearance within a certain transcendental disclosure of being. To put it in a brutally simplified way, Heidegger's true problem is not Being but the status of the ontic outside a horizon of Being. (This is why some partisans of object-oriented-ontology are right to replace "ontology" with "onticology.") Thus, when Heidegger talks about god, he limits himself to how divinity appears to us, humans, in different epochal disclosures of Being. In this sense, Heidegger obviously deplores the rise of the "god of philosophy," the abstract notion of *causa sui*:

> This is the right name for the god of philosophy. Man can neither pray nor sacrifice to this god. Before the *causa sui*, man can neither fall to his knees in awe nor can he play music and dance before this god.[11]

Again, the question here is not which figure of god is more true, it is strictly about different epochal appearances of god. And, similarly, in spite of his newfound respect for religion, Habermas, Heidegger's great opponent, insists that we are required to adopt an *agnostic* attitude to religious beliefs—agnostic, i.e., leaving the question open, not excluding the existence of god.[12]

Today, we thus don't just live in an era of the proclaimed end of philosophy—we live in an era of the *double* end of philosophy. The prospect of a "wired brain" is a kind of final point of the naturalization of human thought: when our process of thinking can directly interact with a digital machine, it effectively becomes an object in reality; it is no longer "our" inner thought as opposed to external reality. On the other hand, with today's transcendental historicism, "naïve" questions about reality are accepted precisely as "naïve," which means they cannot provide the ultimate cognitive frame of our knowledge. A scientist may snap back: OK, but cannot a historical anthropology describe how, in the course of evolution, different shapes of *episteme* arise out of tradition and concrete social circumstances? Does Marxism not provide a quite convincing account of how new ideologies and sciences emerge in a complex social totality? Habermas is right here to insist that we cannot get out of the hermeneutic circle: the evolutionary explanation of human cognitive faculties already presupposes a certain epistemic approach to reality. The result is thus that a parallax is irreducible here: at some obvious "naïve" realist level, it is clear that humans evolved out of a vast field of reality; however, the circle of including ourselves in reality cannot ever be fully closed since every explanation of our place in reality already relies on a certain horizon of meaning—what to do here?

Heidegger gave to the transcendental approach an existential turn: philosophy as transcendental-phenomenological ontology does not inquire into the nature of reality, it analyses how all of reality appears to us in a given epochal constellation. In today's age of techno-science, we consider as "really existing" only what can be an object of scientific research—all other entities are reduced to illusory subjective experiences, just imagined things, etc. Heidegger's point is not that such a view is more or less "true" than a premodern view, but that, with the new disclosure of being that characterizes modernity, the very criteria of what is "true" or "false" changed … It is not difficult to grasp the paradox of such an approach: while Heidegger is perceived as a thinker uniquely focused on the question of Being, he leaves completely out of consideration what we understand by this question in our "naïve" pre-transcendental stance: how do things exist independently of the way we relate to them, independently of how they appear to us?

Is this enough, however? If the transcendental dimension is the irreducible frame or horizon through which we perceive (and, in a strict Kantian sense which has nothing to do with ontic creation, constitutes reality), how can we move beyond (or beneath) the couple of reality and its transcendental horizon? Is there a zero-level where these two dimensions overlap? The search for this level is the big topic of German Idealism: Fichte found it in the self-positing of the absolute I (transcendental Self), while Schelling found it in the intellectual intuition in which subject and object, activity and passivity, intellect and intuition immediately coincide.

Following the failure of these attempts, our starting point should be that the zero-level of reality and its transcendental horizon is not to be sought in some kind of synthesis of the two but in the very rupture between the two. Since today scientific realism is the hegemonic view, the question to be raised is: can the transcendental dimension be accounted for in these terms? How can the transcendental dimension arise/explode in reality? The reply is not a direct realist reduction but another question: what has to be constitutively excluded (primordially repressed) from our notion of reality? In short, what if the transcendental dimension is the "return of the repressed" of our notion of reality?

Man as a *Katastrophe*

This, then, is our deadlock: we have two ends of philosophy, the one in positive science occupying the field of old metaphysical speculations, and the one with Heidegger who brought the transcendental approach to its radical conclusion, reducing philosophy to the description of the historical "events," modes of disclosure of Being. The two do not complement each other, they are mutually exclusive, but the immanent insufficiency of each of them opens up the space for the other: science cannot close the circle and ground in its object the approach it uses when analyzing its object; only transcendental philosophy can do this; transcendental philosophy which limits itself to describing different disclosures of Being has to ignore the ontic question (how are entities outside of the horizon of their appearing to us), and science fills in this void with its claims about the nature of things. Is this parallax the ultimate stand of our thinking, or can we reach beyond (or, rather, beneath) it?

Heidegger's typical move when confronted with the prospect of a catastrophe is to move back from the ontic level to its ontological horizon. In the 1950s, when we were all haunted by the prospect of nuclear war, Heidegger wrote that the true danger is not actual nuclear war but the disclosure of Being in which scientific domination over nature is what matters—only within this horizon can an eventual nuclear self-destruction take place. To parody his jargon, one might say that the essence of a catastrophe is the catastrophe of/in the essence itself. Such an approach seems to me too short: it ignores the fact that the eventual self-destruction of humanity would simultaneously annihilate *Da-Sein* as the only site of the disclosure of Being.

Although Heidegger is the ultimate transcendental philosopher, there are mysterious passages where he ventures into this pre-transcendental domain. In the elaboration of this notion of an untruth */lethe/* older than the very dimension of truth, Heidegger emphasizes how man's "stepping into the essential unfolding of truth" is a "transformation of the being of man in the sense of a derangement */Ver-rueckung—*going mad"/ of his position among beings."[13] The "derangement" to which Heidegger refers is, of course, not a psychological or clinical category of madness: it signals a much more radical, properly ontological reversal/ aberration, when, in its very foundation, the universe itself is in a way "out of joint," thrown off its rails. What is crucial here is to remember that Heidegger wrote these lines in the years of his intensive reading of Schelling's *Treatise on Human Freedom*, a text which discerns the origin of Evil precisely in a kind of ontological madness, in the "derangement" of man's position among beings (his self-centeredness), as a necessary intermediate step ("vanishing mediator") in the passage from "prehuman nature" to our symbolic universe: "man, in his very essence, is a *katastrophe—*a reversal that turns him away from the genuine essence. Man is the only catastrophe in the midst of beings."[14]

However, at this crucial point where in some sense everything is decided, I think that we should take a step further with regard to Heidegger's formulation—"a derangement of his position among beings"—a step indicated by some other formulations of Heidegger himself. It may appear clear what Heidegger aims at by the quoted formulation: man as *Da-Sein* (the "being-there" of Being, the place of the disclosure of Being) is an entity irreducibly rooted in his body (I use here the masculine form since it is at work in Heidegger). With a little bit of rhetorical exaggeration, one can say that Heidegger's "no Being without Being-There as the place of its disclosure" is his version of Hegel's "one should grasp the Absolute not only as Substance but also as Subject." However, if the disclosure of the entire domain of entities is rooted in a singular entity, then something "deranged" is taking place: a particular entity is the exclusive site at which all entities appear, acquire their Being—so, to put it brutally, you kill a man and you simultaneously "kill Being" ... This short-circuit between the Clearance of Being and a particular entity introduces a catastrophic de-rangement into the order of beings: because man, rooted in his body, cannot look at entities from outside, every disclosure of Being, every Clearance, has to be grounded in untruth (concealment/hiddenness). The ultimate cause of the de-rangement that pertains to *Da-Sein* thus resides in the fact that *Dasein* is by definition embodied, and, towards the end of his life, Heidegger conceded that, for philosophy, "the body phenomenon is the most difficult problem":

> The bodily /*das Leibliche*/ in the human is not something animalistic. The manner of understanding that accompanies it is something that metaphysics up till now has not touched on.[15]

One is tempted to risk the hypothesis that it is precisely psychoanalytic theory which was the first to touch on this key question: is not the Freudian eroticized body, sustained by libido, organized around erogenous zones, precisely the non-animalistic, non-biological body? Is not *this* (and not the animalistic) body the proper object of psychoanalysis? Heidegger totally misses this dimension when in his *Zollikoner Seminare*, he dismisses Freud as a causal determinist:

> He postulates for the conscious human phenomena that they can be explained without gaps, i.e. the continuity of causal connections. Since there are no such connections "in the consciousness," he has to invent "the unconscious," in which there have to be the causal links without gaps.[16]

This interpretation may appear correct: is it not that Freud tries to discover a causal order in what appears to our consciousness as a confused and contingent array of mental facts (slips of tongue, dreams, clinical symptoms) and, in this way, to close the chain of causal links that run our psyche? However, Heidegger completely misses the way the Freudian "unconscious" is grounded in the traumatic encounter of an Otherness whose intrusion precisely *breaks*, interrupts, the continuity of the causal link: what we get in the "unconscious" is not a complete, uninterrupted, causal link, but the repercussions, the after-shocks, of traumatic interruptions.

What Freud calls "symptoms" are ways to deal with a traumatic cut, while "fantasy" is a formation destined to cover up this cut. That's why for Heidegger a finite human being *a priori* cannot reach the inner peace and calm of Buddhist Enlightenment (nirvana). A world is disclosed to us against the background of an ontological catastrophe: "man is the only catastrophe in the midst of beings."

But, again, here we have to risk a step further: if man is the only catastrophe, does this mean that, prior to the arrival of humanity, there was no catastrophe, that nature was a balanced order derailed only by human *hubris*? (By catastrophe I don't mean ontic disasters like asteroids hitting the earth but more radical de-rangement of the entire network of forms of life.) The problem is that if man is the only catastrophe "in the midst of beings," and if beings are only disclosed to us as humans, then the very space of non-catastrophic beings that surround humans is already ontologically grounded in the catastrophe that is the rise of man.

Now we face the key question: is man as the only catastrophe in the midst of beings as exception, so that if we assume the impossible point of view of looking at the universe from a safe distance, we see a universal texture of beings just not deranged by catastrophes (since man is a catastrophe only from his own standpoint, as the exception that grounds his access to beings)? In this case, we are back at the Kantian position: reality "in itself," outside the Clearing within which it appears to us, is unknowable, we can only speculate about it the way Heidegger himself does when he plays with the idea that there is a kind of ontological pain in nature itself. Or should we take Heidegger's speculation seriously, so that the catastrophe is not only man but already nature in itself, and in man as the being-of-speech this catastrophe that grounds reality in itself only comes to word? (Quantum physics offers its own version of a catastrophe that grounds reality: the broken symmetry, the disturbance of the void, quantum oscillations; theosophical speculations offer another version: the self-division or Fall of Godhead itself which gives birth to our world.)

In a debate with a theology student, Richard Dawkins[17] said that he takes seriously what departments of theology are doing when they are engaged in research on the historical origins of a religion and its development—we get here a solid anthropological study—but he doesn't take seriously, for example, the debates of theologians about the exact nature of transubstantiation in Christian ritual (the miraculous change by which, according to Roman Catholic and Eastern Orthodox dogma, the eucharistic elements at their consecration become the body and blood of Christ while keeping only the appearances of bread and wine). I think, on the contrary, that such debates should also be taken extremely seriously and not reduced to mere metaphors—they not only allow access to the basic ontological premises of theology; they can also often be used to throw a new light onto some Marxist notions. Fredric Jameson was right to proclaim predestination the most interesting theological concept for Marxism: predestination indicates the retroactive causality which characterizes a properly dialectical historical process. In a similar way, we should not be afraid to search for the traces of meta-transcendental (dialectical materialist) approach in theosophical speculations of Meister Eckhart, Jacob Boehme or F.W.J. Schelling. For a Kantian, of course, such speculations are nothing more than empty *Schwarmerei*, enthusiastic blah-blah about nothing, while for us, it is only here that we touch the Real.

If we endorse this option, then we have to draw the only consequent conclusion: every image or construction of "objective reality," of the way it is in itself, "independently of us," is one of the ways being is disclosed to us, and is as such already in some basic sense "anthropocentric," grounded in (and at the same time obfuscating) the catastrophe that constitutes us. The main candidates for getting close to how reality is "in itself" are formulas of relativity theory and quantum physics—the result of complex experimental and intellectual work to which nothing corresponds in our direct experience of reality ... The only "contact" we have with the Real "independent of us" is our very separation from it, the radical de-rangement—what Heidegger calls catastrophe. The paradox is that what unites us with the Real "in itself" is the very gap that we experience as our separation from it.

The same goes for Christianity where the only way to experience unity with god is to identify with Christ suffering on the cross, i.e., with the point at which god is divided from himself. The basic premise of what I call "materialist theology" or "Christian atheism" is that the fall of man from god is simultaneously the fall of god from itself, and that there is nothing that precedes this fall: "god" is the retroactive effect of its own fall. And this move of experiencing the gap itself as the point of unity is the basic feature of Hegel's dialectic—which is why the space beyond Heidegger's thought that we designated as the space beyond the transcendental is the space to which Hegelian thought belongs. This is also the space for thinking which cannot be reduced to science—here is Heidegger's own ambiguous formulation of this obscure point:

> I often ask myself—this has for a long time been a fundamental question for me—what nature would be without man—must it not resonate through him in order to attain its ownmost potency.[18]

Note that this passage is from the time immediately after Heidegger's lectures on *The Fundamental Concepts of Metaphysics* from 1929–30, where he also formulates a Schellingian hypothesis that, perhaps, animals are, in a hitherto unknown way, aware of their lack—of the "poorness" of their relating to the world. Perhaps, there is an infinite pain pervading the entirety of living nature:

> if deprivation in certain forms is a kind of suffering, and poverty and deprivation of the world belongs to the animal's being, then a kind of pain and suffering would have to permeate the whole animal realm and the realm of life in general.[19]

So when Heidegger speculates about pain in nature itself taken independently of man, how can we read this claim without committing ourselves to anthropocentric-teleological thinking? The answer was indicated by none other than Marx who, in his introduction to *Grundrisse*, wrote:

> Bourgeois society is the most developed and the most complex historic organization of production. The categories which express its relations, the comprehension of its structure, thereby also allows insights into the structure and the relations of production of all the vanished social formations out of whose ruins and elements it built itself up, whose partly still unconquered remnants are carried along within it, whose mere

nuances have developed explicit significance within it, etc. Human anatomy contains a key to the anatomy of the ape. The intimations of higher development among the subordinate animal species, however, can be understood only after the higher development is already known.[20]

In short, to paraphrase Pierre Bayard,[21] what Marx is saying here is that the anatomy of the ape, although it was formed earlier in time than the anatomy of man, nonetheless in a way *plagiarizes by anticipation the anatomy of man*. There is no teleology here, the effect of teleology is strictly retroactive: *once capitalism is here* (emerging in a wholly contingent way), it provides a universal key for all other formations. Teleology resides precisely in evolutionary progressism where the key to the anatomy of man is the anatomy of ape. Alenka Zupančič pointed out that the same holds for Lacan's *il n'y a pas de rapport sexuel*: this doesn't mean that in nature, among apes and other animals, there is a harmonious (instinctually regulated) sexual relationship, while with the arrival of humans disharmony explodes. There is no sexual relationship already among apes etc., their complex mating rituals demonstrate this, but this disharmony remains "in itself," it is a simple fact (probably experienced as painful), while with humans the failure is registered as such, "for itself." In this sense the pain in nature points towards the symbolic order that registers it.[22]

Along these lines, one can also understand why Kant claims that, in some sense, the world was created so that we can fight our moral struggles in it: when we are caught in an intense struggle which means everything to us, we experience it as if the whole world will collapse if we fail; the same holds also when we fear the failure of an intense love affair. There is no direct teleology here; our love encounter is the result of a contingent encounter, so it could easily also not have happened—but once it does happen, it decides how we experience the whole of reality. When Benjamin wrote that a big revolutionary battle decides not only the fate of the present but also of all past failed struggles, he mobilizes the same retroactive mechanism that reaches its climax in religious claims that, in a crucial battle, not only our fate but also the fate of god himself is decided. Only Hegel allows us to think this paradox.

To somewhat simplify the overall picture, the basic feature of the dialectically materialist vision is that of irreducible reflexivity inscribed in the universe: the external difference (say, between content and its form) is inscribed in content itself, so that external difference coincides with the internal one. Think about the reflexivity between form and content that is sometimes found in sculptures where the "unfinished" sculpture portrays a man trying to break out of the stone out of which his (unfinished) corpse is carved: the heroic effort of displaying strength is not just what the statue "represents," it is inscribed in the very relationship between what the statue represents and how this represented form relates to its matter.[23] For this reason, the basic model of a dialectical reversal is not some big struggle against opposite (Mao's totally non-Hegelian notion of "contradiction") but a small displacement (or, rather, reversal) within the same which miraculously changes everything. The simple reversal of the subject and predicate of a statement can radically change its meaning, as is clear from the reversal of the title of Pedro Calderon de la Barca's play "Life is dream/*La* vida es sueño/" which means something like "our life is a lifeless miserable appearance with no substantial vitality"; if, however, I say "dream is life," I say something totally different: "we are only fully alive in a dream, dream has the full vitality in contrast to the constraints of our miserable existence." In a homologous way, if I say "sex is death," I indicate that I consider sexual pleasure something false, obfuscating the fact that sex is a sinful decadent thing which brings corruption and death; but if I say "death is sex," I indicate that dying itself can be sexy, that it can bring unexpected pleasure. And, finally, with regard to Hegel, if I say "subject is substance," I imply that the true substance of reality is subject, that subject is the ground which generates all reality, but if I say "substance is subject," I indicate that substance is in itself "subjective" (market by cuts, inconsistencies, incomplete).

Hegel's dialectic is neither a dynamized transcendental dimension (the succession of all possible ways reality can appear to us, as Brandom and Pippin claim), nor the "objective" dialectical process of reality itself (as Marxist "dialectical materialists" as well as objective idealists claim); its hidden resource is the experience of the irreducible gap that precedes the two. In this way, we can also clarify to some degree the difference between naturalist ("mechanic") materialism, idealism and dialectical materialism: "mechanic" materialism covers the wide area from pre-Platonic materialists to today's scientific naturalism and object-oriented-ontology (even if it characterizes itself as "immaterialist")—all of them approach reality as something given, ignoring its transcendental constitution; idealism is characterized by the predominance of the transcendental approach; dialectical materialism appears when we move into the obscure domain beyond the transcendental, as it was done by the post-Kantian turn of Schelling and Hegel, by some theosophical speculations (including those of Walter Benjamin), by some tentative formulations of Lacan, as well as by some speculative readings of quantum physics.[24] That's why we should not be afraid to use the term "theology" to circumscribe the obscure area that eludes any ontology, transcendental or naively realist. Crazy as it may sound, sometimes it is only a materialist theology that can help us break out of philosophical idealism.

Why do I call the position towards which all these different approaches tend "dialectical materialism," a term that is difficult to dissociate from the Stalinist tradition—a term which stands for philosophical ideology at its most stupid, for a philosophy that has no cognitive value but just serves to justify political decisions? Because I think what I have in mind here is ultimately unnamable, there is no "proper" name for it, so the only solution is to use a term which signals as clearly as possible its own inadequacy. In other words, the claim "Hegel is a dialectical materialist" should be read as a new version of the speculative statement "the Spirit is a bone": taken directly, the claim is an obvious nonsense, there is an infinite gap between Hegel's thought and dialectical materialism—however, *Hegel's thought is precisely the thought of this gap.*

"We Must Live Till We Die"

It is only against the background of this global vision of human beings as a catastrophe that we can approach the question towards which the whole of this book is moving: is there a subjective gesture through which we can escape the vicious cycle of surplus-enjoyment? The space whose contours we outlined above, the space beyond Heidegger's thought (beyond the transcendental in our radical sense of the term), is the space which enables the subject to enact subjective destitution. If Heidegger's space is the space of being-towards-death, this space is the space of living-dead. As is often the case, the condensed formula of the solution is provided by a song by Rammstein.

Polish graffiti from the glorious age of early Solidarnosc says: "What is life? A disease transmitted by sexual intercourse which always ends in death." So is there life which avoids these coordinates? Yes, the life of the living dead. The central theme of Rammstein's song "Dalai Lama" is one of falling further and further into a state of ruin but, crucially, having to keep on living—this is death-drive at its purest, not death itself but the fact that we have to LIVE till we die, this endless dragging of life, this endless compulsion to repeat.[25] The song sounds like what in France they call a *lapalissade* (an emptautological wisdom like "a minute before he died, Monsieur la Palice was still alive"). But Rammstein turns around the obvious wisdom "no matter how long you live, at the end you will die": till you die, you have to live. What makes the Rammstein version not an empty tautology is the ethical dimension: before we die we are not just (obviously) alive, we HAVE to live: life is not organic continuation; with us, humans, it is a decision, an active obligation—we can lose this will. However, the lesson of "Dalai Lama" is not that we should succumb to the seductively calming voice of angels and accept death, like Death itself which invites the girl in Schubert 's "Death and the Maiden": "Give me your hand, you lovely, tender creature. / I am your friend, and come not to chastise. / Be of good courage. I am not cruel; / you shall sleep softly in my arms." But neither is the lesson of the song that we should desperately cling to life and avoid death. The lesson is that, although we cannot escape death, even accepting death is not the solution: the ultimate negation (death) itself fails, we still have to live till we die, and this living just drags on.

"There are weeks when decades happen," Lenin said about the Russian revolution. The pandemic in 2020 and 2021 is just the opposite: a year when a week happened—with some oscillations, the same week was replayed again and again. This is how Castrillon and Marchevsky describe the disruptive effect of the pandemic, with a gentle swipe at me: "It is a castration that fundamentally disrupts the imagined arc of our lives, but we have not yet made it disruptive enough of hyper-modernity and digital commodity capitalism to serve as any kind of revolution (with our apologies to Žižek)."[26] My reply is that yes, the revolutionary disruption didn't happen, but its prospect threw a shadow over the entire year: the only way to account for what *did* effectively happen is to interpret it as a desperate reaction to this threat—not the threat of the pandemic itself but the threat of the only adequate way to confront the pandemic (with universal global healthcare, universal basic income, etc.). Plus I disagree with the designation of the disruptive effect of the pandemic as a form of castration: if we use this term in the strict Lacanian sense, then the impact of the pandemic was almost the exact opposite of castration. One should bear in mind the liberating aspect of (symbolic) castration: castration is a liberating loss, a loss which opens up the space for creative distance, and the absence of castration means a psychotic suffocation in which the symbolic falls into the real. This, exactly, is what happened with the outbreak of the pandemic: the opening of our social space sustained by the big Other (partially, at least) collapsed, the over-proximity of others became a mortal threat.

In a critical move against Agamben who sees in the measures against the pandemic a mere continuation of the state of exception, Zsuzsa Barros formulated in a simple but precise way the difference between the standard notion of the state of exception and the state of exception triggered by the pandemic: "The state of exception (if this term still applies) in the case of this 'novel' virus is not the exercise of power over life as bare life but, on the contrary, an extreme (exceptional) self-defensive measure and immune reaction by the political body to an invading life form that is not even properly alive."[27] In the case of the pandemic, it is not the state authority which invaded civil society, submitting it to a total control; it is an invading life form (or, rather, not even a true form of life but just a self-reproducing chemical mechanism) which invaded and disturbed the political body, throwing it into a panic and rendering its impotence visible.

In the US and Europe, the new barbarians were precisely those who violently protested against anti-pandemic measures in defense of personal freedom and dignity—those like Jared Kushner, back in April 2020, who bragged that Trump was taking the country "back from the doctors."[28] Sergio Benvenuto succinctly formulated the obscenity of the idea that the protective measures against the pandemic demand from us too great a sacrifice in having to forsake basic human rights: "To consider this sacrifice as unbearable, when there are those who are risking their lives in hospitals to save ours, is not only offensive; it is ridiculous."[29]

Rammstein's "we have to live till we die" outlines a way out of this deadlock: to fight against the pandemic, we should live with utmost intensity. Is there anyone more ALIVE today than millions of healthcare workers who, with full awareness, risk their lives on a daily basis? Many of them died, but *till they died they were alive.* They did not just sacrifice themselves for us, getting our hypocritical praise. And they were even less survival machines reduced to bare life—they were those who are today most alive. So what is, more closely, the existential stance advocated by Rammstein in the song? It is a version of what Lacan called subjective destitution, the concluding moment of the psychoanalytic process.

From Being-Towards-Death to Undeadness

Our premise here is that what Heidegger designated as "being-towards-death" is not the ultimate existential experience—it is possible to pass through it into a dimension for which perhaps the best name is undeadness. In order to make this passage somewhat clearer, let's turn our attention towards a perhaps unexpected topic: the symphonies of Dmitri Shostakovich. The most popular among them is his Fifth Symphony whose fate was very curious: written after the devastating critique of Shostakovich's opera *Lady Macbeth* in *Pravda*, the Fifth is usually perceived as a conscious compromise, a return to more traditional music to ensure the composer's political rehabilitation. However, long after Stalin's demise, it remains his most popular and most frequently performed symphony in the West also. A couple of years ago, it was voted by a critical panel as the only twentieth-century work among the ten greatest symphonies of all time (which it is definitely not: in its own genre, the Eighth and the Tenth are much better). But what interests us here are Shostakovich's last two symphonies, the Fourteenth and Fifteenth, which directly tackle death or, more precisely, the passage from death to undeadness (in this regard, the passage from the Fourteenth to the Fifteenth Symphony is homologous to the passage from *Vertigo* and *Psycho* in Hitchcock's opus or the passage from the third to the fourth movement of Sibelius's fourth symphony).[30] Apropos the Fourteenth, Shostakovich openly declared his obsession with death:

> "Death is in store for all of us and I for one do not see any good in the end of our lives. Death is terrifying. There is nothing beyond it." Shostakovich was arguing against the view that death is some glorious beginning to the afterlife. He disagreed with all the composers who had portrayed death with music that was beautiful, radiant, and ecstatic.[31]

An incident at the premiere of the symphony echoes in an uncanny way this non-glorious, even mischievous, approach to death:

> Shostakovich had spoken about the need for a special silence whilst listening to this work. His supporters were therefore particularly angry when, during one of the quietest moments, a huge crash was heard in the auditorium and a man made a hasty and clumsy exit. When it was revealed afterwards that this man was none other than Pavel Ivanovitch Apostolov, a party organiser and one of Shostakovich's main critics and aggressive persecutors during the late 1940s, people assumed that his protest had been carefully planned for maximum distraction. Only later did it become known that it was during this performance that Apostolov had in fact suffered a heart attack; he was dead within a month. The irony was not lost on anyone.[32]

No wonder Solzhenitsyn himself was horrified by the symphony's dark and irreverent tone with no hope of redemption—but was he right? The first thing to note is that the Fourteenth "is not about death but about unnatural death; death caused by murder, oppression, and war."[33] The second thing is that the Fourteenth does not culminate in an apotheosis of a meaningless death: its climax is undoubtedly "Delvig," the most "sincere" song in the symphony, with no irony—even optimistic in a way. It sets to music a poem by Wilhelm Küchelbecker dedicated to the death (in 1831) of his friend Anton Delvig, a poet friendly with the Decembrists who failed in their rebellion—the poem "is a celebration of the artists' power and the importance of their friendship in the face of tyranny." (Küchelbecker himself was sent to Siberia for his part in the failed Decembrist uprising against the Tsar in 1825, where he died deaf and blind in 1846.) Significantly this lament for the death of a poet is composed in a traditional mode, in contrast to all other songs in the symphony: "Like an idée fixe, the twelve-note system haunts all the movements of the Fourteenth Symphony"—except "Delvig" which is "written in a very pure major key, whereas all the others show a predominance of atonal lines, capricious, sinuous and often grotesque."[34]

It is important that "Delvig" follows "Letter to Sultan," an extraordinary song which comes closest to the domain of politics in the entire symphony; it stages a revolt against higher authority as an act of brutal obscenity. Shostakovich decided to put in musical form a crazy document from the Russian past: in 1676, Sultan Mehmed IV wrote a letter to Zaporozhian Cossacks, calling them to submit themselves to his rule; the Cossacks' reply came as a stream of invective and vulgar rhymes:

Zaporozhian Cossacks to the Turkish Sultan! O sultan, Turkish devil and damned devil's kith and kin, secretary to Lucifer himself. What the devil kind of knight are thou, that canst not slay a hedgehog with your naked arse? The devil shits, and your army eats. Thou shalt not, thou son of a whore, make subjects of Christian sons. We have no fear of your army; by land and by sea we will battle with thee. Fuck thy mother. Thou Babylonian scullion, Macedonian wheelwright, brewer of Jerusalem, goat-fucker of Alexandria, swineherd of Greater and Lesser Egypt, pig of Armenia, Podolian thief, catamite of Tartary, hangman of Kamyanets, and fool of all the world and underworld, an idiot before God, grandson of the Serpent, and the crick in our dick. Pig's snout, mare's arse, slaughterhouse cur, unchristened brow.

Screw thine own mother! So the Zaporozhians declare, you lowlife. You won't even be herding pigs for the Christians. Now we'll conclude, for we don't know the date and don't own a calendar; the moon's in the sky, the year with the Lord. The day's the same over here as it is over there; for this kiss our arse! *Koshovyi otaman Ivan Sirko, with the whole Zaporozhian Host.*[35]

Furthermore, "Letter to Sultan" is preceded by "Prison" sets puts to music Guillaume Apollinaire's description of a man imprisoned alone in a cell. In the middle of this song, we get an orchestral interlude which marks a break in the subjective stance of the suffering prisoner—after this interlude, the first words are: "I am not the man I was." So we can see the meaning of the order of these three songs: despair in the prison which makes the subject a different man and pushes him to brutal rebellion, followed by lament when the rebellion is crushed. (In a further analysis one could reconstruct the narrative line that unites all 11 songs of the symphony: the first two are the introduction and the last two the finale (which begins with the same motif as the introduction); the following songs then vary the motif of "death and the maiden"— the femme fatale causes the death of her lovers, she kills herself . . . with a gradual shift towards the corpses of young men on the battlefield, and then the man is reduced to a number in prison which triggers the rebellion.)

But, as we have seen, "Delvig," the emotional culmination of the symphony, cancels the premise that "death is terrifying. There is nothing beyond it." Beyond death there is poetry which makes death in all its meaninglessness a noble event. What comes after death if we really accept that there is nothing beyond it? Shostakovich provides the answer in his Fifteenth Symphony which was played continuously on the set of *Blue Velvet*. David Lynch wanted to signal the atmosphere he wanted in the movie: "I wrote the script to Shostakovich: No. 15 in A major. I just kept playing the same part of it, over and over again." During its filming, Lynch placed speakers on set and played the symphony in order to convey the mood he wanted. He later requested that Angelo Badalamenti compose a score for the film that was "like Shostakovich."[36] Kurt Sanderling, who debuted the symphony in

East Germany, heard the music as being about loneliness and death, and that no other work by Shostakovich seemed to him so "radically horrible and cruel"; others see playful optimism in it, while Shostakovich himself characterized it as a "wicked symphony." The mixture of voices heard in it can well be read as a crazy interaction of "objects as comrades": "We hear hospital equipment, electric shock treatment, vulgarity and satire; he brings in serialism, a vast array of quotations—everything from Rossini's *William Tell* to Wagner's *Tristan* and *Ring*—which come across like the crazy voices in your head when you are delirious."[37] But this delirious interaction does not happen within a soul, its space is only opened by subjective destitution: if the Fourteenth Symphony culminates in the lyrical confession of a soul (Delvig), the Fifteenth is soulless—a monstrous mix of childish playfulness and undeadness.

Revolutionary Self-Destitution . . .

Here, perhaps, we can also locate Shostakovich's limitation: subjective destitution does not appear only as such a monstrous mixture, and is also not constrained to the clinical experience—it has a political dimension described by Brecht. In the lines from his *Beggar's Opera* quoted in the previous chapter, Brecht condenses four basic existential stances (the longing for everyday joys, brutal reality, religious feeling, cynical wisdom) into two, with joyful cynicism as the last word.[38] However, this was not Brecht's own last word: with a breath-taking consequence, Brecht added in his learning plays (*Jasager, Die Massnahme*) another subjective position—that of a purely formal gesture of self-sacrifice grounded in no deeper meaning or goal. The implicit logic here is that one cannot overcome cynical wisdom with some positive ethical ideal: cynicism can undermine them all; it is only a totally meaningless self-sacrificial act that undermines the cynical distance itself. The Freudian name for such an act is, of course, death-drive, and its Hegelian name self-relating negativity. However, we should be very careful here: Brecht makes it clear that this act is not a kind of pure excessive suicidal gesture of stepping out of the symbolic space (something that belongs more to the theory of Bataille). In yet another case of "infinite judgment," death-drive coincides with its opposite, with radical alienation in the symbolic order. Along these same lines, Saroj Giri described "revolutionary self-destitution, self-objectification" as a specific form of subjectivity:

> A specific, individual life, a unique human being, is now an object, a mere object who can be taken down any time: The "comrade as object" is a continuation of de-classing and de-personification, now taken to the point of revolutionary destitution, involving the courage to die, death. To the extent that the comrade is a living human being, his or her objectification will and must involve the openness to death. Life is hanging in a balance, and the vulnerability to death is a constant presence. You are never safe and the willingness to sacrifice life is best embraced graciously.[39] (11)

Siri establishes here a double link with the past, recent and more ancient. Recent: the idea of objectification and destitution is close to the idea of Fanon's idea of declivity: "an utterly naked declivity is where an authentic upheaval is born." Or when he says, "the Negro is a zone of non-being, an extraordinarily sterile and arid region, an utterly declining declivity" (22). Ancient past: Buddhist revolutionary self.[40] The void (of destitution) "as the 'path,' the rupture/opening to a 'new world' can be found in the Buddha's nibbana. Nibbana is often known as Awakening or Enlightenment, but actually nibbana is, in the first instance, extinction, the blowing out, the vanishing" (14).

What Giri calls subjective destitution is therefore not just a new form of political subjectivity but simultaneously something that concerns our basic existential level, "a different way of being, involving a different modality of life and death" (15). In his afterword to Peter Hallward's collection *Think Again*, Badiou approvingly quotes Lin Biao: "The essence of revisionism is the fear of death."[41] This existential radicalization of the political opposition between orthodoxy and revisionism throws new light on the old '68 motto "the personal is political": here, the political becomes personal, the ultimate root of political revisionism is located in the intimate experience of the fear of death. Badiou's version of it would be that, since "revisionism" is, at its most basic, the failure to subjectivize oneself, to assume fidelity to a Truth-Event, being a revisionist means remaining within the survivalist horizon of the "human animal."

There is, however, an ambiguity that clings to Lin Biao's statement: it can be read as saying that the root of political revisionism lies in human nature which makes us fear death; but it can also be read as saying that, since there is no unchangeable human nature, our very intimate fear of death is already politically overdetermined, for it arises in an individualist and egotistical society with little sense of communal solidarity; which is why, in a Communist society, people would no longer fear death.

"Comrade as object" does not imply that we should observe and manipulate ourselves from a cold "objective" distance. It is to be supplemented by its inversion, "object as comrade": "Instead of going over to the fetishistic powers of the commodity, one had to go towards the 'hidden' engineering/artistic powers of things, objects and materials: this would, as it were, allow the object to commune and speak, providing us the first contours of the 'object as comrade'" (6). This "object as comrade" displays what Giri calls idealism in the (material) thing itself, of what we may call spiritual corporeality as opposed to the fetishist idealism which imposes on a thing from outside a social dimension as its reified property: to treat an object as "comrade" means to open oneself up to virtual potentials of an object in an intense interaction with it. Maybe, a surprising link can help us understand what is meant by "object as comrade" which supplements "comrade as object": today's object-oriented-ontology. Here is Graham Harman's concise description of the basic stance of Object-oriented-ontology:

> The arena of the world is packed with diverse objects, their forces unleashed and mostly unloved. Red billiard ball smacks green billiard ball. Snowflakes glitter in the light that cruelly annihilates them, while damaged submarines rust along the ocean floor. As flour emerges from mills and blocks of limestone are compressed by earthquakes, gigantic mushrooms spread in the Michigan forest. While human philosophers bludgeon each other over the very possibility of "access" to the world, sharks bludgeon tuna fish and icebergs smash into coastlines.[42]

Such a way of treating object as a "comrade" also opens up a new way of being ecological: to accept our environment in all its complexity that includes what we perceive as trash or pollution, as well as what we cannot directly perceive since it is too large or too minuscule (Timothy Morton's "hyperobjects"). Along these lines, for Morton, being ecological

> is not about spending time in a pristine nature preserve but about appreciating the weed working its way through a crack in the concrete, and then appreciating the concrete. It's also part of the world, and part of us. Reality is populated with "strange strangers"—things that are "knowable yet uncanny." This strange strangeness, Morton writes, is an irreducible part of every rock, tree, terrarium, plastic Statue of Liberty, quasar, black hole, or marmoset one might encounter; by acknowledging it, we shift away from trying to master objects and toward learning to respect them in their elusiveness. Whereas the Romantic poets rhapsodized about nature's beauty and sublimity, Morton responds to its all-pervading weirdness; they include in the category of the natural everything that is scary, ugly, artificial, harmful, and disturbing.[43]

Is not a perfect example of such a mixture the fate of rats in Manhattan during the pandemic? Manhattan is a living system of humans, cockroaches ... and millions of rats. Lockdown at the peak of the pandemic meant that, since all restaurants were closed, rats who lived off the trash from restaurants were deprived of one their food sources. This caused mass starvation; many rats were found eating their offspring ... A closure of restaurants which changed the eating habits of humans but posed no threat to them was a catastrophe for rats, rats as comrades. Another similar accident from recent history could be called "sparrow as comrade." In 1958, at the beginning of the Great Leap Forward, the Chinese government declared that "birds are public animals of capitalism" and set in motion a major campaign to eliminate sparrows which were suspected of consuming approximately four pounds of grain per sparrow per year. Sparrow nests were destroyed, eggs were broken, and chicks were killed; millions of people organized into groups, and hit noisy pots and pans to prevent sparrows from resting in their nests, with the goal of causing them to drop dead from exhaustion. These mass attacks depleted the sparrow population, pushing it to near extinction. However, by April 1960, Chinese leaders were forced to realize that sparrows also ate large quantities of insects in the fields, so that, rather than increasing, rice yields after the campaign substantially decreased: the extermination of sparrows upset the ecological balance, and insects destroyed crops as a result of the absence of natural predators. By this time, however, it was too late: with no sparrows to eat them, locust populations ballooned, swarming the country and compounding the ecological problems already caused by the Great Leap Forward, including widespread deforestation and misuse of poisons and pesticides. Ecological imbalance is credited with exacerbating the Great Chinese Famine, in which 15–45 million people died of starvation. The Chinese government eventually resorted to importing 250,000 sparrows from the Soviet Union to replenish their population.[44]

Three examples from the cinema of Joris Ivens perfectly exemplify this dimension of object as comrade. Is his documentary *Regen* (*Rain*, 1929), a portrayal of Amsterdam during rainfall, not a portrait of rain as comrade? One should mention here Hanns Eisler's *Fourteen Ways of Describing the Rain*, a twelve-minute exercise in dodecaphony for flute, clarinet, string trio, and piano, written as a musical accompaniment to Ivens's *Regen*. Then, there is Ivens's "Pour le Mistral" (1966): wind as a comrade—scenes of life and landscape in Provence where a cold wind called the Mistral blows down the valley of the Rhône to the Mediterranean. There is also another portrayal of wind as a comrade: "A Tale of the Wind" (1988), shot in China, old and sick Ivens's attempt to depict the insight that "the secret of breathing lies in the rhythm of the autumn wind."

However, we have to bear in mind something that Object-oriented-ontology ignores which Giri is fully aware of: while subjective destitution (a term Giri took from Lacan), reduction to an object, does not mean de-subjectivization, it *does* mean de-humanization: after subjective destitution a subject is no longer "human" (in the sense of the depth of personality, of "rich inner life" as opposed to external reality and similar psychic baggage). Only in and through destitution subject in its purity (a capitalized Subject) emerges:

> The activist-comrade as object is still a Subject—a subject who perhaps speaks in the name of History and invokes the "metanarrative" of the "stages of History," but whose self-destitution and self-objectification open up a revolutionary possibility by creating a null point, a void in History itself. (13)

Through subjective destitution, we do not enter a happy interaction of "object as comrade" and "comrade as object" in which a destitute subject deals with objects that surround him as his equal interlocutors, renouncing acting as their master who exploits them. In subjective destitution, subject is not simply immersed in the flux of reality; he is rather reduced to a void, a null point, a gap in reality. It is only through this reduction to a void, from the subjective position of that void, that a subject can perceive and experience the interaction of comrade as object and object as comrade. In other words, through subjective destitution subject is radically divided: into a pure void and the object that he is. In this way, we overcome mortality and enter undeadness: not life after death but death in life, not dis-alienation but extreme self-abolishing alienation—we leave behind the very standard by means of which we measure alienation, the notion of a normal warm daily life, of our full immersion in the safe and stable world of customs. The way to overcome the topsy-turvy world is not to return to normality but to embrace turvy without topsy.

Already from this brief description it is clear that the phenomenon of subjective destitution assumes many forms which cannot be reduced to the same inner experience. There is the Buddhist nirvana, a disconnection from external reality which enables us to acquire a distance from our cravings and desires—I assume a kind of impersonal stance, my thoughts are thoughts without thinker. Then there are so-called mystical experiences which should not be confused with nirvana: although they also involve a kind of subjective destitution, but this destitution takes the form of a direct identity between me and a higher Absolute (typical formula: the eyes through which I see god are the eyes through which god sees himself)—my innermost desire gets depersonalized, it overlaps with the will of god himself, so that the big Other lives through me. In short, while in nirvana one steps out of the "wheel of desire," the mystical experience enacts the overlapping of our enjoyment with the enjoyment of the big Other. Then there is the subjective stance described by Giri: the destitution of a revolutionary agent who reduces itself to an instrument-object of the process of radical social change—he obliterates his personality, inclusive of the fear of death, so that revolution lives through him. Then there is the explosion of self-destructive social nihilism—think of *Joker*, but also of a scene in Eisenstein's *October* in which a revolutionary mob penetrates the wine cellar of the Winter Palace and engages in an orgy of massive destruction of hundreds of bottles of expensive champagne. And, last but not least, subjective destitution in its psychoanalytic (Lacanian) sense of traversing the fantasy, which is a much more radical gesture than it may appear: for Lacan, fantasy is not opposed to reality but provides the coordinates of what we experience as reality, plus the coordinates of what we desire—the two coordinates are not the same, but they are intertwined (when our fundamental fantasy dissolves, we experience the loss of reality which also impedes our ability to desire). (We should also recall that traversing the fantasy is not Lacan's final word: in the final years of his teaching, he proposed as the final moment of the analytic process identification with the symptom, a gesture that enables us a moderately acceptable form of life.)

How are these versions related? They seem to form a kind of Greimasian semiotic square since there are two axes along which they are disposed: active engagement (self-destructive social explosion; revolutionary destitution described by Giri) versus disengagement (nirvana, mystical experience); self-contraction (destructive explosion against external reality; nirvana) versus reliance on a big Other (God in mystical experience, History in revolutionary destitution). In a destructive explosion, we contract into ourselves by way of destroying our environment; in nirvana, we just withdraw into ourselves leaving reality the way it is. In mystical experience, we disengage from reality by immersing ourselves in divinity; in revolutionary destitution, we renounce our Self by engaging in the historical process of revolutionary change.

(From the Lacanian standpoint, these last two stances court the danger of falling into a perverse position of conceiving oneself as an object-instrument of the big Other.)

What Lacan calls subjective destitution is the zero level, the neutral abyss in the center of this square. Here one should be very precise: what we reach in subjective destitution is not the absolute Void out of which everything springs but the very disturbance of this Void, not the inner peace of withdrawal but the imbalance of the Void—not the fall of the Void into finite material reality but the antagonism/tension in the very heart of the Void which causes the emergence of material reality out of the Void. The other four versions of subjective destitution structurally come second, they are attempts to pacify the antagonism ("self-contradiction") of the Void.

The question that arises here is: how should destitution in its politically engaged form avoid the fall into perversity? The answer is clear: it should suspend its reliance on the big Other (on historical necessity, etc.). Hegel constrained philosophy to grasping "what is," but for Hegel "what is" is not just a stable state of things, it is an open historical situation full of tensions and potentials—one should therefore link Hegel's insight with Saint-Just's claim: "*Ceux qui font des révolutions ressemblent au premier navigateur instruit par son audace* (Revolutionaries are akin to a first navigator guided his audacity alone)." Isn't this the implication of Hegel's confinement of the conceptual grasp to the past? As engaged subjects, we have to act with a view to the future, but for *a priori* reasons we cannot base our decisions on a rational pattern of historical progress (as Marx thought), so we have to improvise and take risks. Was this also the lesson Lenin learned from reading Hegel in 1915? The paradox is that what Lenin took from Hegel—who is usually decried as *the* philosopher of historical teleology, of inexorable and regular progress towards freedom—was the utter contingency of the historical process.[45]

The common-sense counter-argument that arises here is: subjective destitution is such a radical gesture that it is limited to an enlightened elite, and remains an impossible ethical ideal for the masses, except in rare episodes of revolutionary enthusiasm. But I think that this reproach misses the point: Giri emphasizes that subjective destitution is not an elitist stance of Leaders, but, on the contrary, a stance displayed by numerous ordinary combatants, like—once again—thousands who risk their life in the struggle against COVID-19.

... versus Religious Fundamentalism

But are we in this way not coming dangerously close to a fundamentalist's disregard for survival? Let's turn to what goes on now—in the middle of August 2021—in Afghanistan: the Taliban is smoothly taking over the country, cities are falling like dominoes, although government forces are much better equipped and trained, and also more numerous (300,000 versus 80,000 Taliban fighters). When the Taliban approaches, government forces mostly melt away: they surrender and/or run away, displaying no stomach for a fight— why? Media bombard us with a couple of explanations. The first is directly racist: the people there are simply not mature enough for democracy, they long for religious fundamentalism ... a ridiculous claim if there ever was one: half a century ago, Afghanistan was a (moderately) enlightened country with a very strong Communist Party which even took power for some years. (As befits a true Communist party, the People's Democratic Party of Afghanistan (PDPA) was for most of its existence split between the hardline *Khalq* and moderate *Parcham* factions.) The country became religiously fundamentalist only later, as a reaction to the Soviet occupation which tried to prevent the collapse of the Communist power.

The media bombard us with a couple of explanations. The first is terror: the Taliban ruthlessly executes those who oppose its politics. The second is faith: the Taliban simply believes its acts fulfill the task imposed on them by god, so that its final victory is guaranteed and they can afford to be patient—they can wait; time is on their side ... A more complex and realist explanation is that the situation in Afghanistan is chaotic, with ongoing war and corruption, so that even if the Taliban regime ultimately brings oppression and Sharia law, it will at least guarantee safety and order.

But all these explanations seem to avoid the basic fact, which is traumatic for the liberal Western view: the Taliban's disregard for survival, the readiness of its fighters to undertake "martyrdom," to die not just in a battle but even in suicidal acts. The explanation that the Taliban as fundamentalists "really believe" that they will enter paradise if they die as martyrs is not enough: it fails to capture the difference between belief in the sense of intellectual insight ("I know I will go to heaven, it's a fact") and belief as an engaged subjective position. In other words, it fails to take into account the material power of an ideology—in this case, the power of faith—which is not simply grounded in the strength of our convictions but in how we are directly existentially committed to our belief: we are not subjects choosing this or that belief, we "are" our belief in the sense of this belief impregnating our life. It was due to this feature that Michel Foucault was, in 1978, so fascinated by the Khomeini revolution that he twice visited Iran. What fascinated him there was not just the stance of accepting martyrdom, of indifference with regard to losing one's own life—he was "engaged in a very specific telling of the 'history of truth', emphasizing a partisan and agonistic form of truth-telling, and transformation through struggle and ordeal, as opposed to the pacifying, neutralizing, and normalizing forms of modern Western power. Crucial for understanding this point is the conception of *truth* at work in historico-political discourse, a conception of truth as *partial*, as reserved for *partisans*."[46] As Foucault himself put it,

if this subject who speaks of right (or rather, rights) is speaking the truth, that truth is no longer the universal truth of the philosopher. It is true that this discourse about the general war, this discourse that tries to interpret the war beneath peace, is indeed an attempt to describe the battle as a whole and to reconstruct the general course of the war. But that does not make it a totalizing or neutral discourse; it is always a perspectival discourse. It is interested in the totality only to the extent that it can see it in one-sided terms, distort it and see it from its own point of view. The truth is, in other words, a truth that can be deployed only from its combat position, from the perspective of the sought for victory and ultimately, so to speak, of the survival of the speaking subject himself.[47]

Can such an engaged discourse be dismissed as a sign of premodern "primitive" society which has not yet entered modern individualism?

And is its revival today to be dismissed as a sign of Fascist regression (in the way I was a couple of times proclaimed a Leftist Fascist)?[48] To anyone minimally acquainted with Western Marxism, the answer is clear: Georg Lukacs demonstrated how Marxism is "universally true" not in spite of its partiality but *because* it is "partial," accessible only from a particular subjective position. Heidegger often repeated a critique of Marx's thesis 11: when we want to change the world, this change has to be grounded in a new interpretation, and Marx ignores this presupposition, although his work does exactly this—offering a new historical-materialist interpretation of history as the history of class struggles . . .[49] Does this reproach hit the mark? One can argue that Marx has in mind something different: an interpretation to which the demand for change is immanent, i.e., an interpretation which is not neutral or impartial since it is only available to those who are already engaged in an effort to change reality.

We may agree or disagree with this view, but the fact is that what Foucault was looking for in far-away Iran—the agonistic ("war") form of truth-telling—was already forcefully present in the Marxist view that being caught in the class struggle is not an obstacle to "objective" knowledge of history but its condition. The usual positivist notion of knowledge as an "objective" (non-partial) approach to reality which is not distorted by a particular subjective engagement—what Foucault characterized as "the pacifying, neutralizing, and normalizing forms of modern Western power"—is ideology at its purest: the ideology of the "end of ideology." On the one hand, we have non-ideological "objective" expert-knowledge; on the other hand, we have dispersed individuals each of whom is focused on his/her idiosyncratic "care of the Self" (the term Foucault used when he abandoned his Iranian experience), small things that bring pleasure to his/her life. From this standpoint of liberal individualism, universal commitment, especially if it includes risk of life, is suspicious and "irrational" . . .

Here we encounter an interesting paradox: while it is doubtful if traditional Marxism can provide a convincing account of the success of the Taliban, it provided a perfect European example of what Foucault was looking for in Iran (and of what fascinates us now in Afghanistan), an example which did not involve any religious fundamentalism but just a collective engagement for a better life. After the triumph of global capitalism, this spirit of collective engagement was repressed, and now this repressed stance seems to return in the guise of religious fundamentalism.

This brings us back to the mystery of what went on in Afghanistan: at Kabul airport, thousands were desperately trying to leave the country, individuals hanging on to planes as they took off and falling from them when the planes were in the air ... as if we witness the latest tragic example of the ironic supplement to old anti-colonialist motto: "Yankee go home!"—Yankee go home ... and take me with you! The true enigma is here in what was a surprise for the Taliban itself: how quickly the army's resistance melted away. If thousands are now desperately trying to catch a flight out of the country and are ready to risk their life to escape, why didn't they *fight* against the Taliban? Why did they prefer falling to their death from the sky to death in battle? The easy answer to this is that those who crowded Kabul airport were the corrupted minority of the American collaborators ... However, what about the thousands of women who stay at home frightened? Are they also collaborators? The fact is that the US occupation of Afghanistan gradually created some kind of secular civil society with many women educated, employed, aware of their rights and also with an important independent intellectual life. When Goran Therborn visited Kabul and Herat a couple of years ago, giving talks on Western Marxism, hundreds of people appeared for the talk to the surprise of the organizers. Yes, the Taliban are now stronger than ever, stronger than 20 years ago when Western powers came to Afghanistan to liberate the country from them, which clearly demonstrates the futility of the entire operation, but should we for that reason ignore the (partially, at least, unintended) progressive consequences of their intervention?

Yanis Varoufakis touched this difficult point in his latest tweet: "On the day liberal-neocon imperialism was defeated once and for all, DiEM25's thoughts are with the women of Afghanistan. Our solidarity probably means little to them but it is what we can offer— for the time being. Hang in there sisters!"[50] How are we to read the two parts of his tweet, i.e., why the defeat of liberal imperialism came with the regression of women's (and other) rights? Do we (those who count ourselves as the global Left's opponents of neocolonial imperialism) have the right to ask Afghan women to sacrifice their rights so that global liberal capitalism can suffer a major defeat? When Varoufakis was accused of subordinating women's liberation to anti-imperialist struggle, he tweeted back: "We predicted how neocon imperialism would strengthen Misogynist Islamic Fundamentalism (MIF). It did! How did the neocons react? By blaming MIF's triumph on ... us. Cowards as well as war criminals."[51]

I must say that I find this blaming of the neocons a little bit problematic: neocons can easily find a common language with the Taliban—remember that Trump invited the Taliban to Camp David and made a pact with them which opened up the path towards the US capitulation. Plus there are already neocon reactions to the fall of Kabul which read it as the ultimate defeat of the Western tradition of secular Enlightenment and individualist hedonism ... No, it was not neocons who boosted Islamic fundamentalism; this fundamentalism grew in a reaction to the influence of Western liberal secularism and individualism. Decades ago, Ayatollah Khomeini wrote: "We're not afraid of sanctions. We're not afraid of military invasion. What frightens us is the invasion of Western immorality." The fact that Khomeini talks about fear, about what a Muslim should fear most in the West, should be taken literally: Muslim fundamentalists do not have any problems with the brutality of economic and military struggles, their true enemy is not Western economic neocolonialism and military aggression but its "immoral" culture. In many African and Asian countries, the gay movement is also perceived as an expression of the cultural impact of capitalist globalization and of its undermining of traditional social and cultural forms, so that, consequently, the struggle against gays appears as an aspect of the anti-colonial struggle. Does the same not hold for, say, Boko Haram? For its members, the liberation of women appears as the most visible feature of the destructive cultural impact of capitalist modernization, so that Boko Haram (whose name can be roughly and descriptively translated as "Western education is forbidden," specifically education for women) can perceive and portray itself as an agent fighting the destructive impact of modernization, by way of imposing hierarchic regulation of the relationship between the sexes. The enigma is thus: why do Muslims, who have undoubtedly been exposed to exploitation, domination, and other destructive and humiliating aspects of colonialism, target in their response what is (for us, at least) the best part of the Western legacy: our egalitarianism and personal freedoms, inclusive of a healthy dose of irony and a mocking of all authorities? The obvious answer is that their target is well chosen. What for them makes the liberal West so unbearable is not only that it practices exploitation and violent domination but that, to add insult to injury, it presents this brutal reality in the guise of its opposite: freedom, equality and democracy.

So once again we have to learn Marx's crucial lesson: true, capitalism systematically violates its own rules ("human rights and freedoms")—just remember that, at the beginning of the modern era which celebrates human freedoms, capitalism resuscitated slavery in its colonies ... But capitalism at the same time provided standards to measure its own hypocrisy, so we should not say "since human rights are a mask of exploitation, let's drop human rights" but: "Let's take human rights more seriously than those who found the ideology of human rights!" This is what Socialism meant from the very beginning.

The American or European populist Right fanatically opposes Muslim fundamentalism, in which it sees the main threat to Western Christian civilization—as they like to say, Europe is on the verge of becoming Europastan, and the US withdrawal from Afghanistan is for them the ultimate humiliation of the US ... However, something new has taken place lately. According to recent analysis from the SITE Intelligence Group, an American non-governmental organization that tracks online activity of white supremacist and jihadist organizations, some supremacists are

> commending the Taliban's takeover as "a lesson in love for the homeland, for freedom, and for religion." Neo-Nazi and violent accelerationists—who hope to provoke what they see as an inevitable race war, which would lead to a Whites-only state—in North America and Europe are praising the Taliban for its anti-Semitism, homophobia, and severe restrictions on women's freedom. For example, a quote taken from the Proud Boy to Fascist Pipeline Telegram channel, said: "These farmers and

minimally trained men fought to take back their nation back from globohomo. They took back their government, installed their national religion as law, and executed dissenters . . . If white men in the west had the same courage as the Taliban, we would not be ruled by Jews currently." "Globohomo" is a derogatory word used to insult "globalists," the term used by conspiracy promoters to describe their enemy (the evil global elite who control the media, finance, political system, etc.).[52]

American Rightist populists who sympathize with the Taliban are more right than they think: what we see in Afghanistan is what our populists want, just purified to its extreme version. It is clear what features the two sides share: opposition to "globohomo," to the new global elite which spreads LGBT+ and multicultural values eroding the established way of life of local communities. The opposition between populist Right and Muslim fundamentalists is thus relativized: Rightist populist can easily imagine the co-existence of a different way of life. This is why the new Right is anti-Semitic and pro-Zionist at the same time, saying no to Jews who want to stay in their land and assimilate, but yes to Jews who return to their land— or, as Reinhardt Heydrich himself, the mastermind of the Holocaust, wrote in 1935: "We must separate the Jews into two categories, the Zionists and the partisans of assimilation. The Zionists profess a strictly racial concept and, through emigration to Palestine, they help to build their own Jewish State . . . our good wishes and our official goodwill go with them."[53]

What may appear (but is not) more surprising is that some Leftists also, in a limited way, join this bandwagon: although they deplore the fate of women under the Taliban, they nonetheless perceive the US withdrawal as a great defeat of global capitalist neocolonialism, of Western powers used to imposing their notions of freedom and democracy on others.

"Les non-dupes errent"

This proximity is not limited to the stance towards the Taliban: we also find it among those who opposite vaccines and social regulations as measures against the pandemic. The recent discovery of the Pegasus program was just a further confirmation of our general distrust regarding how we are socially controlled, and it can help us understand why many of us resist vaccination: if everything, all the flow of data and all our social activities, is controlled, the inside of our body appears as the last island that should escape this control, and with the vaccination, state apparatuses and corporations seem to invade even this last island of free intimacy ... We may thus say that the resistance to vaccination is the misdirected price we are paying for being exposed to Pegasus in all its versions. And since science is widely used to justify measures, since vaccines are a great scientific achievement, resistance to vaccination is also grounded in the suspicion that science is in the service of social control and manipulation.

We have lately been witnessing a gradual decay of the authority of what Jacques Lacan called "the big Other," the shared space of public values within which only our differences and identities can thrive—a phenomenon often falsely characterized as "post-truth era." Liberal resistance against vaccination on behalf of human rights makes one nostalgic for Leninist "democratic Socialism" (free democratic debate, but once a decision is taken, everybody has to obey it). One should interpret this democratic Socialism in the sense of Kant's formula of Enlightenment: not "Don't obey, think freely!" but: "Think freely, state your thoughts publicly, *and obey*!" The same holds for vaccine doubters: debate, publish your doubts, but obey regulations once the public authority imposes them. Without such practical consensus we will slowly drift into a society composed of tribal factions.

In Slovenia (my own country), we now (in September 2021) endure the catastrophic consequences of a liberal approach to vaccination: we are now the worst area of Europe, designated as dark-red. The approach of the government was not only that every individual should be free to choose whether to be vaccinated or not, but people were also even given a choice of vaccine (many choosing Janssen because the authorities proclaimed that one shot would be enough for full protection). When trouble appeared (a young student died because of the blood clots caused by Janssen), it was possible to say "you made a choice, so it's your responsibility" ... At the same time, the government was making vaccination de facto obligatory in all public services etc., so it was no wonder that the result was a wide anti-vaccination protest movement that led to violent clashes with police and journalists. It is obvious what the right strategy would have been simply to impose obligatory universal vaccination the way this was done decades ago in case of other infectious diseases—this would have given people a sense of purposeful stability, depoliticizing the entire topic of vaccination. Now the Rightist-nationalist government is accusing the Leftist opposition of fomenting anti-vaccination protests, interpreting the failure of its strategy as the result of a dark Leftist plot, and we are where we are.

Here we can see clearly the link between individual freedom and social cohesion: the freedom to choose whether to be vaccinated or not is, of course, a formal kind of freedom; however, to reject vaccination effectively implies limiting my actual freedom as well as the freedom of others. Within a community, being vaccinated means I am a much lesser threat to others (and others to me), so I can to a much greater degree exercise my social freedoms to mix with others in the usual way. My freedom is only actual as freedom within a certain social space regulated by rules and prohibitions. I can walk freely along a busy street because I can be reasonably sure that others on the street will behave in a civilized way towards me and will be punished if they attack me, if they insult me, etc.—and it is exactly the same with vaccination. Of course, we can strive to change the rules of common life—there are situations when these rules can be relaxed, but also strengthened (as in the conditions of a pandemic), but a domain of rules is needed as the very terrain of our freedoms.

Therein resides the Hegelian difference between abstract and concrete freedom: in a concrete life-world, abstract freedom changes into its opposite since it narrows our actual exercise of freedom. Let's take the case of freedom to speak and communicate with others: I can only exert this freedom if I obey the commonly established rules of language (with all their ambiguities and inclusive of the unwritten rules of messages between the lines). The language we speak is, of course, not ideologically neutral, it embodies many prejudices and makes it impossible for us to formulate clearly certain uncommon thoughts—as, again, Hegel knew it, thinking always occurs in language and it brings with itself a common-sense metaphysics (view of reality), but to truly think, we have to think in a language against this language. The rules of language can be changed in order to open up new freedoms, but the trouble with Politically Correct newspeak clearly shows that the direct imposition of new rules can lead to ambiguous results and give birth to new more subtle forms of racism and sexism.

The disintegration of public space is at its worst in the US, and it can be nicely illustrated by a detail of common culture. In Europe, the ground floor in a building is counted as 0, so that the floor above it is the first floor, while in the US, the first floor is on the street level. In short, Americans start to count with 1, while Europeans know that 1 is already a stand-in for 0. Or, to put it in more historical terms, Europeans are aware that, prior to beginning a count, there has to be a 'ground' of tradition, a ground which is always-already given and, as such, cannot be counted, while the US, a land with no pre-modern historical tradition proper, lacks such a ground. Things begin there directly with the self-legislated freedom: the past is erased or transposed onto Europe.[54] Perhaps, we should thus begin by assuming again the lesson of Europe and learn to count from 0 . . . Should we really? The catch is, of course, that 0 is never neutral but the shared space of ideological hegemony traversed by inherent antagonisms and inconsistencies. Even the "post-truth" space of rumors is still a form of the big Other, just different from the big Other of dignified public space which. So we have to put our claim in a more specific and precise way: ignoring the ground floor obfuscates an even stronger form of the big Other.

Some Lacanians (Jacques-Alain Miller included) often advocate the idea that today, in the era of "fake news," the big Other really no longer exists—but is this true? What if it exists more than ever, just in a new form? Our big Other is no longer the public space clearly distinguished from the obscenities of private exchanges, but the very *public* domain in which "fake news" circulates, in which we exchange rumors and conspiracy theories. One should not lose sight of what is so surprising about this rise of the shameless obscenity of the alt-right so well noted and analyzed by Angela Nagle.[55] Traditionally (or in our retroactive view of tradition, at least), shameless public obscenity worked as subversive, as an undermining of traditional domination, as depriving the Master of his false dignity. What we are getting today, with the exploding public obscenity, is not the disappearance of domination, of Master figures, but its forceful reappearance.[56]

In this more precise sense, the US is today *the* country of the new obscene big Other: the 0 that they more and more lack is the 0 of public dignity, of a shared commitment. Furthermore, this obscene big Other is supplemented (although often in a conflictual way) by the big Other of neutral expertise in its different forms (state apparatuses, legal order, science), and here the true problem emerges: can we trust this big Other, even in its scientific form? Is not science caught in the procedures of technological domination and exploitation, and of capitalist interests? Did not science long ago lose its neutrality? Was this neutrality from the very beginning not a mask of social domination? Applied to the pandemic, does this insight not compel us to problematize the scientific-medical justification of lockdown measures and other reactions to the pandemic? The most consequent partisan of Marxist COVID-scepticism is Fabio Vighi who argues that, if we join the dots provided by the close analysis of the financial background of the pandemic, we "might see a well-defined narrative outline emerge":

lockdowns and the global suspension of economic transactions were intended to 1) allow the Fed to flood the ailing financial markets with freshly printed money while deferring hyperinflation; and 2) introduce mass vaccination programs and health passports as pillars of a neo-feudal regime of capitalist accumulation ... The mainstream narrative should therefore be reversed: the stock market did not collapse (in March 2020) because lockdowns had to be imposed; rather, lockdowns had to be imposed because financial markets were collapsing ... SARS-CoV-2 is the name of a special weapon of psychological warfare that was deployed in the moment of greatest need ... The aim of the printing-spree was to plug calamitous liquidity gaps. Most of this "magic-tree money" is still frozen inside the shadow banking system, the stock exchanges, and various virtual currency schemes that are *not* meant to be used for spending and investment. Their function is solely to provide cheap loans for financial speculation. This is what Marx called "fictitious capital," which continues to expand in an orbital loop that is now completely independent of economic cycles on the ground. The bottom line is that all this cash cannot be allowed to flood the real economy, for the latter would overheat and trigger hyperinflation.[57]

In short, it is not the pandemic which put the capitalist order into an emergency state, it is global capitalism itself which needed an emergency state to avoid a debilitating crisis much stronger than the 2008 meltdown, and the pandemic was fabricated as a welcome excuse for the emergency state. In contrast to Agamben who focused on how the pandemic justified the permanent state of emergency with an unheard-of strengthening of biopolitics, Vighi puts forward capital's reproduction. The passage from neoliberal global capitalism to corporate neo-feudal capitalism is the basic process that uses historical contingencies as excuses, and Vighi is not afraid to add to this series of excuses ecologically grounded lockdowns: far from just confronting capitalism with its fateful limitations, ecological crises can and will also be used as a scientifically grounded way to discipline and control the population—"green capitalism" is not just a humanitarian mask of the global order, it is also a way for big corporate capital to control small capital.

Vighi takes into account the complexity of the situation: the interests of pharmaceutical corporations, the way the expert "scientific" insights that ground anti-pandemic measures justify new forms of social control and regulation which discipline the behavior of the population, etc. His line of argumentation contains many perspicuous insights, and the basic premise of his economic analysis hits the mark. The economic growth during the pandemic provides a case of the already-mentioned Lauderdale paradox: there was an enormous rise of production in the pharma-industry, not just vaccines but also masks, medical instruments, etc., which formally count as economic growth although they actually make people poorer. And one can be sure global warming will generate even more of such "economic growth."

I therefore thoroughly appreciate Vighi's work, but what I find problematic is his inverted causality: as we can see in the passages quoted above, instead of the "official" story of the pandemic triggering lockdown and other healthcare measures, he makes the needs of capital the determining agent which uses (or, in some of his formulations, even directly produces) the pandemic in order to justify lockdown measures. Especially when he also adds ecological crises to the elements justifying lockdowns, I think he proceeds too fast. The pandemic is not a fake invention or an exaggeration of the danger posed by a version of the flu; the danger is real, measures against it had to be taken. Science that investigates it is not a science in quotation marks but actual science. Science and the measures proposed by health authorities are, of course, twisted by corporate interests and by the interests of social control and domination, but therein, precisely, resides the problem: the only agencies we have to fight a real threat are kidnapped and twisted by the establishment, which is what makes the situation so tragic. So, in reality we are blackmailed: yes, the enforced measures are twisted, but they are the only thing we have, we cannot ignore them. To put it in another way, the mistake of the approach focused on the Real of capital's movement and interests is that (implicitly, if not openly) it reduces the "apparent" reality of the pandemic and the suffering it causes to just that, an appearance that can be safely ignored—however, even if the pandemic is invented and manipulated by interests of capital, it has actual material consequences which have to be met at the level of medical measures etc. What we cannot do is precisely the step implicitly advocated by Vighi: break out of the spell of the official narrative which justifies emergency measures and return to our everyday normality.

To perceive such a catastrophic by-product of capitalism as a moment of larger-than-life plan comes too close to a paranoiac construct. It presupposes that China is somehow, in spite of all geopolitical and economic conflicts with the West, part of the same capitalist mega-plot. It presupposes that science in many different countries is so easily manipulated by the establishment. Vighi's critique of the predominant notion of the pandemic is, of course, resolutely *not* paranoiac: he remains firmly within rational reasoning—he just comes dangerously close to it.

In what, then, resides the difference between conspiracy theories and critical thinking: although both begin with distrust of official ideology, conspiracy theories take a fateful step further not (just) in the sense of manipulating facts but at the very formal level. Recall Lacan's claim (to which I often refer) about jealousy: if what a jealous husband claims about his wife (that she sleeps around with other men) is all true, his jealousy is still pathological: the pathological elements is the husband's need for jealousy as the only way to retain his dignity, identity even. Along the same lines, one could say that, even if most of the Nazi claims about the Jews were true (they exploited Germans, they seduced German girls ...)— which they were not, of course—their anti-Semitism would still be (and was) a pathological phenomenon because it repressed the true reason why the Nazis needed anti-Semitism in order to sustain their ideological position. In the Nazi vision, their society was an organic Whole of harmonious collaboration, so an external intruder was needed to account for divisions and antagonisms. The same holds for how, today, anti-immigrant populists deal with the "problem" of refugees: they approach it in an atmosphere of fear, of the incoming struggle against the Islamization of Europe, and they get caught in a series of obvious absurdities. Alenka Zupančič[58] perspicuously applies this formula to conspiracy theories: "even though some conspiracies really exist, there is still something pathological that pertains to conspiracy theories, some surplus investment that is not reducible to these or those facts." She identifies three interconnected features of this pathology. First, conspiracy theories are "inherently connected with enjoyment— connected with what Lacan called *jouis-sens* (a world play with *jouissance* [enjoyment]), 'enjoy-meant' or the enjoyment of meaning": COVID-sceptics like to claim that they just want a free debate, a readiness to listen to all sides and to make up their own mind, against the dogmatism of experts and science in the service of establishment. They begin with scepticism, doubting all official theories, but then they (almost magically) abolish this doubt by way of providing a unified total explanation—and this overcoming of doubt by a total explanation, a meaning of it all, provides an immense surplus-enjoyment.

The motto of conspiracy theories "Do your research!" (i.e., don't trust authorities, think for yourself) de facto means its exact opposite: *do not think!* That is to say: how, concretely, do we do "our own research"? Since we are motivated by the distrust of the official view, "research" means a Google search—and, of course, we search for the COVID-denying sites which are on the top of our list ... "Do your research!" thus means: expose yourself to conspiracy theories which you are in no position to test. Recall Karl Popper's famous falsification theory of scientific knowledge: scientists should attempt to disprove a theory rather than attempt to continually prove it, since even if there are numerous instances that confirm it, it only takes one counter-observation to falsify it—scientific knowledge progresses when a theory is shown to be wrong and a new theory is introduced which better explains the phenomena. (Popper is aware that in concrete scientific research, things get more complex.) A conspiracy theory appears to be Popperian, it looks for instances that falsify it—however, it treats falsifications as additional proofs of its own truth: what appears as falsification just proves the strength of the deceiving big Other.

This brings us to the second feature: the common perception that conspiracy theories are part of our relativist post-truth era in which each group promotes its own subjective truth is simply wrong. Conspiracy theorists fanatically believe in Truth, "they take the category of truth very seriously. They believe that there is Truth; they are just convinced that this truth is different or other than the official one." The third feature (which makes conspiracy theories totally at odds with Marxism) is that this Truth is not just an objective social process but a conspiracy, a plot, of an active all-powerful agent whose main goal is to deceive us, a "subject supposed to deceive (us)" behind the apparent chaos (to add yet another variation to Lacan's notion of "subject supposed to know"). As Zupančič notes, there is a kind of theology of an evil god at work here:

we are basically dealing with a desperate attempt to preserve the agency of the big Other in the times of its disintegration into a generalized relativism, an attempt that can succeed only at the price of moving the big Other to the zone of malevolence and evil? The consistency of the big Other (its not being 'barred') can no longer manifest itself in anything else but in the Other successfully deceiving us. A consistent big Other can only be a big Deceiver (a big Fraud or Cheat), an evil Other. A consistent God can only be an evil God; nothing else adds up. Yet, better an evil God than no God.

(Only in its extreme Stalinist version does Marxism act like this: the presupposition of the Stalinist purges was that there is one big reactionary plot that unites all those who oppose the Stalinist party line.) In his analysis of the paranoia of the German judge Schreber, Freud reminds us that what we usually consider as madness (the paranoiac scenario of the conspiracy against the subject) is effectively already an attempt at recovery: after the complete psychotic breakdown, the paranoiac construct is an attempt of the subject to reestablish a kind of order in his universe, a frame of reference enabling him to acquire a "cognitive mapping." Does exactly the same not hold for today's conspiracy theories? They are attempts to recover a global cognitive mapping after the breakdown of the big Other.

There are, of course, cracks which immediately appear in this edifice: the abolished uncertainty returns in the way the "dogmatic" conspiracy theories are as a rule inconsistent and follow the logic of the joke about the borrowed kettle evoked by Freud: (1) I never borrowed a kettle from you; (2) I returned it to you unbroken; (3) the kettle was already broken when I got it from you. Such an enumeration of inconsistent arguments, of course, confirms by negation what it endeavors to deny—that I returned your kettle broken ... In the case of COVID-sceptics, they also effortlessly combine a series of contradictory claims: there is no COVID-19 virus; this virus was deliberately created (to reduce the population, to strengthen control over people, to boost capitalist economy ...); it is a natural disease much milder than the media say; vaccines are more dangerous than the virus ...

In this strange paranoiac world, Trump is telling the truth while Greta Thunberg is an agent of big capital ... I personally know people who died of COVID, I know researchers who are analyzing the virus from different perspectives (medical, statistical, etc.), I know their doubts and limitations which they openly confess and which are part of their scientific approach. For them, trust in science is the very opposite of dogmatic orthodoxy: it is the trust in exploration which is constantly progressing.

For all these reasons, I think that the idea of a mega-plot in the service of capital is infinitely less believable than the idea of the brutal reality of the pandemic as a contingent event deftly exploited by the establishment, but in a way which is in itself contradictory: the pandemic which obviously calls for greater cooperation and social coordination at the same time triggers a defensive reaction of capital, a reaction which comes second and is an attempt to control the damage. I find especially problematic the idea that the ecological threat has a similar status of being invented (or at least exaggerated) to strengthen the emerging neo-feudal capitalism. Global warming is a traumatic real which obviously calls for socialization of the economy; the largely predominant tendency of the capitalist establishment is to downplay the threat, and the fact that it is (to a very limited degree) astutely used by the global order is a limited secondary fact.

Another moment that should draw our attention is how, at the start of 2020, COVID suddenly exploded as a central topic in our media, eclipsing all other illnesses and even political news (although other illnesses and misfortunes were causing far more suffering and deaths). Now infections are still very high, but there are far fewer lockdowns and other defensive measures—the model is here the UK which abandoned all regulations of public life and shifted responsibility to individuals themselves (in this way, the government returned us our freedom with a price: we are ourselves guilty for any infections ...). Media call this "learning to live with COVID" ... Can this shift (which is obviously out of sync with the reality of the pandemic) be accounted for by the claim that the establishment decided we can return to a limited normality since lockdown played its economic and social role and social control is well entrenched? The weird normality we are entering now could be much better explained by crowd-psychology: in traumatic situations, the temporality of the reaction does not follow reality, people get exhausted by the permanent emergency state, a tired indifference begins to predominate.

But one has to take a step further here. Panic as well as its opposite, tiredness and indifference, are not just categories of psychic life, they can only emerge (in the form they are taking today) as moments in the social process of the change in the status of the big Other. A year and a half ago we were in a panic because of the disintegration of the big Other that we could share and trust: there was no authority able to provide a global cognitive mapping of the situation. The importance of this dimension—of the shifts in the mode of symbolic production—was neglected already by Marx: to fight pandemic and global warming, a new big Other—a new space of solidarity grounded in science and emancipation—is needed.

In the ongoing struggles and conflicts, it is crucial to make the right choice. To characterize an epoch, the question to ask is not what unites it but what is the division that defines it—the "difference that makes difference." Advocates of the idea that class struggle is out often claim that today's big division is a new one, say, between the liberal establishment and populist resistance. For Jean-Claude Milner, the division that replaced class struggle is that between Zionism and anti-Semitism, and it appears that these days, towards the end of 2021, the division that matters, at least in the developed world, is the that between partisans of anti-pandemic measures and those who resist them. It is precisely at this point that we should insist on the primacy of class struggle as the factor which "in last instance" determines the whole. With anti-Semitism, this link is clear: anti-Semitism is distorted anti-capitalism; it "naturalizes" capitalist profiteering and exploitation in the figure of "the Jew," an external intruder who brings antagonism into social body. But what if the same goes for COVID deniers and sceptics? Are COVID-denying conspiracy theories not vaguely similar to anti-Semitic theories, at least in their Rightist-populist version where anti-capitalism is displaced onto distrust of science as serving the financial-corporate-medical establishment? In both cases, it is crucial to draw the line of distinction between the basic antagonism and its ideological displacement.

The conflict between COVID-sceptics and advocates of anti-pandemic measures therefore cannot be directly translated into our basic political struggle, so even a radical Leftist has to make a choice. On September 9 2021, Biden announced "policies requiring most federal employees to get COVID-19 vaccinations and pushing large employers to get their workers inoculated or tested weekly. These new measures will apply to about two-thirds of all

US employees. "'We've been patient,' Biden told the tens of millions of Americans who have declined to get coronavirus shots. 'But our patience is wearing thin, and your refusal has cost all of us.'"[59] Is this a move destined to assert state control over individuals and to foster interests of big capital? No: I "naively" accept it will help millions.

Vighi here takes the side of Agamben who, in an interview attached to his collection of texts on the pandemic *Where are we now?*,[60] replied to the critical observation that, in his opposition to lockdown measures, he comes close to Trump and Bolsonaro, with the claim that a truth is a truth whether articulated by Right or Left. Agamben here ignores the tension between truth and knowledge: yes, a piece of knowledge (truth in the sense of adequately rendering a particular fact) is a piece of knowledge, but the horizon of meaning can give a totally different spin to this piece of knowledge. In the fact that there were many Jews among art critics in Germany around 1930 resonates a different "truth" if we mean it as a confirmation that Jews have great sensibility for art, or alternatively if we mean it as a confirmation that Jews control our artistic production and push it in the direction of *"entartete Kunst"* (degenerate art). Although Vighi endeavors to do precisely this—to discern social truth beneath the medical knowledge that justifies measures against the pandemic—he ignores the complex social and material background of the pandemic. The circular movement of capitalist self-reproduction takes place at three interconnected levels: the speculative dance of capital itself; the social implications of this dance (the distribution of wealth and poverty, exploitation, the dissolution of social links); the material process of production and exploitation of our environment which affects our entire life-world and culminates in "capitalocene" as a new geological era on the Earth. The other side of the mad dance of fictitious capital which ignores reality are the real facts of immense heaps of plastic trash, of forest fires and global warming, of toxic pollution of hundreds of millions of people.

The moment we also take this third level fully into account, we can see how pandemic and global warming emerge as the material product of global capitalist economy. Yes, capitalism did produce the pandemic and the ecological threat—not as part of a brutal tactic to survive its own crisis but as the result of its immanent contradictions. The best formula to characterize COVID-sceptics is therefore Lacan's *les non-dupes errent* (those who are not duped err most).[61] Sceptics who distrust the public narrative of a catastrophe (pandemic, global warming . . .) and see a deeper plot in it err the most, missing the actual process that gave birth to it. Vighi is thus all too optimistic: there is no need to invent pandemics and weather catastrophes, the system produces them by itself.

Lambs to the Slaughter

Les non-dupes errent should be generalized into the basic mode of how ideology functions today, as the obverse—or, rather, the practical implication—of the ongoing process of social disintegration. Jill Filipovic (CNN) reported on October 19, 2021 a "mind-bogglingly horrific" event from Philadelphia: a woman was raped on a Southeastern Pennsylvania Transport Authority train while onlookers recorded the event with their cellphones but did not intervene or call 911: "It suggests not only a total disregard for women's safety and wellbeing, but social disintegration; a disturbing impulse to filter terrible events through the lens of entertainment and shock value, and the disturbing ability to dehumanize suffering by mediating it through a screen."[62] The list of causes is very precise: disregard for women, wider social disintegration, and, a key feature all too often ignored, filtering of violent events through a screen which somehow derealizes and dehumanizes them. This social disintegration in the form of the lack of elementary solidarity is a global phenomenon—it was noted a couple of years ago even in China. When people witness a horrible event of one person causing pain to another, many of them react in four ways of descending amorality: they run away so as not to witness the event; they walk by and just avert their gaze, ignoring it; they eagerly observe the event; or they record the event. The last two ways obviously generate a surplus-enjoyment of its own: what makes us, observers, guilty is not just the fact that we do nothing (through fear or for whatever other reason), but this enjoyment is embodied in our eager gaze.

Is something similar not at work in how our media report on violence against women? Jacqueline Rose recently made a key point when she dealt with the question: is the widespread talk about violence against women in our mainstream media an indication that there is more of this violence in real life, or is it just that this violence became more visible because, on account of the growing feminist awareness, we apply higher ethical standards which qualify as violence what was before considered part of a normal state of things? Rose pointed out that this higher visibility is profoundly ambiguous: it signals the fact that feminist awareness has penetrated general culture, but it also neutralizes the impact of violence against women, rendering it tolerable and standardized—we see it all around, we protest against it, and life goes on . . .

Let's take a case of the direct "critical" depiction of the oppressive atmosphere of an imagined conservative-fundamentalist rule. The new TV version of Margaret Atwood's *The Handmaid's Tale* confronts us with the weird pleasure of fantasizing a world of brutal patriarchal domination—of course, nobody would openly admit the desire to live in such nightmarish world, but this assurance that we really don't want it makes fantasizing about it, imagining all the details of this world, all the more pleasurable. Yes, we feel pain while experiencing this pleasure, but Lacan's name for this pleasure-in-pain is *jouissance* . . . And, at an even more general level, the same goes for many critical (or fictional) reports on the horrors of capitalism: it is as if the brutal and open critique of capitalism is immediately co-opted, included in the capitalist self-reproduction. Let's take *Squid Game*, the gigantic global hit produced by Netflix: its "not-so-subtle message" is:

> runaway capitalism is bad. Alas, I am not sure executives at Netflix are particularly bothered. They are far too busy raking in all the cash that Squid Game has made them. As it turns out, a scathing critique of capitalism may help push Netflix into becoming a trillion-dollar company. Squid Game has boosted Netflix stock's market value by $19 billion since it launched it in mid-September; it has also created $900m in "impact value", which is a metric Netflix uses to assess the performance of individual shows. The streaming platform is shamelessly trying

to squeeze every last penny it can out of the show: it's even selling Squid Game hoodies on its online store.[63]

However, this immediate co-option goes deeper and reaches well beyond the immense profits the series is generating. What perhaps matters even more is the formal aspect: *Squid Game* transposes brutal capitalist exploitation and competition (which are features of the system as such) into a game run by hidden organizers, and thereby makes us, spectators—observers who fully enjoy the tensions and reversals of the plot.

So how can we counteract an ideology which takes into account the very fact that individuals don't trust it? A possible solution came recently from Greece, and its simple redoubled spin confirms that Greece is the origin of our civilization. On October 2021, Greek media reported that a scam involving over 100,000 anti-vaxxers and 200–300 doctors and nurses was discovered: "anti-vaxxers would pay doctors €400 for fake vaccinations. Basically they would ask them to inject them with a dose of, e.g., plain tap water, instead of the vaccine. However, the doctors involved in the scheme would then out-scheme them, by switching in the last minute the 'fake' liquid with the real thing, and thus would actually inject them with the real vaccine, unbeknownst to the anti-vaxxer. The (now simultaneously both corrupt and ethical) doctor would still keep the bribe! And now for the final hilarious twist : the 'secretly' vaxxed anti-vaxxer would naturally get, and would describe to others, the vaccine's side-effects, without, however, being able to explain how or why they would occur, since the anti-vaxxer would still believe that he or she had tricked the system."[64] Although I condemn the doctors participating in this scam, I cannot judge them too harshly. When they issued the document confirming the vaccination to an anti-vaxxer, they were not cheating: the person really was vaccinated. The only person who was effectively cheated was the one who wanted to cheat, i.e., to enjoy the benefits of vaccination without getting vaccinated, but he was cheated by means of truth itself: what he didn't know is that he really is what he pretended to be (vaccinated) ... Is, then, the problem that the doctor not only lied to his patient (promising him that he would not really be vaccinated), but also pocketed the bribe

(400 euros)? Even here, one might argue that if the doctor were not to accept the bribe, his patient might suspect that he would not be really not-vaccinated. The true ethical concern resides in the fact that the patient was vaccinated against his explicit will—which, in this situation, I consider a rather minor misdemeanor since the patient's intention was to cheat, i.e., while not being vaccinated he wanted an official document confirming that he had been vaccinated, which is why he was a threat not just to himself but also to others.

Many of those who oppose vaccination argue that obligatory vaccination is not only an attack on our personal freedom of choice but also a violent intrusion into our bodies comparable to rape— when I get vaccinated, I am raped by the public (not only) medical authority ... as if our body is ever really just ours? There was recently in Slovenia a case of a very old lady who was slowly dying in a hospital, unable to feed herself, kept alive by six or seven simultaneous infusions. When asked if she would like to get vaccinated, she ferociously resisted, saying that she didn't know what was in the vaccine and didn't want to have any foreign stuff injected into her body ... Is this not the situation for all of us: vaccinated or not, we are already controlled and manipulated in ways we are unaware of, in the same way that, although some rich Jews are exploiting us, our exploitation also goes on with full force without Jews.

However, the true interest of this anecdote is that, whether true or not, it functions as an exemplum in Pierre Bayard's sense, rendering in a pure form rarely encountered in social reality the way we are controlled and manipulated: while we think we cheat the public authority, our cheating is already included in the cycle of the self-reproduction of public authority. So we are in a way acting even worse than a lamb to the slaughter: we act like a lamb which eagerly pays for its own slaughter. Again, as Lacan put it, *les non-dupes errent*, like the white lower class members who were not duped by the liberal establishment and ended up voting for Trump. One should also note how the logic of "lamb to the slaughter" applies to both sides of the ongoing struggle: for COVID-sceptics, lambs to the slaughter were the people who waited in line to get vaccinated, or, when the vaccines were difficult to get, even bribing the doctors to get vaccinated. For (for the time being, at least) the majority of lambs to the slaughter are the COVID-deniers who pose a threat to their own life and the lives of others by their refusal to comply with the anti-pandemic measures.

One often hears that the anti-vaccination protests are not just a display of anti-scientific irrationality: they condense a series of other dissatisfactions (with exploding control over our lives, with the power of medical and other corporations, etc.), so we should enter into a dialogue with them, not just dismiss them with contempt . . . The problem I see here is that exactly the same can be said about anti-Semitism (it expresses a protest against financial exploitation, etc.), or even about violence against women (men who abuse women often in order to vent their frustration at being humiliated in their social life). What, in all these cases, undermines such a "benevolent" and "understanding" view is the surplus-enjoyment generated by the movement in question: brutalizing women obviously brings a perverted enjoyment, the same goes for anti-Semitic pogroms, and anti-vaccination conspiracy theories also generate an enjoyment of their own. So we should here supplement Lacan's formula of psychoanalytic ethics "the only thing you can be guilty of is to compromise your desire" with: you are always guilty/responsible for your enjoyment, even when what brings you to enjoy is externally imposed on you.

Therein resides the material power of ideology: it not only trains us to tolerate power, or even to actively participate in our own submission. It cheats on us by the very act of warning us against being cheated, i.e., it does not count on our trust (in the public order and its values) but on our very distrust—its underlying message is: "Don't trust those in power, you are being manipulated, and here is how you can avoid being duped!"

The Two Faces of Anachronism

Perhaps the deepest rift we are dealing with here is the rift between the image of reality offered by science and common-sense normality, the way of life we are used to: normality, inclusive of all the intuitions of how our life works, is on the side of vaccine-deniers. They simply cannot accept that the problems we are facing now—pandemic, global warming, social unrest ...—will lead to the end of our way of life. I have spoken to people who need regular dialysis to survive, and they all told me that the most traumatic thing to accept is that their very survival depends on this prosthesis: there is a big machine out there, in front of me, and my bodily functioning depends on its regular use and smooth functioning. The prospect of vaccination confronts us with the same shattering experience: my survival hinges on the success of being jabbed repeatedly.

What the populist Right and the libertarian Left share is a distrust of the entire space of public authorities: police regulations, healthcare control and regulations sustained by medical and pharmaceutical institutions, big corporations and banks ... They both want to resist this pressure, to maintain a space of freedom—on behalf of what? The Left—if it still deserves this name—should take a step further here: it is not enough to resist (whatever we perceive as) the establishment on behalf of some more authentic mode of existence: one should also mobilize the mechanism of the "critique of critique" and problematize the "authentic" position on behalf of what we resist. It is easy to recognize that the populist resistance to vaccination in the US acts in defense of the "American way of life" with its rampant individualism, carrying guns in public, racism, etc. The Leftist vision which sustains vaccine-sceptics is as a rule that of direct democracy of small groups that want to live in a transparent society without alienated centers of power. The problematic nature of the Taliban vision goes by itself. The paradox is thus that, to defeat the external threat (of globalist domination), one should begin by sacrificing the very heart of what we feel is threatened.

We should learn to trust science: it is only with the help of science that we can overcome our problems (caused, among other things, by science in the service of power). We should learn to trust public authority: only such an authority makes it possible to confront dangers such as pandemics and environmental catastrophes by way of imposing necessary measures. We should learn to trust the big Other, the shared space of basic values: without it, solidarity is not possible. We don't need the freedom to be different, we need the freedom to choose how to be the same in a new way. And, perhaps most difficult, we should be ready to abandon many of the common-sense beliefs and practices that form our way of life. To be truly conservative today, to fight for what is worth saving in our traditions, means to engage in a radical change. The old conservative motto "some things have to change so that everything remains the same" has acquired a new weight today: many things will have to change radically for us to remain human.

The critique we hear again and again is that the West failed in Afghanistan because it tried to implement its own idea of democracy and freedom there, ignoring specific local circumstances and traditions. However, on a closer look, one can see that the West was trying precisely to establish links with local formations—and the result was pacts with local warlords, etc. The long-term outcome of such attempts can only be a combination of global capitalism and local nationalism, as we see it in Turkey—no wonder the Taliban has good relations with the Turkish government. Afghanistan did not get too much modernity, it mostly got all that has gone wrong in our modernity, beginning with Soviet occupation—as Juergen Habermas put it decades ago, modernity is an unfinished project, and the Taliban are the proof of it. So to understand properly phenomena like the Taliban, one has to resuscitate the dialectical notion of anachronism:[65] no system can be purely contemporaneous with itself, it has to include trans-functionalized elements of the past. Why did the British nobility remain in power in state apparatuses even when Great Britain became a highly developed capitalist country? Marx explained this apparent anachronism: the bourgeoisie allowed this because capitalists were aware that nobility is the best representative of the capitalist class as such, as a whole—left to itself, the capitalist class would get lost in factional struggles. And the same goes for the rise of fundamentalist movements like the Taliban: they are not simply anachronistic, they stand for tradition which never existed, a tradition reinvented to counteract the destructive consequences of modernization—the Taliban fill in the lack of failed capitalist modernity.

However, one should oppose here the anachronism which enables the present order to complete its hegemony to the anachronism which disrupts the present order and points towards an alternate future. We are in the midst of a process that is "not only destined to make labor more flexible but to eradicate the reality of labor as a collective form of life and struggle in order to make it a mere private affair for individuals managing their 'human capital',"[66] and in this situation, the hegemonic ideology desperately tries to dismiss all signs of the persistence of class struggle (trade unions, strikes, etc.) as "anachronisms." The moment a more radical Leftist orientation emerges (as was the case with Corbyn in the UK and Sanders in the US), it is immediately attacked as out of time, as a remainder of the "old Left" which ignores the new conditions. From an authentic Leftist standpoint, of course, class struggle remains the encompassing unity in this shift from still visible class struggle to each of us as a manager of his/her human capital—which means that the very disappearance of class struggle from public discourse indicates the victory of the ruling side in the class struggle, or, to quote none other than Warren Buffet: "There's class warfare, all right, but it's my class, the rich class, that's making war, and we're winning."[67]

Such a notion of anachronism is grounded in what I call materialist theology—what is theology here? Walter Benjamin (who can also be called a materialist theologian) provided the answer: "What science has 'determined' remembrance can modify. Such mindfulness can make the incomplete (happiness) into something complete, and the complete (suffering) into something incomplete. That is theology."[68] Science "determines" things, it aims to establish the full continuous causal link among them, and in this way an image of reality emerges in which happiness is always "incomplete," thwarted, while suffering remains what it is, a fact of life. What Benjamin calls "theology" breaks up the causal continuity of time: it "completes" happiness and "incompletes" suffering in one and the same move: by way of establishing a direct trans-temporal link between past, present and future. A present emancipatory struggle is posited as something in which past failed struggles resonate and repeat themselves, and this struggle opens itself upon a different future. In this perspective, present, past, and future are not successive states in a historical continuum, they are all different strata of a contemporary event. As Benjamin put it, the present struggle is a struggle through which the past itself will be redeemed, which means that past and future are not external opposites: there is a future dimension inscribed into the past itself.

Arthur Rimbaud's famous line "*il faut etre absolument moderne*" is today perhaps more actual than ever. Those who see our predicament as the final outcome of modern subjectivity which objectivizes and tries to dominate all reality, like to propose a shift from Subject to humans: we, humanity, are not the Subject elevated above all reality, we are humans rooted in a given historical and environmental context which makes us human ... We should gather the courage to turn around this idea: the ongoing crises impose on us the urge to sacrifice our historical form of humanity, of what it means to be human to us now, and to assert ourselves as pure abyssal subject.

The Taliban and vaccine-deniers are not an irrational extremism, they are the two extreme expressions of resistance to modernity. It is relatively easy to dismiss them as a freakish outgrowth, but it is much more difficult to render problematic the basic stance which grounds them: the idea that our multicultural globalized societies are societies whose spirit is tired (as Nietzsche put it), unable to engage in a large-scale passionate project which may demand from us that we even risk our lives. Recall the Taliban victory in Afghanistan: there was no passionate engagement to fight the Taliban advocated by Left liberals, the only passion emerged after the Taliban takeover when our media became obsessed with the fate of the victims who remained in Afghanistan and were threatened by Taliban rule (women, Western collaborators . . .).

More generally, the only passion we can recognize today is the negative passion to identify and fight racist, sexist, etc. prejudices. Effectively there is a nihilist dimension in this perverted passion which stands for the hermeneutic of suspicion at its most extreme: the frantic effort to bring out a patriarchal, homophobic, Eurocentric, etc. bias in every positive project. "Globohomo" is an ideal combination of corporate capitalism with a Politically Correct personality. What one has to fear is that the "open" democratic West will display the same inability to act as the pro-Western residents of big cities in Afghanistan did, unable to really mobilize against the nationalist-populist threat—is this not already happening? We are witnessing again and again the weird oscillation of the "democratic" forces in the EU, endlessly postponing clear confrontation with the Hungarian and Polish governments.

In this context, the position of European nationalist populists cannot but appear as well-grounded: what is more normal than to fight globalism with local roots, way of life, commitment to one's community, etc., as a protection against "globohomo" lifeless nihilism? However, as we have already seen, *this* is the temptation to be avoided at any price. Today's multiple crises (from pandemics to ecology) require a global commitment totally at odds with global-capitalist modernity. And the only path to this new committed universality leads through an even more radical nihilism, the nihilism which clearly perceives the vacuity of liberal universalism. In Nietzsche's terms, we have to take a step from passive nihilism to active nihilism—an outburst of self-destructive negativity whose figure in our popular culture is Joker.

So what should Americans have done in Afghanistan? Yes, they messed up the situation, but after they did it, they lost the right to just run away from the mess they created. They should have stayed and start to act differently—how? Let me just conclude with a reversal of the well-known metaphor of how, when we are throwing out the dirty water from a bathtub, we should be careful not to lose the clean and healthy baby. Racists are doing this when they realize that the Western interventions designed to spread human rights and freedoms to the poor and dirty Third World countries miserably fail: OK, so let's throw out of the bathtub of human rights and freedoms the dirty water of Third World people who are not mature enough for secular democracy, and let's just keep in the pure white baby . . . Perhaps, we should do the exact opposite: throw out the pure white baby and be careful not to lose the dirty water of the poor and exploited in the Third World who really deserve human rights and not just our sympathy and charity.

So can we imagine a return of the repressed in its proper form of collective emancipatory engagement? Not only can we imagine it—it is already knocking on our doors with great force. Let's just mention the global warming catastrophe—it calls for large-scale collective actions which will demand their own forms of martyrdom, sacrificing many pleasures we have got used to. If we really want to change our entire way of life, the individualist "care of the Self" which focuses of our use of pleasures will have to be superseded. Expert science alone will not do the job—it will have to be a science rooted in the deepest collective engagement. *This* should be our answer to the Taliban: a "subjective destitution" much stronger than that of religious fundamentalists.

Destructive Nihilism

It is crucial to note here that subjective destitution as the emergence of a radical gap in the continuity of History is here not an explosion of destructive violence which can only in a later stage be transformed into a pragmatic and realist construction of a new order: Giri describes subjective destitution as a stance which enables us to engage in a construction of a new social order. As such, revolutionary subjective destitution should be strictly separated from the outbursts of radical negativity which appear as self-destructive political nihilism. There is no better example of this topic in art than Todd Phillips' *Joker*—one cannot but express admiration for a Hollywood in which it is possible to make a film like *Joker*, and for the public which turned it into a mega blockbuster.

However, the reason for the film's popularity resides in its meta-fictional dimension: it provides the dark genesis of the Batman story, a genesis that has to remain invisible for the Batman myth to function. Let's try to imagine *Joker* without this reference to the Batman myth, just as the story of a victimized kid who adopts the mask of a clown to survive his predicament—it simply wouldn't work, it would have been just another realist drama. *Time Out* characterized *Joker* as "a truly nightmarish vision of late-era capitalism," and categorized it as a "social horror film." This would have seemed unimaginable until recently—a combination of two genres which are perceived as totally disparate, the realist depiction of social misery and fantasized horror—a combination which, of course, only works when social reality acquires dimensions of horror fiction.

The three main stances towards the film in our media perfectly mirror the tripartite division of our political space: conservatives worry that it may incite viewers to acts of violence; Politically Correct liberals discerned in it racist and other clichés (in the opening scene, a group of boys who beat Arthur appear black), plus also an ambiguous fascination with blind violence; Leftists celebrate it for faithfully rendering the conditions of the rise of violence in our societies. But does *Joker* really incite spectators to imitate Arthur's acts in real life? Emphatically no—for the simple reason that Arthur-Joker is not presented as a figure of identification—the whole film works on the premise that it is impossible for us, viewers, to identify with him.[69] He remains a stranger up to the end.

Before *Joker* was released, the media warned the public that it may incite violence; the FBI itself specifically warned that the film may inspire violence from Clowncels, an Incel subgroup obsessed with clowns such as Pennywise from *It* and *Joker*. (There were no reports of violence inspired by the film.) After the film was released, critics were not sure how to categorize it: is *Joker* just a piece entertainment (as is the entire Batman series), an in-depth study of the genesis of pathological violence, or an exercise in social criticism.

Since *Joker* depicts radical rebellion against the existing order as a self-destructive orgy of violence with no positive vision underlying it, it can also be read as anti-Leftist—for Tyler Cowen, the film "quite explicitly portrays the egalitarian instinct as a kind of barbaric violent atavism, and it is pointedly critical of Antifa and related movements, showing them as representing a literal end of civilization. Only the wealthy are genteel and urbane and proper."[70] The lesson of the film is thus: no radical steps, we can only count on the benevolent charity of the rich to gradually improve things. The Leftist answer to this reading is that the self-destructive rebellion portrayed in *Joker* is that such a nihilist explosion of brutal rage precisely signals that we remain within the coordinates of the existing order, and that a more radical shift of political imagination is needed. From his radical Leftist standpoint, Michael Moore found *Joker* to be "a timely piece of social criticism and a perfect illustration of the consequences of America's current social ills": when it explores how Arthur Fleck became Joker, it brings out the role of bankers, the collapse of healthcare, and the divide between rich and poor. Moore is therefore right to mock those who feared the film's release: "Our country is in deep despair, our constitution is in shreds, a rogue maniac from Queens has access to the nuclear codes—but for some reason, it's a movie we should be afraid of ... The greater danger to society may be if you DON'T go see this movie ... This movie is not about Trump. It's about the America that gave us Trump—the America which feels no need to help the outcast, the destitute." Consequently, "the fear and outcry over Joker is a ruse. It's a distraction so that we don't look at the real violence tearing up our fellow human beings—30 million Americans who don't have health insurance is an act of violence. Millions of abused women and children living in fear is an act of violence."

However, *Joker* not only depicts this America, it also raises a "discomfiting question": "What if one day the dispossessed decide to fight back? And I don't mean with a clipboard registering people to vote. People are worried this movie may be too violent for them. Really? Considering everything we're living through in real life?" In short, the film tries to "understand why innocent people turn into Jokers after they can no longer keep it together": rather than feeling incited to violence, a spectator "will thank this movie for connecting you to a new desire—not to run to the nearest exit to save your own ass but rather to stand and fight and focus your attention on the nonviolent power you hold in your hands every single day."[71]

But does it really work like that? The "new desire" Moore mentions is not Joker's desire—to see this, one has to introduce here the psychoanalytic distinction between drive and desire. Drive is compulsively-repetitive, in it, we are caught in the loop of turning again and again around the same point, while desire enacts a cut; it opens up a new dimension. Joker remains a being of drive: at the film's end, he is powerless, and his violent outbursts are just impotent explosions of rage, actings-out of his basic powerlessness. In order for the desire described by Moore to arise, one step further is needed: an additional change of subjective stance is to be accomplished if we are to pass from Joker's outbursts to becoming able to "stand and fight and focus your attention on the nonviolent power you hold in your hands every single day"—when you become aware of this power you can renounce brutal bodily violence. The paradox is that you become truly violent (in the sense of posing a threat to the existing system) only when you renounce physical violence.

This does not mean that Joker's act is a dead-end to be avoided—it is rather a kind of Malevich-moment, reduction to a zero point of minimal frame of protest. Malevich's famous black square on white surface is not some kind of self-destructive abyss we should beware of not being swallowed by, but a point through which we should pass to gain a new beginning. It is the moment of death-drive which opens up the space for sublimation. And in the same way that, in his minimalist paintings like Black Square, Malevich reduced a painting to its minimal opposition of frame and background, Joker reduced protest to its minimal content-less self-destructive form. An additional twist is needed to pass from drive to desire, to leave behind the nihilist point of self-destruction, to make this zero-point function as a new beginning. However, the lesson of *Joker* is that we have to go through this zero-point to get rid of the illusions that pertain to the existing order.[72]

This zero-point is today's version of what was once called a proletarian position, the experience of those who have nothing to lose—or, to quote Arthur from the film: "I've got nothing left to lose. Nothing can hurt me anymore. My life is nothing but a comedy." This is where the idea that Trump is a kind of Joker in power finds its limit: Trump definitely did not go through this zero-point. He may be an obscene clown in his own way, but he is not a Joker figure—it's an insult to Joker to compare him with Trump. In the film, Wayne the father is a "joker" in the simple sense of the agent who displays the obscenity of power.

Now we can see where M.L. Clark goes ridiculously wrong when he reads my own philosophy as a version of Joker's nihilist stance: "Žižek's Hegelian-philosophy-meets-flimsy-pop-science relentlessly insists that the only objective reality is not the Nothingness from which Something was created, but rather the tension between the true nothing-burger underpinning existence, and the moral depravity of our every, inevitable attempt to impose meaning upon it." In short, for me, the basic ontological fact is the tension between the ultimate meaningless void/crack and our (humanity's) attempts to impose some universal meaning onto this chaotic crack—such a position is nothing special, it simply reproduces a certain existential humanism which perceives humans as beings who heroically endeavor to impose some meaning onto the chaos of the world into which we are thrown. However, according to Clark, I here take a step further in the Joker direction: since all attempts to impose meaning onto the primordial chaotic Void obfuscate this void and are thus hypocritical, i.e., since they escape from the basic nonsense of existence, they are acts of moral depravity—or, to bring this point to extreme, morality itself (attempts to impose a universal meaning onto reality) is a form of moral depravity. The only consequent moral stance is thus one of full nihilism, of joyfully endorsing the violent destruction of every attempt to impose a moral order onto our chaotic life, of renouncing every universal humanist project that would enable us to surmount our discords:

> no matter how much we might want to insist that our shared humanity is stronger than our momentary discords and our abiding individual differences . . . the Jokers and Žižeks are never quite going to be persuaded. Their respective ideological frameworks require them to keep pointing to the social tensions that remain: the chaos that will always be a part of our collective press towards a better-synthesized societal whole.[73]

I, of course, consider this stance of radical nihilism not only totally at odds with my clear political engagements but also self-contradictory: it needs its fake-moral opponent to assert itself in its nihilistic destruction and in the unmasking of its hypocrisy. Therein resides the limit of all the desperate attempts to reverse tragedy into triumphant comedy practiced by Incels, Clowncels and Joker himself who, just before shooting Murray, his TV host, tells him: "Have you seen what it's like out there, Murray? Do you ever actually leave the studio? Everybody just yells and screams at each other. Nobody's civil anymore! Nobody thinks what it's like to be the other guy. You think men like Thomas Wayne ever think what it's like to be someone like me? To be somebody but themselves? They don't. They think that we'll just sit down and take it like good little boys! That we won't werewolf and go wild!" The assertion of joyful destruction remains parasitic on this complaint. Joker doesn't go "too far" in the destruction of the existing order, he remains stuck in what Hegel called "abstract negativity," unable as he is to propose its concrete negation.

Insofar as the Freudian name for this negativity is death-drive, we should thus be careful not to characterize Donald Trump's self-destructive defense against the attempts to impeach him as manifestations of death-drive.[74] Yes, while Trump rejects the accusations against him, he simultaneously confirms (and even boasts of) the very crimes he is accused of and breaks the law in his very defense—but does he not thereby just enact (more openly than usual, true) the paradox that is constitutive of the rule of the law, i.e., the fact that the very agency that regulates the application of the law has to exempt itself from its reign? So yes, Trump is obscene in acting the way he acts, but in this way he merely brings out the obscenity that is the obverse of the law itself; the "negativity" of his acts is totally subordinated to (his perception of) his ambitions and well-being, he is far from the self-destruction of the existing order enacted by Joker. There is nothing suicidal about Trump's boasting about his breaking the rules, it is simply part of his message that he is a tough guy president beset by corrupt elites and boosting the US abroad, and that his transgressions are necessary because only a rule breaker can crush the power of the Washington swamp. To read this well-planned and very rational strategy in terms of death-drive is yet another example of how it is Left liberals who are really on a suicidal mission, giving rise to the impression that they are engaged in bureaucratic-legal nagging while the President is doing a good job for the country.

In Christopher Nolan's *The Dark Knight*, Joker is the only figure of truth: the goal of his terrorist attacks on Gotham City is made clear: they will stop when Batman takes off his mask and reveal his true identity. What, then, is Joker who wants to disclose the truth beneath the Mask, convinced that this disclosure will destroy the social order? He is not a man without mask, but, on the contrary, a man fully identified with his mask, a man who *is* his mask—there is nothing, no "ordinary guy," beneath his mask. This is why Joker has no back-story and lacks any clear motivation: he tells different people different stories about his scars, mocking the idea that he should have some deep-rooted trauma that drives him. It may appear that *Joker* aims precisely at providing a kind of socio-psychological genesis of Joker, depicting the traumatic events which made him the figure he is.[75] The problem is that thousands of young boys who grew up in ruined families and were bullied by their peers suffered the same fate, but only one "synthesized" this circumstances into the unique figure of Joker. In other words, yes, Joker is the result of a set of pathogenic circumstances, but these circumstances can be described as the causes of this unique figure only retroactively, once Joker is already here. In one of the early novels about Hannibal Lecter, the claim that Lecter's monstrosity is the result of unfortunate circumstances is rejected: "Nothing happened *to* him. *He* happened."

However, one can (and should) also read *Joker* in the opposite sense and claim that the act that constitutes the main figure as "Joker" is an autonomous act by means of which he surpasses the objective circumstances of his situation. He identifies himself with his fate, but this identification is a free act: in it, he posits himself as a unique figure of subjectivity . . ."[76] We can locate this reversal at a precise moment in the film when the hero says: "You know what really makes me laugh? I used to think that my life was a tragedy. But now I realize, it's a fucking comedy." One should take note of the exact moment when Arthur says this: while, standing by the side of his mother's bed, he takes her pillow and uses it to smother her to death. Who, then, is his mother? Here is how Arthur describes her presence: "She always tells me to smile and put on a happy face. She says I was put here to spread joy and laughter." Is this not maternal superego at its purest? No wonder she calls him Happy, not Arthur. He gets rid of his mother's hold (by killing her) through fully identifying with her command to laugh.

This, however, does not mean that Joker lives in a maternal world: his mother is a half-dead impassive victim of paternal violence, obsessed with the ultra-rich Wayne as the father of her child, hoping to the end that he will help her and Arthur.[77] (The film elegantly leaves it open as to whether Wayne is Arthur's father or not.) Arthur's sad fate is thus not the result of an over-strong maternal presence—far from being guilty, his mother is herself the victim of extreme male brutality. Apart from Wayne, there is another paternal figure in the film: Murray, the comedian who invites Arthur to his popular TV show and thus gives him a chance of social integration and public recognition. One is almost tempted to say that this duality of Wayne and Murray enacts the opposition between "bad" and "good" father (in this case, the father who ignores Arthur and the father who recognizes him), but the integration fails, Arthur sees through Murray's hypocrisy and shoots him in the midst of the TV show, and it is only at this, after repeating the murder of his mother in the public murder of a paternal figure that he fully becomes Joker. (In yet another elegant move, Arthur does not kill Wayne, his putative father, himself—this act is left to an anonymous man wearing a clown mask, a member of Joker's new tribe. Both Oedipal enigmas, the question of who is Arthur's father and the question of who enacts the parricide, are thus left in dark.)

Because of his act, Joker may not be moral, but he definitely is ethical. Morality regulates how we relate to others with regard to our shared common Good, while ethics concerns our fidelity to the Cause which defines our desire, a fidelity which reaches beyond the pleasure-principle. Morality in its basic sense is not opposed to social customs, it is an affair of what in ancient Greece was called *eumonia*, the harmonious well-being of the community. One should recall here how, at the beginning of *Antigone*, the chorus reacts to the news that someone (at this point one doesn't yet know who) violated Creon's prohibition and performed funeral rites on Polynices' body—it is Antigone herself who is implicitly castigated as the "cityless outcast" engaged in excessive demonic acts which disturb the *eumonia* of the state, fully reasserted in the last lines of the play:

> The most important part of happiness / is therefore wisdom— not to act impiously / towards the gods, for boasts of arrogant men / bring on great blows of punishment / so in old age men can discover wisdom.

From the standpoint of *eumonia*, Antigone is definitely demonic/ uncanny: her defying act expresses a stance of de-measured excessive insistence which disturbs the "beautiful order" of the city; her unconditional ethics violates the harmony of the *polis* and is as such "beyond human boundary." The irony is that, while Antigone presents herself as the guardian of the immemorial laws that sustain human order, she acts as a freakish and ruthless abomination— there definitely is something cold and monstrous about her, as is rendered by the contrast between her and her warmly human sister Ismene. If we want to grasp the stance that leads Antigone to perform the funeral of Polynices, we should move forwards from the over-quoted lines about the unwritten laws to one of her later speeches where she specifies what she means by the law that she cannot not obey—here is the standard correct translation:

> I'd never have done it
> for children of my own, not as their mother,
> nor for a dead husband lying in decay—
> no, not in defiance of the citizens.
> What law do I appeal to, claiming this?
> If my husband died, there'd be another one,
> and if I were to lose a child of mine.
> I'd have another with some other man.
> But since my father and my mother, too,
> are hidden away in Hades' house,
> I'll never have another living brother.
> That was the law I used to honor you.

These lines caused a scandal for centuries, with many interpreters claiming that they must be a later interpolation. Even the translation of the first sentence varies. There are some which totally turn around its meaning, like the following: "Whether a mother of children or a wife, I'd always take up this struggle and go against the city's laws." Then there are translations which delete the brutal mention of rotting corpses, with Antigone just stating that she would never violate the public laws for a dead husband or child. Then there is the correct above-quoted translation which does mention corpses decaying corpses, but just as a fact, not as something Antigone subjectively assumes. But one has to add here David Feldshuh's translation which fully renders Antigone's subjective stance—although it is not true to the original, one should say that it is in some sense better than the original, more faithful to the original's repressed message: "For Creon's law, I would bow to it if / A husband or a son had died. I'd let their bodies / Rot in the steaming dust unburied and alone."[78] "I'd let their bodies rot"—as Alenka Zupančič pointed out in her ground-breaking study on *Antigone*, this is not just a statement of the fact that an unburied corpse is rotting in the open but the expression of her active stance towards it—she would let the body rot.[79]

It is clear from this passage that Antigone is at the very opposite end of just applying to her dead brother the general unwritten primordial rule of the respect for the dead. Therein resides the predominant reading of *Antigone*: she enacts a universal rule deeper than all social and political regulations. (Although this rule is supposed to allow for no exception, its partisans usually oscillate when one confronts them with a case of extreme evil: should Hitler also be given a proper funeral? Cornel West likes to call people he writes about "brothers"—say, in his course on Chekhov, he always referred to him as "brother Anton"—but when I heard him saying this, I was tempted to ask him if he would also, when talking about Hitler, refer to him as "brother Adolph" . . .) Judith Butler tries to save the day by here by deftly pointing out that the reference to a brother who cannot be replaced is ambiguous: Oedipus himself is her father but also her brother (they share the same mother); but I don't think we can extrapolate this opening into a new universality of respect for all those who are marginal, excluded from the public order of community. Another way to save the day is to claim that any person who dies is for some other(s) in a position of exception as defined by Antigone: even for Hitler, there must have been somebody for whom he was irreplaceable. (Let's not forget that, for the citizens of Thebes, Polynices *was* a criminal.)[80] In this way, we can claim that Antigone's "exception" ("only for my brother am I ready to break the public law") is really universal: when we are facing death, the dead is always in a position of exception.

However, such a reading fails to avoid the paradox: Antigone must have been aware that, for hundreds (at least) who died in the battle for Thebes, the same holds as for Polynices. Plus her reasoning is very strange: if her husband or her child were to die, she would let them rot only because she would be able to replace them . . . Why should respect for the dead be unconditional only for those who cannot be replaced? Doesn't the process of replacement she evokes (she can find another husband, breed another child) strangely ignore the uniqueness of each person? Why should another husband be able to replace a husband whom she would love in his singularity? Kathrin H. Rosenfield described in detail how Antigone's exception is grounded in her unique family situation: her privileging of her brother only makes sense against the background of all the misadventures that befell Oedipus's family.[81] Far from being a simple ethical act expressing utter devotion to one's family, her act is penetrated by obscure libidinal investments and passions. It is only in this way that we can explain the weird mechanical reasoning that justifies her exception (her brother cannot be replaced): her reasoning is the superficial mask of a deeper passion.

So the fact remains that what Antigone does is something quite unique: her universal rule is "let the bodies rot," and she fully honors this rule with only the exception of her particular case. The law that she obeys in properly burying Polynices is the law of exception, and this is a very brutal law, far from any human reconciliation. This brings us back to the distinction between examples and exemplum: Antigone's monstrous act is not an example of anything, it clearly violates the universal law, but it is nonetheless its exemplum, the exemplum which not only functions as an exception with regard to this law but which *turns this exception itself into a law of its own*. Antigone thus takes a Hegelian step further with regard to the triad of law, its examples and its exemplum: she transposes the gap that separates exemplum from examples back into the universal domain of the law itself. She demonstrates how the consequent actualization of the universal law has to turn it into its opposite. Instead of opposing the pure law (respect for the dead) to its factual violations (we often let them rot), she elevates these violations themselves into a universal law (let them all rot) and elevates the law of respecting the dead into an exception. Antigone's stance is thus incompatible with any project of a new world-ethics that should unite all of humanity beyond all particular world-views around a set of basic axioms: don't kill, respect the dead, follow the golden rule (don't do to others what you don't want others to do to you), etc. The most elaborated project in this direction is the Global Ethic Project that arose out of the thought of the Swiss theologian Hans Kung:

> In order for people from different cultures, religions, and nations to be able to live together in a constructive way, common basic values which connect us all are needed. This is true in regards to the smaller structures of families as well as in schools, companies,

and society as a whole. Unifying values and norms—independent of culture, religion or nationality—are becoming more and more important in the age of the internet, global politics and economies, and increasingly multicultural societies.[82]

Among the big translations of *Antigone*, Friedrich Hölderlin's is deservedly praised as unique, and one cannot but note how her exception (her readiness to perform the proper funeral of her brother) can be read in the light of a specific feature of Hölderlin's late poetry: instead of first describing a state of things and then mentioning the exception ("but"), he often begins a sentence directly by "aber" ("but") in German, without indicating which is the "normal" state disturbed by the exception, as in the famous lines from his hymn *Andenken*: "Was bleibet aber, stiften die Dichter" / "But poets establish what remains." The standard reading, of course, is that, after events, poets are able to perceive the situation from a mature standpoint, i.e. from a safe distance when the historical meaning of the events become clear. What if, however, there is nothing before the "but," just a nameless chaos, and a world (concocted by a poet) emerges as a "but," as an act of disturbing a chaotic void? What if at the beginning there is a "but"? So what if we read Hölderlin's line literally? "But poets establish what remains"—poets donate/create/establish (*stiften*) a "strophe," the opening line of a poem, which is that which remains after what? After the *katastrophe* of the pre-ontological gap/rupture.

In this sense, Antigone's choice (of brother) is a primordial ethical act: it does not disturb a preceding universal ethical law, it just interrupts the pre-ethical chaos of "letting them rot" ... The pre-ethical chaos is cut short by "*aber mein Brueder ...*" ("but my brother ..."). However, is it not that Antigone's act is so problematic because it *does* disturb a pre-existing order of customs? There is only one conclusion to be drawn here: with her act, with her "but," Antigone herself devalues the preceding order of customs, reducing it to a chaos or rotting corpses. An act does not just introduce order into chaos, it simultaneously annihilates a preceding order, denouncing it as a false mask of chaos. Insofar as "ethics" is at its most basic dimension the network of customs that regulate our communal life, and insofar as Antigone's act suspends the communal ethical substance, this act can be characterized not as the ethical suspension of the political (the insistence on the ethics when a political decision violates a basic ethical principle), but, on the contrary, as a moment of the *political suspension of the ethical*. The political is at its most basic the suspension of the predominant ethical substance. Today, we need such acts more than ever. Antigone's act is not an exception to universality, it is an exception that is itself elevated into universality, this is why her stance is not masculine (in the sense of Lacan's formulas of sexuality: a universality grounded in its exception) but feminine: universality is not-all because there are only exceptions.

Antigone is thus ethical but not moral in the same sense as Joker. One should also take note of Arthur's family name, Fleck, which in German means stain/spot—Arthur is a disharmonious stain in the social edifice, something with no proper place in it. But what makes him a stain is not just his miserable marginal existence but primarily a feature of his subjectivity, his propensity to compulsive and uncontrollable outbursts of laughter. The status of this laughter is paradoxical: it is quite literally ex-timate (to use Lacan's neologism), intimate and external. Arthur insists that it forms the very core of his subjectivity: "Remember you used to tell me that my laugh was a condition, that there was something wrong with me? It isn't. That's the real me." But precisely as such, it is external to him, to his personality, experienced by him as an autonomized partial object that he cannot control and that he ends up fully identifying with—a clear case of what Lacan called "identification with a symptom" (or, rather, "sinthome": not a bearer of meaning, of a coded message from the unconscious but a cypher of enjoyment, the elementary formula of subject's enjoyment. The paradox here is that in the standard Oedipal scenario, it is the Name-of-the-Father which enables an individual to escape the clutches of maternal desire; with Joker, paternal function is nowhere to be seen, so that the subject can outdo mother only by over-identifying with her superego command.

The film provides not only the socio-psychological genesis of Joker, it also implies the condemnation of the society in which a protest can only assume the form of a new tribe led by Joker. There is a subjective act in this Joker's move, but no new political subjectivity arises through it: at the film's end, we get Joker as a new tribal leader, but with no political program, just an explosion of negativity—in his conversation with Murray, Arthur insists twice that his act is not political. Referring to his clown makeup, Murray asks him: "What's with the face? I mean, are you part of the protest?" Arthur's reply: "No, I don't believe any of that. I don't believe in anything. I just thought it'd be good for my act." And, again, later: "I'm not political. I'm just trying to make people laugh."

Not political? In a famous over four-minute long but superbly made publicity spot for Heineken (the Dutch beer in green bottles with a red star on the cover) from 2017,[83] people with opposite views meet (a patriarchal man opposes a transgender person, etc.), talk and seal their friendship through sharing a bottle of Heineken. Although the spot plays with levels of complexity (roles are played by actors who step out of their roles, etc.), the basic message is clear: even if we are politically and ideologically opposed, we are beneath these superficial conflicts all the same warm humans and can debate even the toughest issues by sharing a good beer . . . Needless to add, this notion of shared humanity is ideology at its purest: a closer look reveals that shared "humanity" is always twisted in a certain political direction (rather obviously Left-liberal, in the sense of Politically Correct corporatism, in this case—it is a commodity (a bottle of beer) which embodies and cements friendly relations). As Alenka Zupančič put it,[84] the first step of the critique of ideology is not just to engage in emancipatory politics but to *emancipate politics*, proper political struggle, as such. When interviewed for TV, a protester against pandemic regulations in Slovenia recently claimed that she was not interested in any politics, she just wanted to protect her freedom and maintain control over her body . . . what freedom, what politics? What are our basic rights and freedoms is the outcome of a political struggle, the ignorance of political struggle always serves the establishment.

Today's hegemonic ideology can easily tolerate the idea that politics is a space of corruption, of cheating and lying, etc., and that it's best to keep politics at a distance. What it finds intolerable is the idea that all politics is not the same, that there is something that cannot but be called a politics of truth, not just a mess of conflicting opinions. We should add here another question: what might happen if the buddies were just to go on until they were completely drunk? There are two basic options here: either the formula of Brecht's *Mr Puntila and his Man Matti* (in which Puntila is warm, friendly and loving when drunk, but cold, cynical and penny-pinching when sober—similar to the relationship between the Tramp and the Millionaire in Charlie Chaplin's *City Lights*), or, when the two were to become fully drunk, things would get really nasty, as their oppressed brutal sexist, racist, etc. prejudices would return in all their raw force, no longer restrained by rules of politeness.

Therein resides the difference between Joker's jokes, everyday common jokes, and the reason why every dialectician likes to envelop his/her theory within jokes. Why do I so compulsively tell jokes in my texts? A meme circulating now on the web gives a correct hint: it tells of an Oak Hill couple sitting at home on Saturday evening—they discover there is a thief in their home after the man tells his wife a joke and they hear a laugh coming from upstairs.[85] So the point is not just to amuse the public but to make the "thief" (the ideological enemy) among them betray himself by his laughter—how? The enemy is not a stupid guy who doesn't get a joke: he gets it and he laughs at the right moment for the wrong reason—in order to reassert his sexist, racist, etc. prejudices. In short, the enemy laughs at others. Joker descends to a zero-level where he just laughs, while a dialectician ultimately laughs at him/herself.

A.O. Scott (in *New York Times*) therefore misses the point when he dismissed *Joker* as "a story about nothing": "The look and the sound ... connote gravity and depth, but the movie is weightless and shallow." There is effectively no "gravity and depth" in Joker's final stance—his revolt is "weightless and shallow," and that's the utterly desperate point of the film. There is no militant Left in the film's universe, it's just a flat world of globalized violence and corruption. Charity events are depicted as what they are: if a Mother Theresa figure were to be there she would for sure participate in the charity event organized by Wayne, a humanitarian amusement of the privileged rich. Every authentic Leftist should put on the wall above his bed or table the opening paragraph of Oscar Wilde's "The Soul of Man under Socialism" where he points out that "it is much more easy to have sympathy with suffering than it is to have sympathy with thought." People find themselves surrounded by hideous poverty, by hideous ugliness, by hideous starvation. It is inevitable that they should be strongly moved by all this ... Accordingly, with admirable, though misdirected intentions, they very seriously and very sentimentally set themselves to the task of remedying the evils that they see. But their remedies do not cure the disease: they merely prolong it. Indeed, their remedies are part of the disease ... The proper aim is to try and reconstruct society on such a basis that poverty will be impossible. And the altruistic virtues have really prevented the carrying out of this aim ... It is immoral to use private property in order to alleviate the horrible evils that result from the institution of private property.

The last sentence provides a concise formula of what is wrong with Bill and Melinda Gates' foundation. It is not enough just to point out that the Gates charity is based on brutal business practice[86]— one should go a step further and also denounce the ideological foundation of the Gates charity, the vacuity of its pan-humanitarianism. The title of Sama Naami's collection of essays—*Refusal of Respect: Why We Should Not Respect Foreign Cultures. And Our Own Also Not*—hits the nail on its head: it is the only authentic stance with regard to the other three variations of the same formula. The Gates' charity implies the formula: respect all cultures, your own and others. The Rightist nationalist formula is: respect your own culture and despise others which are inferior to it. The Politically Correct formula is: respect other cultures, but despise your own which is racist and colonialist (that's why Politically Correct woke culture is always anti-Eurocentric). The correct Leftist stance is: bring out the hidden antagonisms of your own culture, link it to the antagonisms of other cultures, and then engage in a common struggle of those who fight here against the oppression and domination at work in our culture and those who do the same in other cultures.

What this means is something which may sound shocking, but one should insist on it: you don't have to respect or love immigrants—what you have to do is to change the situation so that they will not have to be what they are. The citizen of a developed country who wants fewer immigrants and is ready to do something so that they will not have to come to this place which they mostly don't even like is much better than a humanitarian who preaches openness to immigrants while silently participating in the economic and political practices which brought the countries where immigrants are from to ruin.

However, it's difficult to imagine a more stupid critique of *Joker* than the reproach that it doesn't portray a positive alternative to the Joker revolt. Just imagine a film shot along these lines: an edifying story about how the poor, unemployed, with no healthcare coverage, the victims of street gangs and police brutality, etc., organize non-violent protests and strikes to mobilize public opinion—a new non-racial version of Martin Luther King ... and an extremely boring film, lacking the crazy excesses of Joker which makes the film so attractive for viewers.

Here we touch the crux of the matter: since it seems obvious to a Leftist that such non-violent protests and strikes are the only way to proceed, i.e., to exert an efficient pressure onto those in power, are we dealing here with a simple gap between political logic and narrative efficiency (to put it bluntly, brutal outbursts like those of Joker are politically a deadlock but they make a story interesting), or is there also an immanent political necessity in the self-destructive stance embodies by Joker? My hypothesis is that one has to go through the self-destructive zero-level for which Joker stands—not actually, but one has to experience it as a threat, as a possibility. Only in this way can one break out of the coordinates of the existing system and envisage something really new. Joker's stance is a blind alley, a total deadlock, superfluous and non-productive, but the paradox is that one has to go through it to perceive its superfluous character—there is no direct way from the existing misery to its constructive overcoming. Or, insofar as Joker is obviously a kind of madman, one should recall here Hegel for whom madness is not an accidental lapse, distortion, "illness" of human spirit, but something which is inscribed into individual spirit's basic ontological constitution: to be a human means to be potentially mad:

> This interpretation of insanity as a necessarily occurring form or stage in the development of the soul is naturally not to be

understood as if we were asserting that *every* mind, *every* soul, must go through this stage of extreme derangement. Such an assertion would be as absurd as to assume that because in the *Philosophy of Right* crime is considered as a necessary manifestation of the human will, therefore to commit crime is an inevitable necessity for *every* individual. Crime and insanity are *extremes* which the human mind *in general* has to overcome in the course of its development.[87]

Although not a factual necessity, madness is a formal possibility constitutive of the human mind: it is something whose threat has to be overcome if we are to emerge as "normal" subjects, which means that "normality" can only arise as the overcoming of this threat. This is why, as Hegel put it a couple of pages later, "insanity must be discussed before the healthy, intellectual consciousness, although it has that consciousness for its *presupposition*."[88] In short, we do not all have to be mad in reality, but madness is the reality of our psychic lives, a point to which our psychic lives necessarily refer in order to assert themselves as "normal." And it is the same with Joker: we are not all Jokers in reality, but the position of Joker is something the human mind *in general* has to overcome in the course of its development. The elegance of *Joker* is that, in order to articulate a new positive political vision, we don't have actually to become Jokers—the film does it for us. The film stages the madness, confronts us with it, and thereby enables us to overcome it.

The Return of Vanishing Mediators

Is this madness not an exemplary case of what Fredric Jameson calls the "vanishing mediator" between the old and the new? "Vanishing mediator" designates a specific feature in the process of a passage from the old order to a new order: when the old order is disintegrating, unexpected things happen, not just the horrors mentioned by Gramsci but also bright utopian projects and practices. Once the new order is established, a new narrative arises and, within this new ideological space, mediators disappear from view.[89] Suffice it to take a look at the passage from Socialism to

Capitalism in Eastern Europe. When in the 1980s, people protested against the Communist regimes in Eastern Europe, what the large majority had in mind was not capitalism. They wanted social security, solidarity, a rough kind of justice; they wanted the freedom to live their lives outside of state control, to come together and talk as they pleased; they wanted a life of simple honesty and sincerity, liberated from primitive ideological indoctrination and the prevailing cynical hypocrisy ... in short, the vague ideals that led the protesters were, to a large extent, taken from Socialist ideology itself. And, as we learned from Freud, what is repressed returns in a distorted form. In Europe, the Socialism repressed in the dissident imaginary returned in the guise of Right populism.

Although, as to their positive content, the Communist regimes were a failure, they at the same time opened up a certain space, the space of utopian expectations which, among other things, enabled us to measure the failure of the really existing Socialism itself. When dissidents like Vaclav Havel denounced the existing Communist regime on behalf of authentic human solidarity, they (unknowingly, for the most part) spoke from the place opened up by Communism itself—which is why they tend to be so disappointed when the "really existing capitalism" does not meet the high expectations of their anti-Communist struggle. At a recent reception in Poland, a nouveau riche capitalist congratulated Adam Michnik for being a doubly successful capitalist (he helped destroy Socialism and he also heads a highly profitable publishing empire). Deeply embarrassed, Michnik replied: "I am not a capitalist; I am a socialist who is unable to forgive socialism that it did not work."[90]

Why mention this vanishing mediator today? Is it not clear that it was just an explosion of irrelevant utopian hope? In his interpretation of the fall of East European Communism, Jürgen Habermas proved to be the ultimate Left Fukuyamist, silently accepting that the existing liberal-democratic order is the best one possible, and that, while we should strive to make it more just, we should not challenge its basic premises. This is why he welcomed precisely what many leftists saw as the big deficiency of the anti-Communist protests in Eastern Europe: the fact that these protests were not motivated by any new visions of the post-Communist future. As he put it, the central and eastern European revolutions were just "rectifying" or "catch-up" (*nachholende*) revolutions, their aim being to enable those societies to gain what the western Europeans already possessed; in other words, to rejoin the West European normality.

However, the ongoing wave of protests in different parts of the world tends to question this very frame—and this is why figures like "jokers" accompany them (just think of the "violent excesses" of Black Lives Matter). When a movement questions the fundamentals of the existing order, its basic normative foundations, it is almost impossible to get solely peaceful protests without violent excesses. The "*gilets jaunes*" in France, protests in Spain and other similar protests today are definitely NOT catch-up movements. They embody the weird reversal that characterizes today's global situation. The old antagonism between "ordinary people" and financial-capitalist elites is back with a vengeance, with "ordinary people" erupting in protest against the elites, who are accused of being blind to their suffering and demands. However, what is new is that the populist Right has proved to be much more adept in channeling these eruptions in its direction than the Left. Alain Badiou was thus fully justified to say apropos the *gilets jaunes*: "*Tout ce qui bouge n'est pas rouge*"—all that moves (makes unrest) is not red.

Here, then, is the paradox we have to confront: the populist disappointment at liberal democracy is a proof that 1990 was not just a catch-up revolution, that it aimed at more than the liberal-capitalist normality. Freud spoke about *Unbehagen in der Kultur*, the discontent or unease in culture; today, thirty years after the fall of the Wall, the ongoing new wave of protests bears witness to a kind of *Unbehagen* in liberal capitalism, and the key question is: who will articulate this discontent? Will it be left to nationalist populists to exploit it? Therein resides the big task of the Left. This discontent is not something new. I wrote about it more than thirty years ago in "Eastern Europe's Republics of Gilead" (a reference to the *Handmaid's Tale*) which was published in *New Left Review* back in 1990—may I quote myself?

The dark side of the processes current in Eastern Europe is thus the gradual retreat of the liberal-democratic tendency in the face of the growth of corporate national populism with all its usual elements, from xenophobia to anti-Semitism. The swiftness of this process has been surprising: today, we find anti-Semitism in East Germany (where one attributes to Jews the lack of food, and to Vietnamese the lack of bicycles) and in Hungary and in Romania (where the persecution of the Hungarian minority also continues). Even in Poland we can perceive signs of a split within Solidarity: the rise of a nationalist-populist faction that imputes to the "cosmopolitan intellectual" (the old regime's codeword for Jews) the failure of the recent government's measures.[91]

This dark side is now re-emerging forcefully, and its effects are felt in the Rightist rewriting of history. This is why we should remember vanishing mediators: today the global capitalist order is approaching a crisis again, and the vanished radical legacy will have to be resuscitated. This legacy is not just the vast array of utopian hopes; it is also the self-destructive drive that sustains them. The way in which destructive fury clears the space for the creation of new sublime forms is made clear by Lacan who insisted on the link between death-drive and sublimation[92]—suffice it to recall Andrei Platonov's masterpiece, *The Foundation Pit*. Is the foundation pit—this gigantic hole in the earth which will never be filled in with the new Communist building, this symbol of meaningless expenditure of labor which plays no role in the struggle for survival or for better life—not a spectacular monument to death-drive as a social category?

And this brings us back to *Joker*: the elegance of the film resides in how the crucial move from self-destructive drive to what Moore called a "new desire" for an emancipatory political project is absent from its storyline. We, the spectators, are solicited to fill in this absence ... Or are we? Will *Joker* not turn out to be just another proof that today's sphere of culture and entertainment can easily integrate even the most "subversive" anti-capitalist messages and practices? Just imagine a biennale whose program does not question Eurocentrism or the all-pervasive reign of financial capital or our destruction of environment? Why should *Joker* be different from paintings which destroy themselves, from galleries which "make us think" by displaying rotten animal corpses or sacred images soaked in urine? Maybe, it's not as simple as that. Maybe, what makes *Joker* so unsettling is that it does not engage itself in calling for a political action—it leaves the decision to us. Visiting an "anti-capitalist" art performance or engaging in social charity makes us feel good—seeing *Joker* definitely does not do that, and that's our hope. Joker practices what Giorgio Agamben called the courage of hopelessness (whose exemplary case of today's afro-pessimism)—in short, he enacts a version of subjective destitution.

The crucial question here is, of course, how does self-destructive violence relate to other figures of subjective destitution, especially to the political destitution described by Giri? One should avoid the trap of placing them in some hierarchic order like a pseudo-Hegelian triad that seems to offer itself: in the misery of peaceful times, we have recourse to nirvana or mystical experience; when crisis arises, we explode in self-destructive violence; finally, we transform nihilism into revolutionary practice focused on a positive project ... The figures of subjective destitution form an irreducible mixture echoing in each other, passing into each other, without any prospect of one of them sublating the others.

All these forms of destitution are by definition states of exception with regard to (what one cannot but call) normal daily life—does this not limit the scope of our analysis? No, because (as Hegel pointed out apropos madness) such exceptions are a possibility, a potential, with regard to which what we experience as normal daily life constitutes itself. And that's our problem today, in the age of pandemics, ecological crises and social unrests: these crises pose a threat to our normal daily life, they destabilize it. Different forms of denial of these threats are ultimately just desperate defenses of this normal daily life, and what is needed today is the courage to go through the purifying fire of exception, of subjective destitution.

The main voices of renormalization are so-called "rational optimists" like Matt Ridley who bombard us with good news: the 2010s were the best decade in human history, poverty is declining in Asia and Africa, pollution is decreasing, etc. If this is the case, then where does the growing atmosphere of apocalypse come from? Is it not an outgrowth of a self-generated pathological need for unhappiness? When rational optimists tell us that we are overly scared about minor problems, our answer should be that, on the contrary, we are not scared enough. As Alenka Zupančič formulates the paradox: "Apocalypse has already begun, but it seems that we still *prefer to die* than to allow the apocalyptic threat to scare us to death." In the Spring of 2020, the lieutenant governor of Texas Dan Patrick said that grandparents like him don't want to sacrifice the country's economy during the coronavirus crisis: "No one reached out to me and said, 'as a senior citizen, are you willing to take a chance on your survival in exchange for keeping the America that all America loves for your children and grandchildren?'" Patrick said. "And if that's the exchange, I'm all in."[93] Even if it was meant seriously, such a gesture of self-sacrifice is not an act of true courage but an act of cowardice—it fits exactly Zupančič's words: Patrick prefers to die rather than to courageously confront the threat of catastrophe. Since we are today in a kind of war for our survival, we can conclude with G.K. Chesterton's description of the paradox of courage:

> A soldier surrounded by enemies, if he is to cut his way out, needs to combine a strong desire for living with a strange carelessness about dying. He must not merely cling to life, for then he will be a coward, and will not escape. He must not merely wait for death, for then he will be a suicide, and will not escape. He must seek his life in a spirit of furious indifference to it; he must desire life like water and yet drink death like wine.[94]

To seek one's life in a spirit of furious indifference to it—this is how subjective destitution works. Sometimes, the passage through such a furious indifference is the only way to establish a new livable normality—without this passage, normality itself falls apart.

Notes

Ouverture: Living in a Topsy-Turvy World

1. In this sense, Thomas Carlyle wrote in his *History of Friedrich II of Prussia* about a "sudden topsy-turvying of his plans."
2. Not-Mother: On Freud's Verneinung—Journal #33, March 2012—e-flux (e-flux.com).
3. See "The Dark Side of Wellness: The Overlap Between Spiritual Thinking and Far-right Conspiracies", *The Guardian*, October 17, 2021.
4. Quoted from www.e-flux.com/journal/97/251199/apocalypse-without-kingdom/.
5. For a more detailed account of this notion, see "The Varieties of Surplus" in my *Incontinence of the Void*, Cambridge: MIT Press 2017.
6. One should nonetheless not deny the notion of ethical progress. The TV series *Vikings* deserves praise for directly depicting the brutality of that era (eighth century), with senseless killings and terrible torture (like the "blood eagle"). (One should nonetheless note that this extreme torture is not a wild act of cruelty but performed as a sacred ritual, in some sense even honoring the victim.) The very fact that we (or most of us, at least) feel uneasy at such scenes is an indication of some kind of ethical progress—it is difficult for us fully to identify even with the "good guys" in this cruel world, as they all regularly commit acts that are silently passed over in other movies on Vikings.
7. See "Good luck, Mr. Gorsky" true or false? *Parkes Champion-Post*, Parkes, NSW (parkeschampionpost.com.au).
8. Roger Scruton, *Fools, Frauds and Firebrands—The Thinkers of The New Left*, London: Bloomsbury 2019, p. 260.
9. I rely here on Eduardo Cadava and Sara Nadal-Melsio, *Politically Red*, Cambridge: MIT Press 2022.

10. Quoted from www.haujournal.org/index.php/hau/article/view/ hau7.2.021/2980.

11. Not only this—I am sometimes reproached for "self-plagiarizing" (which, incidentally, makes as much sense as to call masturbation a self-rape). It is true that I sometimes include in my new texts short passages from previously published texts, but a careful reader can always note the violence of this operation: I tear a fragment out of its original context and insert it into a new context which imposes a new reading of the fragment, sometimes even the opposite of the "original" one.

12. See Canadian professor canned for opinion that biological sex is a real thing, The College Fix. thecollegefix.com.

13. See www.wsws.org/en/articles/2021/10/11/she1-o11.html.

1 Where is the Rift? Marx, Capitalism and Ecology

1. Kohei Saito, *Karl Marx's Ecosocialism*, New York: Monthly Review Press 2017. Numbers in brackets refer to the pages of this book.

2. *Coronavirus, Psychoanalysis, and Philosophy*, edited by Fernando Castrillón and Thomas Marchevsky, London: Routledge 2021, pp. 153–4.

3. 2% of Elon Musk's wealth could solve world hunger, says director of UN food scarcity organization—CNN.

4. Facebook whistleblower Frances Haugen calls for urgent external regulation, Facebook, *The Guardian*.

5. Private exchange.

6. See Peter Sloterdijk, *Was geschah im 20.Jahrhundert?*, Frankfurt: Suhrkamp 2016.

7. Quoted from https://edition.cnn.com/2019/10/21/asia/china-hong-kong-chile-spain-protests-intl-hnk/index.html.

8. Available online at America Against America—DOKUMEN.PUB.

9. See Carlo Ginzburg, "The Bond of Shame," in *New Left Review* 120 (November/December 2019), pp. 35–44.

10. Immanuel Kant, "What is Enlightenment?," in Isaac Kramnick, *The Portable Enlightenment Reader*, New York: Penguin Books 1995, p. 5.

11. V.I. Lenin, "Better Few, But Better" (1923), quoted from Better Fewer, But Better (marxists.org).

12. Quoted from www.marxists.org/archive/lenin/works/1922/feb/x01. htm.

13. See Former Bolivian V P Álvaro García Linera on How Socialists Can Win (jacobinmag.com).

14. I owe this idea to Robin Dolar.

15. See Disaster patriarchy: how the pandemic has unleashed a war on women, *The Guardian.*

16. One should nonetheless add that one argument for "dialectical materialism" is that it fits better than Western Hegelian Marxism with the topic of ecology since it treats nature as an autonomous sphere with its global laws and thereby avoids the Hegelian-Marxist trap of reducing nature to a social category, as the young Lukacs put it. As for Althusser, one should add that in his late writings he saw already in Hegel elements for the Marxist notion of a "process without subject."

17. Quoted from www.academia.edu/3035436/John_Rosenthal_The_ Myth_of_Dialectics_Reinterpreting_the_Marx-Hegel_Relation.

18. See www.marxists.org/archive/marx/works/1867-c1/appendix.htm.

19. Gerard Lebrun, *L'envers de la dialectique.* Paris: Editions du Seuil 2004, p. 311.

20. Quoted from Rebecca Carson, Chapter 6 of her dissertation: "Marx's Social Theory of Reproduction" (unpublished manuscript 2021).

21. One should also note here the homology between the Hegelian process of alienation and its overcoming through the subjective mediation, i.e., reflexive re-appropriation, of the alienated substantial content, and the Freudian process of repression and its overcoming through the analytic process where the patient is brought to recognize its own content in what appeared to him as weird formations of the unconscious. (The two most systematic articulations of this homology are found in Habermas's *Interest and Human Knowledge,* and in Helmut Dahmer's *Libido und Gesellschaft.*) Like Hegelian reflection, psychoanalysis does not generate neutral-objective knowledge, but a "practical" knowledge which, when subjectively assumed, radically changes its bearer. And we should add that what Lacan did in his "return to Freud" is that he reformulated the basic coordinates of psychoanalysis in the same way in which we try to provide a new reading of Hegel outside of the "subject appropriates the substance" paradigm.

22. G.W.F. Hegel, *Phenomenology of Spirit*, New York: Oxford University Press 1977, pp. 18–19.

23. See www.marxists.org/archive/marx/works/1867-c1/ch07.htm.

24. An exemplary case of a rift in premodern societies is provided by Iceland: it was fully forested when Norwegians arrived there in eighth century, and soon afterwards it was totally deforested.

25. See Jason Moore, *Capitalism in the Web of Life*, London: Verso Books 2015.

26. Etienne Balibar "Towards a New Critique of Political Economy: From Generalized Surplus-value to Total Subsumption," in *Capitalism: Concept, Idea, Image*, Kingston: CRMEP Books 2019.

27. Balibar, op. cit., p. 51.

28. Op. cit., p. 53.

29. Op. cit., p. 57.

30. See Timothy Morton's *Ecology Without Nature*, Cambridge: Harvard University Press 2007.

31. Morton, op. cit., p. 35.

32. I dealt with this topic in more detail in the chapter "*Unbehagen in der Natur*" of my *In Defense of Lost Causes*, London: Verso Books, 2008.

33. Jacques Lacan, *Écrits*, New York: Norton 1997, p. 738.

34. See www.marxists.org/archive/marx/works/1857/grundrisse/ch01.htm.

35. Marx, op. cit.

36. David Harvey, *A Companion to Marx's* Capital, London: Verso Books 2010, p. 29.

37. Anson Rabinbach, "From Emancipation to the Science of Work: The Labor Power Dilemma" (quoted from the manuscript).

38. Op. cit.

39. See www.marxists.org/archive/marx/works/1867-c1/ch07.htm.

40. Op. cit.

41. See www.youtube.com/watch?v=MS4hoppZPG0.

42. Quoted from Rebecca Carson, Chapter 6 of her dissertation: "Marx's Social Theory of Reproduction" (unpublished manuscript 2021).

43. See www.marxists.org/archive/marx/works/1867-c1/ch01.htm#S4.

44. Karl Marx, *Grundrisse*, available online at www.marxists.org/archive/marx/works/1857/grundrisse/ch01.htm#3.

45. Marx, op. cit.

46. Marx, op. cit.

47. See Aaron Bastani, *Fully Automated Luxury Communism*, London: Verso Books 2019.

48. Quoted from www.nytimes.com/2019/06/11/opinion/fully-automated-luxury-communism.html.

49. Quoted from www.marxists.org/archive/marx/works/1868/letters/index.htm.

50. Incidentally, the same holds for market competition: a participant never has access to complete data about supply and demand which would enable him/her to make optimal decisions, and this incompleteness (the fact that individuals are compelled to decide without full information) is not just an empirical complication, it is (to put it in Hegelese) part of the very notion of market competition.

51. See Pierre Bayard, *Comment parler des faits qui ne se sont pas produits?*, Paris: Les editions de Minuit 2020.

52. Bayard's final example case is the mass panic caused by Orson Welles's performance of *The War of the Worlds* as a radio show: here also, the reality (millions taking the radio fiction as truth and fleeing their homes) is far from truth.

53. Economic Manuscripts: Capital Vol. I—Chapter 6 (marxists.org).

54. See www.academia.edu/38109734/The_Logic_of_Capital._Interview_with_Chris_Arthur.

55. Rebecca Carson, "Time and Schemas of Reproduction" (manuscript).

56. Inside WallStreetBets, the Reddit army that's rocking Wall Street—CNN.

57. Alexandria Ocasio-Cortez on Twitter. .

58. Analysis: Hedge funds bitching about Reddit can cry me a river—CNN.

59. Op. cit.

60. Robert Brandom, *The Spirit of Trust*, Cambridge: Harvard University Press 2019, p. 501.

61. Op. cit., p. 506.

62. When we are shocked by what some politicians like Trump or Modi say, we explode in critical rage: "How is this possible? It is unacceptable and outrageous!" However, by reacting in this way, we miss the point: the big Other (the moral authority we are addressing and relying on) is no longer here, our complaint is pointless, there is no one listening to it. When there was a war in Bosnia almost three

decades ago, I remember the reports on the suicides of raped women: they survived the rape; what kept them alive was the conviction that they must live to tell their story to their community. But it often happened that nobody in their community was ready to listen to them—they were viewed with suspicion, treated as participating in and co-responsible for their humiliation, and this experience drove them to suicide. Something similar awaits those who explode in rage about today's political obscenities.

63. Victoria Fareld and Hannes Kuch, *From Marx to Hegel and Back*, London: Bloomsbury 2020, p. 13.

64. See www.marxists.org/archive/marx/works/1867-c1/ch01.htm#S3.

65. See "Something is very wrong": Alien-like slime is invading Turkey's waters (cnn.com).

66. I owe this line of thought to Alenka Zupančič.

67. See www.academia.edu/38109734/The_Logic_of_Capital._Interview_with_Chris_Arthur.

68. Lebrun, op. cit., p. 311.

69. See Frank Ruda, *Abolishing Freedom*, Winnipeg: Bison Books 2016.

70. See www.spectator.co.uk/2020/01/fight-fire-with-fire-controlled-burning-could-have-protected-australia/.

71. See https://bible.org/seriespage/lesson-63-believing-seeing-seeing-not-believing-john-1138-57.

72. See www.raystedman.org/new-testament/john/gods-strange-ways.

73. See www.theguardian.com/world/2021/aug/09/smoke-siberia-wildfires-reaches-north-pole-historic-first.

74. See Climate change is frying the Northern Hemisphere with unprecedented heat, hundreds dead and a town destroyed—CNN.

75. "Heat dome" probably killed 1bn marine animals on Canada coast, experts say, *The Guardian*.

76. See https://edition.cnn.com/2021/08/26/world/blob-chile-megadrought-study-intl-hnk-scli-scn/index.html.

77. See www.theguardian.com/environment/2021/aug/05/climate-crisis-scientists-spot-warning-signs-of-gulf-stream-collapse.

78. See The IPCC report is clear: nothing short of transforming society will avert catastrophe, Patrick Vallance, *The Guardian*.

79. Alain Badiou, "Prefazione all'edizione italiana," in *Metapolitica*, Napoli: Cronopio 2002, p. 14.

80. See Andreas Malm, *How to Blow Up a Pipeline*, London: Verso Books 2021.

81. See Herbert H. Haines, "Radical Flank Effects," in The Wiley-Blackwell *Encyclopedia of Social and Political Movements*, Hoboken: Blackwell Publishing 2013.

82. Joanna Lumley says wartime-style rationing could help solve climate crisis, *The Guardian*.

2 A Non-Binary Difference? Psychoanalysis, Politics, and Philosophy

1. The fight to whitewash US history: "A drop of poison is all you need," *The Guardian*.

2. Jean-Pierre Dupuy, *La Catastrophe ou la vie—Pensées par temps de pandémie*, Paris: Editions du Seuil 2021, p. 16.

3. See www.theguardian.com/world/2016/apr/16/canada-first-nations-suicide-crisis-attawapiskat-history.

4. Op. cit.

5. More unmarked graves found near another school that housed Indigenous children in Canada—CBS News.

6. France Catholic church abuse scandal: 216,000 minors sexually abused, report finds—CNN.

7. In Search of Common Ground: Conversations with Erik H. Erikson and Huey P. Newton, New York: Norton 1973, p. 69.

8. Quoted from Theodor Herzl and the trajectory of Zionism, openDemocracy.

9. Gabriel Tupinamba, *The Desire of Psychoanalysis* (to appear with Northwestern University Press). All quotes from Tupinamba are taken from this source.

10. In my critical remarks, I refer to (what I see as) the simplified core of Tupinamba's argumentation, often neglecting its complexity as well as the graphs and formulas he uses to elaborate his position. Plus, I have to add that I consider these remarks part of an ongoing dialogue: in his book, Tupinamba treats me very respectfully—even too respectfully since I think I am an implicit target of what he critically calls "structural dialectics," so I want to bring our differences into the open.

11. See Docile to Trans—The Lacanian Review (thelacanianreviews.com).

12. All these data are taken from Wikipedia.

13. Claude Levi-Strauss, "Do Dual Organizations Exist?," in *Structural Anthropology* (New York: Basic Books 1963), pp. 131–63; the drawings are on pages 133–4.

14. A further example is provided by the well-known fact that, when victims of torture, rape, or a similar traumas are asked to report on their experiences, their reports are always uncertain, ambiguous, even self-contradictory. However, this inexactitude, this partial discord with objective facts, is in itself an argument for the veracity of the report. A measured and precise report on what happened would be much more suspicious.

15. See Işık Barış Fidaner, https://zizekanalysis.wordpress.com/2019/07/06/exigency-and-enjoyment-isik-baris-fidaner. What group to choose as the stand-in for the proletarian struggle is thus a matter of strategic decision. "El Baile de los que Sobran" ("The dance of those who are left over") by the Chilean rock band *Los Prisioneros*, for decades a kind of anthem of social protests in Chile, is distinguished by the clever choice of those who stand for the proletarian position, the position of those who "are left over," the social group for which there is no proper place in the social edifice. It is not the wage workers, not even the unemployed in general, but those who have completed their studies and cannot get a job, so they just walk around in search of a post and kick stones on the street. This aimless wandering around in the evening, after a day lost, is at the level of music magically coordinated into a collective dance—not in the sense of aesthetization (we forget our troubles in a collective trance of dancing rhythm), but as a strictly political gesture of building a collective out of individual despair. This choice is *politically correct*: among many groups of those who are "left over," it chooses that which best indicates the crisis of today's global capitalism. So maybe, we should rehabilitate the term "political correctness" in a more literal and simple meaning of a political decision that is correct in a given situation—in this sense, most of Political Correctness is not politically correct since it hampers the effectiveness of emancipatory struggle.

16. Michel Foucault, "Truth and Power," in *Power/Knowledge: Selected Interviews and Other Writings*, New York: Random House 1980, p. 118.

17. See Peter Sloterdijk, *Den Himmel zum Sprechen bringen: Über Theopoesie*, Frankfurt: Suhrkamp 2020.

18. Jacques Lacan, *Écrits*, p. 872.

19. Op. cit., p. 874.

20. "Not that good": Montreal restaurant's brutally honest menu pulls in the customers, *The Guardian*.

21. Op. cit., p. 869.

22. Quoted from 1938: Dialectical and Historical Materialism (marxists.org).

23. Lacan, op. cit., p. 738.

24. See www.theguardian.com/commentisfree/2020/nov/14/coupledom-couple-norm-social-change.

25. See, for example, Laura Kipnis, *Against Love*, New York: Random House 2005.

26. See www.theguardian.com/commentisfree/2020/mar/10/i-wish-everyone-strength-however-they-identify-suzanne-moore.

27. Furthermore, as Alenka Zupančič has pointed out, there is a homologous shift to that from sex to gender at work in much of today's social theory: the shift from politics to power—the topic of political antagonisms is to a large extent replaced by the notion of apolitical power games.

28. See Katherine Angel, *Tomorrow Sex Will Be Good Again*, London: Verso Books 2021.

29. Quoted from www.versobooks.com/books/3743-tomorrow-sex-will-be-good-again. [My emphases.]

30. Unacknowledged rape: the sexual assault survivors who hide their trauma—even from themselves, *The Guardian*.

31. Taliban tell Afghan women to stay home because soldiers are "not trained" to respect them—CNN.

32. See www.boredpanda.com/afghanistan-1960-bill-podlich-photography/?utm_source=google&utm_medium=organic&utm_campaign=organic.

33. This, of course, in no way implies that there is no emancipatory potential in such daily rituals. The only thing I like about the list of the places proclaimed by UNESCO as part of the world cultural heritage are those which do *not* belong to the category of "big" monuments of the past (cathedrals, etc.), like Neapolitan pizza, camel racing and Finnish sauna. Algar, a city of about 1,400 people in Southern Spain, wants its own cultural tradition added to that list:

almost every evening after the sun sets, neighbors and family sit outside their homes in narrow streets and share stories from their day—the tradition known as *charlas al fresco* (fresh air chats). (See https://www.npr.org/2021/08/14/1027689265/a-small-town-in-spain-launches-unesco-bid-for-its-outdoor-chats?t=1629259768042.) This for me is true culture—small rituals woven into daily life, and it is only at this level that I agree that we should preserve our way of life.

34. One should also note that the film's plot focuses on the attempt of the Erudite (intellectuals) to carry out a coup d'etat, taking power by way of using the Dauntless ("brave" soldiers) to depose the Abnegations who run society—in Lacanese, an attempt of university discourse to replace the discourse of the Master. Beneath this plot is the correct insight into how university discourse is more oppressive than the reign of a Master: "totalitarianism" has the structure of a university discourse.

35. Sigmund Freud, *Three Essays on the Theory of Sexuality*, New York: Basic Books 1962, p. 155.

36. Jean Laplanche, "Sexuality and Attachment in Metapsychology," in *Infantile Sexuality and Attachment*, edited by D. Widlöcher, New York: Other Press 2002, p. 49.

37. In the domain of cinema, recall *Gilda* (1946, Charles Vidor): the convoluted plot full of "queer" sadist and homoerotic sexual undertones finishes with an unconvincing happy ending in which all the perversity magically disappears—what is truly queer is this libidinally unconvincing ending.

38. *Resident Alien*, created by Chris Sheridan (main writer), produced by Jocko Productions, Universal Content Productions, Dark Horse Entertainment, and Amblin Television. Original network: Syfy (2021).

39. Due to the limitations of my knowledge, I cannot deal here with this topic.

40. But is this eternalized superego the ultimate truth of Christianity? There is an alternate option which defines what I call Christian atheism/materialism: what if we imagine Christ's death on the Cross not as an act of deliberate sacrifice but as an act of endorsing one's death and impotence? Christ's death sets us free because it deprives us of any transcendent support, because it exposes us to a weak impotent god who can only offer sympathy for our suffering.

41. Quoted from (PDF) *The Night of the Iguana*, Gazi Shamsher Ahmad—Academia.edu.

42. Roger Boyes, "Final forgiveness for spy who betrayed his wife to the Stasi," *The Times*, January 6 2007.

43. Homeland Series Finale Ending Explained by Showrunner (collider. com).

44. Deployed in Alain Badiou, *La vraie vie*, Paris: Fayard 2016.

45. The question that nonetheless has to be raised here is the old one first raised in all its clarity by the German idealists: how should pre-human "external reality" be structured so that something like symbolic order with its self-thwarted circular structure can emerge in it? I elaborate this topic in detail in *Sex and the Failed Absolute* (London: Bloomsbury 2019).

46. See Jacques Lacan, *The Four Fundamental Concepts of Psychoanalysis*, New York: Norton quotes1998, p. 103.

47. See Chapter 4 of my *Like a Thief in Broad Daylight*, London: Penguin Books 2018.

48. Other strange things happen in the use of term "kurc" in Slavic languages. There is a vulgar Serb phrase "Boli me kurac!" which literally translates "I have a pain in my prick!"; it signals indifference—when somebody tells me "But you should do something, help us!", and I snap back "Boli me kurac!", it means: "Fuck off, I don't care!" In everyday language, this phrase is gender-neutral, men and woman use it—so when I hear a woman saying it, my automatic reaction is to reproach her for having a phantom limb sensation which disavows castration, as if she (still) has her penis. (From a strict Lacanian standpoint, of course, such a reading is wrong: the phallus is as such a kind of phantom limb whose movement is uncontrollable.) Incidentally, Slovene feminists now do have their version of the term: "Puca mi muca! ("My pussy is bursting!)"

49. See www.mamamia.com.au/fk-it-therapy-because-nothings-really-worth-worrying-about/.

50. Jacques Lacan, *Four Fundamental Concepts of Psycho-Analysis*, New York: Norton 1998, p. 95.

51. Stephen Hawking's illness confirms this special status of erection: he was totally incapacitated, suffering from ALS (amyotrophic lateral sclerosis), but he was capable of having an erection because ALS affects motor neurons while sexual activity/organs are controlled by the parasympathetic nervous system. People with ALS (and many quadriplegics in general) are usually fully capable of having sex.

52. Quoted from www.bpi.edu/ourpages/auto/2014/11/11/40818641/
    Anouilh_Antigone%20Full%20Text.pdf.

53. See Alenka Zupančič, "Oedipus or the Excrement of the Signifier," in
    Ojdip v Kolonu (in Slovene), Ljubljana: *Analecta* 2018.

54. Op. cit., p. 171.

55. Quoted from https://nosubject.com/Oedipus_at_Colonus.

56. Terry Eagleton, *Trouble with Strangers*, Oxford: Wiley-Blackwell 2008,
    p. 201.

57. See https://lyricstranslate.com/en/lo-eterno-eternal-one.html.

58. Available online at www.slate.com/id/2107100.

59. See https://en.wikipedia.org/wiki/Here%27s_to_You_(song).

60. Wolfram Hogrebe, *Die Wirklichkeit des Denkens*, Heidelberg: Winter
    Verlag 2007, pp. 64–72.

61. Maximilien Robespierre, *Virtue and Terror*, London: Verso Books
    2007, Robespierre, p. 129.

3 Surplus-Enjoyment, or, why we Enjoy our Oppression

1. Resumed from https://screenrant.com/vikings-season-4-ragnar-
   death-revenge-explained/.

2. Did something similar not happen in Poland in 1989 when the
   military government negotiated with Solidarnosc? Unexpectedly,
   General Jaruzelski, the head of the government, and Adam Michnik,
   one of the main dissident figures, became personal friends. Their
   families met regularly until Jaruzelski's death. (On his deathbed, none
   other than Lech Walesa visited him.) Today, with Jaroslaw Kaczynski
   in power, such a friendship is not imaginable . . . In short, we can also
   have polite revolutionaries—a welcome contrast to the obscene
   brutality of those in power.

3. I have to ignore here the perverse repetition of the intense
   relationship between Ragnar and Athelstan in season 5, in the
   relationship of mutual fascination between Ivar the Boneless, Ragnar's
   brutal psychotic son, and bishop Huahmund, a fanatic proto-Jesuit
   figure of a warrior-monk. He is, like Athelstan, not killed but
   kidnapped by Ivar who brings him home to Norway.

4. Another version of the Id-machine is found in Barry Levinson's
   Sphere (1998).

5. I resume here my reading of *Solaris* in www.lacan.com/zizekthing. htm.

6. Stanislaw Lem, *Solaris*, New York: Harcourt, Brace & Company 1978, p. 30.

7. The formula of Tonya Howe (University of Michigan, Ann Arbor), on whose excellent seminar paper "*Solaris* and the Obscenity of Presence" I rely here.

8. See Jacques-Alain Miller, "Des semblants dans la relation entre les sexes," in *La Cause freudienne 36,* Paris 1997, pp. 7–15.

9. Quoted from Antoine de Vaecque, *Andrei Tarkovski*, Cahiers du Cinema 1989, p. 108.

10. Created and directed by Baltasar Kormákur and Sigurjón Kjartansson, Netflix 2021. The story is resumed from "Katla" Netflix Review: Stream It or Skip It? (decider.com) and 'KATLA' Ending, & Folklore Origins Explained, DMT (dmtalkies.com).

11. Jacques Ranciere, "Anachronism and the Conflict of Times," in *Diacritics* Vol. 48 (2, 2020), p. 121.

12. I've dealt more in detail with this prospect in Slavoj Žižek, *Hegel in a Wired Brain*, London: Bloomsbury 2020.

13. See, again, my *Hegel in a Wired Brain.*

14. Sigmund Freud, "The Ego and the Id," quoted from www. sigmundfreud.net/the-ego-and-the-id-pdf-ebook.jsp.

15. Freud, op. cit.

16. Étienne Balibar, "The Invention of the Superego: Freud and Kelsen, 1922," in Citizen Subject, New York: Fordham University Press 2016, pp. 227–55.

17. Jacques Lacan, *Ethics of Psychoanalysis*, p. 310.

18. I developed these distinctions in my *How to Read Lacan*, London: Granta 2006.

19. There is a crucial difference here between Kant and Hegel: for Kant (and Kelsen as a neo-Kantian) empirical perversions are secondary, while for Hegel they arise from the immanent tensions of the notion itself—absolute freedom necessarily turns into terror, the honor of serving the Master who personifies a Cause into hypocritical flattery (as in the passage from Lenin to Stalin).

20. For a detailed analysis of this topic, see Jamadier Esteban Uribe Muñoz and Pablo Johnson, "El pasaje al acto de Telémaco:

psicoanálisis y política ante el 18 de octubre chileno," to appear in *Política y Sociedad* (Madrid).

21. See Adrian Johnston, "Divine Ignorance: Jacques Lacan and Christian Atheism"(unpublished manuscript). Non-accredited quotes that follow are from this text.

22. Johnston, op. cit.

23. Jacques-Alain Miller, "La psychanalyse, la cité, les communautés," *La cause freudienne* 68 (February 2008), p. 109.

24. Nicolas Fleury, Le réel insensé: Introduction à la pensée de Jacques-Alain Miller, Paris: Germina 2010, p. 96.

25. Fleury, *Le réel insensé*, p. 95 (quotations from Miller, op. cit.).

26. Charles Baudelaire, *Journaux intimes*. Paris: Les Éditions G. Cres et Cie 1920, p. 3.

27. Hannah Arendt, "The Crisis of Education," in *Between Past and Future*, New York: Viking Press 1961, p. 191.

28. See Gerard Miller, *Les Pousse-au-jouir du Marechal Petain*, Paris: Points 2004.

29. Documentation Center of Cambodia (DC-Cam).

30. Another form of total prohibition which gets close to psychotic *Verwerfung* occurs when some words become unmentionable. Say, the fact that the N-word is unmentionable in today's public discourse, that its use cannot be justified even as a part of a critical interpretation of racism, unmistakably signals that its status is that of a real: in it, the symbolic falls into the real, it is impervious to any symbolic mediation.

31. Duane Rousselle, personal communication.

32. See Ben Burgis, *Canceling Comedians While the World Burns: A Critique of the Contemporary Left*, London: Zero Books 2021.

33. Saroj Giri, "Introduction. From the October Revolution to the Naxalbari Movement: Understanding Political Subjectivity," in K. Murali, *Of Concepts and Methods*, Keralam: Kanal Publication Center 2020, p. 29.

34. California unveils new woke math program, encouraging teachers to punish good students by holding them back—RT USA News.

35. See Herbert Marcuse, *Eros and Civilization*, Boston: Beacon Press 1974.

36. Sigmund Freud and Josef Breuer, *Studies in Hysteria*, in *Standard Edition*, Vol. II, London: Vintage Press 1999, p. 305.

37. See Martin Hagglund, *This Life: Why Mortality Makes Us Free*, London: Profile Books 2019.

38. See www.msn.com/en-gb/entertainment/movies/kevin-bacon-ive-been-told-im-more-well-known-for-being-well-known-than-for-anything-ive-acted-in/ar-BB19T5pi?ocid=msedgntp.

39. Matthew Flisfeder, "Renewing Humanism Against the Anthropocene: Towards a Theory of the Hysterical Sublime" (manuscript).

40. See Mladen Dolar, "Oedipus at Colonus," in *Ojdip v Kolonu* (in Slovene), Ljubljana: Analecta 2018.

41. See the chapter on Self-Consciousness in www.marxists.org/reference/archive/hegel/works/ph/pinkard-translation-of-phenomenology.pdf.

42. See Yanis Varoufakis, *Another Now. Dispatches from an Alternative Present*, London: The Bodley Head 2020. Numbers in brackets refer to the pages of this book.

43. Jean-Pierre Dupuy, Avions-nous oublie le mal? Penser la politique après le 11 septembre, Paris: Bayard 2002.

44. See John Rawls, *A Theory of Justice*, Cambridge (Ma): Harvard University Press 1971 (revised edition 1999).

45. See www.marxists.org/reference/archive/hegel/help/findlay4.htm.

46. Aaron Schuster, "Beyond Satire," in William Mozzarella, Eric Santner, Aaron Schuster, *Sovereignty Inc. Three Inquiries in Politics and Enjoyment*, Chicago: The University of Chicago Press 2020.

47. Jacques Lacan, *Écrits*, New York: Norton, 2006, p. 699.

48. See lyricstranslate.com/en/erstes-dreigroschenfinale-%C3%BCber-die-unsicherheit-menschlicher-verh%C3%A4ltnisse-first-final-o.html#footnote2_g19jfds.

49. Original version available at www.youtube.com/watch?v=TF_jtz0kP9s&list=TLPQMjQxMDIwMjBNari4iHpmQw&index=1.

50. Russell Sbriglia (private communication).

51. An insurrection of upper-middle class white people, Will Bunch (inquirer.com).

52. See Todd MacGowan, *Capitalism and Desire*, Cambridge UP 2016.

53. Philosophy of Mind, 315.

54. Jacques Lacan, *The Four Fundamental Concepts of Psycho-Analysis*, New York: Norton 1998, p. 275.

55. Hannah Arendt, "The Concentration Camps," in *Partisan Review*, July 1948.

56. Adrian Johnston, "The Self-Cleaning Fetish: Repression Under the Shadow of Fictitious Capital," manuscript.

57. Frank Ruda, *Abolishing Freedom*, Lincoln and London: University of Nebraska Press 2016. Numbers in brackets refer to the pages of this book.

58. Robert Pippin, *Fatalism in American Film Noir*, Charlottesville: University of Virginia Press 2012, pp. 48–9.

59. Op. cit., p. 97.

60. Ecologists like to point out how the introduction of a foreign species into a specific life-world can fatally destabilize its: a new predator eating local animal species disturbs the entire cycle of life, a new plant suffocates other plants and destroys the entire food chain, etc. What they often forget to mention is that we are the main intruders—we humans—the human species, whose explosive growth devastates life-worlds, so that nature has to establish new fragile ecological balances.

61. The correct designation for the stance advocated here is not Christian atheism but atheist Christianity: Christian atheism reduces "Christian" to one of the possible predicates/versions of atheism, while "atheist Christianity" implies a stronger claim that Christianity is at its core atheist, i.e., that this is what distinguishes Christianity from other religions.

62. See www.stillnessspeaks.com/wp-content/uploads/2015/09/MeisterEckhartThePoorMan.pdf.

63. Op. cit.

64. Op. cit.

65. G.K. Chesterton, *Orthodoxy*, San Francisco: Ignatius Press 1995, p. 139.

66. Op. cit., p. 145.

67. Ibid.

68. See Catherine Malabou, *Le plaisir effacé. Clitoris et pensee*, Paris: Bibliotheque Rivages 2020.

69. See The Butterfly Effect—Wikipedia.

Finale: Subjective Destitution as a Political Category

1. Martin Heidegger, *Logic as the Question Concerning the Essence of Language*, Albany: SUNY Press 2009, p. 73.

2. See Grant Farred, *Martin Heidegger Saved My Life*, Minneapolis: University of Minnesota Press 2015.

3. Living with the ghost of Martin Heidegger—University of Minnesota Press Blog (uminnpressblog.com).

4. In this global crisis, there's one consolation: the beauty of the universe, *The Guardian*.

5. The late Friedrich Engels made a similar remark apropos his "dialectics of nature" manuscripts.

6. Available in English in Martin Heidegger, "The End of Philosophy and the Task of Thinking," in *On Time and Being*, New York: Harper and Row 1972.

7. See Huw Price, Naturalism without representationalism—PhilPapers.

8. Similarly, following the 1917 October Revolution, Soviet philosophy found itself divided between two factions: the "dialecticians" headed up by Abram Deborin who referred to Hegel as the model of dialectical thinking, and the "mechanists" whose leading figure was the philosopher Lyubov Axelrod (Nikolai Bukharin was also seen as their member) and who modelled Marxist materialism on natural sciences. However, they both conceived philosophy as a general view of reality, as providing the universal structure of all there is—Deborin also rejected the transcendental turn enacted by Georg Lukacs and Karl Korsch.

9. Karen Barad, *Meeting the Universe Halfway: Quantum Physics and the Entanglement of Matter and Meaning*, Durham: Duke University Press 2007, p. 25.

10. Jürgen Habermas, "The Language Game of Responsible Agency and the Problem of Free Will: How Can Epistemic Dualism be Reconciled with Ontological Monism?," *Philosophical Explorations* 10, No. 1 (March 2007), p. 31.

11. Martin Heidegger, *Identity and Difference*, New York: Torchbooks 1975, p. 72.

12. See Juergen Habermas, *Between Naturalism and Religion,* Cambridge: Polity 2008.

13. Martin Heidegger, *Beitraege zur Philosophie*, in *Gesamtausgabe*, Frankfurt: Vittorio Klostermann 1975 ff., Vol. 65, p. 338.

14. Martin Heidegger, Hölderlin's Hymne, "Der Ister," *Gesamtausgabe 53*, Frankfurt: Vittorio Klostermann 1984, p. 94.

15. Martin Heidegger, *Heraclitus Seminar* (with Eugen Fink), Tuscaloosa: University of Alabama Press 1979, p. 146.

16. Martin Heidegger, *Zollikoner Seminare*, Frankfurt: Vittorio Klostermann 2017, p. 260.

17. See www.youtube.com/watch?v=yHoK6ohqNo4.

18. Letter from October 11, 1931, *Martin Heidegger—Elisabeth Blochmann. Briefwechsel 1918–1969*, Marbach: Deutsches Literatur-Archiv 1990, p. 44.

19. Martin Heidegger, *The Fundamental Concepts of Metaphysics*, Bloomington: Indiana University Press 1995, p. 271.

20. Quoted from www.marxists.org/archive/marx/works/1857/grundrisse/ch01.htm#3.

21. See Pierre Bayard, *Le plagiat par anticipation*, Paris: Editions de Minuit 2009.

22. See Alenka Zupančič, *What IS Sex?*, Cambridge: MIT Press 2017.

23. Similarly, there are cases in classical music where the main motif is not simply presented: it gradually emerges out of the mixture of sounds, as if it is struggling to liberate itself from the vocal mess. Instead of beginning with a motif and then proceeding to its variations, the motif comes at the end, as the culmination of a long painful process.

24. Fichte's position is here subtly ambiguous: even when he talks about the absolute I positing the not-I, he is not claiming that the absolute I creates objects in the direct causal sense. The only thing that the subject creates is the mysterious "impetus" which pushes it to "posit" reality, and this impetus is his version of what Lacan calls *objet a*.

25. nI deal in more detail with Rammstein's "Dalai Lama" in my *Heaven in Disorder*, New York: OR Books 2021.

26. *Coronavirus, Psychoanalysis, and Philosophy*, edited by Fernando Castrillón and Thomas Marchevsky, London: Routledge 2021, p. 2.

27. Op. cit., p. 60.

28. See https://edition.cnn.com/2020/10/28/politics/woodward-kushner-coronavirus-doctors/index.html.

29. *Coronavirus, Psychoanalysis, and Philosophy*, edited by Fernando Castrillón and Thomas Marchevsky, London: Routledge 2021, p. 95.

30. I developed this parallel in Chapter 9 of my *Less Than Nothing*, London: Verso Books 2013.

31. Mark's notes on Shostakovich Symphony No. 14—Mark Wigglesworth.

32. Op. cit.
33. Op. cit.
34. AJ0378.pdf (chandos.net).
35. Reply of the Zaporozhian Cossacks—Wikipedia.
36. Symphony No. 15 (Shostakovich)—Wikipedia.
37. An introduction to Shostakovich's Symphony No. 15—Classical Music (classical-music.com).
38. Such a cynical stance implies that we should not dismiss the new Right populists as a bunch of primitive fundamentalists who cannot stand obscenity, irony and promiscuity. The new Right made a dangerous pact with many "neutral" experts, managers, journalists, and artists whose basic stance is "I don't care about politics, I just want to do my job in peace!" However, their "neutrality" is the same as that of some German conservative artists after 1945: if they were invited to perform at an event organized by Leftists, they refused, claiming that they didn't want to get involved in politics; if they were invited to perform at an event organized by Rightists, they accepted for exactly the same reason, claiming that they didn't care about politics and just wanted to perform ...
39. Saroj Giri, "Introduction," in K. Murali, *Of Concepts and Methods*, Keralam: Kanal Publishing Center 2021. Numbers in brackets refer to the pages of this book.
40. Saroj Giri, "The Buddhist Ineffable Self and a Possible Indian Political Subject," *Political Theology*, 19:8 (2018), pp. 734–50.
41. Peter Hallward, ed., *Think Again: Alain Badiou and the Future of Philosophy*, London: Continuum 2004, p. 257.
42. Quoted from Timothy Morton's Hyper-Pandemic, *The New Yorker*.
43. Quoted from op. cit.
44. See https://en.wikipedia.org/wiki/Four_Pests_campaign.
45. In spite of my occasional critical comments on Lenin, I must emphasize that the only bad Lenin for me is Lenin Moreno, the president of Ecuador who delivered Julian Assange to the UK police.
46. See https://journals.sagepub.com/doi/full/10.1177/0191453718794751#.
47. Michel Foucault, "Society Must Be Defended," in *Lectures at the Collège de France 1975–1976*, New York: Picador 2003, p. 52.
48. See https://jacobinmag.com/2011/07/the-power-of-nonsense.

49. Among others, in an interview available on Martin Heidegger—Ein Interview 1/2—YouTube.

50. Yanis Varoufakis on Twitter: "On the day liberal-neocon imperialism was defeated once and for all, DiEM25's thoughts are with the women of Afghanistan. Our solidarity probably means little to them but it is what we can offer—for the time being. Hang in there sisters!" / Twitter.

51. See https://twitter.com/yanisvaroufakis/status/1427210155767353348.

52. See https://edition.cnn.com/2021/09/01/politics/far-right-groups-praise-taliban-takeover/index.html.

53. Quoted from Heinz Hoehne, *The Order of the Death's Head: The Story of Hitler's SS*, London: Penguin, 2000, p. 333.

54. I've dealt with this more in detail in my part of *The Monstrosity of Christ* (co-written with John Millbank), Cambridge (Ma): MIT Press 2009.

55. See Angela Nagle, *Kill All Normies*, New York: Zero Books 2017.

56. I've dealt with this new figure of the big Other in more detail in *Pandemic 2: Chronicles of a Time Lost,* Cambridge: Polity Press 2021.

57. A Self-Fulfilling Prophecy: Systemic Collapse and Pandemic Simulation—The Philosophical Salon.

58. Quotes that follow are from Alenka Zupančič, "A Short Essay on Conspiracy Theories" (manuscript).

59. Attacking anti-vaccine movement, Biden mandates widespread COVID shots, tests, Reuters.

60. See Giorgio Agamben, *Where are We Now?*, London: Eris 2021.

61. I owe to Russell Sbriglia (private conversation) the idea of using this formula of Lacan to characterize COVID-sceptics.

62. See A woman is raped and onlookers record it: the story beyond the outrage (opinion)—CNN.

63. Netflix's Squid Game savagely satirises our money-obsessed society—but it's capitalism that is the real winner, Arwa Mahdawi, *The Guardian*.

64. Nikitas Fessas, personal communication. The journalist who made the story known is Vasilis G. Lampropoulos.

65. See Jacques Ranciere, "Anachronism and the Conflict of Times," in *Diacritics* Vol. 48 (2, 2020).

66. Jacques Ranciere, "Anachronism and the Conflict of Times," in *Diacritics* Vol. 48 (2, 2020), p. 123.

67. Quoted in Ben Stein, "In class warfare, guess which class is winning," *New York Times*, November 26, 2006.

68. Walter Benjamin, The Arcades Project, Cambridge (Ma): Harvard University Press 1999, p. 471.

69. The most one can argue is that the film incites us, the viewers, to act through the Joker: the Joker acts for us, he actualizes our brutal rage against the social order, thus enabling us to go on living as usual, since we have vented out our frustration through him.

70. Quoted from https://marginalrevolution.com/ marginalrevolution/2019/10/the-joker.html.

71. Quoted from www.good.is/the-five-most-powerful-lines-from-michael-moores-masterful-joker-review.

72. Recall the already-quoted Fanon's claim that "the Negro is a zone of non-being, an extraordinarily sterile and arid region, an utterly declining declivity": is the experience that grounds today's "afro-pessimism" not a similar one? Is the insistence of afro-pessimists that black subordination is much more radical than that of other underprivileged groups (Asians, LGBT+, women . . .), i.e., that black people should not be put into the series with other forms of "colonization," not grounded in the act of assuming that one belongs to such a "zone of non-being"? Is this not the ultimate meaning of the "X" in Malcolm X's name? This is why Fredric Jameson is right when he insists that one cannot understand class struggle in the US without taking into account anti-black racism: any talk which equalizes white and black proletarians is a fake.

73. See www.patheos.com/blogs/ anotherwhiteatheistincolombia/2019/10/tribelessness-secular-zizek-joker/.

74. See https://www.lrb.co.uk/v41/n20/judith-butler/genius-or-suicide.

75. Before seeing the movie and just being aware of the critical reactions to it, I thought it would provide the social genesis of the figure of Joker. Now, having seen it, I must admit, in the spirit of Communist self-criticism, that I was wrong: the passage from passive victimhood to a new form of subjectivity is the pivotal moment of the film.

76. Clowncels are also not just determined by their circumstances: even more than incels in general, they enact a symbolic gesture of turning their suffering into a form of enjoyment—they obviously enjoy their predicament, parading it proudly, and are therefore responsible for it, not just victims of unfortunate circumstances.

77. I rely here on Matthew Flisfeder (private exchange).

78. Antigone book (bcscschools.org).

79. I rely here on Alenka Zupančič's extraordinary study on Antigone, *Let Them Rot*, New York: Fordham University Press 2022. Her booklet is a true game-changer: nothing will remain the same in the vast field of *Antigone* studies after its appearance.

80. Another way to domesticate Antigone is to ignore the fact that Polynices was a traitor to his people. A couple of years ago, Jenin Freedom Theatre, an independent Palestinian West Bank theatre, staged a contemporary version of Antigone. The premise was that Antigone is a daughter of a large Palestinian family whose brother participated in anti-Israeli resistance and was killed by Israeli soldiers; the Israeli occupation authority prohibits his funeral, and Antigone defies the prohibition ... I intervened in the debate about this staging and pointed out that the parallel is wrong and misleading: *Antigone* stages a family conflict, and Polynices attacks Thebes together with a foreign invasion force. Consequently, in today's occupied Palestine, Creon is not the Israel state authority but the head of Antigone's family—the situation should be that Polynices collaborated with Israeli occupiers and was disowned and killed by his own family as a traitor, and Antigone wants to bury him properly against the wishes of her family. I've dealt with this more in detail in my *Antigone*, London: Bloomsbury Press 2015.

81. See Kathrin H. Rosenfield, "Getting into Sophocles's Mind Through Hölderlin's *Antigone*," available online at 000932216.pdf;sequence=1 (ufrgs.br).

82. Quoted from Global Ethic—Global Ethic (global-ethic.org).

83. Available online at www.youtube.com/watch?v=etIqln7vT4w. I owe this example to Douane Rousselle (personal communication).

84. Personal communication.

85. See https://knowyourmeme.com/photos/1079755-funny-news-headlines.

86. See Paul Vallely's "How philanthropy benefits the super-rich," available online at How philanthropy benefits the super-rich, *The Guardian*.

87. Hegel, *Encyclopaedia,* Para. 408, Addition. Quoted from The Subjective Spirit (marxists.org).

88. Ibid.

89. I dealt with this notion in detail in my *For They Not Know What They Do*, London: Verso Books 2008.

90. I owe this anecdote to Adam Chmielewski, who was present when it occurred.

91. Slavoj Žižek, quoted from Slavoj Zizek, Eastern Europe's Republics of Gilead, NLR I/183, September–October 1990 (newleftreview.org).

92. See Part I of Jacques Lacan, *Seminar VII: The Ethics of Psychoanalysis*, London: Routledge 2007.

93. Quoted from COVID-19: Texas official suggests elderly willing to die for economy (usatoday.com).

94. Gilbert Keith Chesterton, *Orthodoxy,* San Francisco: Ignatius Press 1999, p. 99.

Index

The letter *f* after an entry indicates a page that includes a figure.

Dreigroschenoper (*Threepenny
    Opera*; *Beggar's Opera*) 236–8,
    285
Weininger, Otto 191, 192
Welles, Orson 95
Welt, Die 13
West, the 297–8, 318
West, Cornell 331
Western Marxism 19, 89
"What is Enlightenment?" (Kant,
    Immanuel) 25–6
"What Is to Be Done?" (Lenin,
    Vladimir) 29
Where are we now? (Agamben,
    Giorgio) 311
white supremacists 298–9
Wilcox, Fred
    Forbidden Planet, The 190
Wilde, Oscar
    "Soul of Man under Socialism,
    The" 336–7
William Tell (Rossini, Gioachino) 285
Winnebago, the 132–3
Winterson, Jeanette
    Frankissstein: A Love Story 150
Wiseman, Eva 4
woke capitalism 217
Wollenberger, Knud 167
women 257, 258 *see also* feminist
    ideology
    Afghanistan 296–7
    betrayal 168–9
    Boko Haram 2978
    clitoris, the 257–8
    desire 151
    education 297
    feminine enjoyment 134–6
    femme a postiche 193–4
    "having it" 193–4
    identity 166
    Islam 155, 156
    lack 193–4
    liberation 297
    love 168–9
    as male fantasy 191

male identity 194
Miller, Jacques-Alain 193
motherhood 258–9
reproduction 165–6
Taliban, the 154–5
violence against 151, 153–6,
    312–13, 316
vulgar expressions 355 n.
    48
Weininger, Otto 191, 192
worker, the 71, 73 *see also* labor
    automation 70, 71–3
    classism 158–9
    film portrayals 158–9
workforce 49, 87 *see also* labor
Worstward Ho (Beckett, Samuel) 27

xenophobia 342

yolo (You Only Live Once) 80

Zaporozhian Cossacks 283–4
zero-point 325
Zeuxis and Parrhasius anecdote
    171
Zionism 110, 299, 310
Žižek, Slavoj 12–13, 102
    Clark, M.L. 325–6
    COVID-19 pandemic 280
    "Eastern Europe's Republics of
    Gilead" 341–2
    Less Than Nothing 12
    psychoanalysis 119–20
    self-plagiarism accusations 346 n.
    11
    wealth 119–20
Zollikoner Seminare (Heidegger,
    Martin) 272
Zuckerberg, Mark 21
Zupančič, Alenka 241, 242, 244, 245,
    276
    Antigone 330
    apocalypse 344
    conspiracy theories 306–8
    ideology 335